Praise fo

A *Booklist* Top

"First-rate adventure writing from the nineteenth century. . . . Such variety promises something to please every shade of taste for armchair adventure."   —Brad Hooper, *Booklist*

"In our 21st-century, when travel is often sanitized by cruise ships, tour packages and guidebooks that leave nothing to the imagination, these tales ring with an almost unimaginable sense of intensity, danger, and accomplishment."   —Christian Martin, *Bellingham Weekly*

"A deep sense of awe runs through every single account collected here. It's fascinating, beautifully written material, and Whybrow has done an admirable job of researching and presenting it."
—Nicola Smith, *Valley News*

"This captivating collection conveys the excitement, dangers and uncertainty of exploration in the 19th century, when much of the world remained uncharted and mysterious. Whybrow . . . has compiled diverse material with an emphasis on first-person stories of adventure and survival that remain powerful and immediate."   —*Tampa Tribune*

"Readers . . . will be rewarded by multiple evocations of a challenging and untamed world."   —*Kirkus Reviews*

"Whybrow's collection of excerpts from these 32 still-exhilarating stories will encourage readers to seek out the originals in their entirety."
—*Library Journal*

"32 riveting accounts of geographic discovery, personal odyssey and lifelong quests that take you all over the 19th-century globe."   —*The Oregonian*

"Carefully chosen from the original works, these excerpts from the 19th century's outdoor superstars represent literary excellence and gripping adventure."   —Michael Anastasi, *Woodland Hills Daily News*

Happy Birthday!

Much love,

Joel & Erin

June 2005

DEAD RECKONING

Tales of the

Great Explorers,

1800–1900

EDITED BY HELEN WHYBROW

Outside
BOOKS

W. W. Norton & Company • New York • London

Selection from *The Journals of Lewis and Clark* reprinted from *The Journals of the Lewis and Clark Expedition, Volume 4: April 7–July 17, 1805*, edited by Gary E. Moulton, by permission of the University of Nebraska Press. Copyright © 1976 by the University of Nebraska Press.

The text of this book is composed in Fairfield LH with the display set in Akzidenz Grotesk
Composition by Carole Desnoes
Manufacturing by The Haddon Craftsmen, Inc.
Book design by JoAnne Metsch

The Library of Congress has cataloged the hardcover edition as follows:

Library of Congress Cataloging-in-Publication Data

Dead reckoning : great adventure writing from the golden age of exploration, 1800–1900 / edited by Helen Whybrow. — 1st ed.
p. cm. — (Outside books)
Includes bibliographical references (p.   ).
ISBN 0-393-01054-6 (hardcover)
1. Voyages and travels—History—19th century. 2. Travelers—History—19th century. 3. Travelers' writings. I. Whybrow, Helen. II. Series.
G465.D42 2002
910.4'09'034—dc21
2002010867

ISBN 0-393-32653-5 pbk.

W. W. Norton & Company, Inc., 500 Fifth Avenue, New York, N.Y. 10110
www.wwnorton.com

W. W. Norton & Company Ltd., Castle House, 75/76 Wells Street, London W1T 3QT

1 2 3 4 5 6 7 8 9 0

To my sister Kate,

this book is affectionately dedicated

The man wants to wander, and he must do so, or he
shall die. . . . The world was "all before me" and there was
pleasant excitement in plunging single-handed into its
chilling depths.

—SIR RICHARD FRANCIS BURTON

I am excessively weak, and but for the donkey, could not
move a hundred yards. It is not all pleasure, this exploration.

—DR. DAVID LIVINGSTONE

Contents

Acknowledgments

No journey is undertaken entirely alone, and certainly my efforts to collect this anthology were made easier by the help of many people. My first and greatest thanks go to my editor, John Barstow, who initiated this project and gave me his enthusiastic support and expert suggestions at every stage. I am grateful to Hal Espen, editor of *Outside*, and his colleagues at the magazine for their endorsement and their valuable advice as the collection took shape. I am also grateful to David Roberts for his excellent advice early in the process and to John O'Brien for his supply of books and ideas throughout. Others who led me to material I may not have otherwise found and gave generously of their enthusiasm are: Jim Babb, Jim Collins, Garrett and Alexandra Conover, Bill Coperthwaite, Greg Glade, Bob Howells, Sandra Miller, David Noland, Linda Peavy, David Quammen, John Rousmaniere, Ursula Smith, Laura Waterman, and Donovan Webster. The research and illustration of this book would not have been possible without the generous assistance of Jan Turner and Clive Coward of the Royal Geographic Society, and Phil Cronenwett, Sarah Hartwell, Joshua Shaw and the rest of the staff at the Rauner Special Collections at Dartmouth College. Finally, this year of exploration has been enriched and sustained by the love and support of my family, and of Peter.

Introduction

The recounting of a journey and its ensuing mysteries and hardships is the oldest form of storytelling, and yet it never feels worn. In the telling, as well as in the going, there are good journeys and bad, yet the act of leaving the familiar to seek the unknown and unpredictable—whether it be the first ascent of Everest or a first summer in the Sierra Nevada—remains timeless. We read about journeys of any age to find the world's edges and our own, to learn the best and worst of ourselves, to be scared witless, to bolster our courage, to be in awe. We need them, and for that reason adventure stories endure.

The focus of this anthology is adventure travel narratives of the nineteenth century. During the 1800s, the Western world's knowledge of the earth's geography, natural sciences, indigenous peoples, and flora and fauna took a quantum leap. In the century's youth, no one knew where the Nile had its source, or what effect altitude had on the body, or whether the North and South Poles consisted of land or sea, or whether the Northwest Passage through North America to Asia was real or imagined. There was no such thing as radar or radio, an icebreaker or artificial oxygen, synthetic clothing or nylon rope. If you lost your compass and the sky was cloudy, you resorted to dead reckoning, divining your direction by its relation to something fixed, such as the motion of the waves, a distant mountain or even a log thrown overboard. And if your journey didn't go as planned, such as for Robert O'Hara Burke and William Wills who missed a relief party by just eight hours and starved to death in the Australian outback, your prospects of survival were slim to none.

In the face of the extravagant hardships possible in such vast unknowns—one couldn't prepare for what one didn't know existed—risk hardly had to be sought; it was part of the package. The depth of isolation possible up until the early 1900s can scarcely be imagined in modern times. Because travel was by boat, pack-animal, and primarily on foot, wilderness journeys of any significance took years, sometimes many years, to complete. These explorers were entirely on their own when it came to medical help, foraging for food when supplies ran out, navigating without instruments, plotting their own maps, understanding the customs and languages of native people, burying their dead.

One of the most famous stories of the nineteenth century is that of Sir John Franklin, a British admiral who in 1848 departed for the Arctic with 129 men and two boats, the *Erebus* and the *Terror,* on a search for the Northwest Passage. They never returned. For eleven years their fate was unknown, and during that time more than thirty rescue expeditions from England and America were sent in search of them, many of which experienced disastrous journeys themselves with considerable loss of life. In 1859 Leopold M'Clintock found the wreckage and skeletons of Franklin's expedition strewn along the coast of King William Island. The men had abandoned their ship to its prison of ice (1846 was the coldest winter on record), and then died a slow and excruciating death from lead poisoning, scurvy, and starvation, some resorting to cannibalism in a futile effort to save themselves. Franklin's fate was a shocking one, even in the era of high-risk exploration. His had been the most elaborately and expensively outfitted polar expedition ever launched, and yet all had disappeared without a trace not long after leaving England's shores. The

Franklin story illustrates how much larger and labyrinthine the globe must have seemed in the 1800s, with all of its blank spaces and empty quarters. Imagine: it took thirty expeditions and eleven years to find even a trace of those 129 men. It turns out they were not far into Canada's arctic archipelago, where icebreaker luxury cruises routinely take tourists today.

As time and space have been compressed by technology, the quality and nature of adventure have changed inestimably. The voices of adventure, too, have changed. In the dwindling of geographic conquests left to make, our celebration of individual achievement has grown, and modern adventure writing is more personal and psychological than in the past. The mountaineers and travelers and scientists of the nineteenth century tended to downplay their achievements, stiff upper lips being the custom of the day. Hence, epic first ascents were published in volumes called *Scrambles* or *Hours of Exercise* and landmark discoveries jotted in journals or described as "Incidents of Travel." Yet there are more similarities than differences between the adventure stories of the nineteenth century and today. In all the best travel stories there is a vivid intensity to the writing, as if in facing the edge of survival or seeing nature at its most elemental the writer is stripped of the vestiges of his or her era and can write from a place starkly human and pure. The explorers of the 1800s had a different perception of the world and their relation to it than do adventurers today—and indeed their world was a very different place— and yet the intimacy we feel with these writers as they face their essential aloneness and humanness unite us across time.

• • •

The stories I have chosen from among the many classics of the era are all written with verve and wit and an irrepressible curiosity for the unknown. Many of these books were bestsellers in their day; some are still in print over 100 years later. Others were forgotten and are reprinted here for the first time in many decades. The stories are often desperate ones, such as George Melville's account of his journey on board the American vessel *Jeannette,* which was crushed in the Arctic icepack, leaving him and his crew marooned on the north coast of Siberia for three and a half years. Martin Amis once said, "all writers maintain a vampiric attitude to disaster; and having survived it, are unreservedly grateful for the experience." There is nothing quite like danger to crystallize the mind, and indeed the passages of peril in these books often begged to be excerpted, being so cleanly written and electrifying to read. Lifelong explorer David Livingstone wrote in his journal, "The mere animal pleasure of traveling in a wild unexplored country is very great . . . The effect of travel on a man whose heart is in the right place is that the mind is made more self-reliant: it becomes more confident of its own resources—there is greater presence of mind."

The adventure stories of the nineteenth century are compelling not only for their grim realities and show of human bravery. Many of them are not grim at all, but full of wonder and wise observation. These stories take us to a much wilder world, one that is gone forever. In many cases, the men and women were describing places that no European had ever seen or imagined, that had never before been put on the page. It is a stirring thing to read Francis Parkman describe hundreds of grizzlies feeding in a river channel on the Great Plains, or Alfred Russel Wallace paint in words the plumage of a rare and splendid paradise bird, and then to realize that such scenes are no longer of this world.

This project, I admit, became something of an obsession. Each old volume I read led me to several more, and the pile of slips I handed in at library desks grew and grew until I had read well over a hundred books. Together with editors at *Outside* and W. W. Norton, we put together some guidelines for what went to the copy machine and what didn't. First of all, the work had to be great storytelling, of a style that would be engaging to modern readers. No arcane Victorian literature, however classic the book was in its day (hence the omission of Kinglake's *Eothen* and Doughty's *Arabia Deserta*). Important, but less so, was that the excerpt described a journey of historical importance. We did not attempt to make this collection a record of the century's great geographical discoveries at the expense of its being an exciting read. We wanted the excerpt to be in the first person, and we did not alter the writer's original spelling or syntax. We've retained original footnotes and added others where a term or reference needed to be explained. Finally, the journey had to be made before the turn of the century, a boundary that is admittedly more convenient than historically useful. The age of exploration, during which vast blank areas of the world map were filled in, began in earnest at the end of the Napoleonic Wars in 1815 and ended with the start of the First World War in 1914. So, although Sir Ernest Shackleton and Robert Falcon Scott's journeys in Antarctica have much more in common with the adventures of the nineteenth century than with those of twentieth, they are not included here.

Ultimately, we chose the stories that most stirred our blood.

A curious thing happened to me in the course of editing this book. I started out determined to be organized, and to arrange my studies of the literature by geography—the Arctic, Africa, North America, and so forth. When that discipline began to break down I structured my reading chronologically, thinking that arranging the anthology by year would give readers a feel for the unfolding of the century. But that too was abandoned. One day, when I handed my slips to Phil Cronenwett at the Rauner Special Collections at Dartmouth College, he looked at my request for Francis Parkman's *Oregon Trail* and Cook's *Through the Antarctic Night* and said to me (with a smile), "You can't do this. You're all over the globe and all over the century." Well, that was how excited I was about this material. One can't be orderly! I realized how much I wanted readers to share my sense of intimacy with these writers and their lives—beyond history, beyond geography.

So, I divided the book into three parts by theme. The first, Voyages of Discovery, includes the explorations of those sent out by governments or institutions on a quest for worldly knowledge: Lewis and Clark, Darwin, Stanley. But I saw from the beginning that not every story worthy of inclusion would come from the annals of exploration. Some, like Robert Louis Stevenson's delightful *Travels with a Donkey in the Cévennes* and Joshua Slocum's *Voyage of the* Liberdade are engrossing travelogues that embody the personal quest at its finest. Others, such as Richard Henry Dana's *Two Years Before the Mast,* are stories about livelihood—journeys that combined hard work with a chance to live close to the edge. These and other stories make up the second part, Personal Odysseys. The third part, Lifelong Quests, gives homage to people like John Muir, Isabella Bird, Sven Hedin, and others for whom adventure was an all-consuming way of life, essential to their very souls. Lest readers think that this is a compendium of doomed polar explorers marooned on icebergs and camel trains dying of thirst in the desert, I want to emphasize that many in the collection are lighthearted, funny, and full of the ecstasy of the open road.

With any anthology, especially one with material as boundless and rich as this subject has to offer, it is hard to know when to stop. There is always more to read, more to consider, and the nagging awareness that every reader might have a favorite that was left out. Goodness, I myself had favorites I had to leave out! These were written a touch too early or too late, overlapped too closely with another top contender, told of a famous voyage but were a tad dry, or smacked more of tourism than adventure. I must admit that it was difficult to part with a book called *On Sledge and Horseback to Outcast Siberian Lepers,* or to pass up the early-twentieth-century mountaineer Annie Smith Peck, who penned one of the best lines in any travel book: "To possess an imagination is a great advantage to a writer, but for comfort in travelling one is better off without."

A deeper regret is that the collection does not have greater cultural diversity. I considered slave narratives and Native American oral accounts of the "trail of tears," but I felt I would demean the great injustices inherent in such journeys by inserting them in a collection of adventure writing. There is no getting around the fact that the English and Americans dominated world travel in the nineteenth century, and that many approached the indigenous peoples they found in these "blank spaces" of the globe with a deep-seated arrogance, even disdain. Yet there are notable exceptions, as you'll find in George Kennan's sympathetic *Tent Life in Siberia* and Mary Kingsley's *Travels in West Africa,* both excerpted here. (Kennan, in fact, was so moved by his experience living with nomadic tribes in Siberia that we went on to become America's leading expert on Russia and her indigenous peoples and an outspoken opponent of the Siberian exile system.)

In significant ways, the explorers of the nineteenth century shaped the character of modern adventure. At some point in the century, a gradual shift occurred that remains the essence of adventure, and adventure writing, to this day: What do these strange and novel landscapes and cultures have to teach us? explorers began to ask. How can we return home changed, with new knowledge not just of the world but of ourselves?

PART I

Voyages of Discovery

We are now about to penetrate a country at least two thousand miles in width, on which the foot of civilized man had never trodden; the good or evil it had in store for us was for experiment yet to determine. . . . Entertaining as I do the most confident hope of succeeding in a voyage which had formed a darling project of mine for the last ten years, I could but esteem this moment of my departure as among the most happy of my life.

—MERIWETHER LEWIS

MERIWETHER LEWIS

(1774–1809)

From *The Journals of Lewis and Clark*

When Lewis and Clark set out from Saint Louis, Missouri, with their Corps of Discovery in 1804, they went with Thomas Jefferson's words, "the object of your mission is single, the direct water communication from sea to sea." Yet the Lewis and Clark Expedition became much more than a search for a terrestrial Northwest Passage. Lewis sent back specimens of hundreds of plants and dozens of animals no naturalist had recorded, described landscapes and peoples no other American knew existed, and mapped one of the vast blank spaces on the map of North America.

The Journals are deeply moving, if only because they describe a West that will never again be as fecund or formidable. They describe in vivid but straightforward language a journey of such magnitude that it has become a national legend. Teddy Roosevelt said of the famous pair: "Few explorers who saw and did so much that was absolutely new have written of their deeds with such quiet absence of boastfulness, and have drawn their description with such complete freedom from exaggeration."

The following entries from Lewis's notebooks are some of the most thrilling. They describe the days just prior to a critical moment in the outward journey. Lewis and Clark must chose the fork of the Missouri that will lead them to the Continental Divide before winter, and the answer is determined by the position of the Great Falls, as described to them by the Hidatsa Indians. When Lewis goes alone to scout one fork of the river, he comes across a series of waterfalls so awe-inspiring that for once he struggles to find words to tell his story. On the long walk back that night, he has a series of dangerous and "curious adventures" with wild animals.

There are many editions of the journals. This passage is taken from the University of Nebraska Press edition, edited by Gary Moulton. The Footnotes are his. He retained Lewis's imaginative spelling from the original notebooks.

[Lewis]   **Thursday June 13th 1805.**

This morning we set out about sunrise after taking breakfast off our venison and fish. we again ascended the hills of the river and gained the level country. the country through which we passed for the first six miles tho' more roling than that we had passed yesterday might still with propryety be deemed a level country; our course as yesterday was generally S. W. the river from the place we left it appeared to make a considerable bend to the South. from the extremity of this roling country I overlooked a most beatifull and level plain of great extent or at least 50 or sixty miles; in this there were infinitely more buffaloe than I had ever before witnessed at a view. nearly in the direction I had been travling or S. W. two curious mountains presented themselves of square figures,† the sides rising perpendicularly to the hight of 250 feet and appeared to be formed of yellow clay; their tops appeared to be level plains; these inac-

---

† These are probably buttes just south of Black Horse Lake along Highway 87 north of Great Falls, Cascade County, Montana.

cessible hights appeared like the ramparts of immence fortifications; I
have no doubt but with very little assistance from art they might be rendered impregnable. fearing that the river boar to the South and that I
might pass the falls if they existed between this an the snowey mountains I altered my course nealy to the South leaving those insulated hills
to my wright and proceeded through the plain; I sent Feels on my right
and Drewyer and Gibson on my left with orders to kill some meat and
join me at the river where I should halt for dinner. I had proceded on
this course about two miles with Goodrich at some distance behind me
whin my ears were saluted with the agreeable sound of a fall of water
and advancing a little further I saw the spray arrise above the plain like a
collumn of smoke which would frequently dispear again in an instant
caused I presume by the wind which blew pretty hard from the S. W. I
did not however loose my direction to this point which soon began to
make a roaring too tremendious to be mistaken for any cause short of
the great falls of the Missouri. here I arrived about 12 OClock having
traveled by estimate about 15 Miles. I hurryed down the hill which was
about 200 feet high and difficult of access, to gaze on this sublimely
grand specticle.† I took my position on the top of some rocks about 20
feet high opposite the center of the falls. this chain of rocks appear once
to have formed a part of those over which the waters tumbled, but in the
course of time has been seperated from it to the distance of 150 yards
lying prarrallel to it and forming a butment against which the water after
falling over the precipice beats with great fury; this barrier extends on
the right to the perpendicular clift which forms that board [bound? border?] of the river but to the distance of 120 yards next to the clift it is
but a few feet above the level of the water, and here the water in very

---

† Lewis had arrived at the Great Falls, first of a series of five falls in Cascade
Country northeast of the present city of Great Falls. The spectacle he saw has been
considerably reduced by Ryan Dam. The cliffs surrounding the Falls of the Missouri
are composed of the lower Cretaceous Kootenai Formation. It contains light-brown
and red-brown sandstone, red-to-purple shale, and green shale. The gorge was cut
during the glacial period when ice diverted the Missouri from its former course.

high tides appears to pass in a channel of 40 yds. next to the higher part of the ledg of rocks; on the left it extends within 80 or ninty yards of the lard. Clift which is also perpendicular; between this abrupt extremity of the ledge of rocks and the perpendicular bluff the whole body of water passes with incredible swiftness. immediately at the cascade the river is about 300 yds. wide; about ninty or a hundred yards of this next the Lard. bluff is a smoth even sheet of water falling over a precipice of at least eighty feet, the remaining part of about 200 yards on my right formes the grandest sight I ever beheld, the hight of the fall is the same of the other but the irregular and somewhat projecting rocks below receives the water in it's passage down and brakes it into a perfect white foam which assumes a thousand forms in a moment sometimes flying up in jets of sparkling foam to the hight of fifteen or twenty feet and are scarcely formed before large roling bodies of the same beaten and foaming water is thrown over and conceals them. in short the rocks seem to be most happily fixed to present a sheet of the whitest beaten froath for 200 yards in length and about 80 feet perpendicular. the water after decending strikes against the butment before mentioned or that on which I stand and seems to reverberate and being met by the more impetuous courant they role and swell into half formed billows of great hight which rise and again disappear in an instant. this butment of rock defends a handsom little bottom of about three acres which is deversified and agreeably shaded with some cottonwood trees; in the lower extremity of the bottom there is a very thick grove of the same kind of trees which are small, in this wood there are several Indian lodges formed of sticks. a few small cedar grow near the ledge of rocks where I rest. below the point of these rocks at a small distance the river is divided by a large rock which rises several feet above the water, and extends downwards with the stream for about 20 yards. about a mile before the water arrives at the pitch it decends very rappidly, and is confined on the Lard. side by a perpendicular clift of about 100 feet, on Stard. side it is also perpendicular for about three hundred yards above the pitch where it is then broken by the discharge of a small ravine, down which the buffaloe have a large beaten road to the water, [NB:

Qu.] for it is but in very few places that these anamals can obtain water near this place owing to the steep and inaccessible banks. I see several skelletons of the buffaloe lying in the edge of the water near the Stard. bluff which I presume have been swept down by the current and precipitated over this tremendious fall. about 300 yards below me there is another butment of solid rock with a perpendicular face and abot 60 feet high which projects from the Stard. side at right angles to the distance of 134 yds. and terminates the lower part nearly of the bottom before mentioned; there being a passage arround the end of this butment between it and the river of about 20 yardes; here the river again assumes it's usual width soon spreading to near 300 yards but still continues it's rappidity. from the reflection of the sun on the spray or mist which arrises from these falls there is a beatifull rainbow produced which adds not a little to the beauty of this majestically grand senery. after wrighting this imperfect discription I again viewed the falls and was so much disgusted with the imperfect idea which it conveyed of the scene that I determined to draw my pen across it and begin agin, but then reflected that I could not perhaps succeed better than pening the first impressions of the mind; I wished for the pencil of Salvator Rosa [*EC: a Titian*] or the pen of Thompson,† that I might be enabled to give to the enlightened world some just idea of this truly magnificent and sublimely grand object, which has from the commencement of time been concealed from the view of civilized man; but this was fruitless and vain. I most sincerely regreted that I had not brought a crimee obscura†† with me by the assistance of which even I could have hoped to have done better but alas this was also out of my reach; I therefore with the assistance of my pen only indeavoured to trace††† some of the

---

† Salvator Rosa, seventeenth-century Italian landscape painter, generally painted wild desolate scenes. James Thomson, eighteenth-century Scottish poet, was a forerunner of the English Romantic movement; his best-known poem was "The Seasons."

†† A camera obscura, basically a box with a lens mounted on one wall; light entering through the lens would project an image on the opposite wall of the dark box, which an artist could then trace, getting an almost photographic image.

††† No drawing of the falls by Lewis has ever been known to exist.

stronger features of this seen by the assistance of which and my recollection aided by some able pencil. I hope still to give to the world some
faint idea of an object which at this moment fills me with such pleasure
and astonishment, and which of it's kind I will venture to ascert is second to but one in the known world. I retired to the shade of a tree where
I determined to fix my camp† for the present and dispatch a man in the
morning to inform Capt. C. and the party of my success in finding the
falls and settle in their minds all further doubts as to the Missouri. the
hunters now arrived loaded with excellent buffaloe meat and informed
me that they had killed three very fat cows about 3/4 of a mile hence. I
directed them after they had refreshed themselves to go back and
butcher them and bring another load of meat each to our camp determining to employ those who remained with me in drying meat for the
party against their arrival. in about 2 hours or at 4 OClock P.M. they set
out on this duty, and I walked down the river about three miles to discover if possible some place to which the canoes might arrive or at
which they might be drawn on shore in order to be taken by land above
the falls; but returned without effecting either of these objects; the river
was one continued sene of rappids and cascades which I readily perceived could not be encountered with our canoes, and the Clifts still
retained their perpendicular structure and were from 150 to 200 feet
high; in short the river appears here to have woarn a channel in the
process of time through a solid rock. on my return I found the party at
camp; they had butchered the buffaloe and brought in some more meat
as I had directed. Goodrich had caught half a douzen very fine trout††
and a number of both species of the white fish. these trout [NB: *caught
in the falls*] are from sixteen to twenty three inches in length, precisely
resemble our mountain or speckled trout in form and the position of
their fins, but the specks on these are of a deep black instead of the red
or goald colour of those common to the U.' States. these are furnished

---

† Near the Great Falls, on the north side of the river, in Cascade County.
†† The cutthroat trout, *Salmo clarkii* after William Clark, a species new to science.

long sharp teeth on the pallet and tongue and have generally a small dash of red on each side behind the front ventral fins; the flesh is of a pale yellowish red, or when in good order, of a rose red.—

I am induced to believe that the Brown, the white and the Grizly bear of this country are the same species only differing in colour from age or more probably from the same natural cause that many other anamals of the same family differ in colour. one of those which we killed yesterday was of a creemcoloured white while the other in company with it was of the common bey or rdish brown, which seems to be the most usual colour of them. the white one appeared from it's tallons and teath to be the youngest; it was smaller than the other, and although a monstrous beast we supposed that it had not yet attained it's growth and that it was a little upwards of two years old. the young cubs which we have killed have always been of a brownish white, but none of them as white as that we killed yesterday. one other that we killed sometime since which I mentioned sunk under some driftwood and was lost, had a white stripe or list of about eleven inches wide entirely arround his body just behind the shoalders, and was much darker than these bear usually are. the grizly bear we have never yet seen. I have seen their tallons in possession of the Indians and from their form I am perswaded if there is any difference between this species and the brown or white bear it is very inconsiderable. There is no such anamal as a black bear in this open country or of that species generally denominated the black bear

my fare is really sumptuous this evening; buffaloe's humps, tongues and marrowbones, fine trout parched meal pepper and salt, and a good appetite; the last is not considered the least of the luxuries.

[Lewis]   Friday June 14th 1805.
This morning at sunrise I dispatched Joseph Fields with a letter to Capt. Clark and ordered him to keep sufficiently near the river to observe it's situation in order that he might be enabled to give Capt. Clark an idea of the point at which it would be best to halt to make our portage. I set one

man about preparing a saffold and collecting wood to dry the meat. Sent the others to bring in the ballance of the buffaloe meat, or at least the part which the wolves had left us, for those fellows are ever at hand and ready to partake with us the moment we kill a buffaloe; and there is no means of puting the meat out of their reach in those plains; the two men shortly after returned with the meat and informed me that the wolves had devoured the greater part of the meat. about ten OClock this morning while the men were engaged with the meat I took my Gun and espontoon[1] and thought I would walk a few miles and see where the rappids termineated above, and return to dinner. accordingly I set out and proceeded up the river about S.W. after passing one continued rappid and three small cascades of abut for or five feet each at the distance of about five miles I arrived at a fall of about 19 feet; the river is here about 400 yds. wide. this pitch which I called the crooked falls[†] occupys about three fourths of the width of the river, commencing on the South side, extends obliquly upwards about 150 yds. then forming an accute angle extends downwards nearly to the commencement of four small Islands lying near the N. shore; among these Islands and between them and the lower extremity of the perpendicular pitch being a distance of 100 yards or upwards, the water glides down the side of a sloping rock with a velocity almost equal to that of it's perpendicular decent. just above this rappid the river makes a suddon bend to the right or Northwardly. I should have returned from hence but hearing a tremendious roaring above me I continued my rout across the point of a hill a few hundred yards further and was again presented by one of the most beatifull objects in nature, a cascade of about fifty feet perpendicular streching at rightangles across the river from side to side to the distance of at least a quarter of a mile.[††] here the river pitches over a shelving rock, with an edge as regular and as

[†] Crooked Falls still bears that name.
[††] Rainbow Falls, Lewis and Clark's "Handsom Falls," now greatly altered by Rainbow Dam.

[1] A club, most often used by Lewis as a walking stick.

streight as if formed by art, without a nich or brake in it; the water decends in one even and uninterupted sheet to the bottom wher dashing against the rocky bottom rises into foaming billows of great hight and rappidly glides away, hising flashing and sparkling as it departs the sprey rises from one extremity to the other to 50 f. I now thought that if a skill-full painter had been asked to make a beautifull cascade that he would most probably have pesented the precise immage of this one; nor could I for some time determine on which of those two great cataracts to bestoe the palm, on this or that which I had discovered yesterday; at length I determined between these two great rivals for glory that this was *pleasingly beautifull*, while the other was *sublimely grand*. I had scarcely infixed my eyes from this pleasing object before I discovered another fall above at the distance of half a mile;[†] thus invited I did not once think of returning but hurried thither to amuse myself with this newly discovered object. I found this to be a cascade of about 14 feet possessing a perpendicular pitch of about 6 feet. this was tolerably regular streching across the river from bank to bank where it was about a quarter of a mile wide; in any other neighbourhood but this, such a cascade would probably be extoled for it's beaty and magnifficence, but here I passed it by with but little attention, determining as I had proceded so far to continue my rout to the head of the rappids if it should even detain me all night. at every rappid cateract and cascade I discovered that the bluffs grew lower or that the bed of the river rose nearer to a level with the plains. still pursuing the river with it's course about S. W. passing a continued sene of rappids and small cascades, at the distance of 2 1/2 miles I arrived at another cataract of 26 feet.[††] this is not immediately perpendicular, a rock about 1/3 of it's decent seems to protrude to a small distance and receives the water in it's passage downwards and gives a curve to the

---

† Colter Falls (now submerged).
†† Black Eagle Falls, just below the present town of Black Eagle, Cascade County, Montana. The eagle's nest on the island below the falls, a distinguishing feature referred to by the Hidatsas in their directions to the captains, was still there in 1860.

water tho' it falls mostly with a regular and smoth sheet. the river is near six hundred yards wide at this place, a beatifull level plain on the S. side only a few feet above the level of the pitch; on the N. side where I am the country is More broken and immediately behind me near the river a high hill. below this fall at a little distance a beatifull little Island well timbered is situated about the middle of the river. in this Island on a Cottonwood tree an Eagle has placed her nest; a more inaccessable spot I beleive she could not have found; for neither man nor beast dare pass those gulphs which seperate her little domain from the shores. the water is also broken in such manner as it decends over this pitch that the mist or sprey rises to a considerable hight. this fall is certainly much the greatest I ever behald except those two which I have mentioned below. it is incomparably a geater cataract and a more noble interesting object than the celibrated falls of Potomac or Soolkiln† &c. just above this is another cascade of about 5 feet, above which the water as far as I could see began to abate of it's valosity, and I therefore determined to ascend the hill behind me which promised a fine prospect of the adjacent country, nor was I disappointed on my arrival at it's summit. from hence I overlooked a most beatifull and extensive plain reaching from the river to the base of the Snowclad mountains to the S. and S. West; I also observed the missoury streching it's meandering course to the South through this plain to a great distance filled to it's even and grassey brim; another large river flowed in on it's Western side about four miles above me and extended itself though a level and fertile valley of 3 miles in width a great distance to the N. W. rendered more conspicuous by the timber which garnished it's borders. in these plains and more particularly in the valley just below me immence herds of buffaloe are feeding. the missouri just above this hill makes a bend to the South where it lies a smoth even and unruffled sheet of water of nearly a mile in width bearing on it's watry bosome vast flocks of geese which feed at pleasure in the delightfull pasture on either border. the young geese are now completely feathered

† Probably the Schuylkill River in Pennsylvania.

except the wings which both in the young and old are yet deficient. after feasting my eyes on this ravishing prospect and resting myself a few minutes I determined to procede as far as the river which I saw discharge itself on the West side of the Missouri convinced that it was the river which the Indians call *medicine river*† and which they informed us fell into the Missouri just above the falls   I decended the hills and directed my course to the bend of the Missouri near which there was a herd of at least a thousand buffaloe; here I thought it would be well to kill a buffaloe and leave him untill my return from the river and if I then found that I had not time to get back to camp this evening to remain all night here there being a few sticks of drift wood lying along shore which would answer for my fire, and a few sattering cottonwood trees a few hundred yards below which would afford me at least a semblance of a shelter. under this impression I scelected a fat buffaloe and shot him very well, through the lungs; while I was gazeing attentively on the poor anamal discharging blood in streams from his mouth and nostrils, expecting him to fall every instant, and having entirely forgotton to reload my rifle, a large white, or reather brown bear, had perceived and crept on me within 20 steps before I discovered him; in the first moment I drew up my gun to shoot, but at the same instant recolected that she was not loaded and that he was too near for me to hope to perform this opperation before he reached me, as he was then briskly advancing on me; it was an open level plain, not a bush within miles nor a tree within less than three hundred yards of me; the river bank was sloping and not more than three feet above the level of the water; in short there was no place by means of which I could conceal myself from this monster until I could charge my rifle; in this situation I thought of retreating in a brisk walk as fast as he was advancing untill I could reach a tree about 300 yards below me, but I had no sooner terned myself about but he pitched at me, open mouthed and full speed, I ran about 80 yards and found he gained on me fast, I then run into the water   the idea struk me to get into the water to such

---

† Today's Sun River, which meets the Missouri at the present city of Great Falls.

debth that I could stand and he would be obliged to swim, and that I could in that situation defend myself with my espontoon; accordingly I ran haistily into the water about waist deep, and faced about and presented the point of my espontoon, at this instant he arrived at the edge of the water within about 20 feet of me; the moment I put myself in this attitude of defence he sudonly wheeled about as if frightened, declined the combat on such unequal grounds, and retreated with quite as great precipitation as he had just before pursued me. as soon as I saw him run of[f] in that manner I returned to the shore and charged my gun, which I had still retained in my hand throughout this curious adventure. I saw him run through the level open plain about three miles, till he disappeared in the woods on medecine river; during the whole of this distance he ran at full speed, sometimes appearing to look behind him as if he expected pursuit. I now began to reflect on this novil occurrence and indeavoured to account for this sudden retreat of the bear. I at first thought that perhaps he had not smelt me before he arrived at the waters edge so near me, but I then reflected that he had pursued me for about 80 or 90 yards before I took the water and on examination saw the grownd toarn with his tallons immediately on the impression of my steps; and the cause of his allarm still remains with me misterious and unaccountable.— so it was and I feelt myself not a little gratifyed that he had declined the combat. My gun reloaded I felt confidence once more in my strength; and determined not to be thwarted in my design of visiting medicine river, but determined never again to suffer my peice to be longer empty than the time she necessarily required to charge her. I passed through the plain nearly in the direction which the bear had run to medecine river, found it a handsome stream, about 200 yds. wide with a gentle current, apparently deep, it's waters clear, and banks which were formed principally of darkbrown and blue clay† were about the hight of

---

† The north bank of the Sun River is alluvium derived from dark-gray shales of the Blackleaf Formation. The south bank is composed of clay, silt, and sand deposited in Glacial Lake, Great Falls, during the glacial period.

those of the Missouri or from 3 to 5 feet; yet they had not the appearance of ever being overflown, a circumstance, which I did not expect so immediately in the neighbourhood of the mountains, from whence I should have supposed, that sudden and immence torrants would issue at certain seasons of the year; but the reverse is absolutely the case. I am therefore compelled to beleive that the snowey mountains yeald their warters slowly, being partially effected every day by the influence of the sun only, and never suddonly melted down by haisty showers of rain.—

having examined Medecine river I now determined to return, having by my estimate about 12 miles to walk. I looked at my watch and found it was half after six P.M.— in returning through the level bottom of Medecine river and about 200 yards distant from the Missouri, my direction led me directly to an anamal that I at first supposed was a wolf;[†] but on nearer approach or about sixty paces distant I discovered that it was not, it's colour was a brownish yellow; it was standing near it's burrow, and when I approached it thus nearly, it couched itself down like a cat looking immediately at me as if it designed to spring on me. I took aim at it and fired, it instantly disappeared in it's burrow; I loaded my gun and exmined the place which was dusty and saw the track from which I am still further convinced that it was of the tiger kind. whether I struck it or not I could not determine, but I am almost confident that I did; my gun is true and I had a steady rest by means of my espontoon, which I have found very serviceable to me in this way in the open plains. It now seemed to me that all the beasts of the neighbourhood had made a league to distroy me, or that some fortune was disposed to amuse herself at my expence, for I had not proceded more than three hundred yards from the burrow of this tyger cat, before three bull buffaloe, which wer feeding with a large herd about half a mile from me on my left, seperated from the herd and ran full speed towards me, I thought at least to give them some amusement and altered my direction to meet them; when they arrived within a hundred yards they mad a halt, took a good

† Perhaps a wolverine, *Gulo luscus* (or *G. gulo*).

view of me and retreated with precipitation. I then continued my rout homewards passed the buffaloe which I had killed, but did not think it prudent to remain all night at this place which really from the succession of curious adventures wore the impression on my mind of inchantment; at sometimes for a moment I thought it might be a dream, but the prick-ley pears which pierced my feet very severely once in a while, particularly after it grew dark, convinced me that I was really awake, and that it was necessary to make the best of my way to camp.† it was sometime after dark before I returned to the party; I found them extremely uneasy for my safety; they had formed a thousand conjectures, all of which equally forboding my death, which they had so far settled among them, that they had already agreed on the rout which each should take in the morning to surch for me. I felt myself much fortiegued, but eat a hearty supper and took a good night's rest.— the weather being warm I had left my leather over shirt and had woarn only a yellow flannin one.

† Evidently the same as the previous night's camp.

JOHN WESLEY POWELL

(1834–1902)

From *The Exploration of the Colorado River and Its Canyons*

Setting out on a scientific expedition that was to become one of the most epic adventures of our nation's history, John Wesley Powell took nine men down the Colorado River in the summer of 1869. They were a ragtag crew of ox-drivers and mountainmen, none of whom had ever run rapids before, let alone anything as formidable as the narrow, twisting canyons of the Colorado Plateau. Their leader was a young professor of geology, an amateur naturalist with an undying curiosity for the western landscape, and a Civil War veteran with one arm.

Their ninety-nine-day journey is the essence of bravery. At each new breathless bend in the river they wondered when "we shall come to a fall in these canyons which we cannot pass, where the walls rise from the water's edge so that we cannot land, and where the water is so swift that we cannot return."

Finally this anxiety of the unknown dangers grew too much for three of the men, who left the party only to die in the desert. Powell's expedition ended in tatters, and he returned to the East to read his own obituary in the papers. Yet he would return to explore the Colorado and the tribes of the surrounding mesas twice more and to go on to have a long career as the head of both the United States Geological Survey and the Bureau of Ethnicity. One hundred and twenty-five years after it was published, his account of his experiences on the Colorado is not only a gripping read but a lyrical and observant memorial to a once ferocious river that is now famous for never reaching the sea.

August 13.—We are now ready to start on our way down the Great Unknown. Our boats,[1] tied to a common stake, chafe each other as they are tossed by the fretful river. They ride high and buoyant, for their loads are lighter than we could desire. We have but a month's rations remaining. The flour has been resifted through the mosquito-net sieve; the spoiled bacon has been dried and the worst of it boiled; the few pounds of dried apples have been spread in the sun and reshrunken to their normal bulk. The sugar has all melted and gone on its way down the river. But we have a large sack of coffee. The lightening of the boats has this advantage: they will ride the waves better and we shall have but little to carry when we make a portage.

We are three quarters of a mile in the depths of the earth, and the great river shrinks into insignificance as it dashes its angry waves against the walls and cliffs that rise to the world above; the waves are but puny ripples, and we but pigmies, running up and down the sands or lost among the boulders.

We have an unknown distance yet to run, an unknown river to explore. What falls there are, we know not; what rocks beset the channel, we know not; what walls rise over the river, we know not. Ah, well! we may conjecture many things. The men talk as cheerfully as ever; jests are bandied about freely this morning; but to me the cheer is somber and the jests are ghastly.

---

[1] The expedition took four boats. These were 21-feet long, and shaped like a broad-bottomed canoe with enclosed bulkheads fore and aft.

With some eagerness and some anxiety and some misgiving we enter the canyon below and are carried along by the swift water through walls which rise from its very edge. They have the same structure that we noticed yesterday—tiers of irregular shelves below, and, above these, steep slopes to the foot of marble cliffs. We run six miles in a little more than half an hour and emerge into a more open portion of the canyon, where high hills and ledges of rock intervene between the river and the distant walls. Just at the head of this open place the river runs across a dike; that is, a fissure in the rocks, open to depths below, was filled with eruptive matter, and this on cooling was harder than the rocks through which the crevice was made, and when these were washed away the harder volcanic matter remained as a wall, and the river has cut a gateway through it several hundred feet high and as many wide. As it crosses the wall, there is a fall below and a bad rapid, filled with boulders of trap; so we stop to make a portage. Then on we go, gliding by hills and ledges, with distant walls in view; sweeping past sharp angles of rock; stopping at a few points to examine rapids, which we find can be run, until we have made another five miles, when we land for dinner.

Then we let down with lines over a long rapid and start again. Once more the walls close in, and we find ourselves in a narrow gorge, the water again filling the channel and being very swift. With great care and constant watchfulness we proceed, making about four miles this afternoon, and camp in a cave.

August 14.—At daybreak we walk down the bank of the river, on a little sandy beach, to take a view of a new feature in the canyon. Heretofore hard rocks have given us bad river; soft rocks, smooth water; and a series of rocks harder than any we have experienced sets in. The river enters the gneiss! We can see but a little way into the granite gorge, but it looks threatening.

After breakfast we enter on the waves. At the very introduction it inspires awe. The canyon is narrower than we have ever before seen it; the water is swifter; there are but few broken rocks in the channel; but

the walls are set, on either side, with pinnacles and crags; and sharp, angular buttresses, bristling with wind- and wave-polished spires, extend far out into the river.

Ledges of rock jut into the stream, their tops sometimes just below the surface, sometimes rising a few or many feet above; and island ledges and island pinnacles and island towers break the swift course of the stream into chutes and eddies and whirlpools. We soon reach a place where a creek comes in from the left, and, just below, the channel is choked with boulders, which have washed down this lateral canyon and formed a dam, over which there is a fall of 30 or 40 feet; but on the boulders foothold can be had, and we make a portage. Three more such dams are found. Over one we make a portage; at the other two are chutes through which we can run.

As we proceed the granite rises higher, until nearly a thousand feet of the lower part of the walls are composed of this rock.

About eleven o'clock we hear a great roar ahead, and approach it very cautiously. The sound grows louder and louder as we run, and at last we find ourselves above a long, broken fall, with ledges and pinnacles of rock obstructing the river. There is a descent of perhaps 75 or 80 feet in a third of a mile, and the rushing waters break into great waves on the rocks, and lash themselves into a mad, white foam. We can land just above, but there is no foothold on either side by which we can make a portage. It is nearly a thousand feet to the top of the granite; so it will be impossible to carry our boats around, though we can climb to the summit up a side gulch and, passing along a mile or two, descend to the river. This we find on examination; but such a portage would be impracticable for us, and we must run the rapid or abandon the river. There is no hesitation. We step into our boats, push off, and away we go, first on smooth but swift water, then we strike a glassy wave and ride to its top, down again into the trough, up again on a higher wave, and down and up on waves higher and still higher until we strike one just as it curls back, and a breaker rolls over our little boat. Still on we speed, shooting past projecting rocks, till the little boat is caught in a whirlpool and spun round several times. At last we pull out again into the stream. And now the other boats have passed us. The open compartment of the "Emma Dean" is filled with water and every breaker rolls over us. Hurled back from a rock, now on this side, now on that, we are carried into an eddy, in which we struggle for a few minutes, and are then out again, the breakers still rolling over us. Our boat is unmanageable, but she cannot sink, and we drift down another hundred yards through breakers—how, we scarcely know. We find the other boats have turned into an eddy at the foot of the fall and are waiting to catch us as we come, for the men have seen that our boat is swamped. They push out as we come near and pull us in against the wall. Our boat bailed, on we go again.

The walls now are more than a mile in height—a vertical distance difficult to appreciate. Stand on the south steps of the Treasury building in Washington and look down Pennsylvania Avenue to the Capitol; measure this distance overhead, and imagine cliffs to extend to that altitude, and you will understand what is meant; or stand at Canal Street in New York and look up Broadway to Grace Church, and you have about the distance; or stand at Lake Street bridge in Chicago and look down to the Central Depot, and you have it again.

A thousand feet of this is up through granite crags; then steep slopes and perpendicular cliffs rise one above another to the summit. The gorge is black and narrow below, red and gray and flaring above, with crags and angular projections on the walls, which, cut in many places by side canyons, seem to be a vast wilderness of rocks. Down in these grand, gloomy depths we glide, ever listening, for the mad waters keep up their roar; ever watching, ever peering ahead, for the narrow canyon is winding and the river is closed in so that we can see but a few hundred yards, and what there may be below we know not; so we listen for falls and watch for rocks, stopping now and then in the bay of a recess to admire the gigantic scenery; and ever as we go there is some new pinnacle or tower, some crag or peak, some distant view of the upper plateau, some strangely shaped rock, or some deep, narrow side canyon.

Then we come to another broken fall, which appears more difficult than the one we ran this morning. A small creek comes in on the right, and the first fall of the water is over boulders, which have been carried down by this lateral stream. We land at its mouth and stop for an hour or two to examine the fall. It seems possible to let down with lines, at least a part of the way, from point to point, along the right-hand wall. So we make a portage over the first rocks and find footing on some boulders below. Then we let down one of the boats to the end of her line, when she reaches a corner of the projecting rock, to which one of the men clings and steadies her while I examine an eddy below. I think we can pass the other boats down by us and catch them in the eddy. This is soon done, and the men in the boats in the eddy pull us to their side. On the shore of this little eddy there is about two feet of gravel beach above the water. Standing on this beach, some of the men take the line of the little boat and let it drift down against another projecting angle. Here is a little shelf, on which a man from my boat climbs, and a shorter line is passed to him, and he fastens the boat to the side of the cliff; then the second one is let down, bringing the line of the third. When the second boat is tied up, the two men standing on the beach above spring into the last boat, which is pulled up alongside of ours; then we let down the boats for 23 or 30 yards by walking along the shelf, landing them again in the mouth of a side canyon. Just below this there is another pile of boulders, over which we make another portage. From the foot of these rocks we can climb to another shelf, 40 or 50 feet above the water.

On this bench we camp for the night. It is raining hard, and we have no shelter, but find a few sticks which have lodged in the rocks, and kindle a fire and have supper. We sit on the rocks all night, wrapped in our *ponchos,* getting what sleep we can.

August 15.—This morning we find we can let down for 300 or 400 yards, and it is managed in this way: we pass along the wall by climbing from projecting point to point, sometimes near the water's edge, at other places 50 or 60 feet above, and hold the boat with a line while two men remain aboard and prevent her from being dashed against the rocks and keep the line from getting caught on the wall. In two hours we have brought them all down, as far as it is possible, in this way. A few yards below, the river strikes with great violence against a projecting rock and our boats are pulled up in a little bay above. We must now manage to pull out of this and clear the point below. The little boat is held by the bow obliquely up the stream. We jump in and pull out only a few strokes, and sweep clear of the dangerous rock. The other boats follow in the same manner and the rapid is passed.

It is not easy to describe the labor of such navigation. We must prevent the waves from dashing the boats against the cliffs. Sometimes, where the river is swift, we must put a bight of rope about a rock, to prevent the boat from being snatched from us by a wave; but where the plunge is too great or the chute too swift, we must let her leap and catch her below or the undertow will drag her under the falling water and sink her. Where we wish to run her out a little way from shore through a channel between rocks, we first throw in little sticks of drift-wood and watch their course, to see where we must steer so that she will pass the channel in safety. And so we hold, and let go, and pull, and lift, and ward—among rocks, around rocks, and over rocks.

And now we go on through this solemn, mysterious way. The river is very deep, the canyon very narrow, and still obstructed, so that there is no steady flow of the stream; but the waters reel and roll and boil, and we are scarcely able to determine where we can go. Now the boat is carried to the right, perhaps close to the wall; again, she is shot into the stream, and perhaps is dragged over to the other side, where, caught in a whirlpool, she spins about. We can neither land nor run as we please. The boats are entirely unmanageable; no order in their running can be preserved; now one, now another, is ahead, each crew laboring for its own preservation. In such a place we come to another rapid. Two of the boats run it perforce. One succeeds in landing, but there is no foothold by which to make a portage and she is pushed out again into the stream. The next minute a great reflex wave fills the open compartment; she is water-logged, and drifts unmanageable. Breaker after breaker rolls over her and one capsizes her. The men are thrown out; but they cling to the boat, and she drifts down some distance alongside of us and we are able to catch her. She is soon bailed out and the men are aboard once more; but the oars are lost, and so a pair from the "Emma Dean" is spared. Then for two miles we find smooth water.

Clouds are playing in the canyon to-day. Sometimes they roll down in great masses, filling the gorge with gloom; sometimes they hang aloft from wall to wall and cover the canyon with a roof of impending storm, and we can peer long distances up and down this canyon corridor, with its cloud-roof overhead, its walls of black granite, and its river bright with the sheen of broken waters. Then a gust of wind sweeps down a side gulch and, making a rift in the clouds, reveals the blue heavens, and a stream of sunlight pours in. Then the clouds drift away into the distance, and hang around crags and peaks and pinnacles and towers and walls, and cover them with a mantle that lifts from time to time and sets them all in sharp relief. Then baby clouds creep out of side canyons, glide around points, and creep back again into more distant gorges. Then clouds arrange in strata across the canyon, with intervening vista views to cliffs and rocks beyond. The clouds are children of the heavens, and when they play among the rocks they lift them to the region above.

It rains! Rapidly little rills are formed above, and these soon grow into brooks, and the brooks grow into creeks and tumble over the walls in innumerable cascades, adding their wild music to the roar of the river. When the rain ceases the rills, brooks, and creeks run dry. The waters that fall during a rain on these steep rocks are gathered at once into the river; they could scarcely be poured in more suddenly if some vast spout ran from the clouds to the stream itself. When a storm bursts over the canyon a side gulch is dangerous, for a sudden flood may come, and the inpouring waters will raise the river so as to hide the rocks.

Early in the afternoon we discover a stream entering from the north— a clear, beautiful creek, coming down through a gorgeous red canyon. We land and camp on a sand beach above its mouth, under a great, over-spreading tree with willow-shaped leaves.

August 16.—We must dry our rations again to-day and make oars.

The Colorado is never a clear stream, but for the past three or four days it has been raining much of the time, and the floods poured over the walls have brought down great quantities of mud, making it exceedingly turbid now. The little affluent which we have discovered here is a clear, beautiful creek, or river, as it would be termed in this western country, where streams are not abundant. We have named one stream, away above, in honor of the great chief of the "Bad Angels," and as this is in beautiful contrast to that, we conclude to name it "Bright Angel."

Early in the morning the whole party starts up to explore the Bright Angel River, with the special purpose of seeking timber from which to make oars. A couple of miles above we find a large pine log, which has been floated down from the plateau, probably from an altitude of more than 6,000 feet, but not many miles back. On its way it must have passed over many cataracts and falls, for it bears scars in evidence of the rough usage which it has received. The men roll it on skids, and the work of sawing oars is commenced.

This stream heads away back under a line of abrupt cliffs that terminates the plateau, and tumbles down more than 4,000 feet in the first mile or two of its course; then runs through a deep, narrow canyon until it reaches the river.

Late in the afternoon I return and go up a little gulch just above this creek, about 200 yards from camp, and discover the ruins of two or three old houses, which were originally of stone laid in mortar. Only the foundations are left, but irregular blocks, of which the houses were constructed, lie scattered about. In one room I find an old mealing-stone, deeply worn, as if it had been much used. A great deal of pottery is strewn around, and old trails, which in some places are deeply worn into the rocks, are seen.

It is ever a source of wonder to us why these ancient people sought such inaccessible places for their homes. They were, doubtless, an agricultural race, but there are no lands here of any considerable extent that they could have cultivated. To the west of Oraibi, one of the towns in the Province of Tusayan, in northern Arizona, the inhabitants have actually built little terraces along the face of the cliff where a spring gushes out, and thus made their sites for gardens. It is possible that the ancient inhabitants of this place made their agricultural lands in the same way. But why should they seek such spots? Surely the country was not so crowded with people as to demand the utilization of so barren a region. The only solution suggested of the problem is this: We know that for a century or two after the settlement of Mexico many expeditions were sent into the country now comprising Arizona and New Mexico, for the purpose of bringing the town-building people under the dominion of the Spanish government. Many of their villages were destroyed, and the inhabitants fled to regions at that time unknown; and there are traditions among the people who inhabit the pueblos that still remain that the canyons were these unknown lands. It may be these buildings were erected at that time; sure it is that they have a much more modern appearance than the ruins scattered over Nevada, Utah, Colorado, Arizona, and New Mexico. Those old Spanish conquerors had a monstrous greed for gold and a wonderful lust for saving souls. Treasures they must have, if not on earth, why, then, in heaven; and when they failed to find heathen temples bedecked with silver, they propitiated Heaven by seizing the heathen themselves. There is yet extant a copy of a record made by a heathen artist to express his conception of the demands of the conquerors. In one part of the picture we have a lake, and near by stands a priest pouring water on the head of a native. On the other side, a poor Indian has a cord about his throat. Lines run from these two groups to a central figure, a man with beard and full Spanish panoply. The interpretation of the picture-writing is this: "Be baptized as this saved heathen, or be hanged as that damned heathen." Doubtless, some of these people preferred another alternative, and rather than be baptized or hanged they chose to imprison themselves within these canyon walls.

August 17.—Our rations are still spoiling; the bacon is so badly injured that we are compelled to throw it away. By an accident, this morning, the saleratus[2] was lost overboard. We have now only musty flour sufficient for ten days and a few dried apples, but plenty of coffee. We must make all haste possible. If we meet with difficulties such as we have encoun-

2 Sodium bicarbonate, used for leavening their bread.

tered in the canyon above, we may be compelled to give up the expedition and try to reach the Mormon settlements to the north. Our hopes are that the worst places are passed, but our barometers are all so much injured as to be useless, and so we have lost our reckoning in altitude, and know not how much descent the river has yet to make.

The stream is still wild and rapid and rolls through a narrow channel. We make but slow progress, often landing against a wall and climbing around some point to see the river below. Although very anxious to advance, we are determined to run with great caution, lest by another accident we lose our remaining supplies. How precious that little flour has become! We divide it among the boats and carefully store it away, so that it can be lost only by the loss of the boat itself.

We make ten miles and a half, and camp among the rocks on the right. We have had rain from time to time all day, and have been thoroughly drenched and chilled; but between showers the sun shines with great power and the mercury in our thermometers stands at 115°, so that we have rapid changes from great extremes, which are very disagreeable. It is especially cold in the rain to-night. The little canvas we have is rotten and useless; the rubber *ponchos* with which we started from Green River City have all been lost; more than half the party are without hats, not one of us has an entire suit of clothes, and we have not a blanket apiece. So we gather driftwood and build a fire; but after supper the rain, coming down in torrents, extinguishes it, and we sit up all night on the rocks, shivering, and are more exhausted by the night's discomfort than by the day's toil.

August 18.—The day is employed in making portages and we advance but two miles on our journey. Still it rains.

While the men are at work making portages I climb up the granite to its summit and go away back over the rust-colored sandstones and green-ish-yellow shales to the foot of the marble wall. I climb so high that the men and boats are lost in the black depths below and the dashing river is a rippling brook, and still there is more canyon above than below. All about me are interesting geologic records. The book is open and I can read as I run. All about me are grand views, too, for the clouds are playing again in the gorges. But somehow I think of the nine days' rations and the bad river, and the lesson of the rocks and the glory of the scene are but half conceived.

I push on to an angle, where I hope to get a view of the country beyond, to see if possible what the prospect may be of our soon running through this plateau, or at least of meeting with some geologic change that will let us out of the granite; but, arriving at the point, I can see below only a labyrinth of black gorges.

August 19.—Rain again this morning. We are in our granite prison still, and the time until noon is occupied in making a long, bad portage.

After dinner, in running a rapid the pioneer boat is upset by a wave. We are some distance in advance of the larger boats. The river is rough and swift and we are unable to land, but cling to the boat and are carried down stream over another rapid. The men in the boats above see our trouble, but they are caught in whirlpools and are spinning about in eddies, and it seems a long time before they come to our relief. At last they do come; our boat is turned right side up and bailed out; the oars, which fortunately have floated along in company with us, are gathered up, and on we go, without even landing. The clouds break away and we have sunshine again.

Soon we find a little beach with just room enough to land. Here we camp, but there is no wood. Across the river and a little way above, we see some driftwood lodged in the rocks. So we bring two boat loads over, build a huge fire, and spread everything to dry. It is the first cheerful night we have had for a week—a warm, drying fire in the midst of the camp, and a few bright stars in our patch of heavens overhead.

August 20.—The characteristics of the canyon change this morning. The river is broader, the walls more sloping, and composed of black slates that stand on edge. These nearly vertical slates are washed out in places—

that is, the softer beds are washed out between the harder, which are left standing. In this way curious little alcoves are formed, in which are quiet bays of water, but on a much smaller scale than the great bays and buttresses of Marble Canyon.

The river is still rapid and we stop to let down with lines several times, but make greater progress, as we run ten miles. We camp on the right bank. Here, on a terrace of trap, we discover another group of ruins. There was evidently quite a village on this rock. Again we find mealing-stones and much broken pottery, and up on a little natural shelf in the rock back of the ruins we find a globular basket that would hold perhaps a third of a bushel. It is badly broken, and as I attempt to take it up it falls to pieces. There are many beautiful flint chips, also, as if this had been the home of an old arrow-maker.

August 21.—We start early this morning, cheered by the prospect of a fine day and encouraged also by the good run made yesterday. A quarter of a mile below camp the river turns abruptly to the left, and between camp and that point is very swift, running down in a long, broken chute and piling up against the foot of the cliff, where it turns to the left. We try to pull across, so as to go down on the other side, but the waters are swift and it seems impossible for us to escape the rock below; but, in pulling across, the bow of the boat is turned to the farther shore, so that we are swept broadside down and are prevented by the rebounding waters from striking against the wall. We toss about for a few seconds in these billows and are then carried past the danger. Below, the river turns again to the right, the canyon is very narrow, and we see in advance but a short distance. The water, too, is very swift, and there is no landing-place. From around this curve there comes a mad roar, and down we are carried with a dizzying velocity to the head of another rapid. On either side high over our heads there are overhanging granite walls, and the sharp bends cut off our view, so that a few minutes will carry us into unknown waters. A way we go on one long, winding chute. I stand on deck, supporting myself with a strap fastened on either side of the gunwale. The boat glides rapidly where the water is smooth, then, striking a wave, she leaps and bounds like a thing of life, and we have a wild, exhilarating ride for ten miles, which we make in less than an hour. The excitement is so great that we forget the danger until we hear the roar of a great fall below; then we back on our oars and are carried slowly toward its head and succeed in landing just above and find that we have to make another portage. At this we are engaged until some time after dinner.

Just here we run out of the granite. Ten miles in less than half a day, and limestone walls below. Good cheer returns; we forget the storms and the gloom and the cloud-covered canyons and the black granite and the raging river, and push our boats from shore in great glee.

Though we are out of the granite, the river is still swift, and we wheel about a point again to the right, and turn, so as to head back in the direction from which we came; this brings the granite in sight again, with its narrow gorge and black crags; but we meet with no more great falls or rapids. Still, we run cautiously and stop from time to time to examine some places which look bad. Yet we make ten miles this afternoon; twenty miles in all to-day.

. . .

August 24.—The canyon is wider to-day. The walls rise to a vertical height of nearly 3,000 feet. In many places the river runs under a cliff in great curves, forming amphitheaters half-dome shaped.

Though the river is rapid, we meet with no serious obstructions and run 20 miles. How anxious we are to make up our reckoning every time we stop, now that our diet is confined to plenty of coffee, a very little spoiled flour, and very few dried apples! It has come to be a race for a dinner. Still, we make such fine progress that all hands are in good cheer, but not a moment of daylight is lost.

. . .

August 26.—The canyon walls are steadily becoming higher as we advance. They are still bold and nearly vertical up to the terrace. We still see evidence of the eruption discovered yesterday, but the thickness of the basalt is decreasing as we go down stream; yet it has been reinforced at points by streams that have come down from volcanoes standing on the terrace above, but which we cannot see from the river below.

Since we left the Colorado Chiquito we have seen no evidences that the tribe of Indians inhabiting the plateaus on either side ever come down to the river; but about eleven o'clock to-day we discover an Indian garden at the foot of the wall on the right, just where a little stream with a narrow flood plain comes down through a side canyon. Along the valley the Indians have planted corn, using for irrigation the water which bursts out in springs at the foot of the cliff. The corn is looking quite well, but it is not sufficiently advanced to give us roasting ears; but there are some nice green squashes. We carry ten or a dozen of these on board our boats and hurriedly leave, not willing to be caught in the robbery, yet excusing ourselves by pleading our great want. We run down a short distance to where we feel certain no Indian can follow, and what a kettle of squash sauce we make! True, we have no salt with which to season it, but it makes a fine addition to our unleavened bread and coffee. Never was fruit so sweet as these stolen squashes.

After dinner we push on again and make fine time, finding many rapids, but none so bad that we cannot run them with safety; and when we stop, just at dusk, and foot up our reckoning, we find we have run 35 miles again. A few days like this, and we are out of prison.

We have a royal supper—unleavened bread, green squash sauce, and strong coffee. We have been for a few days on half rations, but now have no stint of roast squash.

August 27.—This morning the river takes a more southerly direction. The dip of the rocks is to the north and we are running rapidly into lower formations. Unless our course changes we shall very soon run again into the granite. This gives some anxiety. Now and then the river turns to the west and excites hopes that are soon destroyed by another turn to the south. About nine o'clock we come to the dreaded rock. It is with no little misgiving that we see the river enter these black, hard walls. At its very entrance we have to make a portage; then let down with lines past some ugly rocks. We run a mile or two farther, and then the rapids below can be seen.

About eleven o'clock we come to a place in the river which seems much worse than any we have yet met in all its course. A little creek comes down from the left. We land first on the right and clamber up over the granite pinnacles for a mile or two, but can see no way by which to let down, and to run it would be sure destruction. After dinner we cross to examine on the left. High above the river we can walk along on the top of the granite, which is broken off at the edge and set with crags and pinnacles, so that it is very difficult to get a view of the river at all. In my eagerness to reach a point where I can see the roaring fall below, I go too far on the wall, and can neither advance nor retreat. I stand with one foot on a little projecting rock and cling with my hand fixed in a little crevice. Finding I am caught here, suspended 400 feet above the river, into which I must fall if my footing fails, I call for help. The men come and pass me a line, but I cannot let go of the rock long enough to take hold of it. Then they bring two or three of the largest oars. All this takes time which seems very precious to me; but at last they arrive. The blade of one of the oars is pushed into a little crevice in the rock beyond me in such a manner that they can hold me pressed against the wall. Then another is fixed in such a way that I can step on it; and thus I am extricated.

Still another hour is spent in examining the river from this side, but no good view of it is obtained; so now we return to the side that was first examined, and the afternoon is spent in clambering among the crags and pinnacles and carefully scanning the river again. We find that the lateral streams have washed boulders into the river, so as to form a dam, over which the water makes a broken fall of 18 or 20 feet; then there is a rapid, beset with rocks, for 200 or 300 yards, while on the other side, points of the wall project into the river. Below, there is a second fall; how great, we cannot tell. Then there is a rapid, filled with huge rocks, for 100 or 200 yards. At the bottom of it, from the right wall, a great rock projects quite halfway across the river. It has a sloping surface extending up stream, and the water, coming down with all the momentum gained in the falls and rapids above, rolls up this inclined plane many feet, and tumbles over to the left. I decide that it is possible to let down over the first fall, then run near the right cliff to a point just above the second, where we can pull out into a little chute, and, having run over that in safety, if we pull with all our power across the stream, we may avoid the great rock below. On my return to the boat I announce to the men that we are to run it in the morning. Then we cross the river and go into camp for the night on some rocks in the mouth of the little side canyon.

After supper Captain Howland asks to have a talk with me. We walk up the little creek a short distance, and I soon find that his object is to remonstrate against my determination to proceed. He thinks that we had better abandon the river here. Talking with him, I learn that he, his brother, and William Dunn have determined to go no farther in the boats. So we return to camp. Nothing is said to the other men.

For the last two days our course has not been plotted. I sit down and do this now, for the purpose of finding where we are by dead reckoning. It is a clear night, and I take out the sextant to make observation for latitude, and I find that the astronomic determination agrees very nearly with that of the plot—quite as closely as might be expected from a meridian observation on a planet. In a direct line, we must be about 45 miles from the mouth of the Rio Virgen.[3] If we can reach that point, we know that there are settlements up that river about 20 miles. This 45 miles in a direct line will probably be 80 or 90 by the meandering line of the river. But then we know that there is comparatively open country for many miles above the mouth of the Virgen, which is our point of destination.

As soon as I determine all this, I spread my plot on the sand and wake Howland, who is sleeping down by the river, and show him where I suppose we are, and where several Mormon settlements are situated.

We have another short talk about the morrow, and he lies down again; but for me there is no sleep. All night long I pace up and down a little path, on a few yards of sand beach, along by the river. Is it wise to go on?

---

[3] Almost certainly the Virgin River, which enters the Colorado near Lake Mead.

I go to the boats again to look at our rations. I feel satisfied that we can get over the danger immediately before us; what there may be below I know not. From our outlook yesterday on the cliffs, the canyon seemed to make another great bend to the south, and this, from our experience heretofore, means more and higher granite walls. I am not sure that we can climb out of the canyon here, and, if at the top of the wall, I know enough of the country to be certain that it is a desert of rock and sand between this and the nearest Mormon town, which, on the most direct line, must be 75 miles away. True, the late rains have been favorable to us, should we go out, for the probabilities are that we shall find water still standing in holes; and at one time I almost conclude to leave the river. But for years I have been contemplating this trip. To leave the exploration unfinished, to say that there is a part of the canyon which I cannot explore, having already nearly accomplished it, is more than I am willing to acknowledge, and I determine to go on.

I wake my brother and tell him of Howland's determination, and he promises to stay with me; then I call up Hawkins, the cook, and he makes a like promise; then Sumner and Bradley and Hall, and they all agree to go on.

August 28.—At last daylight comes and we have breakfast without a word being said about the future. The meal is as solemn as a funeral. After breakfast I ask the three men if they still think it best to leave us. The elder Howland thinks it is, and Dunn agrees with him. The younger Howland tries to persuade them to go on with the party; failing in which, he decides to go with his brother.

Then we cross the river. The small boat is very much disabled and unseaworthy. With the loss of hands, consequent on the departure of the three men, we shall not be able to run all of the boats; so I decide to leave my "Emma Dean."

Two rifles and a shotgun are given to the men who are going out. I ask them to help themselves to the rations and take what they think to be a fair share. This they refuse to do, saying they have no fear but that they can get something to eat; but Billy, the cook, has a pan of biscuits pre-pared for dinner, and these he leaves on a rock.

Before starting, we take from the boat our barometers, fossils, the min-erals, and some ammunition and leave them on the rocks. We are going over this place as light as possible. The three men help us lift our boats over a rock 25 or 30 feet high and let them down again over the first fall, and now we are all ready to start. The last thing before leaving, I write a letter to my wife and give it to Howland. Sumner gives him his watch, directing that it be sent to his sister should he not be heard from again. The records of the expedition have been kept in duplicate. One set of these is given to Howland; and now we are ready. For the last time they entreat us not to go on, and tell us that it is madness to set out in this place; that we can never get safely through it; and, further, that the river turns again to the south into the granite, and a few miles of such rapids and falls will exhaust our entire stock of rations, and then it will be too late to climb out. Some tears are shed; it is rather a solemn parting; each party thinks the other is taking the dangerous course.

My old boat left, I go on board of the "Maid of the Canyon." The three men climb a crag that overhangs the river to watch us off. The "Maid of the Canyon" pushes out. We glide rapidly along the foot of the wall, just grazing one great rock, then pull out a little into the chute of the second fall and plunge over it. The open compartment is filled when we strike the first wave below, but we cut through it, and then the men pull with all their power toward the left wall and swing clear of the dangerous rock below all right. We are scarcely a minute in running it, and find that, although it looked bad from above, we have passed many places that were worse.

The other boat follows without more difficulty. We land at the first practicable point below, and fire our guns, as a signal to the men above that we have come over in safety. Here we remain a couple of hours, hop-ing that they will take the smaller boat and follow us. We are behind a curve in the canyon and cannot see up to where we left them, and so we wait until their coming seems hopeless, and then push on.

And now we have a succession of rapids and falls until noon, all of which we run in safety. Just after dinner we come to another bad place. A little stream comes in from the left, and below there is a fall, and still below another fall. Above, the river tumbles down, over and among the rocks, in whirlpools and great waves, and the waters are lashed into mad, white foam. We run along the left, above this, and soon see that we cannot get down on this side, but it seems possible to let down on the other. We pull up stream again for 200 or 300 yards and cross. Now there is a bed of basalt on this northern side of the canyon, with a bold escarpment that seems to be a hundred feet high. We can climb it and walk along its summit to a point where we are just at the head of the fall. Here the basalt is broken down again, so it seems to us, and I direct the men to take a line to the top of the cliff and let the boats down along the wall. One man remains in the boat to keep her clear of the rocks and prevent her line from being caught on the projecting angles. I climb the cliff and pass along to a point just over the fall and descend by broken rocks, and find that the break of the fall is above the break of the wall, so that we cannot land, and that still below the river is very bad, and that there is no possibility of a portage. Without waiting further to examine and determine what shall be done, I hasten back to the top of the cliff to stop the boats from coming down. When I arrive I find the men have let one of them down to the head of the fall. She is in swift water and they are not able to pull her back; nor are they able to go on with the line, as it is not long enough to reach the higher part of the cliff which is just before them; so they take a bight around a crag. I send two men back for the other line. The boat is in very swift water, and Bradley is standing in the open compartment, holding out his oar to prevent her from striking against the foot of the cliff. Now she shoots out into the stream and up as far as the line will permit, and then, wheeling, drives headlong against the rock, and then out and back again, now straining on the line, now striking against the rock. As soon as the second line is brought, we pass it down to him; but his attention is all taken up with his own situation, and he does not see that we are passing him the line. I stand on a projecting rock, waving my hat to gain his attention, for my voice is drowned by the roaring of the falls. Just at this moment I see him take his knife from its sheath and step forward to cut the line. He has evidently decided that it is better to go over with the boat as it is than to wait for her to be broken to pieces. As he leans over, the boat sheers again into the stream, the stem-post breaks away and she is loose. With perfect composure Bradley seizes the great scull oar, places it in the stern rowlock, and pulls with all his power (and he is an athlete) to turn the bow of the boat down stream, for he wishes to go bow down, rather than to drift broadside on. One, two strokes he makes, and a third just as she goes over, and the boat is fairly turned, and she goes down almost beyond our sight, though we are more than a hundred feet above the river. Then she comes up again on a great wave, and down and up, then around behind some great rocks, and is lost in the mad, white foam below. We stand frozen with fear, for we see no boat. Bradley is gone! so it seems. But now, away below, we see something coming out of the waves. It is evidently a boat. A moment more, and we see Bradley standing on deck, swinging his hat to show that he is all right. But he is in a whirlpool. We have the stem-post of his boat attached to the line. How badly she may be disabled we know not. I direct Sumner and Powell to pass along the cliff and see if they can reach him from below. Hawkins, Hall, and myself run to the other boat, jump aboard, push out, and away we go over the falls. A wave rolls over us and our boat is unmanageable. Another great wave strikes us, and the boat rolls over, and tumbles and tosses, I know not how. All I know is that Bradley is picking us up. We soon have all right again, and row to the cliff and wait until Sumner and Powell can come. After a difficult climb they reach us. We run two or three miles farther and turn again to the northwest, continuing until night, when we have run out of the granite once more.

August 29.—We start very early this morning. The river still continues swift, but we have no serious difficulty, and at twelve o'clock emerge from the Grand Canyon of the Colorado. We are in a valley now, and low

mountains are seen in the distance, coming to the river below. We recognize this as the Grand Wash.

. . .

To-night we camp on the left bank, in a mesquite thicket.

The relief from danger and the joy of success are great. When he who
has been chained by wounds to a hospital cot until his canvas tent seems
like a dungeon cell, until the groans of those who lie about tortured with
probe and knife are piled up, a weight of horror on his ears that he cannot throw off, cannot forget, and until the stench of festering wounds
and anæsthetic drugs has filled the air with its loathsome burthen,—
when he at last goes out into the open field, what a world he sees! How
beautiful the sky, how bright the sunshine, what "floods of delirious
music" pour from the throats of birds, how sweet the fragrance of earth
and tree and blossom! The first hour of convalescent freedom seems rich
recompense for all pain and gloom and terror.

Something like these are the feelings we experience to-night. Ever
before us has been an unknown danger, heavier than immediate peril.
Every waking hour passed in the Grand Canyon has been one of toil. We
have watched with deep solicitude the steady disappearance of our scant
supply of rations, and from time to time have seen the river snatch a portion of the little left, while we were a-hungered. And danger and toil were
endured in those gloomy depths, where ofttimes clouds hid the sky by
day and but a narrow zone of stars could be seen at night. Only during
the few hours of deep sleep; consequent on hard labor, has the roar of
the waters been hushed. Now the danger is over, now the toil has ceased,
now the gloom has disappeared, now the firmament is bounded only by
the horizon, and what a vast expanse of constellations can be seen!

The river rolls by us in silent majesty; the quiet of the camp is sweet;
our joy is almost ecstasy. We sit till long after midnight talking of the
Grand Canyon, talking of home, but talking chiefly of the three men who
left us. Are they wandering in those depths, unable to find a way out? Are
they searching over the desert lands above for water? Or are they nearing
the settlements?

CLARENCE KING

(1842–1901)

From *Mountaineering in the Sierra Nevada*

---

*As a young man, fresh from Yale with a degree in chemistry, Clarence
King landed the most romantic, adventurous job he could imagine. In
1863 he headed west as the assistant geologist on the first survey of the
high Sierra. During many happy and distinguished years as a geologist
(he later was head of the United States Geological Survey), he traveled
throughout the West, climbing and measuring peaks, and finding
important fossils that helped solve the puzzle about the Sierra Nevada's
age. A person of versatile intellect and insatiable curiosity, he was also
an artist and respected literary critic. His friend Henry Adams called
him "the most many-sided genius of his day."*

*As you'll see in this heart-stopping account of his desperate climb of
Mount Tyndall, King was also an athletic daredevil to the point of
madness—even if you don't believe everything he wrote. Though he
was notorious for weaving a yarn, there is no dispute that King was the
first to reach the top of many of the Sierra Nevada's highest mountains,
including Whitney, Tyndall, and Shasta. Like John Muir after him,
King was enthralled by everything about those mountains, and in a*

similar state of ecstasy, he could seemingly live on air and light and reg-
ular doses of death-defying adventures. Although King's prose is less
reverent and more antic than Muir's—his approach to Nature more
that of boyish conquest than spiritual immersion—his enthusiasm is no
less profound.

King's travel essays, first serialized in the Atlantic Monthly *in 1871*
and still in print today, combine engrossing storytelling about moun-
taineering and frontier life with an artist's aesthetic sense of the land-
scape and a scientist's observations of the natural world.

Morning dawned brightly upon our bivouac among a cluster of dark firs in the mountain corridor opened by an ancient glacier of King's River into the heart of the Sierras. It dawned a trifle sooner than we could have wished, but Professor Brewer and Hoffman[1] had breakfasted before sunrise, and were off with barometer and theodolite[2] upon their shoulders, purposing to ascend our amphitheatre to its head and climb a great pyramidal peak which swelled up against the eastern sky, closing the view in that direction.

We who remained in camp spent the day in overhauling campaign materials and preparing for a grand assault upon the summits. For a couple of hours we could descry our friends through the field-glasses, their minute black forms moving slowly on among piles of giant *débris;* now and then lost, again coming into view, and at last disappearing altogether.

It was twilight of evening and almost eight o'clock when they came back to camp, Brewer leading the way, Hoffman following; and as they sat down by our fire without uttering a word, we read upon their faces terrible fatigue.

So we hastened to give them supper of coffee and soup, bread and

---

[1] Professor William H. Brewer, head of the expedition, and Charles Hoffman, chief topographer.

[2] A surveyor's instrument for measuring angles.

venison, which resulted, after a time, in our getting in return the story of the day.

· For eight whole hours they had worked up over granite and snow, mounting ridge after ridge, till the summit was made about two o'clock.

These snowy crests bounding our view at the eastward we had all along taken to be the summits of the Sierra, and Brewer had supposed himself to be climbing a dominant peak, from which he might look eastward over Owen's Valley and out upon leagues of desert. Instead of this a vast wall of mountains, lifted still higher than his peak, rose beyond a tremendous cañon which lay like a trough between the two parallel ranks of peaks. Hoffman showed us on his sketch-book the profile of this new range, and I instantly recognized the peaks which I had seen from Mariposa, whose great white pile had led me to believe them the highest points of California.

For a couple of months my friends had made me the target of plenty of pleasant banter about my "highest land," which they lost faith in as we climbed from Thomas's Mill,[3]—I too becoming a trifle anxious about it; but now that the truth had burst upon Brewer and Hoffman they could not find words to describe the terribleness and grandeur of the deep cañon, nor for picturing those huge crags towering in line at the east. Their peak, as indicated by the barometer, was in the region of thirteen thousand four hundred feet, and a level across to the farther range showed its crests to be at least fifteen hundred feet higher. They had spent hours upon the summit scanning the eastern horizon, and ranging downward into the labyrinth of gulfs below, and had come at last with reluctance to the belief that to cross this gorge and ascend the eastern wall of peaks was utterly impossible.

Brewer and Hoffman were old climbers, and their verdict of impossible oppressed me as I lay awake thinking of it; but early next morning I

---

[3] Thomas's Sawmill Ranch, on the edge of the mountains, was where they made their first camp to get a sense of the range's topography.

had made up my mind, and, taking Cotter[4] aside, I asked him in an easy manner whether he would like to penetrate the Terra Incognita with me at the risk of our necks, provided Brewer should consent. In a frank, courageous tone he answered after his usual mode, "Why not?" Stout of limb, stronger yet in heart, of iron endurance, and a quiet, unexcited temperament, and, better yet, deeply devoted to me, I felt that Cotter was the one comrade I would choose to face death with, for I believed there was in his manhood no room for fear or shirk.

It was a trying moment for Brewer when we found him and volunteered to attempt a campaign for the top of California, because he felt a certain fatherly responsibility over our youth, a natural desire that we should not deposit our triturated remains in some undiscoverable hole among the feldspathic granites; but, like a true disciple of science, this was at last over-balanced by his intense desire to know more of the unexplored region. He freely confessed that he believed the plan madness, and Hoffman, too, told us we might as well attempt to get on a cloud as to try the peak.

As Brewer gradually yielded his consent, I saw by his conversation that there was a possibility of success; so we spent the rest of the day in making preparations.

Our walking-shoes were in excellent condition, the hobnails firm and new. We laid out a barometer, a compass, a pocket-level, a set of wet and dry thermometers, note-books, with bread, cooked beans, and venison enough to last a week, rolled them all in blankets, making two knapsack-shaped packs strapped firmly together with loops for the arms, which, by Brewer's estimate, weighed forty pounds apiece.

Gardner[5] declared he would accompany us to the summit of the first range to look over into the gulf we were to cross, and at last Brewer and Hoffman also concluded to go up with us.

Quite too early for our profit we all betook ourselves to bed, vainly

---

[4] King's personal friend, Richard Cotter, was a jack-of-all-trades on the expedition.
[5] James T. Gardner, assistant surveyor.

hoping to get a long refreshing sleep from which we should arise ready for our tramp.

Never a man welcomed those first gray streaks in the east gladder than I did, unless it may be Cotter, who has in later years confessed that he did not go to sleep that night. Long before sunrise we had done our breakfast and were under way, Hoffman kindly bearing my pack, and Brewer Cotter's.

Our way led due east up the amphitheatre and toward Mount Brewer, as we had named the great pyramidal peak.

Awhile after leaving camp, slant sunlight streamed in among gilded pinnacles along the slope of Mount Brewer, touching here and there, in broad dashes of yellow, the gray walls, which rose sweeping up on either hand like the sides of a ship.

Our way along the valley's middle ascended over a number of huge steps, rounded and abrupt, at whose bases were pools of transparent snow-water edged with rude piles of erratic glacier blocks, scattered companies of alpine firs, of red bark and having cypress-like darkness of foliage, with fields of snow under sheltering cliffs, and bits of softest velvet meadow clouded with minute blue and white flowers.

As we climbed, the gorge grew narrow and sharp, both sides wilder; and the spurs which projected from them, nearly overhanging the middle of the valley, towered above us with more and more severe sculpture. We frequently crossed deep fields of snow, and at last reached the level of the highest pines, where long slopes of *débris* swept down from either cliff, meeting in the middle. Over and among these immense blocks, often twenty and thirty feet high, we were obliged to climb, hearing far below us the subterreanean gurgle of streams.

Interlocking spurs nearly closed the gorge behind us; our last view was out a granite gateway formed of two nearly vertical precipices, sharp-edged, jutting buttress-like, and plunging down into a field of angular boulders which fill the valley bottom.

The eye ranged out from this open gateway overlooking the great King's Cañon with its moraine-terraced walls, the domes of granite upon

Big Meadows, and the undulating stretch of forest which descends to the plain.

The gorge turning southward, we rounded a sort of mountain promontory, which, closing the view behind us, shut us up in the bottom of a perfect basin. In front lay a placid lake reflecting the intense black-blue of the sky. Granite stained with purple and red, sank into it upon one side, and a broad spotless field of snow came down to its margin upon the other.

From a pile of large granite blocks, forty or fifty feet up above the lake margin, we could look down fully a hundred feet through the transparent water to where boulders and pebbles were strewn upon the stone bottom. We had now reached the base of Mount Brewer and were skirting its southern spurs in a wide open corridor surrounded in all directions by lofty granite crags from two to four thousand feet high; above the limits of vegetation, rocks, lakes of deep heavenly blue, and white trackless snows were grouped closely about us. Two sounds, a sharp little cry of martens, and occasional heavy crashes of falling rock, saluted us.

Climbing became exceedingly difficult, light air—for we had already reached twelve thousand five hundred feet—beginning to tell upon our lungs to such an extent that my friend, who had taken turns with me in carrying my pack, was unable to do so any longer, and I adjusted it to my own shoulders for the rest of the day.

After four hours of slow laborious work we made the base of the *débris* slope which rose about a thousand feet to a saddle pass in the western mountain wall, that range upon which Mount Brewer is so prominent a point. We were nearly an hour in toiling up this slope over an uncertain footing which gave way at almost every step. At last, when almost at the top, we paused to take breath, and then all walked out upon the crest, laid off our packs, and sat down together upon the summit of the ridge, and for a few moments not a word was spoken.

The Sierras are here two parallel summit ranges. We were upon the crest of the western ridge, and looked down into a gulf five thousand feet deep, sinking from our feet in abrupt cliffs nearly or quite two thousand feet, whose base plunged into a broad field of snow lying steep and smooth for a great distance, but broken near its foot by craggy steps often a thousand feet high.

Vague blue haze obscured the lost depths, hiding details, giving a bottomless distance out of which, like the breath of wind, floated up a faint tremble, vibrating upon the senses, yet never clearly heard.

Rising on the other side, cliff above cliff, precipice piled upon precipice, rock over rock, up against sky, towered the most gigantic mountain-wall in America, culminating in a noble pile of Gothic-finished granite and enamel-like snow. How grand and inviting looked its white form, its untrodden, unknown crest, so high and pure in the clear strong blue! I looked at it as one contemplating the purpose of his life; and for just one moment I would have rather liked to dodge that purpose, or to have waited, or have found some excellent reason why I might not go; but all this quickly vanished, leaving a cheerful resolve to go ahead.

From the two opposing mountain-walls singular, thin, knife-blade ridges of stone jutted out, dividing the sides of the gulf into a series of amphitheatres, each one a labyrinth of ice and rock. Piercing thick beds of snow, sprang up knobs and straight isolated spires of rock, mere obelisks curiously carved by frost, their rigid, slender forms casting a blue, sharp shadow upon the snow. Embosomed in depressions of ice, or resting on broken ledges, were azure lakes, deeper in tone than the sky, which at this altitude, even at midday, has a violet duskiness.

To the south, not more than eight miles, a wall of peaks stood across the gulf, dividing the King's, which flowed north at our feet, from the Kern River, that flowed down the trough in the opposite direction.

I did not wonder that Brewer and Hoffman pronounced our undertaking impossible; but when I looked at Cotter there was such complete bravery in his eye that I asked him if he was ready to start. His old answer, "Why not?" left the initiative with me; so I told Professor Brewer that we would bid him good by. Our friends helped us on with our packs in silence, and as we shook hands there was not a dry eye in the party. Before he let go of my hand Professor Brewer asked me for my plan, and I had to own that I had but one, which was to reach the highest peak in the range.

After looking in every direction I was obliged to confess that I saw as yet no practicable way. We bade them a "good by," receiving their "God bless you" in return, and started southward along the range to look for some possible cliff to descend. Brewer, Gardner, and Hoffman turned north to push upward to the summit of Mount Brewer, and complete their observations. We saw them whenever we halted, until at last, on the very summit, their microscopic forms were for the last time discernible. With very great difficulty we climbed a peak which surmounted our wall just to the south of the pass, and, looking over the eastern brink, found that the precipice was still sheer and unbroken. In one place, where the snow lay against it to the very top, we went to its edge and contemplated, the slide. About three thousand feet of unbroken white, at a fearfully steep angle, lay below us. We threw a stone over and watched it bound until it was lost in the distance; after fearful leaps we could only detect it by the flashings of snow where it struck, and as these were, in some instances, three hundred feet apart, we decided not to launch our own valuable bodies, and the still more precious barometer, after it.

There seemed but one possible way to reach our goal; that was to make our way along the summit of the cross ridge which projected between the two ranges. This divide sprang out from our Mount Brewer wall, about four miles to the south of us. To reach it we must climb up and down over the indented edge of the Mount Brewer wall. In attempting to do this we had a rather lively time scaling a sharp granite needle, where we found our course completely stopped by precipices four and five hundred feet in height. Ahead of us the summit continued to be broken into fantastic pinnacles, leaving us no hope of making our way along it; so we sought the most broken part of the eastern descent, and began to climb down. The heavy knapsacks, beside wearing our shoulders gradually into a black-and-blue state, overbalanced us terribly, and kept us in constant danger of pitching headlong. At last, taking them off, Cotter climbed down until he had found a resting-place upon a cleft of rock, then I lowered them to him with our lasso, afterwards descending cautiously to his side, taking my turn in pioneering downward, receiving the freight of knapsacks by lasso as before. In this manner we consumed more than half the afternoon in descending a thousand feet of broken, precipitous slope; and it was almost sunset when we found ourselves upon the fields of level snow which lay white and thick over the whole interior slope of the amphitheatre. The gorge below us seemed utterly impassable. At our backs the Mount Brewer wall either rose in sheer cliffs or in broken, rugged stairway, such as had offered us our descent. From this cruel dilemma the cross divide furnished the only hope, and the sole chance of scaling that was at its junction with the Mount Brewer wall. Toward this point we directed our course, marching wearily over stretches of dense frozen snow, and regions of *débris,* reaching about sunset the last alcove of the amphitheatre, just at the foot of the Mount Brewer wall. It was evidently impossible for us to attempt to climb it that evening, and we looked about the desolate recesses for a sheltered camping-spot. A high granite wall surrounded us upon three sides, recurring to the southward in long elliptical curves; no part of the summit being less than two thousand feet above us, the higher crags not unfrequently reaching three thousand feet. A single field of snow swept around the base of the rock, and covered the whole amphitheatre, except where a few spikes and rounded masses of granite rose through it, and where two frozen lakes, with their blue ice-disks, broke the monotonous surface. Through the white snow-gate of our amphitheatre, as through a frame, we looked eastward upon the summit group; not a tree, not a vestige of vegetation in sight,—sky, snow, and granite the only elements in this wild picture.

After searching for a shelter we at last found a granite crevice near the margin of one of the frozen lakes,—a sort of shelf just large enough for Cotter and me,—where we hastened to make our bed, having first filled the canteen from a small stream that trickled over the ice, knowing that in a few moments the rapid chill would freeze it. We ate our supper of cold venison and bread, and whittled from the sides of the wooden barometer-case shavings enough to warm water for a cup of miserably

tepid tea, and then, packing our provisions and instruments away at the
head of the shelf, rolled ourselves in our blankets and lay down to enjoy
the view.

After such fatiguing exercises the mind has an almost abnormal clear-
ness: whether this is wholly from within, or due to the intensely vitalizing
mountain air, I am not sure; probably both contribute to the state of exal-
tation in which all alpine climbers find themselves. The solid granite
gave me a luxurious repose, and I lay on the edge of our little rock niche
and watched the strange yet brilliant scene.

All the snow of our recess lay in the shadow of the high granite wall to
the west, but the Kern divide which curved around us from the southeast
was in full light; its broken sky-line, battlemented and adorned with
innumerable rough-hewn spires and pinnacles, was a mass of glowing
orange intensely defined against the deep violet sky. At the open end of
our horseshoe amphitheatre, to the east, its floor of snow rounded over in
a smooth brink, overhanging precipices which sank two thousand feet
into the King's Cañon. Across the gulf rose the whole procession of summit peaks, their lower halves rooted in a deep sombre shadow cast by the
western wall, the heights bathed in a warm purple haze, in which the
irregular marbling of snow burned with a pure crimson light. A few fleecy
clouds, dyed fiery orange, drifted slowly eastward across the narrow zone
of sky which stretched from summit to summit like a roof. At times the
sound of waterfalls, faint and mingled with echoes, floated up through
the still air. The snow near by lay in cold ghastly shade, warmed here and
there in strange flashes by light reflected downward from drifting clouds.
The sombre waste about us; the deep violet vault overhead; those far
summits, glowing with reflected rose; the deep impenetrable gloom
which filled the gorge, and slowly and with vapor-like stealth climbed the
mountain wall extinguishing the red light, combined to produce an effect
which may not be described; nor can I more than hint at the contrast
between the brilliancy of the scene under full light, and the cold, death-
like repose which followed when the wan cliffs and pallid snow were all
over-shadowed with ghostly gray.

A sudden chill enveloped us. Stars in a moment crowded through the dark heaven, flashing with a frosty splendor. The snow congealed, the brooks ceased to flow, and, under the powerful sudden leverage of frost, immense blocks were dislodged all along the mountain summits and came thundering down the slopes, booming upon the ice, dashing wildly upon rocks. Under the lee of our shelf we felt quite safe, but neither Cotter nor I could help being startled, and jumping just a little, as these missiles, weighing often many tons, struck the ledge over our heads and whizzed down the gorge, their stroke resounding fainter and fainter, until at last only a confused echo reached us.

The thermometer at nine o'clock marked twenty degrees above zero. We set the "minimum" and rolled ourselves together for the night. The longer I lay the less I liked that shelf of granite; it grew hard in time, and cold also, my bones seeming to approach actual contact with the chilled rock; moreover, I found that even so vigorous a circulation as mine was not enough to warm up the ledge to anything like a comfortable tempera- ture. A single thickness of blanket is a better mattress than none, but the larger crystals of orthoclase, protruding plentifully, punched my back and caused me to revolve on a horizontal axis with precision and frequency. How I loved Cotter! how I hugged him and got warm, while our backs gradually petrified, till we whirled over and thawed them out together! The slant of that bed was diagonal and excessive; down it we slid till the ice chilled us awake, and we crawled back and chocked ourselves up with bits of granite inserted under my ribs and shoulders. In this pleasant position we got dozing again, and there stole over me a most comfortable ease. The granite softened perceptibly. I was delightfully warm and sank into an industrious slumber which lasted with great soundness till four, when we rose and ate our breakfast of frozen venison.

The thermometer stood at two above zero; everything was frozen tight except the canteen, which we had prudently kept between us all night. Stars still blazed brightly, and the moon, hidden from us by western cliffs, shone in pale reflection upon the rocky heights to the east, which rose, dimly white, up from the impenetrable shadows of the cañon.

Silence,—cold, ghastly dimness, in which loomed huge forms,—the biting frostiness of the air, wrought upon our feelings as we shouldered our
packs and started with slow pace to climb toward the "divide."

Soon, to our dismay, we found the straps had so chafed our shoulders
that the weight gave us great pain, and obliged us to pad them with our
handkerchiefs and extra socks, which remedy did not wholly relieve us
from the constant wearing pain of the heavy load.

Directing our steps southward toward a niche in the wall which
bounded us only half a mile distant, we travelled over a continuous snow-
field frozen so densely as scarcely to yield at all to our tread, at the same
time compressing enough to make that crisp frosty sound which we all
used to enjoy even before we knew from the books that it had something
to do with the severe name of regelation.

As we advanced, the snow sloped more and more steeply up toward
the crags, till by and by it became quite dangerous, causing us to out
steps with Cotter's large bowie-knife,—a slow, tedious operation, requiring patience of a pretty permanent kind. In this way we spent a quiet
social hour or so. The sun had not yet reached us, being shut out by the
high amphitheatre wall; but its cheerful light reflected downward from a
number of higher crags, filling the recess with the brightness of day, and
putting out of existence those shadows which so sombrely darkened the
earlier hours. To look back when we stopped to rest was to realize our
danger,—that smooth swift slope of ice carrying the eye down a thousand
feet to the margin of a frozen mirror of ice; ribs and needles of rock piercing up through the snow, so closely grouped that, had we fallen, a miracle
only might save us from being dashed. This led to rather deeper steps,
and greater care that our burdens should be held more nearly over the
centre of gravity, and a pleasant relief when we got to the top of the snow
and sat down on a block of granite to breathe and look up in search of a
way up the thousand-foot cliff of broken surface, among the lines of frac-
ture and the galleries winding along the face.

It would have disheartened us to gaze up the hard, sheer front of
precipices, and search among splintered projections, crevices, shelves,

and snow-patches for an inviting route, had we not been animated by a
faith that the mountains could not defy us.

Choosing what looked like the least impossible way, we started; but,
finding it unsafe to work with packs on, resumed the yesterday's plan,—
Cotter taking the lead, climbing about fifty feet ahead, and hoisting up
the knapsacks and barometer as I tied them to the end of the lasso. Constantly closing up in hopeless difficulty before us, the way opened again
and again to our gymnastics, till we stood together upon a mere shelf, not
more than two feet wide, which led diagonally up the smooth cliff. Edging along in careful steps, our backs flattened upon the granite, we
moved slowly to a broad platform, where we stopped for breath.

There was no foothold above us. Looking down over the course we had
come, it seemed, and I really believe it was, an impossible descent; for
one can climb upward with safety where he cannot downward. To turn
back was to give up in defeat; and we sat at least half an hour, suggesting
all possible routes to the summit, accepting none, and feeling disheartened. About thirty feet directly over our heads was another shelf, which,
if we could reach, seemed to offer at least a temporary way upward. On
its edge were two or three spikes of granite; whether firmly connected
with the cliff, or merely blocks of *débris*, we could not tell from below. I
said to Cotter, I thought of but one possible plan: it was to lasso one of
these blocks, and to climb, sailor-fashion, hand over hand, up the rope.
In the lasso I had perfect confidence, for I had seen more than one Spanish bull throw his whole weight against it without parting a strand. The
shelf was so narrow that throwing the coil of rope was a very difficult
undertaking. I tried three times, and Cotter spent five minutes vainly
whirling the loop up at the granite spikes. At last I made a lucky throw,
and it tightened upon one of the smaller protuberances. I drew the noose
close, and very gradually threw my hundred and fifty pounds upon the
rope; then Cotter joined me, and, for a moment, we both hung our
united weight upon it. Whether the rock moved slightly or whether the
lasso stretched a little we were unable to decide; but the trial must be
made, and I began to climb slowly. The smooth precipice-face against

which my body swung offered no foothold, and the whole climb had
therefore to be done by the arms, an effort requiring all one's determination. When about half-way up I was obliged to rest, and, curling my feet
in the rope, managed to relieve my arms for a moment. In this position I
could not resist the fascinating temptation of a survey downward.

Straight down, nearly a thousand feet below, at the foot of the rocks,
began the snow, whose steep, roof-like slope, exaggerated into an almost
vertical angle, curved down in a long white field, broken far away by
rocks and polished, round lakes of ice.

Cotter looked up cheerfully and asked how I was making it; to which I
answered that I had plenty of wind left. At that moment, when hanging
between heaven and earth, it was a deep satisfaction to look down at the
wild gulf of desolation beneath, and up to unknown dangers ahead, and
feel my nerves cool and unshaken.

A few pulls hand over hand brought me to the edge of the shelf, when,
throwing an arm around the granite spike, I swung my body upon the
shelf and lay down to rest, shouting to Cotter that I was all right, and that
the prospects upward were capital. After a few moments' breathing I
looked over the brink and directed my comrade to tie the barometer to
the lower end of the lasso, which he did, and that precious instrument
was hoisted to my station, and the lasso sent down twice for knapsacks,
after which Cotter came up the rope in his very muscular way without
once stopping to rest. We took our loads in our hands, swinging the
barometer over my shoulder, and climbed up a shelf which led in a zigzag
direction upward and to the south, bringing us out at last upon the thin
blade of a ridge which connected a short distance above with the summit. It was formed of huge blocks, shattered, and ready, at a touch, to
fall.

So narrow and sharp was the upper slope, that we dared not walk, but
got astride, and worked slowly along with our hands, pushing the knapsacks in advance, now and then holding our breath when loose masses
rocked under our weight.

Once upon the summit, a grand view burst upon us. Hastening to step upon the crest of the divide, which was never more than ten feet wide, frequently sharpened to a mere blade, we looked down the other side, and were astonished to find we had ascended the gentler slope, and that the rocks fell from our feet in almost vertical precipices for a thousand feet or more. A glance along the summit toward the highest group showed us that any advance in that direction was impossible, for the thin ridge was gashed down in notches three or four hundred feet deep, forming a procession of pillars, obelisks, and blocks piled upon each other, and looking terribly insecure.

We then deposited our knapsacks in a safe place, and, finding that it was already noon, determined to rest a little while and take a lunch at over thirteen thousand feet above the sea.

West of us stretched the Mount Brewer wall with its succession of smooth precipices and amphitheatre ridges. To the north the great gorge of the King's River yawned down five thousand feet. To the south the valley of the Kern, opening in the opposite direction, was broader, less deep, but more filled with broken masses of granite. Clustered about the foot of the divide were a dozen alpine lakes; the higher ones blue sheets of ice, the lowest completely melted. Still lower in the depths of the two cañons we could see groups of forest trees; but they were so dim and so distant as never to relieve the prevalent masses of rock and snow. Our divide cast its shadow for a mile down King's Cañon in dark blue profile upon the broad sheets of sunny snow, from whose brightness the hard splintered cliffs caught reflections and wore an aspect of joy. Thousands of rills poured from the melting snow, filling the air with a musical tinkle as of many accordant bells. The Kern Valley opened below us with its smooth oval outline, the work of extinct glaciers, whose form and extent were evident from worn cliff-surface and rounded wall; snow-fields, relics of the former *névé*, hung in white tapestries around its ancient birthplace; and, as far as we could see, the broad, corrugated valley, for a breadth of fully ten miles, shone with burnishings wherever its granite surface was not covered with lakelets or thickets of alpine vegetation.

Through a deep cut in the Mount Brewer wall we gained our first view to the westward, and saw in the distance the wall of the South King's Cañon, and the granite point which Cotter and I had climbed a fortnight before. But for the haze we might have seen the plain; for above its farther limit were several points of the Coast Ranges, isolated like islands in the sea.

The view was so grand, the mountain colors so brilliant, immense snow-fields and blue alpine lakes so charming, that we almost forgot we were ever to move, and it was only after a swift hour of this delight that we began to consider our future course.

The King's Cañon, which headed against our wall, seemed untraversable,—no human being could climb along the divide; we had then but one hope of reaching the peak, and our greatest difficulty lay at the start. If we could climb down to the Kern side of the divide, and succeed in reaching the base of the precipices which fell from our feet, it really looked as if we might travel without difficulty among the *roches moutonnées* to the other side of the Kern Valley, and make our attempt upon the southward flank of the great peak. One look at the sublime white giant decided us. We looked down over the precipice, and at first could see no method of descent. Then we went back and looked at the road we had come up, to see if that were not possibly as bad; but the broken surface of the rocks was evidently much better climbing-ground than anything ahead of us. Cotter, with danger, edged his way along the wall to the east, and I to the west, to see if there might not be some favorable point; but we both returned with the belief that the precipice in front of us was as passable as any of it. Down it we must.

After lying on our faces, looking over the brink, ten or twenty minutes, I suggested that by lowering ourselves on the rope we might climb from crevice to crevice; but we saw no shelf large enough for ourselves and the knapsacks too. However, we were not going to give it up without a trial; and I made the rope fast round my breast, and, looping the noose over a firm point of rock, let myself slide gradually down to a notch forty feet below. There was only room beside me for Cotter, so I made him send down the knapsacks first. I then tied these together by the straps with my silk handkerchiefs, and hung them off as far to the left as I could reach without losing my balance, looping the handkerchiefs over a point of rock. Cotter then slid down the rope, and, with considerable difficulty, we whipped the noose off its resting-place above, and cut off our connection with the upper world.

"We're in for it now, King," remarked my comrade, as he looked aloft, and then down; but our blood was up, and danger added only an exhilarating thrill to the nerves.

The shelf was hardly more than two feet wide, and the granite so smooth that we could find no place to fasten the lasso for the next descent; so I determined to try the climb with only as little aid as possible. Tying it round my breast again, I gave the other end into Cotter's hands, and he, bracing his back against the cliff, found for himself as firm a foothold as he could, and promised to give me all the help in his power. I made up my mind to bear no weight unless it was absolutely necessary; and for the first ten feet I found cracks and protuberances enough to support me, making every square inch of surface do friction duty, and hugging myself against the rocks as tightly as I could. When within about eight feet of the next shelf, I twisted myself round upon the face, hanging by two rough blocks of protruding feldspar, and looked vainly for some further hand-hold; but the rock, beside being perfectly smooth, overhung slightly, and my legs dangled in the air. I saw that the next cleft was over three feet broad, and I thought, possibly, I might, by a quick slide, reach it in safety without endangering Cotter. I shouted to him to be very careful and let go in case I fell, loosened my hold upon the rope, and slid quickly down. My shoulder struck against the rock and threw me out of balance; for an instant I reeled over upon the verge, in danger of falling, but, in the excitement, I thrust out my hand and seized a small alpine gooseberry-bush, the first piece of vegetation we had seen. Its roots were so firmly fixed in the crevice that it held my weight and saved me.

I could no longer see Cotter, but I talked to him, and heard the two knapsacks come bumping along till they slid over the eaves above me, and swung down to my station, when I seized the lasso's end and braced myself as well as possible, intending, if he slipped, to haul in slack and help him as best I might. As he came slowly down from crack to crack, I heard his hobnailed shoes grating on the granite; presently they appeared dangling from the eaves above my head. I had gathered in the rope until it was taut, and then hurriedly told him to drop. He hesitated a moment, and let go. Before he struck the rock I had him by the shoulder, and whirled him down upon his side, thus preventing his rolling over-board, which friendly action he took quite coolly.

The third descent was not a difficult one, nor the fourth; but when we had climbed down about two hundred and fifty feet, the rocks were so glacially polished and water-worn that it seemed impossible to get any farther. To our right was a crack penetrating the rock perhaps a foot deep, widening at the surface to three or four inches, which proved to be the only possible ladder. As the chances seemed rather desperate, we concluded to tie ourselves together, in order to share a common fate; and with a slack of thirty feet between us, and our knapsacks upon our backs, we climbed into the crevice, and began descending with our faces to the cliff. This had to be done with unusual caution, for the foothold was about as good as none, and our fingers slipped annoyingly on the smooth stone; besides, the knapsacks and instruments kept a steady backward pull, tending to over-balance us. But we took pains to descend one at a time, and rest wherever the niches gave our feet a safe support. In this way we got down about eighty feet of smooth, nearly vertical wall, reaching the top of a rude granite stairway, which led to the snow; and here we sat down to rest, and found to our astonishment that we had been three hours from the summit.

After breathing a half-minute we continued down, jumping from rock to rock, and, having, by practice, become very expert in balancing ourselves, sprang on, never resting long enough to lose the *aplomb,* and in this manner made a quick descent over rugged *débris* to the crest of a snow-field, which, for seven or eight hundred feet more, swept down in a smooth, even slope, of very high angle, to the borders of a frozen lake.

Without untying the lasso which bound us together, we sprang upon the snow with a shout, and glissaded down splendidly, turning now and then a somersault, and shooting out like cannon-balls almost to the middle of the frozen lake; I upon my back, and Cotter feet first, in a swimming position. The ice cracked in all directions. It was only a thin, transparent film, through which we could see deep into the lake. Untying ourselves, we hurried ashore in different directions, lest our combined weight should be too great a strain upon any point.

With curiosity and wonder we scanned every shelf and niche of the last descent. It seemed quite impossible we could have come down there, and now it actually was beyond human power to get back again. But what cared we? "Sufficient unto the day—" We were bound for that still distant, though gradually nearing, summit; and we had come from a cold shadowed cliff into deliciously warm sunshine, and were jolly, shouting, singing songs, and calling out the companionship of a hundred echoes. Six miles away, with no grave danger, no great difficulty, between us, lay the base of our grand mountain. Upon its skirts we saw a little grove of pines, an ideal bivouac, and toward this we bent our course.

After the continued climbing of the day, walking was a delicious rest, and forward we pressed with considerable speed, our hobnails giving us firm footing on the glittering glacial surface. Every fluting of the great valley was in itself a considerable cañon, into which we descended, climbing down the scored rocks, and swinging from block to block, until we reached the level of the pines. Here, sheltered among *roches moutonnées*, began to appear little fields of alpine grass, pale yet sunny, soft under our feet, fragrantly jewelled with flowers of fairy delicacy, holding up amid thickly clustered blades chalices of turquoise and amethyst, white stars, and fiery little globes of red. Lakelets, small but innumerable, were held in glacial basins, the striæ and grooves of that old dragon's track ornamenting their smooth bottoms.

One of these, a sheet of pure beryl hue, gave us much pleasure from its lovely transparency, and because we lay down in the necklace of grass about it and smelled flowers, while tired muscles relaxed upon warm beds of verdure, and the pain in our burdened shoulders went away, leaving us delightfully comfortable.

After the stern grandeur of granite and ice, and with the peaks and walls still in view, it was relief to find ourselves again in the region of life. I never felt for trees and flowers such a sense of intimate relationship and sympathy. When we had no longer excuse for resting, I invented the palpable subterfuge of measuring the altitude of the spot, since the few clumps of low, wide-boughed pines near by were the highest living trees. So we lay longer with less and less will to rise, and when resolution called us to our feet the getting-up was sorely like Rip Van Winkle's in the third act.

The deep glacial cañon-flutings across which our march then lay proved to be great consumers of time; indeed it was sunset when we reached the eastern ascent, and began to toil up through scattered pines, and over trains of moraine rocks, toward the great peak. Stars were already flashing brilliantly in the sky, and the low glowing arch in the west had almost vanished when we reached the upper trees, and threw down our knapsacks to camp. The forest grew on a sort of plateau-shelf with a precipitous front to the west,—a level surface which stretched eastward and back to the foot of our mountain, whose lower spurs reached within a mile of camp. Within the shelter lay a huge fallen log, like all these alpine woods one mass of resin, which flared up when we applied a match, illuminating the whole grove. By contrast with the darkness outside, we seemed to be in a vast, many-pillared hall. The stream close by afforded water for our blessed teapot; venison frizzled with mild, appetizing sound upon the ends of pine sticks; matchless beans allowed themselves to become seductively crisp upon our tin plates. That supper seemed to me then the quintessence of gastronomy, and I am sure Cotter and I must have said some very good *après-dîner* things, though I long ago forgot them all. Within the ring of warmth, on elastic beds of pine-needles, we curled up, and fell swiftly into a sound sleep.

I woke up once in the night to look at my watch, and observed that the sky was overcast with a thin film of cirrus cloud to which the reflected moonlight lent the appearance of a glimmering tint, stretched from mountain to mountain over cañons filled with impenetrable darkness, only the vaguely lighted peaks and white snow-fields distinctly seen. I closed my eyes and slept soundly until Cotter woke me at half past three, when we arose, breakfasted by the light of our fire, which still blazed brilliantly, and, leaving our knapsacks, started for the mountain with only instruments, canteens, and luncheon.

In the indistinct moonlight climbing was very difficult at first, for we had to thread our way along a plain which was literally covered with glacier boulders, and the innumerable brooks which we crossed were frozen solid. However, our march brought us to the base of the great mountain, which, rising high against the east, shut out the coming daylight, and kept us in profound shadow. From base to summit rose a series of broken crags, lifting themselves from a general slope of *débris*. Toward the left the angle seemed to be rather gentler, and the surface less ragged; and we hoped, by a long *détour* round the base, to make an easy climb up this gentler face. So we toiled on for an hour over the rocks, reaching at last the bottom of the north slope. Here our work began in good earnest. The blocks were of enormous size, and in every stage of unstable equilibrium, frequently rolling over as we jumped upon them, making it necessary for us to take a second leap and land where we best could. To our relief we soon surmounted the largest blocks, reaching a smaller size, which served us as a sort of stairway.

The advancing daylight revealed to us a very long, comparatively even snow-slope, whose surface was pierced by many knobs and granite heads, giving it the aspect of an ice-roofing fastened on with bolts of stone. It stretched in far perspective to the summit, where already the rose of sunrise reflected gloriously, kindling a fresh enthusiasm within us.

Immense boulders were partly embedded in the ice just above us, whose constant melting left them trembling on the edge of a fall. It communicated no very pleasant sensation to see above you these immense missiles hanging by a mere band, and knowing that, as soon as the sun rose, you would be exposed to a constant cannonade.

The east side of the peak, which we could now partially see, was too precipitous to think of climbing. The slope toward our camp was too much broken into pinnacles and crags to offer us any hope, or to divert us from the single way, dead ahead, up slopes of ice and among fragments of granite. The sun rose upon us while we were climbing the lower part of this snow, and in less than half an hour, melting, began to liberate huge blocks, which thundered down past us, gathering and growing into small avalanches below.

We did not dare climb one above another, according to our ordinary mode, but kept about an equal level, a hundred feet apart, lest, dislodging the blocks, one should hurl them down upon the other.

We climbed alternately up smooth faces of granite, clinging simply by the cracks and protruding crystals of feldspar, and then hewed steps up fearfully steep slopes of ice, zigzagging to the right and left to avoid the flying boulders. When midway up this slope we reached a place where the granite rose in perfectly smooth bluffs on either side of a gorge,—a narrow cut, or walled way, leading up to the flat summit of the cliff. This we scaled by cutting ice steps, only to find ourselves fronted again by a still higher wall. Ice sloped from its front at too steep an angle for us to follow, but had melted in contact with it, leaving a space three feet wide between the ice and the rock. We entered this crevice and climbed along its bottom, with a wall of rock rising a hundred feet above us on one side, and a thirty-foot face of ice on the other, through which light of an intense cobalt-blue penetrated.

Reaching the upper end, we had to cut our footsteps upon the ice again, and, having braced our backs against the granite, climb up to the surface. We were now in a dangerous position: to fall into the crevice upon one side was to be wedged to death between rock and ice; to make a slip was to be shot down five hundred feet, and then hurled over the brink of a precipice. In the friendly seat which this wedge gave me, I stopped to take wet and dry observations with the thermometer,—this being an absolute preventive of a scare,—and to enjoy the view.

The wall of our mountain sank abruptly to the left, opening for the first time an outlook to the eastward. Deep—it seemed almost verti-cally—beneath us we could see the blue water of Owen's Lake, ten thou-sand feet down. The summit peaks to the north were piled in titanic confusion, their ridges overhanging the eastern slope with terrible abruptness. Clustered upon the shelves and plateaus below were several frozen lakes, and in all directions swept magnificent fields of snow. The summit was now not over five hundred feet distant, and we started on again with the exhilarating hope of success. But if Nature had intended to secure the summit from all assailants, she could not have planned her defences better; for the smooth granite wall which rose above the snow-slope continued, apparently, quite round the peak, and we looked in great anxiety to see if there was not one place where it might be climbed. It was all blank except in one place; quite near us the snow bridged across the crevice, and rose in a long point to the summit of the wall,—a great icicle-column frozen in a niche of the bluff,—its base about ten feet wide, narrowing to two feet at the top. We climbed to the base of this spire of ice, and, with the utmost care, began to cut our stairway. The material was an exceedingly compacted snow, passing into clear ice as it neared the rock. We climbed the first half of it with comparative ease; after that it was almost vertical, and so thin that we did not dare to cut the footsteps deep enough to make them absolutely safe. There was a constant dread lest our ladder should break off, and we be thrown either down the snow-slope or into the bottom of the crevasse. At last, in order to prevent myself from falling over backwards, I was obliged to thrust my hand into the crack between the ice and the wall, and the spire became so narrow that I could do this on both sides; so that the climb was made as upon a tree, cutting mere toe-holes and embracing the whole column of ice in my arms. At last I reached the top, and, with the greatest cau-tion, wormed my body over the brink, and, rolling out upon the smooth surface of the granite, looked over and watched Cotter make his climb. He came steadily up, with no sense of nervousness, until he got to the narrow part of the ice, and here he stopped and looked up with a forlorn face to me; but as he climbed up over the edge the broad smile came back to his face, and he asked me if it had occurred to me that we had, by and by, to go down again.

We had now an easy slope to the summit, and hurried up over rocks and ice, reaching the crest at exactly twelve o'clock. I rang my hammer upon the topmost rock; we grasped hands, and I reverently named the grand peak MOUNT TYNDALL.

FRIDTJOF NANSEN

(1861–1930)

From *Farthest North*

In 1890, when the young Norwegian explorer Fridtjof Nansen first unveiled his plan to drift in the pack ice across the North Pole, Brigadier General Adolphus Washington Greely called his idea "an illogical scheme of self destruction." Sailing north and getting locked in the ice had been every polar explorer's downfall. What's more, few believed Nansen's theory that the North Pole was neither solid land nor solid ice but a shifting mass of semifrozen currents. Even if his tublike boat, the Fram—which he designed so that the ice would slide off its rounded sides—could withstand the Arctic's dangers, how could it possibly drift so many thousands of miles?

Nansen and his men set out in the summer of 1893 and by September of that year were prisoners of the ice. Life on board an ice-locked boat can get mighty monotonous after hundreds of days, but things got interesting midway into the Fram's journey. By January 1895 Nansen realized that the Arctic currents would never take the boat over the apex of the globe. So, in a momentous decision, he left the ship to try to reach the Pole on foot. He and Hjalmar Johansen took provisions for

100 days, three sledges, two kayaks, and twenty-seven dogs. They knew they would never see the Fram again. The fate of her crew, and their own fate, were equally uncertain. The second volume of Farthest North, which describes Nansen's eighteen-month saga of shifting lanes of rotten ice, white storms, disorientation, monotony, exhaustion, and uncertainty is one of the most suspenseful, intimate, and eloquent Arctic narratives ever written.

Nansen and Johansen toil through the torn ice fields for a month, until they realize that the ice is drifting south almost as fast as they slog north. In May they turn back, knowing that they and their dogs are so low in energy and food that they are almost at the point of no return. And yet, almost inconceivably, they have another year's desperate, hungry journey ahead of them. They reach land in August, but their elation is short-lived. Winter is setting in, making travel south to the depot on the tip of Franz Joseph Land impossible. They are forced to spend the winter in a three-foot-deep stone and dirt hovel covered with walrus skins, living on seal blubber and blood pancakes. The following summer, struggling south along the icy, stormbound coast, they happen upon a British expedition sent to find a land route to the Pole. Naturally, the Brits don't continue after hearing Nansen's stories of the endless Arctic sea, but instead take him and Johansen home. In a miracle of timing, the Fram arrives in Norway a week later, all her crew alive and well.

Nansen's three-year drift in the Fram is now one of the famous success stories of polar exploration. His visionary methods of leadership and his use of dogs and skis inspired a philosophical shift in the way such expeditions would be carried out in the future. When he returned to Norway in 1896, having long ago been given up for dead, he was declared the greatest polar explorer who ever lived. The young Roald Amundsen was inspired by his hero to conquer the Northwest Passage and would later take the Fram to Antarctica. A man of immense moral stature and tireless will, Nansen went on to win the Nobel Peace Prize for his work relocating refugees after the First World War.

This excerpt from Farthest North *begins with some of Nansen's most introspective passages, as he and Johansen prepare to leave the* Fram *and walk to the Pole. It ends several months into their long and anxious journey southward, just as they sight land.*

"Wednesday, January 2, 1895. Never before have I had such strange feelings at the commencement of the new year. It cannot fail to bring some momentous events, and will possibly become one of the most remarkable years in my life, whether it leads me to success or to destruction. Years come and go unnoticed in this world of ice, and we have no more knowledge here of what these years have brought to humanity than we know of what the future ones have in store. In this silent nature no events ever happen; all is shrouded in darkness; there is nothing in view save the twinkling stars, immeasurably far away in the freezing night, and the flickering sheen of the aurora borealis. I can just discern close by the vague outline of the *Fram,* dimly standing out in the desolate gloom, with her rigging showing dark against the host of stars. Like an infinitesimal speck, the vessel seems lost amidst the boundless expanse of this realm of death. Nevertheless, under her deck there is a snug and cherished home for thirteen men undaunted by the majesty of this realm. In there, life is freely pulsating, while far away outside in the night there is nothing save death and silence, only broken now and then, at long intervals, by the violent pressure of the ice as it surges along in gigantic masses. It sounds most ominous in the great stillness, and one cannot help an uncanny feeling as if supernatural powers were at hand, the Jötuns and Rimturser (frost-giants) of the Arctic regions, with whom we may have to engage in deadly combat at any moment; but we are not afraid of them.

"I often think of Shakespeare's Viola, who sat 'like Patience on a monument.' Could we not pass as representatives of this marble Patience, imprisoned here on the ice while the years roll by, awaiting our time? I should like to design such a monument. It should be a lonely man in shaggy wolfskin clothing, all covered with hoar-frost, sitting on a mound

of ice, and gazing out into the darkness across these boundless, ponderous masses of ice, awaiting the return of daylight and spring.

"The ice-pressure was not noticeable after 1 o'clock on Friday night until it suddenly recommenced last night. First I heard a rumbling outside, and some snow fell down from the rigging upon the tent roof as I sat reading; I thought it sounded like packing in the ice, and just then the *Fram* received a violent shock, such as she had not received since last winter. I was rocked backward and forward on the chest on which I was sitting. Finding that the trembling and rumbling continued, I went out. There was a loud roar of ice-packing to the west and northwest, which continued uniformly for a couple of hours or so. Is this the New-year's greeting from the ice?

"We spent New-year's-eve cozily, with a cloudberry punch-bowl, pipes, and cigarettes. Needless to say, there was an abundance of cakes and the like, and we spoke of the old and the new year and days to come. Some selections were played on the organ and violin. Thus midnight arrived. Blessing produced from his apparently inexhaustible store a bottle of genuine 'linje akkevit' (line eau-de-vie), and in this Norwegian liquor we drank the old year out and the new year in. Of course there was many a thought that would obtrude itself at the change of the year, being the second which we had seen on board the *Fram,* and also, in all probability, the last that we should all spend together. Naturally enough, one thanked one's comrades, individually and collectively, for all kindness and good-fellowship. Hardly one of us had thought, perhaps, that the time would pass so well up here. Sverdrup expressed the wish that the journey which Johansen and I were about to make in the coming year might be fortunate and bring success in all respects. And then we drank to the health and well-being in the coming year of those who were to remain behind on board the *Fram.* It so happened that just now at the turn of the year we stood on the verge of an entirely new world. The wind which whistled up in the rigging overhead was not only wafting us on to unknown regions, but also up into higher latitudes than any human foot had ever trod. We felt that this year, which was just commencing, would bring the culminating-point of the expedition, when it would bear its richest fruits. Would that this year might prove a good year for those on board the *Fram;* that the *Fram* might go ahead, fulfilling her task as she has hitherto done; and in that case none of us could doubt that those on board would also prove equal to the task intrusted to them.

"New-year's-day was ushered in with the same wind, the same stars, and the same darkness as before. Even at noon one cannot see the slightest glimmer of twilight in the south. Yesterday I thought I could trace something of the kind; it extended like a faint gleam of light over the sky, but it was yellowish-white, and stretched too high up; hence I am rather inclined to think that it was an aurora borealis. Again to-day the sky looks lighter near the edge, but this can scarcely be anything except the gleam of the aurora borealis, which extends all round the sky, a little above the fog-banks on the horizon, and which is strongest at the edge. Exactly similar lights may be observed at other times in other parts of the horizon. The air was particularly clear yesterday, but the horizon is always somewhat foggy or hazy. During the night we had an uncommonly strong aurora borealis; wavy streamers were darting in rapid twists over the southern sky, their rays reaching to the zenith, and beyond it there was to be seen for a time a band in the form of a gorgeous corona, casting a reflection like moonshine across the ice. The sky had lit up its torch in honor of the new year—a fairy dance of darting streamers in the depth of night. I cannot help often thinking that this contrast might be taken as typical of the Northman's character and destiny. In the midst of this gloomy, silent nature, with all its numbing cold, we have all these shooting, glittering, quivering rays of light.

· · ·

On January 23d I write: "The dawn has grown so much that there was a visible light from it on the ice, and for the first time this year I saw the crimson glow of the sun low down in the dawn." We now took soundings with the lead before I was to leave the vessel; we found 1876 fathoms (3450 metres). I then made some snow-shoes down in the hold; it was important to have them smooth, tough, and light, on which one could make good headway; "they shall be well rubbed with tar, stearine, and tallow, and there shall be speed in them; then it is only a question of using one's legs, and I have no doubt that can be managed.

"Tuesday, January 29th. Latitude yesterday, 83° 30′. (Some days ago we had been so far north as 83° 40′, but had again drifted southward.) The light keeps on steadily increasing, and by noon it almost seems to be broad daylight. I believe I could read the title of a book out in the open if the print were large and clear. I take a stroll every morning, greeting the dawning day, before I go down into the hold to my work at the snow-shoes and equipment. My mind is filled with a peculiar sensation, which I cannot clearly define; there is certainly an exulting feeling of triumph, deep in the soul, a feeling that all one's dreams are about to be realized with the rising sun, which steers northward across the ice-bound waters. But while I am busy in these familiar surroundings a wave of sadness sometimes comes over me; it is like bidding farewell to a dear friend and to a home which has long afforded me a sheltering roof. At one blow all this and my dear comrades are to be left behind forever; never again shall I tread this snow-clad deck, never again creep under this tent, never hear the laughter ring in this familiar saloon, never again sit in this friendly circle.

"And then I remember that when the *Fram* at last bursts from her bonds of ice, and turns her prow towards Norway, I shall not be with her. A farewell imparts to everything in life its own tinge of sadness, like the crimson rays of the sun, when the day, good or bad, sinks in tears below the horizon.

"Hundreds of times my eye wanders to the map hanging there on the wall, and each time a chill creeps over me. The distance before us seems so long, and the obstacles in our path may be many; but then again the feeling comes that we are bound to pull through: it cannot be otherwise; everything is too carefully prepared to fail now, and meanwhile the south-east wind is whistling above us, and we are continually drifting northward nearer our goal. When I go up on deck and step out into the night with its glittering starry vault and the flaring aurora borealis, then all these thoughts recede, and I must, as ever, pause on the threshold of this sanctuary—this dark, deep, silent space, this infinite temple of nature, in which the soul seeks to find its origin. Toiling ant, what matters it whether you reach your goal with your fir-needle or not? Everything disappears none the less in the ocean of eternity, in the great Nirvana; and as time rolls on our names are forgotten, our deeds pass into oblivion, and our lives flit by like the traces of a cloud, and vanish like the mist dispelled by the warm rays of the sun. Our time is but a fleeting shadow, hurrying us on to the end—so it is ordained; and having reached that end, none ever retraces his steps.

"Two of us will soon be journeying farther through this immense waste, into greater solitudes and deeper stillness.

.   .   .

At last by midday on March 14th we finally left the *Fram* to the noise of a thundering salute. For the third time farewells and mutual good wishes were exchanged.[1] Some of our comrades came a little way with us, but Sverdrup soon turned back in order to be on board for dinner at 1 o'clock. It was on the top of a hummock that we two said good-bye to

---

[1] Because of problems with their equipment, Nansen and Johansen returned to the boat twice before finally setting out for good.

each other; the *Fram* was lying behind us, and I can remember how I stood watching him as he strode easily homeward on his snow-shoes. I half wished I could turn back with him and find myself again in the warm saloon; I knew only too well that a life of toil lay before us, and that it would be many a long day before we should again sleep and eat under a comfortable roof; but that that time was going to be so long as it really proved to be, none of us then had any idea. We all thought that either the expedition would succeed, and that we should return home that same year, or—that it would not succeed.

A little while after Sverdrup had left us, Mogstad also found it necessary to turn back. He had thought of going with us till the next day, but his heavy wolfskin trousers were, as he un-euphemistically expressed it, "almost full of sweat, and he must go back to the fire on board to get dry." Hansen, Henriksen, and Pettersen were then the only ones left, and they labored along, each with his load on his back. It was difficult for them to keep up with us on the flat ice, so quickly did we go; but when we came to pressure-ridges we were brought to a standstill and the sledges had to be helped over. At one place the ridge was so bad that we had to carry the sledges a long way. When, after considerable trouble, we had managed to get over it, Peter shook his head reflectively, and said to Johansen that we should meet plenty more of the same kind, and have enough hard work before we had eaten sufficient of the loads to make the sledges run lightly. Just here we came upon a long stretch of bad ice, and Peter became more and more concerned for our future; but towards evening matters improved, and we advanced more rapidly. When we stopped at 6 o'clock the odometer registered a good 7 miles, which was not so bad for a first day's work. We had a cheerful evening in our tent, which was just about big enough to hold all five. Pettersen, who had exerted himself and become overheated on the way, shivered and groaned while the dogs were being tied up and fed, and the tent pitched. He, however, found existence considerably brighter when he sat inside it, in his warm wolfskin clothes, with a pot of smoking chocolate before him, a big lump of butter in one hand and a biscùit in the other, and exclaimed, "Now I am living like a

prince!" He thereafter discoursed at length on the exalting thought that he
was sitting in a tent in the middle of the Polar Sea. Poor fellow, he had
begged and prayed to be allowed to come with us on this expedition; he
would cook for us and make himself generally useful, both as a tinsmith
and blacksmith; and then, he said, three would be company. I regretted
that I could not take more than one companion, and he had been in the
depths of woe for several days, but now found comfort in the fact that he
had, at any rate, come part of the way with us, and was out on this great
desert sea, for, as he said, "not many people have done that."

The others had no sleeping-bag with them, so they made themselves a
cozy little hut of snow, into which they crawled in their wolfskin garments, and had a tolerably good night. I was awake early the next morning; but when I crept out of the tent I found that somebody else was on
his legs before me, and this was Pettersen, who, awakened by the cold,
was now walking up and down to warm his stiffened limbs. He had tried
it now, he said; he never should have thought it possible to sleep in the
snow, but it had not been half bad. He would not quite admit that he had
been cold, and that that was the reason why he had turned out so early.
Then we had our last pleasant breakfast together, got the sledges ready,
harnessed the dogs, shook hands with our companions, and, without
many words being uttered on either side, started out into solitude. Peter
shook his head sorrowfully as we went off. I turned round when we had
gone some little way, and saw his figure on the top of the hummock; he
was still looking after us. His thoughts were probably sad; perhaps he
believed that he had spoken to us for the last time.

We found large expanses of flat ice, and covered the ground quickly,
farther and farther away from our comrades, into the unknown, where we
two alone and the dogs were to wander for months. The *Fram*'s rigging
had disappeared long ago behind the margin of the ice. We often came on
piled-up ridges and uneven ice, where the sledges had to be helped and
sometimes carried over. It often happened, too, that they capsized altogether, and it was only by dint of strenuous hauling that we righted them
again. Somewhat exhausted by all this hard work, we stopped finally at 6

o'clock in the evening, and had then gone about 9 miles during the day. They were not quite the marches I had reckoned on, but we hoped that by degrees the sledges would become lighter and the ice better to travel over. The latter, too, seems to have been the case at first. On Sunday, March 17th, I say in my diary: "The ice appears to be more even the farther north we get; came across a lane, however, yesterday which necessitated a long detour.† At half-past six we had done about 9 miles. As we had just reached a good camping-ground, and the dogs were tired, we stopped. Lowest temperature last night, −45° Fahr. (−42.8° C.)."

---

† It was not advisable, for many reasons, to cross the lanes in the kayaks, now that the temperature was so low. Even if the water in them had not nearly always been covered with a more or less thick layer of ice, the kayaks would have become much heavier from the immediate freezing of the water which would have entered, as they proved to be not absolutely impervious; and this ice we had then no means of dislodging.

The ice continued to become more even during the following days, and our marches often amounted to 14 miles or more in the day. Now and then a misfortune might happen which detained us, as, for instance, one day a sharp spike of ice which was standing up cut a hole in a sack of fish flour, and all the delicious food ran out. It took us more than an hour to collect it all again and repair the damages. Then the odometer got broken through being jammed in some uneven ice, and it took some hours to mend it by a process of lashing. But on we went northward, often over great, wide ice-plains which seemed as if they must stretch right to the Pole. Sometimes it happened that we passed through places where the ice was "unusually massive, with high hummocks, so that it looked like undulating country covered with snow." This was undoubtedly very old ice, which had drifted in the Polar Sea for a long time on its way from the Siberian Sea to the east coast of Greenland, and which had been subjected year after year to severe pressure. High hummocks and mounds are thus formed, which summer after summer are partially melted by the rays of the sun, and again in the winters covered with great drifts of snow, so that they assume forms which resemble ice-hills rather than piles of sea-ice resulting from upheaval.

Wednesday, March 20th, my diary says: "Beautiful weather for travelling in, with fine sunsets; but somewhat cold, particularly in the bag, at nights (it was −41.8° and −43.6° Fahr., or −41° and −42° C.). The ice appears to be getting more even the farther we advance, and in some places it is like travelling over 'inland ice.' If this goes on the whole thing will be done in no time." That day we lost our odometer, and as we did not find it out till some time afterwards, and I did not know how far we might have to go back, I thought it was not worth while to return and look for. It was the cause, however, of our only being able subsequently to guess approximately at the distance we had gone during the day. We had another mishap, too, that day. This was that one of the dogs (it was "Livjægeren") had become so ill that he could not be driven any longer, and we had to let him go loose. It was late in the day before we discovered that he was not with us; he had stopped behind at our camping-ground when we broke up in the morning, and I had to go back after him on snow-shoes, which caused a long delay.

"Thursday, March 21st. Nine in the morning, −43.6° Fahr., or −42° C. (Minimum in the night, −47.2° Fahr., or −44° C.) Clear, as it has been every day. Beautiful, bright weather; glorious for travelling in, but somewhat cold at nights, with the quicksilver continually frozen. Patching Finn shoes in this temperature inside the tent, with one's nose slowly freezing away, is not all pure enjoyment.

"Friday, March 22d. Splendid ice for getting over; things go better and better. Wide expanses, with a few pressure-ridges now and then, but passable everywhere. Kept at it yesterday from about half-past eleven in the morning to half-past eight at night; did a good 21 miles, I hope. We should be in latitude 85°. The only disagreeable thing about it now is the cold. Our clothes are transformed more and more into a cuirass of ice during the day, and wet bandages at night. The blankets likewise. The sleeping-bag gets heavier and heavier from the moisture which freezes on the hair inside. The same clear, settled weather every day. We are both longing now for a change; a few clouds and a little more mildness would be welcome." The temperature in the night, −44.8° Fahr. (−42.7° C.). By an observation which I took later in the forenoon, our latitude that day proved to be 85° 9′ N.

"Saturday, March 23d. On account of observation, lashing the loads on the sledges, patching bags, and other occupations of a like kind, which are no joke in this low temperature, we did not manage to get off yesterday before 3 o'clock in the afternoon. We stuck to it till nine in the evening, when we stopped in some of the worst ice we have seen lately. Our day's march, however, had lain across several large tracts of level ice, so I think that we made 14 miles or so all the same. We have the same brilliant sunshine; but yesterday afternoon the wind from the northeast, which we have had for the last few days, increased, and made it rather raw.

"We passed over a large frozen pool yesterday evening; it looked almost like a large lake." It could not have been long since this was formed, as the ice on it was still quite thin. It is wonderful that these pools can form up there at that time of the year.

From this time forward there was an end of the flat ice, which it had been simple enjoyment to travel over; and now we had often great difficulties to cope with. On Sunday, March 24th, I write: "Ice not so good; yesterday was a hard day, but we made a few miles—not more, though, than seven, I am afraid. This continual lifting of the heavily loaded sledges is calculated to break one's back; but better times are coming, perhaps. The cold is also appreciable, always the same; but yesterday it was increased by the admixture of considerable wind from the northeast. We halted about half-past nine in the evening. It is perceptible how the days lengthen, and how much later the sun sets; in a few days' time we shall have the midnight sun.

"We killed 'Livjægeren' yesterday evening, and hard work it was skinning him." This was the first dog which had to be killed; but many came afterwards, and it was some of the most disagreeable work we had on the journey, particularly now at the beginning, when it was so cold. When this first dog was dismembered and given to the others, many of them went supperless the whole night in preference to touching the meat. But as the days went by and they became more worn out, they learned to appreciate dog's flesh, and later we were not even so considerate as to skin the butchered animal, but served it hair and all.[2]

The following day the ice was occasionally somewhat better; but as a rule it was bad, and we became more and more worn out with the never-ending work of helping the dogs, righting the sledges every time they capsized, and hauling them, or carrying them bodily, over hummocks and inequalities of the ground. Sometimes we were so sleepy in the evenings that our eyes shut and we fell asleep as we went along. My head would drop, and I would be awakened by suddenly falling forward on my snow-

---

[2] When a dog became too ill or exhausted to go on, the men sacrificed it to feed the others. Soon Nansen couldn't bring himself to kill the dogs, so Johansen would take them out of sight and do it where Nansen couldn't see.

shoes. Then we would stop, after having found a camping-ground behind a hummock or ridge of ice, where there was some shelter from the wind. While Johansen looked after the dogs, it generally fell to my lot to pitch the tent, fill the cooker with ice, light the burner, and start the supper as quickly as possible. This generally consisted of "lobscouse" one day, made of pemmican and dried potatoes; another day of a sort of fish rissole substance known as "fiskegratin" in Norway, and in this case composed of fish-meal, flour, and butter. A third day it would be pea, bean, or lentil soup, with bread and pemmican. Johansen preferred the "lobscouse," while I had a weakness for the "fiskegratin." As time went by, however, he came over to my way of thinking, and the "fiskegratin" took precedence of everything else.

As soon as Johansen had finished with the dogs, and the different receptacles containing the ingredients and eatables for breakfast and supper had been brought in, as well as our bags with private necessities, the sleeping-bags were spread out, the tent door carefully shut, and we crept into the bag to thaw our clothes. This was not very agreeable work. During the course of the day the damp exhalations of the body had little by little become condensed in our outer garments, which were now a mass of ice and transformed into complete suits of ice-armor. They were so hard and stiff that if we had only been able to get them off they could have stood by themselves, and they crackled audibly every time we moved. These clothes were so stiff that the arm of my coat actually rubbed deep sores in my wrists during our marches; one of these sores—the one on the right hand—got frostbitten, the wound grew deeper and deeper, and nearly reached the bone. I tried to protect it with bandages, but not until late in the summer did it heal, and I shall probably have the scar for life. When we got into our sleeping-bags in the evening our clothes began to thaw slowly, and on this process a considerable amount of physical *heat* was expended. We packed ourselves tight into the bag, and lay with our teeth chattering for an hour, or an hour and a half, before we became aware of a little of the warmth in our bodies which we so sorely needed. At last our clothes became wet and pliant, only to freeze again a few minutes after we had turned out of the bag in the morning. There was no question of getting these clothes dried on the journey so long as the cold lasted, as more and more moisture from the body collected in them.

How cold we were as we lay there shivering in the bag, waiting for the supper to be ready! I, who was cook, was obliged to keep myself more or less awake to see to the culinary operations, and sometimes I succeeded. At last the supper was ready, was portioned out, and, as always, tasted delicious. These occasions were the supreme moments of our existence—moments to which we looked forward the whole day long. But sometimes we were so weary that our eyes closed, and we fell asleep with the food on its way to our mouths. Our hands would fall back inanimate with the spoons in them and the food fly out on the bag. After supper we generally permitted ourselves the luxury of a little extra drink, consisting of water, as hot as we could swallow it, in which whey-powder had been dissolved. It tasted something like boiled milk, and we thought it wonderfully comforting; it seemed to warm us to the very ends of our toes. Then we would creep down into the bag again, buckle the flap carefully over our heads, lie close together, and soon sleep the sleep of the just. But even in our dreams we went on ceaselessly, grinding at the sledges and driving the dogs, always northward, and I was often awakened by hearing Johansen calling in his sleep to "Pan," or "Barrabas," or "Klapper-slangen": "Get on, you devil, you! Go on, you brutes! Sass, sass! Now the whole thing is going over!" and execrations less fit for reproduction, until I went to sleep again.

In the morning I, as cook, was obliged to turn out to prepare the breakfast, which took an hour's time. As a rule, it consisted one morning of chocolate, bread, butter, and pemmican; another of oatmeal porridge, or a compound of flour, water, and butter, in imitation of our "butter-porridge" at home. This was washed down with milk, made of whey-powder and water. The breakfast ready, Johansen was roused; we sat up in the sleeping-bag, one of the blankets was spread out as a table-cloth, and we fell to work. We had a comfortable breakfast, wrote up our diaries, and then had to think about starting. But how tired we sometimes were, and how often would I not have given anything to be able to creep to the bottom of the bag again and sleep the clock round. It seemed to me as if this must be the greatest pleasure in life, but our business was to fight our way northward—always northward. We performed our toilets, and then came the going out into the cold to get the sledges ready, disentangle the dogs' traces, harness the animals, and get off as quickly as possible. I went first to find the way through the uneven ice, then came the sledge with my kayak. The dogs soon learned to follow, but at every unevenness of the ground they stopped, and if one could not get them all to start again at the same time by a shout, and so pull the sledge over the difficulty, one had to go back to beat or help them, according as circumstances necessitated. Then came Johansen with the two other sledges, always shouting to the dogs to pull harder, always beating them, and himself hauling to get the sledges over the terrible ridges of ice. It was undeniable cruelty to the poor animals from first to last, and one must often look back on it with horror. It makes me shudder even now when I think of how we beat them mercilessly with thick ash sticks when, hardly able to move, they stopped from sheer exhaustion. It made one's heart bleed to see them, but we turned our eyes away and hardened ourselves. It was necessary; forward we must go, and to this end everything else must give place. It is the sad part of expeditions of this kind that one systematically kills all better feelings, until only hard-hearted egoism remains. When I think of all those splendid animals, toiling for us without a murmur, as long as they could strain a muscle, never getting any thanks or even so much as a kind word, daily writhing under the lash until the time came when they could do no more and death freed them from their pangs— when I think of how they were left behind, one by one, up there on those desolate ice-fields, which had been witness to their faithfulness and devotion, I have moments of bitter self-reproach.

· · ·

[April 3] It became more and more of a riddle to me that we did not make greater progress northward. I kept on calculating and adding up our

marches as we went along, but always with the same result; that is to say, provided only the ice were still, we must be far above the eighty-sixth parallel. It was becoming only too clear to me, however, that the ice was moving southward, and that in its capricious drift, at the mercy of wind and current, we had our worst enemy to combat.

"Friday, April 5th. Began our march at three yesterday morning. The ice, however, was bad, with lanes and ridges, so that our progress was but little. These lanes, with rubble thrown up on each side, are our despair. It is like driving over a tract of rocks, and delays us terribly. First I must go on ahead to find a way, and then get my sledge through; then, perhaps, by way of a change, one falls into the water; yesterday, I fell through twice. If I work hard in finding a way and guiding my sledge over rough places, Johansen is no better off, with his two sledges to look after. It is a tough job to get even one of them over the rubble, to say nothing of the ridges; but he is a plucky fellow, and no mistake, and never gives in. Yesterday he fell into the water again in crossing a lane, and got wet up to his knees. I had gone over on my snow-shoes shortly before and did not notice that the ice was weak. He came afterwards without snow-shoes, walking beside one of the sledges, when suddenly the ice gave, and he fell through. Happily he managed to catch hold of the sledge, and the dogs, which did not stop, pulled him up again. These baths are not an unmixed pleasure, now that there is no possibility of drying or changing one's clothes, and one must wear a chain mail of ice until they thaw and dry on the body, which takes some time in this temperature. I took an observation for longitude and a magnetic observation yesterday morning, and have spent the whole fore-noon to-day in calculations (inside the bag) to find out our exact position. I find our latitude yesterday was 86° 2.8′ N. This is very little, but what can we do when the ice is what it is? And these dogs cannot work harder than they do, poor things. I sigh for the sledge-dogs from the Olenek daily now. The longitude for yesterday was 98° 47.15″, variation 44.4°. . . .

"Saturday, April 6th. (Two A.M., −11.4° Fahr. −24.2° C.) The ice grew worse and worse. Yesterday it brought me to the verge of despair, and when we stopped this morning I had almost decided to turn back. I will go on one day longer, however, to see if the ice is really as bad farther northward as it appears to be from the ridge, 30 feet in height, where we are encamped. We hardly made 4 miles yesterday. Lanes, ridges, and endless rough ice, it looks like an endless moraine of ice-blocks; and this continual lifting of the sledges over every irregularity is enough to tire out giants. Curious this rubble-ice. For the most part it is not so very massive, and seems as if it had been forced up somewhat recently, for it is incompletely covered with thin, loose snow, through which one falls suddenly up to one's middle. And thus it extends mile after mile northward, while every now and then there are old floes, with mounds that have been rounded off by the action of the sun in the summer—often very massive ice.

"I am rapidly coming to the conclusion that we are not doing any good here. We shall not be able to get much farther north, and it will be slow work indeed if there be much more of this sort of ice towards Franz Josef Land.[3]

. . .

"Sunday, May 19th. The surprise which the Seventeenth[4] brought us was nothing less than that we found the lanes about here full of narwhals. When we had just got under way, and were about to cross over the lane we had been stopped by the previous day, I became aware of a breathing noise, just like the blowing of whales. I thought at first it must be from the dogs, but then I heard for certain that the sound came from the lane. I listened. Johansen had heard the noise the whole morning, he said, but thought it was only ice jamming in the distance. No; that sound I knew well enough, I thought, and looked over towards an opening in the ice whence I thought it proceeded. Suddenly I saw a movement which could hardly be falling ice, and—quite right—up came the head of a whale;

---

[3] The next day, April 8, they turn around and go south, worried that they won't reach Franz Josef Land before winter.

[4] Norway's independence day.

then came the body; it executed the well-known curve, and disappeared. Then up came another, accompanied by the same sound. There was a whole school of them. I shouted that they were whales, and, running to the sledge, had my gun out in a second. Then came the adjusting of a harpoon, and after a little work this was accomplished, and I was ready to start in pursuit. Meanwhile the animals had disappeared from the opening in the ice where I had first seen them, though I heard their breathing from some openings farther east. I followed the lane in that direction, but did not come within range, although I got rather near them once or twice. They came up in comparatively small openings in the ice, which were to be found along the whole length of the lane. There was every prospect of being able to get a shot at them if we stopped for a day to watch the holes; but we had no time to spare, and could not have taken much with us had we got one, as the sledges were heavy enough already. We soon found a passage over, and continued our journey with the flags hoisted on the sledges in honor of the day. As we were going so slowly now that it was hardly possible for things to be worse, I determined at our dinner-hour that I really would take off the under-runners from my sledge. The change was unmistakable; it was not like the same sledge. Henceforth we got on well, and after a while the under-runners from Johansen's sledge were also removed. As we furthermore came on some good ice later in the day, our progress was quite unexpectedly good, and when we stopped at half-past eleven yesterday morning, I should think we had gone 10 miles during our day's march. This brings us down to latitude 83° 20′ or so.

"At last, then, we have come down to latitudes which have been reached by human beings before us, and it cannot possibly be far to land. A little while before we halted yesterday we crossed a lane or pool exactly like the two previous ones, only broader still. Here, too, I heard the blowing of whales, but although I was not far from the hole whence the noise presumably came, and although the opening there was quite small, I could perceive nothing. Johansen, who came afterwards with the dogs, said that as soon as they reached the frozen lane they got scent of something and wanted to go against the wind. Curious that there should be so many narwhals in the lanes here.

· · ·

"Sunday, June 30th. So this is the end of June, and we are about the same place as when we began the month. And the state of the snow? Well, better it certainly is not; but the day is fine. It is so warm that we are quite hot lying here inside the tent. Through the open door we can see out over the ice where the sun is glittering through white sailing cirrus clouds on the dazzling whiteness. And then there is a Sunday calm, with a faint breeze mostly from the southeast, I think. Ah me, it is lovely at home to-day, I am sure, with everything in bloom and the fjord quivering in the sunlight; and you are sitting out on the point with Liv, perhaps, or are on the water in your boat.[5] And then my eye wanders out through the door again, and I am reminded there is many an ice-floe between now and then, before the time when I shall see it all once more.

"Here we lie far up in the north; two grim, black, soot-stained barbarians, stirring a mess of soup in a kettle and surrounded on all sides by ice; by ice and nothing else—shining and white, possessed of all the purity we ourselves lack. Alas, it is all too pure! One's eye searched to the very horizon for a dark spot to rest on, but in vain. When will it really come to pass? Now we have waited for it two months. All the birds seem to have disappeared to-day; not even a cheery little auk to be seen. They were here until yesterday and we have heard them flying north and south, probably to and from land, where they have gone, I suppose, now that there is so little water about in these parts. If only we could move as easily as they.

· · ·

"Wednesday, July 3rd. Why write again? What have I to commit to these pages? Nothing but the same overpowering longing to be home and away from this monotony. One day just like the other, with the exception, perhaps, that before it was warm and quiet, while the last two days there has

---

[5] Here Nansen addresses his wife, Eva, in his journal. Liv is his two-year-old daughter, an infant when he sailed from Norway.

been a south wind blowing, and we are drifting northwards. Found from a meridian altitude yesterday that we have drifted back to 82° 8.4′ N., while the longitude is about the same. Both yesterday and the day before we had to a certain extent really brilliant sunshine, and this for us is a great rarity. The horizon in the south was fairly clear yesterday, which it has not been for a long time; but we searched it in vain for land. I do not understand it. . . .

. . .

"Saturday, August 3d. Inconceivable toil. We never could go on with it were it not for the fact that we *must*. We have made wretchedly little progress, even if we have made any at all. We have had no food for the dogs the last few days except the ivory-gulls and fulmars we have been able to shoot, and that has been a couple a day. Yesterday the dogs only had a little bit of blubber each.

"Sunday, August 4th. These lanes are desperate work and tax one's strength. We often have to go several hundred yards on mere brash, or from block to block, dragging the sledges after us, and in constant fear of their capsizing into the water. Johansen was very nearly in yesterday, but, as always hitherto, he managed to save himself. The dogs fall in and get a bath continually.

"Monday, August 5th. We have never had worse ice than yesterday, but we managed to force our way on a little, nevertheless, and two happy incidents marked the day: the first was that Johansen was not eaten up by a bear, and the second, that we saw open water under the glacier edge ashore.

"We set off about 7 o'clock yesterday morning and got on to ice as bad it as could be. It was as if some giant had hurled down enormous blocks pell-mell, and had strewn wet snow in between them with water underneath; and into this we sank above our knees. There were also numbers of deep pools in between the blocks. It was like toiling over hill and dale, up and down over block after block and ridge after ridge, with deep clefts in between; not a clear space big enough to pitch a tent on even, and thus it went on the whole time. To put a coping-stone to our misery, there was such a mist that we could not see a hundred yards in front of us. After an exhausting march we at last reached a lane where we had to ferry over in the kayaks. After having cleared the side of the lane from young ice and brash, I drew my sledge to the end of the ice, and was holding it to prevent it slipping in, when I heard a scuffle behind me, and Johansen, who had just turned round to pull his sledge flush with mine,† cried, 'Take the gun!' I turned round and saw an enormous bear throwing itself on him, and Johansen on his back. I tried to seize my gun, which was in its case on the fore-deck, but at the same moment the kayak slipped into the water. My first thought was to throw myself into the water over the kayak and fire from there, but I recognized how risky it would be. I began to pull the kayak, with its heavy cargo, on to the high edge of the ice again as quickly as I could, and was on my knees pulling and tugging to get at my gun. I had no time to look round and see what was going on behind me, when I heard Johansen quietly say, 'You must look sharp if you want to be in time!'

"Look sharp? I should think so! At last I got hold of the butt-end, dragged the gun out, turned round in a sitting posture, and cocked the shot-barrel. The bear was standing not two yards off, ready to make an end to my dog, 'Kaifas.' There was no time to lose in cocking the other barrel, so I gave it a charge of shot behind the ear, and it fell down dead between us.

"The bear must have followed our track like a cat, and, covered by the ice-blocks, have slunk up while we were clearing the ice from the lane and had our backs to him. We could see by the trail how it had crept over a small ridge just behind us under cover of a mound by Johansen's kayak. While the latter, without suspecting anything or looking round, went back and stooped down to pick up the hauling-rope, he suddenly caught

---

† As a rule, we crossed the lanes in this manner; we placed the sledges, with the kayaks on, side by side, lashed them together, stiffened them by running the snow-shoes across under the straps, which also steadied them, and then launched them as they were, with the sledges lashed underneath. When across, we had only to haul them up on the other side.

sight of an animal crouched up at the end of the kayak, but thought it was 'Suggen';[6] and before he had time to realize that it was so big he received a cuff on the ear which made him see fireworks, and then, as I mentioned before, over he went on his back. He tried to defend himself as best he could with his fists. With one hand he seized the throat of the animal, and held fast, clinching it with all his might. It was just as the bear was about to bite Johansen in the head that he uttered the memorable words, "Look sharp!" The bear kept glancing at me continually, speculating, no doubt, as to what I was going to do; but then caught sight of the dog and turned towards it. Johansen let go as quick as thought, and wriggled himself away, while the bear gave 'Suggen' a cuff which made him howl lustily, just as he does when we thrash him. Then 'Kaifas' got a slap on the nose. Meanwhile Johansen had struggled to his legs, and when I fired had got his gun, which was sticking out of the kayak hole. The only harm done was that the bear had scraped some grime off Johansen's right cheek, so that he has a white stripe on it, and had given

[6] At this point, Suggen and Kaifas are the only two surviving dogs.

him a slight wound in one hand; 'Kaifas' had also got a scratch on his nose.

. . .

"The ice was not good; and, to make bad worse, we immediately came on some terrible lanes, full of nothing but tightly packed lumps of ice. In some places there were whole seas of it, and it was enough to make one despair. Among all this loose ice we came on an unusually thick old floe, with high mounds on it and pools in between. It was from one of these mounds that I observed through the glass the open water at the foot of the glacier, and now we cannot have far to go. But the ice looks very bad on ahead, and each piece when it is like this may take a long time to travel over.

"As we went along we heard the wounded bear lowing ceaselessly behind us; it filled the whole of this silent world of ice with its bitter plaint over the cruelty of man. It was miserable to hear it; and if we had had time we should undoubtedly have gone back and sacrificed a cartridge on it. We saw the cubs go off to the place where the mother was lying, and thought to ourselves that we had got rid of them, but heard them soon afterwards, and even when we had camped they were not far off.

"Wednesday, August 7th. At last we are under land; at last the drift-ice lies behind us, and before us is open water—open, it is to be hoped, to the end. Yesterday was the day. When we came out of the tent the evening of the day before yesterday we both thought we must be nearer the edge of the glacier than ever, and with fresh courage, and in the faint hope of reaching land that day, we started on our journey. Yet we dared not think our life on the drift-ice was so nearly at an end. After wandering about on it for five months and suffering so many disappointments, we were only too well prepared for a new defeat. We thought, however, that the ice looked more promising farther on, though before we had gone far we came to broad lanes full of slush and foul, uneven ice, with hills and dales, and deep snow and water, into which we sank up to our thighs. After a couple of lanes of this kind, matters improved a little, and we got on to some flat ice. After having gone over this for a while, it became apparent how much nearer we were to the edge of the glacier. It could not possibly be far off now. We eagerly harnessed ourselves to the sledges again, put on a spurt, and away we went through snow and water, over mounds and ridges. We went as hard as we could, and what did we care if we sank into water till far above our fur leggings, so that both they and our 'komager' filled and gurgled like a pump? What did it matter to us now, so long as we got on?

"We soon reached plains, and over them we went quicker and quicker. We waded through ponds where the spray flew up on all sides. Nearer and nearer we came, and by the dark water-sky before us, which continually rose higher, we could see how we were drawing near to open water. We did not even notice bears now. There seemed to be plenty about, tracks, both old and new, crossing and recrossing; one had even inspected the tent while we were asleep, and by the fresh trail we could see how it had come down wind in lee of us. We had no use for a bear now; we had food enough. We were soon able to see the open water under the wall of the glacier, and our steps lengthened even more. As I was striding along I thought of the march of the Ten Thousand through Asia, when Xenophon's soldiers, after a year's war against superior forces, at last saw the sea from a mountain and cried, 'Thalatta! thalatta!' Maybe this sea was just as welcome to us after our months in the endless white drift-ice.

"At last, at last, I stood by the edge of the ice. Before me lay the dark surface of the sea, with floating white floes; far away the glacier wall rose abruptly from the water; over the whole lay a sombre, foggy light. Joy welled up in our hearts at this sight, and we could not give it expression in words. Behind us lay all our troubles, before us the water-way home. . . ."

GEORGE WALLACE MELVILLE

(1841–1912)

From *In the Lena Delta*

The fate of the naval vessel Jeannette *and her crew is one of the most poignant tragedies in all of Arctic exploration. In 1879, an American team led by navy veteran Captain George Washington De Long set sail from San Francisco toward the North Pole via the Bering Sea. But as happened to so many of the wooden ships that ventured toward the poles, the* Jeannette *was taken prisoner by the ice, and, after nearly two years of frozen exile, crushed in its grip. In this excerpt, Chief Engineer Melville tells of the fateful day—an event that would prove equally so for Sir Ernest Shackleton years later—when the ship is splintered and the men are cast adrift on the ice.*

The situation only got worse. Now without a home, fuel, or provisions, the men set out for the northern coast of Siberia in three small open boats. On the way they met with a ferocious gale, "a white wall of ice and foam," which took one boat to the bottom and separated the other two. Melville rode it to the Lena River delta with ten men just as the Siberian winter was setting in, and spent the next year looking for his companions. Melville's survival came to depend entirely on his *ability to befriend the Yakut natives of the region, who shared with him what little food they had (mostly deer offal and frozen raw fish) and acted as guides on his many overland trips searching for traces of De Long. For much of the winter, Melville's legs were so swollen and blistered from frostbite that he could only crawl on his hands and knees, yet somehow he endured. A person of tireless good humor, ingenuity, and true grit, he kept all his own men alive, although one went mad.*

De Long's group was not so lucky. Melville discovered that they reached shore and started up another branch of the Lena River. But they found little: no game, no people, no relief from the cold. Two men who went ahead to search for help met up with Melville and survived, but the rest died of exposure and starvation.

Although De Long's fatal odyssey was yet another Arctic tragedy with little to show for it, the loss of the Jeannette *had at least one interesting footnote. In 1884, Nansen found pieces of the* Jeannette *washed up in Greenland, many miles from the boat's grave in Siberia. These splinters were key evidence for Nansen's theory about polar currents and led directly to his landmark drift across the top of the world in the* Fram *some years later (See* Farthest North, *page 86).*

We now had new matter for discussion in the little cabin. Indeed there had never been a stagnation of argument there, where all exchanged ideas freely, and courted criticism. Some of the opinions promulgated therein were no less interesting than original. For instance, one of the mess, ever happy and contented, considered it a very fortunate thing indeed that the ship leaked, inasmuch as the men were thereby "trained and exercised"; and it was so cheerful to lie awake in his berth at night listening to the merry "chug" of the pump!

But now we devoted our time to the consideration of the serious circumstances which so thickly beset us. We were all persuaded that the chances of the ship holding together, in the present state of the ice, were not one in a thousand. Yet she might; but what then? This was the

supreme question which constantly presented itself to the minds of all: whether it would not be wiser to abandon the ship at once, and make for the nearest land (New Siberian Islands), instead of tarrying for the fall travel. De Long naturally wished to stay by the ship until the end, or so long as the provisions lasted, proposing that we remain until they had dwindled down to an allowance of ninety days for our retreat. Had a vote been taken of those who gave the matter their undivided thought, there is scarcely any doubt in my mind but that a majority would have decided to abandon the vessel about the middle of June.

However, we had no discretion whatever in the matter. She left us, after sheltering us for so many dreary months; delivering us, Cæsar-like, upon the floe, amid the crashing of her poor old ribs.

On the evening of June 10th the motion of the ice became more violent, the floes far and near cracking and grinding continually. In the silence of the night, when most of the company had retired, the ice started to split around us with fearful frequency; each successive shock being transmitted to the ship as to a centre, and resounding with awful distinctness upon her sides like death strokes. That night it was my tour from nine to twelve P.M., and as officer of the watch it was part of my duty to record the readings of the instruments placed on the ice. Just before the bell struck eight for the midnight hour, and while I was yet on the gang plank making my way towards the observatory, a sharp report like that of a gun rang out on the air, starting the company from their bunks. The floe had split fore and aft on a line with our keel, and the ship, oscillating for a few minutes, came at last to a rest with her starboard side close to the ice, the other floe-piece, on which were the dogs, observatory, and a few small articles, moving off to a distance of a hundred yards or more.

Our situation was now full of peril.

"Well," said De Long in cheery tones to Dunbar, "what do you think of it?"

"She will either be under the floe or on top of it before to-morrow night," replied he.

And so it was.

After the ship had been hauled ahead and fastened within a little cove affording a slight protection, all hands save the watch turned in. Before seven o'clock the next morning the detatched floe-piece, cruelly prolonging our fate, had approached alongside of us, and backed off again. Breakfast over, certain of the men, according to custom, started off hunting, leaving the rest of us to ponder our predicament. Once more the ice drew near, this time closing with the ship and squeezing her gently, as though to test her mettle. The poor *Jeannette* groaned, and the attacking floe, apparently satisfied, eased off. Meanwhile, there were no signs of trepidation among officers or men. The usual signal was given for the return of the hunters, and they came straggling in as if ignorant of the impending disaster. Yet all were aware of it, and fully appreciated how imminent it was. Preparations had been made for such a catastrophe ever since we entered the ice; every officer and man had his appointed duty to perform, and hence there was neither noise nor confusion when it did occur.

About three o'clock in the afternoon the ice was quiet, the sun shining brightly, and the position of the vessel so strikingly picturesque that De Long told me to bring out the camera and photograph her. I had been acting as photographer during the voyage, and had taken a number of fine views,—all of which, however, were lost with the ship. While developing my plate in the dark room, word was passed for all hands to abandon ship, calling every one except the sick to his post. Under Captain De Long's direction, the colors were hoisted to the masthead, the boats lowered, and, together with the sleds, tents, provisions, and general equipment, placed on the ice about five hundred yards back from the edge. Dr. Ambler took charge of the sick, and with the aid of several men rescued his medical stores. Mr. Chipp was the only patient who really required assistance, and this there were many hands to tender, he being a favorite with all. Everything was conducted quietly but vigorously, and superintended by De Long, who stood coolly smoking his pipe on the ship's bridge.

As the ice continued crowding in, the ship heeled over more and more, until it became impossible to stand on deck without clinging to something. The forecastle watch had supped, and the others were about to follow suit, when the water suddenly began to rise, and so swiftly that many could not escape by the ladder and companion-way, but were forced to leap through the deck ventilator. So those of us at work on floe and deck lost the last evening meal.

Every one at length having left the vessel, De Long jumped on the floe, and waving his cap cried, "Good by, old ship!" then commanding that thereafter no one should venture on board of her.

We now set about preparing our camp, tenting, as had been arranged months before, by boat crews, in command of the officers originally detailed, except Lieutenant Chipp; whose tent, by reason of his sickness, was given in charge of Mr. Dunbar. Our boats consisted of the first cutter (to have two tents), the second cutter, the first whale-boat, and the second whale-boat; but considering the long march ahead of us before we might meet with open water, if, indeed, we came up with any at all, Captain De Long very wisely concluded to reserve but three boats; so the second whale-boat, being the most unwieldy, was left hanging at the davits. The tents erected, the coffee made, and supper eaten, we finally turned in.

And here we were, cast out upon the ice five hundred miles from the mouth of the Lena River, our nearest hope of succor; with a sick list, and a limited supply of food. Yet, although the seriousness of our situation was appreciated by all, none were despondent, many merry, and shortly after the boatswain "piped down," the whole camp was lost in slumber.

And thankful were we to make our beds on snow instead of beneath the sea, where honest Jack so often finds his endless rest. Honest Jack! Proverbial for his growling, when the day is fair and life is rosy; for his cheerfulness, in times of danger and distress.

We had slept but a few hours when a loud report like that of a cannon awoke us. The floe had split in every direction, one crack making directly into our camp through the centre of De Long's tent; and had it not been for the weight of the sleepers on either end of the rubber blanket, those in the middle must inevitably have dropped into the sea. As it was, they were rescued with great difficulty; and in an instant the camp was alive again. Although the boats, sleds, and provisions had been placed close to the tents to avoid separation by just such a happening as this, we now found ourselves drifting slowly away from them. Boards were at once thrown across the crack, nimble feet sped back and forth, the sleds and boats were successfully jumped over, and when the gap had widened beyond the length of the planks, a way was discovered around it. The provisions recovered, our tents were quickly shifted farther back from the edge of the floe, and we were soon dozing again in our sleeping-bags. During the early hours of the morning Kühne, the watch, had attentively observed the ship, as she swayed to and fro, creaking and groaning with the movements of the ice. Towards four o'clock, the hour for him to summon relief, he suddenly announced, in addition to his stage whisper to Bartlett, "Turn out, if you want to see the last of the *Jeannette*. There she goes! There she goes!"

Most of us had barely time to arise and look out, when, amid the rattling and banging of her timbers and iron-work, the ship righted and stood almost upright; the floes that had come in and crushed her slowly backed off; and as she sank with slightly accelerated velocity, the yard-arms were stripped and broken upward parallel to the masts; and so, like a great, gaunt skeleton clapping its hands above its head, she plunged out of sight. Those of us who saw her go down, did so with mingled feelings of sadness and relief. We were now utterly isolated, beyond any rational hope of aid; with our proper means of escape, to which so many pleasant associations attached, destroyed before our eyes; and hence it was no wonder we felt lonely, and in a sense that few can appreciate. But we were satisfied, since we knew full well that the ship's usefulness had long ago passed away, and we could now start at once, the sooner the better, on our long march to the south.

It was nearly a week before we were ready to take up our march, and during this time a thorough organization of the crew was effected. No matter what the issue might be, we were all overjoyed when the day of departure at last arrived. Certainly, judging from the marching experiences of all previous Arctic expeditions, we had a most dismal prospect ahead of us. The crew of the *Thegetoff*, it is true, all escaped; but they had been so fortunate as to encounter open water less than one degree of latitude from where they abandoned their ship. And only by a similar good fortune could we hope to make good our retreat; for all these marches were as mere bagatelles compared with the one before us.

Previous to the loss of the ship, Captain De Long had taken accurate observations for position almost daily, and after we were cast out upon the ice they were secured whenever the weather would allow. Our route had long been a subject for discussion among the officers. We had been drifting so rapidly toward the west during the last few months, that the New Siberian Islands were pitched upon as a resting-place on our way to the Lena River, which we had selected for our point of destination, knowing it to be navigated by steamboats, and its banks thickly inhabited. Hence if we could succeed in entering it before winter set in, our difficulties would thereafter be few.

Accordingly, the line of retreat was laid due south, and, at first, "true,"—De Long and Dunbar performing this part of the work with a series of black flags. On the evening of June 16th orders were issued changing our working hours; so that we slept during the day and labored at night. This was done for various reasons, chief of which were that by such an arrangement we avoided snow-blindness from the sun's glare, and could sleep sounder and warmer, while our wet clothes were drying on the boats and tent-tops. Again, it is decidedly less fatiguing to march and haul in the crisp air of night, or when the sun is low, than when it is high and strong. The temperature during the day in summer-time usually runs up to the melting-point of ice,—sometimes as far as forty degrees,—whereas it always freezes at night, even in midsummer, when the sun has been most powerful; and I have often observed the ice melting on the sunny side of the ship while water was freezing on the shady side.

Before turning in on the morning of the 17th, I conveyed, by De Long's orders, a dog-sled load of provisions for our next day's dinner, to what I supposed was the farthest flag; but unfortunately it had fallen down, and the depot I made was nearly half a mile short of it. Our division of labor was as follows: Captain De Long and Mr. Dunbar, as mentioned before, laid out the course and selected the roads; Dr. Ambler had charge of the sick, and with the aid of a dog-team attended to their transportation, as well as that of the medical stores, tent, etc., having also the direction of the road-making, bridging, and rafting; for throughout the entire march we were forced to make our roads, never coming, except once, upon a straight floe-piece more than half a mile long where a horse could be driven without imminent danger of breaking its legs. Owing to the sickness of Chipp and Danenhower, I commanded the working gang. Our first day's work was a hard one, and disastrous to the sledges. It had been imagined that each party could advance its sledge, and then all return in a body for the boats; but upon trial this was found to be utterly impossible, and as De Long thought it best to first haul forward the boats, in order to have at the front the tents, cooking utensils, and sleeping-bags, which were stowed in them, I proceeded to advance the first cutter. Probably two thirds of the working force were equipped with harness, called "ruy ruddies," or double bands of stitched canvas about two inches wide and long enough to pass over one shoulder and under the other arm, after the manner of a baldric; and into an eyelet of which is attached a lanyard made of one inch and a half tarred stuff, furnished with a wooden button at the free end. Aided by these, the men seized the drag-rope, and, surrounding the boat to keep it upright, began hauling it through the deep, soggy snow, which at times reached to our waists. Whooping and singing, we at last carried and dragged it as far as the depot of supplies that I had deposited the day before; but here, very much to our surprise, Mr. Dunbar announced that the farthest flag, to which we were ordered to advance, was still half a mile beyond. Orders are orders, particularly in a fix such as we were in, which allowed of no discretion whatever, so forward we went. The first pull when we were fresh and vigorous had not been especially distressing, but before we had accomplished this second and unexpected march we were all utterly fagged out, two of the men being unable to stand; so they were both left seated in the snow, the one drawn up with cramps in his legs, and the other with a similar attack in his stomach.

We found the camp in a violent state of commotion. Immediately after we had left on our march, the floe whereon the camp was pitched began to break up and run into ridges. When we arrived, De Long, having seen the sick moved forward to the depot of supplies, was with half a dozen of men strenuously trying to get the boats and sleds across the gaping leads in the ice. The state of affairs was very dismal indeed; our beginning was discouraging, and it really looked as though, metaphorically, we would never get to Texas; many even said they didn't care. However, there was need of prompt action; the boats containing the provisions must be bounced across the leads at once; so all hands were placed on one boat or sled at a time, and when the passing floes came together we hurried it over; many of us with a firm grip on the drag-rope dashing into the slush and water "neck and heels," to be hauled out by our companions ahead. Thus, amid roars of laughter and good-humored banter, we succeeded late in the afternoon in again bringing all our baggage together. But the sleds had been so badly damaged that it was necessary to unload and lash them again, besides lightening the freight of the smallest ones. This caused another day's delay. Meanwhile the first cutter was fully half a mile in front of us; but as she lay in the centre of a large, solid floe-piece we were but little alarmed for her welfare. We had now learned several valuable lessons; namely, the importance of keeping ourselves and goods well together, of not permitting too great a distance to intervene between our depots, and of not transporting any of our baggage across a fissure or lead in the ice until we had first brought all of it up to the ferry.

But imagine our chagrin at failing to be able to haul together two of the lightest sleds, and being compelled to advance them singly. By this arrangement, in order to forward our eight pieces of baggage, we must pass over the course thirteen times, or, to make one mile good in a straight line, we must march thirteen. Thus, because of the devious nature of our course, the floe being broken and hummocky, we would toil hard from seven P.M. to six, seven, and often nine A.M., traveling from twenty-five to thirty-two miles to be gladdened by a direct progress of only two or two and a half miles.

Profiting from the experience of the first day, we traveled more easily on the second. In the matter of lashings for the sleds we found hemp to be much better than the raw (walrus) hide, upon which we had relied so much. Perhaps in cold weather walrus hide may make a better lashing, but I doubt it, and am of the opinion that the only advantage attaching to its use is that upon a pinch it can be eaten. Indeed, fresh walrus hide roasted with the hair on is toothsome at any time, and many members of our company feasted on it after consuming their rations of pemmican. We also learned that the mere stupid exertion of strength, upon which, backed by a little "luck," sailors are too prone to depend for the overcoming of their difficulties, was not the proper way for us to accomplish a good day's work. Nursing a weak sled; bridging at certain times; going round a hummock to avoid cutting out a road,—all these expedients served us in good stead.

Our daily toil had little of variety in it. When all hands had been called, the cook of each tent drew three quarters of a pint of alcohol from the doctor, which used in our stoves would in about fifteen minutes bring to a boiling point thirteen pints of water, melted from the moist snow that we found on the high hummocks. The issue of provisions was made by the carpenter, each cook drawing from "Jack-o'-the-dust" his amount of bread, pemmican, sugar, and coffee, and the officer of the tent seeing that the food was equally divided among the men. We also had a half ounce per man per day of Liebig's extract, rations of which were served out to each tent, generally at midnight, for soup, or according as the officer saw fit to dispose of the hot water, the limit of which was governed by the supply of alcohol issued. To secure an impartial distribution of food in tent number four, I detailed Adolf Görtz, seaman, to divide the bread and pemmican into six equal parts, putting each part in a small tin basin or pan. These were then placed in the centre of the tent and each man ordered to take a pan, which most did with astonishing alacrity, Görtz and I appropriating the remaining two.

We usually took up our march at seven o'clock, sharp, continued it until midnight, allowed one hour for dinner and rest, and then endeavored to bring all the boats and sleds together by six A.M., for supper and sleep; but in this we were not always successful, our labors often extending to nine A.M. Then the camp must be made. The ground, generally selected by De Long and Dunbar, must be level, and the ice beneath the snow free of water and cracks. Frequently it was impossible to find such a situation; so a scramble would ensue for the best places upon which to pitch the tents, and this brought about so much contention that every one was at length forbidden to choose any particular spot until all the boats and sleds were in and arranged for the night. Then the word was passed, and several men from each party shouldered the tents, poles and all, and set them up on the best available spots in the near vicinity of the baggage. Camp made, the kettles were put on, each man, officers excepted, serving a week as cook; and, supper over, the sleeping-bags and knapsacks were gotten out. But before turning in we repaired our clothes and moccasins for the next day's march, hanging out such articles as were wet to dry. A watch of one hour for each man was set, beginning with tent one, and continuing on to and through number six, the officers and sick being alone excused from duty. If any of the sleds required lashing, it was done before turning in, unless the work was trivial, when the watch attended to it,—our aim being to permit nothing to check our progress except the necessary halts for rest and repairs.

Next to the labor of hauling the boats and sleds, our greatest hardship consisted in the almost constant wetting we received. True, we carried several extra suits of clothing for general use, but among so many they could be of little advantage, and we soon came to pay no attention to our frequent soakings. Our course was laid out with two rows of flags, between which it was my duty to take the straightest line practicable, and since this rendered it impossible for us to keep dry all day, we argued "as well early as late," and so pushed boldly through the ponds of slush and water which lay knee deep in our path, making detours only with the precious bread sled. As far as our moccasins were concerned, there was not a man in the working force at the end of the first three weeks who wore a tight pair on his feet. Traveling in summer-time through the water and wet snow, the raw hide softens to the consistency of fresh tripe, and then—what with the hauls on the drag-rope and the slipping of feet on the pointed ice—the moccasins are soon gone. Many, many times after a day's march have I seen no less than six of my men standing with their bare feet on the ice, having worn off the very soles of their stockings. Nor would it have been possible to avoid this, since we could not have carried enough "oog-joog" skin, of which moccasin soles are made, to have kept alone our boats in repair.

Many were the devices to which we resorted in order to keep our feet from off the ice. At first we made soles by sewing patch upon patch of "oog-joog." Then we tried the leather of the oar-looms, but it was too slippery, as was also the sheet rubber, which some of the men had thrown away. We used canvas; sewed our knapsack-straps into little patches for our heels and the balls of our feet; platted rope-yarns, hemp, and manilla into a similar protection, with soles of wood; and platted whole mats the shape of our feet. A large number marched with their toes protruding through their moccasins; some with the "uppers" full of holes, out of which the water and slush spurted at every step. Yet no one murmured so long as his feet were clear of the ice, and I have here to say that no ship's company ever endured such severe toil with such little complaint. Another crew, perhaps, may be found to do as well; but *better*—never!

GEORGE KENNAN

(1845–1924)

From *Tent Life in Siberia*

One of the more dubious technological enterprises of the nineteenth century was the attempt, in 1865–67, to build a telegraph line from the United States to Europe via the Bering Strait and Siberia. The first effort to lay an Atlantic cable had failed, and so the Western Union Telegraph Company made a bold stab at a Pacific solution. It was a failure—a successful Atlantic cable laid in 1867 put an end to the race—and has long been forgotten. But a remarkable result of the effort, also largely forgotten, were the experiences of the exploring parties who traversed nearly six thousand miles of wilderness, from Vancouver Island over the Bering Strait and through much of Siberia.

George Kennan, a young American telegraph operator, joined the exploring party—whose ranks consisted of just four men!—at the end of the Civil War. By the end of his travels Kennan was so captivated by Siberia and its people that he returned many times to live with the Koraks, learn local languages, and live by local customs. He published several books about the region including a critique of the exile system, for which he was thrown out of Russia.

Tent Life in Siberia *is an utterly absorbing, vivid adventure tale of life in a wintry wasteland among unfamiliar people. In an age when many explorers looked on their native hosts with a good deal of suspicion and superiority, Kennan's sympathy and genuine interest in the people he meets is all the more remarkable.*

This excerpt begins as Kennan's "tent life" nears its end, in the summer of 1867. He has just heard that the Atlantic cable was successfully laid and that the Siberian operation is to be abandoned. He spends a lovely few last nights in the Far North, and then, just as he is about to set sail, is confronted with "the deadliest peril that we had experienced in more than two years of arctic experience."

On the 15th of July, the Company's bark *Onward* (which should have been named *Backward*) arrived at Gizhiga with orders to sell all of our stores that were salable; use the proceeds in the payment of our debts; discharge our native labourers; gather up our men, and return to the United States. The Atlantic cable had proved to be a complete success, and our Company, after sinking about $3,000,000 in the attempt to build an overland line from America to Europe, had finally decided to put up with its loss and abandon the undertaking. Letters from the directors to Major Abaza, stated that they would be willing to go on with the work, in spite of the success of the Atlantic cable, if the Russian Government would agree to complete the line on the Siberian side of Bering Strait; but they did not think they should be required, under the circumstances, to do all the work on the American side and half of that on the Russian.

Major Abaza,[1] hoping that he could prevail upon the Russian Minister of Ways and Communications to take the Asiatic Division off the hands of the American Company, and thus prevent the complete abandonment of the enterprise, decided at once to go to St. Petersburg overland. He therefore sailed in the *Onward* with me for Okhotsk, intending to disem-

[1] A Russian, and the leader of the expedition.

George Kennan
1868

bark there, start for Yakutsk on horseback, and send me back in the ship
to pick up our working parties along the coast.

The last of July found us becalmed, about fifty miles off the harbour
and river of Okhotsk. I had been playing chess all the evening in the
cabin, and it was almost eleven o'clock when the second mate called to

me down the companionway to come on deck. Wondering if we had taken a favourable slant of wind, I went up.

It was one of those warm, still, almost tropical nights, so rarely seen on northern waters, when a profound calm reigns in the moonless heavens, and the hush of absolute repose rests upon the tired, storm-vexed sea. There was not the faintest breath of air to stir even the reef-points of the motionless sails, or roughen the dark, polished mirror of water around the ship. A soft, almost imperceptible haze concealed the line of the far horizon, and blended sky and water into one great hollow sphere of twinkling stars. Earth and sea seemed to have passed away, and our motionless ship floated, spell-bound, in vacancy—the only earthly object in an encircling universe of stars and planets. The great luminous band of the Milky Way seemed to sweep around beneath us in a complete circle of white, misty light, and far down under our keel gleamed the three bright stars in the belt of Orion. Only when a fish sprang with a little splash out of one of these submarine constellations and shattered it into trembling fragments of broken light could we realise that it was nothing but a mirrored reflection of the heavens above.

Absorbed in the beauty of the scene, I had forgotten to ask the mate why he had called me on deck, and started with surprise as he touched me on the shoulder and said: "Curious thing, ain't it?"

"Yes," I replied, supposing that he referred to the reflection of the heavens in the water, "it's the most wonderful night I ever saw at sea. I can hardly make myself believe that we *are* at sea—the ship seems to be hanging in space with a great universe of stars above and below."

"What do you suppose makes it?" he inquired.

"Makes what—the reflection?"

"No, that light. Don't you see it?"

Following the direction of his outstretched arm, I noticed, for the first time, a bank of pale, diffused radiance, five or six degrees in height, stretching along the northern horizon from about N.N.W. to E.N.E. and resembling very closely the radiance of a faint aurora. The horizon line could not be distinguished; but the luminous appearance seemed to rise in the haze that hid it from sight.

"Have you ever seen anything like it before?" I inquired.

"Never," the mate replied; "but it looks like the northern lights on the water."

Wondering what could be the nature of this mysterious light, I climbed into the shrouds, in order to get a better view. As I watched it, it suddenly began to lengthen out at both ends, like a rapidly spreading fire, and drew a long curtain of luminous mist around the whole northern horizon. Another similar light then appeared in the south-east, and although it was not yet connected with the first, it also seemed to be extending itself laterally, and in a moment the two luminous curtains united, forming a great semi-circular band of pale, bluish-white radiance around the heavens, like a celestial equator belting a vast universe of stars. I could form, as yet, no conjecture as to the cause or nature of this strange phenomenon which looked and behaved like an aurora, but which seemed to rise out of the water. After watching it five or ten minutes, I went below to call the captain.

Hardly had I reached the foot of the companionway when the mate shouted again; "O Kennan! Come on deck quick!" and rushing hastily up I saw for the first time, in all its glorious splendour, the phosphorescence of the sea. With almost incredible swiftness, a mantle of bluish-white fire had covered nearly all the dark water north of us, and its clearly defined edge wavered and trembled for an instant, like the arch of an aurora, within half a mile of the ship. Another lightning-like flash brought it all around us, and we floated, literally, in a sea of liquid radiance. Not a single square foot of dark water could be seen, in any direction, from the maintop, and all the rigging of the ship, to the royal yards, was lighted up with a faint, unearthly, blue glare. The ocean looked like a vast plain of snow, illuminated by blue fire and overhung by heavens of almost inky blackness. The Milky Way disappeared completely in the blaze of light from the sea, and stars of the first magnitude twinkled dimly, as if half hidden by fog.

Only a moment before, the dark, still water had reflected vividly a whole hemisphere of spangled constellations, and the outlines of the ship's spars were projected as dusky shadows against the Milky Way.

Now, the sea was ablaze with opaline light, and the yards and sails were painted in faint tints of blue on a background of ebony. The metamorphosis was sudden and wonderful beyond description! The polar aurora seemed to have left its home in the higher regions of the atmosphere and descended in a sheet of vivid electrical fire upon the ocean. As we stood, silent with amazement, upon the quarter-deck, this sheet of bluish flame suddenly vanished, over at least ten square miles of water, causing, by its almost instantaneous disappearance, a sensation of total blindness, and leaving the sea, for a moment, an abyss of blackness. As the pupils of our eyes, however, gradually dilated, we saw, as before, the dark shining mirror of water around the ship, while far away on the horizon rose the faint luminous appearance which had first attracted our attention, and which was evidently due to the lighting up of the haze by areas of phosphorescent water below the horizon line.

In a moment the mate shouted excitedly: "Here it comes again!" and again the great tide of fire came sweeping up around the vessel, and we floated in a sea of radiance that extended in every direction beyond the limits of vision.

As soon as I had recovered a little from the bewildered amazement into which I was thrown by the first phosphorescent flash, I observed, as closely and carefully as possible, the nature and conditions of the extraordinary phenomenon. In the first place, I satisfied myself beyond question, that the radiance was phosphorescent and not electrical, although it simulated the light of the aurora in the rapidity of its movements of translation from one area to another. When it flashed around the ship the second time, I got down close to the luminous surface and discovered that what seemed, from the deck, to be a mantle of bluish fire was, in reality, a layer of water closely packed with fine bright spangles. It looked like water in which luminous sand was constantly being stirred or churned up. The points of light were so numerous that, at a distance of ten or twelve feet, the eye failed to notice that there was any dark water in the interspaces, and received merely an impression of diffused and unbroken radiance.

In the second place, I became convinced that the myriads of microscopic organisms which pervaded the water did not light up their tiny lamps in response to a mechanical shock, such as would be produced by agitation of the medium in which they floated. There was no breeze, at any time, nor was there the faintest indication of a ripple on the glassy surface of the sea. Between the flashes of phosphorescence, the polished mirror of dark water was not blurred by so much as a breath. The sudden lighting up of myriads of infusorial lamps over vast areas of unruffled water was not due, therefore, to mechanical agitation, and must have had some other and more subtle cause. What the nature was of the impulse that stimulated whole square miles of floating protoplasm into luminous activity so suddenly as to produce the visual impression of an electric flash, I could not conjecture. The officers of the U. S. revenue cutter *McCulloch* observed and recorded in Bering Sea, in August, 1898, a display of phosphorescence which was almost as remarkable as the one I am trying to describe;[†] but in that case the sea was rough; there were no sudden flashes of appearance and disappearance; and the excitation of the light-bearing organisms may have been due—and probably was due—to mechanical shock.

In the third place, I observed that in the intervals between the flashes, when the water was dark, all objects immersed in that water were luminous. The ship's copper was so bright that I could count every tack and seam; the rudder was lighted to its lowest pintle; and medusæ, or jellyfish, drifting past, with slow pulsations, at a depth of ten or twelve feet, looked like submerged moons. It thus appeared that protozoa floating freely in the water lighted their lamps only in response to excitation, of some sort, which affected, almost instantaneously, areas many square miles in extent; while those that were attached to, or in contact with, solid matter kept their lamps lighted all the time.

During one of the periods of illumination, which lasted several minutes, I hauled up a bucketful of the phosphorescent liquid and took it

[†] *N. Y. Sun,* Nov. 11, 1899.

into the cabin. Nothing whatever could be seen in it by artificial light, but when the light had been removed, the inside of the bucket glowed, although the water itself remained dark.

The sea in the vicinity of the ship became phosphorescent three or four times; the sheet of fire in every case, sweeping down upon us from the north at a rate of speed that seemed to be about equal to the speed of sound-waves in air. The duration of the phosphorescence, at each separate appearance, was from a minute and a half to three or four minutes, and it vanished every time with a flash-like movement of translation to another and remoter area. The whole display, so far as we were concerned, was over in about twenty minutes; but long after the sheet of phosphorescence disappeared from the neighbourhood of the ship, we could see it lighting up the overhanging haze as it moved swiftly from place to place beyond the horizon line. At one time, there were three or four such areas of bright water north of us, but as they were below the curve of the earth's convexity we could not see them, and traced them only by the shifting belts or patches of irradiated mist.

WE REACHED OKHOTSK about the 1st of August, and after seeing the Major off for St. Petersburg, I sailed again in the *Onward* and spent most of the next month in cruising along the coast, picking up our scattered working-parties, and getting on board such stores and material as happened to be accessible and were worth saving.

Early in September, I returned to Gizhiga and proceeded to close up the business and make preparations for final departure. Our instructions from the Company were to sell all of our stores that were salable and use the proceeds in the payment of our debts. I have no doubt that this seemed to our worthy directors a perfectly feasible scheme, and one likely to bring in a considerable amount of ready money; but, unfortunately, their acquaintance with our environment was very limited, and their plan, from our point of view, was open to several objections. In the first place, although we had at Gizhiga fifteen or twenty thousand dollars'

worth of unused material, most of it was of such a nature as to be absolutely unsalable in that country. In the second place, the villages of Okhotsk, Yamsk, and Gizhiga, taken together, did not have more than five hundred inhabitants, and it was doubtful whether the whole five hundred could make up a purse of as many rubles, even to ensure their eternal salvation. Assuming, therefore, that the natives wanted our crowbars, telegraph poles, and pickaxes they had little or no money with which to pay for them. However orders were orders; and as soon as practicable we opened, in front of our principal storehouse, a sort of international bazaar, and proceeded to dispose of our superfluous goods upon the best terms possible. We put the price of telegraph wire down until that luxury was within the reach of the poorest Korak family. We glutted the market with pickaxes and long-handled shovels, which we assured the natives would be useful in burying their dead, and threw in a lot of frozen cucumber pickles and other anti-scorbutics which we warranted to fortify the health of the living. We sold glass insulators by the hundred as patent American teacups, and brackets by the thousand as prepared American kindling-wood. We offered soap and candles as premiums to anybody who would buy our salt pork and dried apples, and taught the natives how to make cooling drinks and hot biscuits, in order to create a demand for our redundant lime-juice and baking-powder. We directed all our energies to the creation of artificial wants in that previously happy and contented community, and flooded the whole adjacent country with articles that were of no more use to the poor natives than ice-boats and mouse-traps would be to the Tuaregs of the Saharan desert. In short, we dispensed the blessings of civilisation with a free hand. But the result was not as satisfactory as our directors doubtless expected it to be. The market at last refused to absorb any more brackets and pickaxes; telegraph wire did not make as good fish-nets and dog-harnesses as some of our salesmen confidently predicted that it would; and lime-juice and water, as a beverage, even when drunk out of pressed-crystal insulators, beautifully tinted with green, did not seem to commend itself to the aboriginal mind. So we finally had to shut up our store. We had gathered in—if I remember rightly—about three hundred rubles ($150.), which, with the money that Major Abaza had left us, amounted to something like five hundred. I did not use this cash, however, in the payment of the Company's debts. I expected to have to return to the United States through Siberia, and I did not propose to put myself in such a position that I should be compelled to defray my travelling expenses by peddling lime-juice, cucumber pickles, telegraph wire, dried apples, glass insulators, and baking-powder along the road. I therefore persuaded the Company's creditors, who, fortunately, were not very numerous, to take tea and sugar in satisfaction of their claims, so that I might save all the cash I had for the overland trip from Okhotsk to St. Petersburg.

Our business in Gizhiga was finally adjusted and settled; our working-parties were all called in; and we were just about to sail in the bark *Onward* for Okhotsk, when we were suddenly confronted by the deadliest peril that we had encountered in more than two years of arctic experience. Every explorer who goes into a wild, unknown part of the world to make scientific researches, to find a new route for commerce, or to gratify an innate love of adventure, has, now and then, an escape from a violent death which is so extraordinary that he classifies it under the head of "narrow." The peril that he incurs may be momentary in duration, or it may be prolonged for hours, or even days; but in any case, while it lasts it is imminent and deadly. It is something more than ordinary danger—it is peril in which the chances of death are a hundred and of life only one. Such peril advances, as a rule, with terrifying swiftness and suddenness; and if one be unaccustomed to danger, he is liable to be beaten down and overwhelmed by the quick and unexpected shock of the catastrophe. He has no time to rally his nervous forces, or to think how he will deal with the emergency. The crisis comes like an instantaneous "Vision of Sudden Death," which paralyses all his faculties before he has a chance to exercise them. Swift danger of this kind tests to the utmost a man's inherited or acquired capacity for instinctive and purely automatic action; but as it generally passes before it has been fairly comprehended, it is not so trying, I think, to the nerves and to the character as the danger that is prolonged to the point of full realisation, and that cannot then be averted or lessened by any possible action. It is only when a man has time to understand and appreciate the impending catastrophe, and can do absolutely nothing to avert it, that he fully realises the possibility of death. Action of any kind is tonic, and when a man can fight danger with his muscles or his brain, he is roused and excited by the struggle; but when he can do nothing except wait, watch the suspended sword of Damocles, and wonder how soon the stroke will come, he must have strong nerves long to endure the strain.

Just before we sailed from Gizhiga in the *Onward,* eight of us had an escape from death in which the peril came with great swiftness and suddenness, and was prolonged almost to the extreme limit of nervous endurance. On account of the lateness of the season and the rocky, precipitous, and extremely dangerous character of the coast in the vicinity of Gizhiga, the captain of the bark had not deemed it prudent to run into the mouth of the Gizhiga River at the point of the long A-shaped gulf, but had anchored on a shoal off the eastern coast, at a distance from the beacon-tower of nearly twenty miles. From our point of view on land, the vessel was entirely out of sight; but I knew where she lay, and did not anticipate any difficulty in getting on board as soon as I should finish my work ashore.

I intended to go off to the ship with the last of Sandford's party on the morning of September 11th, but I was detained unexpectedly by the presentation of a number of native claims and other unforeseen matters of business, and when I had finally settled and closed up everything it was four o'clock in the afternoon. In the high latitude of north-eastern Siberia a September night shuts in early, and I felt some hesitation about setting out at such an hour, in an open boat, for a vessel lying twenty miles at sea; but I knew that the captain of the *Onward* was very nervous and anxious to get away from that dangerous locality; the wind, which was blowing a fresh breeze off shore, would soon take us down the coast to the vessel's anchorage; and after a moment of indecision I gave the order to start. There were eight men of us, including Sandford, Bowsher, Heck, and four others whose names I cannot now recall.

Our boat was an open sloop-rigged sail-boat, about twenty-five feet in length, which we had bought from a Russian merchant named Phillipeus. I had not before that time paid much attention to her, but so far as I knew she was safe and seaworthy. There was some question, however, as to whether she carried ballast enough for her sail-area, and at the last moment, to make sure of being on the safe side, I had two of Sandford's men roll down and put on board two barrels of sugar from the Company's storehouse. I then bade good-bye to Dodd and Frost, the comrades who had shared with me so many hardships and perils, took a seat in the stern-sheets of the little sloop, and we were off.

It was a dark, gloomy, autumnal evening, and the stiff north-easterly breeze which came to us in freshening gusts over the snow-whitened crest of the Stanavoi range had a keen edge, suggestive of approaching winter. The sea, however, was comparatively smooth, and until we got well out into the gulf the idea of possible danger never so much as suggested itself to me. But as we left the shelter of the high, iron-bound coast the wind seemed to increase in strength, the sea began to rise, and the sullen, darkening sky, as the gloom of night gathered about us, gave warning of heavy weather. It would have been prudent, while it was still light, to heave the sloop to and take a reef, if not a double reef, in the mainsail; but Heck, who was managing the boat, did not seem to think this necessary, and in another hour, when the necessity of reefing had become apparent to everybody, the sea was so high and dangerous that we did not dare to come about for fear of capsizing, or shipping more green water than we could readily dispose of. So we staggered on before the rising gale, trusting to luck, and hoping every moment that we should catch sight of the *Onward*'s lights.

It has always seemed to me that the most dangerous point of sailing in a small open boat in a high combing sea is running dead before the wind. When you are sailing close-hauled, you can luff up into a squall, if necessary, or meet a steep, dangerous sea bow on; but when you are scudding you are almost helpless. You can neither luff, nor spill the wind out of the sail by slackening off the sheet, nor put your boat in a position to take a heavy sea safely. The end of your long boom is liable to trip as you roll and wallow through the waves, and every time you rise on the crest of a big comber your rudder comes out of water, and your bow swings around until there is imminent danger of an accidental jibe.

Heck, who managed our sloop, was a fairly good sailor, but as the wind increased, the darkness thickened, and the sea grew higher and higher, it became evident to me that nothing but unusually good luck would enable us to reach the ship in safety. We were not shipping any water, except now and then a bucketful of foam and spray blown from the crest of a wave; but the boat was yawing in a very dangerous way as she mounted the high, white-capped rollers, and I was afraid that sooner or later she would swing around so far that even with the most skilful steering a jibe would be inevitable.

It was very dark; I had lost sight of the land; and I don't know exactly in what part of the gulf we were when the dreaded catastrophe came. The sloop rose on the back of an exceptionally high, combing sea, hung poised for an instant on its crest, and then, with a wide yaw to starboard which the rudder was powerless to check, swooped down sidewise into the hollow, rolling heavily to port and pointing her boom high up into the gale. When I saw the dark outline of the leech of the mainsail waver for an instant, flap once or twice, and then suddenly collapse, I knew what was coming, and shouting at the top of my voice, "Look out Heck! She'll jibe!" I instinctively threw myself into the bottom of the boat to escape the boom. With a quick, sudden rush, ending in a great crash, the long heavy spar swept across the boat from starboard to port, knocking Bowsher overboard and carrying away the mast. The sloop swung around into the trough of the sea, in a tangle of sails, sheets, halyards, and standing rigging; and the next great comber came plump into her, filling her almost to the gunwales with a white smother of foam. I thought for a moment that she had swamped and was sinking; but as I rose to a crouching posture and rubbed the saltwater out of my eyes, I saw that she was less than half full, and that if we did not ship another sea too soon, prompt and energetic bailing might yet keep her afloat.

"Bail her out, boys! For your lives! With your hats!" I shouted: and began scooping out the water with my fur hood.

Eight men bailing for life, even with hats and caps, can throw a great deal of water out of a boat in a very short time; and within five or ten minutes the first imminent danger of sinking was over. Bowsher, who was a good swimmer and had not been seriously hurt by the boom, climbed back into the boat; we cut away the standing rigging, freed the sloop from the tangle of cordage, and got the water-soaked mainsail on board; and then, tying a corner of this sail to the stump of the mast, we spread it as well as we could, so that it would catch a little wind and give the boat steerage-way. Under the influence of this scrap of canvas the sloop swung slowly around, across the seas; the water ceased to come into her; and wringing out our wet caps and clothing, we began to breathe more freely.

When the first excitement of the crisis had passed and I recovered my self-possession, I tried to estimate, as coolly as possible, our prospects and our chances. The situation seemed to me almost hopeless. We were in a dismasted boat, without oars, without a compass, without a morsel of food or a mouthful of water, and we were being blown out to sea in a heavy north-easterly gale. It was so dark that we could not see the land on either side of the constantly widening gulf; there was no sign of the *Onward*; and in all probability there was not another vessel in any part of the Okhotsk Sea. The nearest land was eight or ten miles distant; we were drifting farther and farther away from it; and in our disabled and helpless condition there was not the remotest chance of our reaching it. In all probability our sloop would not live through the night in such a gale; and even should she remain afloat until morning, we should then be far out at sea, with nothing to eat or drink, and with no prospect of being picked up. If the wind should hold in the direction in which it was blowing, it would carry us past the *Onward* at a distance of at least three miles; we had no lantern with which to attract the attention of the ship's watch, even should we happen to drift past her within sight; the captain did not know that we were coming off to the bark that night, and would not think of looking out for us; and so far as I could discover, there was not a ray of hope for us in any direction.

How long we drifted out in black darkness, and in that tumbling, threatening, foam-crested sea, I do not know. It seemed to me many hours. I had a letter in my pocket which I had written the day before to my mother, and which I had intended to send down to San Francisco with the bark. In it I assured her that she need not feel any further anxiety about my safety, because the Russian-American telegraph line had been abandoned. I was to be landed by the *Onward* at Okhotsk; I was coming home by way of St. Petersburg over a good post-road; and I should not be exposed to any more dangers. As I sat there in the dismasted sloop, shivering with cold and drifting out to sea before a howling arctic gale, I remembered this letter, and wondered what my poor mother would think if she could read its contents and at the same time see in a mental vision the situation of the writer.

So far as I can remember, there was very little talking among the men during these long, dark hours of suspense. None of us, I think, had any hope; it was hard to make one's voice heard above the roaring of the wind; and we all sat or cowered in the bottom of the boat, waiting for an end which could not be very far away. Now and then a heavy sea would break over us, and we would all begin bailing again with our hats; but aside from this there was nothing to be done. It did not seem to me probable that the half-wrecked sloop would live more than three or four hours. The gale was constantly rising, and every few minutes we were lashed with stinging whips of icy spray, as a fierce squall struck the water to windward, scooped off the crests of the waves, and swept them horizontally in dense white clouds across the boat.

It must have been about nine o'clock when somebody in the bow shouted excitedly, "I see a light!"

"Where away?" I cried, half rising from the bottom of the boat in the stern-sheets.

"Three or four points off the port bow," the voice replied.

"Are you sure?" I demanded.

"I'm not quite sure, but I saw the twinkle of something away over on the Matuga Island side. It's gone now," the voice added, after a moment's pause; "but I saw something."

We all looked eagerly and anxiously in the direction indicated; but strain our vision as we might, we could not see the faintest gleam or twinkle in the impenetrable darkness to leeward. If there was a light visible, in that or in any other direction, it could only be the anchor-light of the *Onward,* because both coasts of the gulf were uninhabited; but it seemed to me probable that the man had been deceived by a sparkle of phosphorescence or the gleam of a white foam-crest.

For fully five minutes no one spoke, but all stared into the thick gloom ahead. Then, suddenly, the same voice cried aloud in a tone of still greater excitement, assurance, and certainty, "There it is again! I knew I saw it! It's a ship's light!"

In another moment I caught sight of it myself—a faint, distant, intermittent twinkle on the horizon nearly dead ahead.

"It's the anchor-light of the *Onward!*" I shouted in fierce excitement. "Spread the corner of the main-sail a little more if you can, boys, so as to give her better steerage-way. We've got to make that ship! Hold her steady on the light, Heck, even if you have to put her in the trough of the sea. We might as well founder as drift past!"

The men forward caught up the loose edges of the mainsail and extended it as widely as possible to the gale, clinging to the thwarts and the stump of the mast to avoid being jerked overboard by the bellying canvas. Heck brought the sloop's head around so that the light was under our bow, and on we staggered through the dark, storm-lashed turmoil of waters, shipping a sea now and then, but half sailing, half drifting toward the anchored bark. The wind came in such fierce gusts and squalls that one could hardly say from what quarter it was blowing; but, as nearly as I could judge in the thick darkness, it had shifted three or four points to the westward. If such were the case, we had a fair chance of making the ship, which lay nearer the eastern than the western coast of the gulf.

"Don't let her head fall off any, Heck," I cried. "Jam her over to the eastward as much as you can, even if the sea comes into her. We can keep her clear with our hats. If we drift past we're gone!"

As we approached the bark the light grew rapidly brighter: but I did not realise how near we were until the lantern, which was hanging in the ship's fore-rigging, swung for an instant behind the jib-stay, and the vessel's illuminated cordage suddenly came out in delicate tracery against the black sky, less than a hundred yards away.

"There she is!" shouted Sandford. "We're close on her!"

The bark was pitching furiously to her anchors, and as we drifted rapidly down upon her we could hear the hoarse roar of the gale through her rigging, and see a pale gleam of foam as the sea broke in sheets of spray against her bluff bows.

"Shall I try to round to abreast of her?" cried Heck to me, "or shall I go bang down on her?"

"Don't take any chances," I shouted. "Better strike her, and go to pieces alongside, than miss her and drift past. Make ready now to hail her—all together—one,—two,—three! Bark aho-o-y! Stand by to throw us a line!"

But no sound came from the huge black shadow under the pitching lantern save the deep bass roar of the storm through the cordage.

We gave one more fierce, inarticulate cry as the dark outline of the bark rose on a sea high above our heads; and then, with a staggering shock and a great crash, the boat struck the ship's bow.

What happened in the next minute I hardly know. I have a confused recollection of being thrown violently across a thwart in a white smother of foam; of struggling to my feet and clutching frantically at a wet, black wall, and of hearing some one shout in a wild, despairing voice: "Watch ahoy! We're sinking! For God's sake throw us a line!"—but that is all.

The water-logged sloop seesawed up and down past the bark's side, one moment rising on a huge comber until I could almost grasp the rail, and the next sinking into a deep hollow between the surges, far below the line of the copper sheathing. We tore the ends of our finger-nails off against the ship's side in trying to stop the boat's drift, and shouted despairingly again and again for help and a line; but our voices were drowned in the roar of the gale, there was no response, and the next sea carried us under the bark's counter. I made one last clutch at the smooth, wet planks; and then, as we drifted astern past the ship, I abandoned hope.

The sloop was sinking rapidly,—I was already standing up to my knees in water,—and in thirty seconds more we should be out of sight of the bark, in the dark, tumbling sea to leeward, with no more chance of res- cue than if we were drowning in mid-Atlantic. Suddenly a dark figure in the boat beside me,—I learned afterward that it was Bowsher,—tore off his coat and waistcoat and made a bold leap into the sea to windward. He knew that it was certain death to drift out of sight of the bark in that sinking sloop, and he hoped to be able to swim alongside until he should be picked up. I myself had not thought of this before, but I saw instantly that it offered a forlorn hope of escape, and I was just poised in the act of following his example when on the quarter-deck of the bark, already twenty feet away, a white ghost-like figure appeared with uplifted arm, and a hoarse voice shouted, "Stand by to catch a line!"

It was the *Onward's* second mate. He had heard our cries in his state-room as we drifted under the ship's counter, and had instantly sprung from his berth and rushed on deck in his night-shirt.

By the dim light of the binnacle I could just see the coil of rope unwind as it left his hand; but I could not see where it fell; I knew that there would be no time for another throw; and it seemed to me that my heart did not beat again until I heard from the bow of the sloop a cheery shout of "All right! I've got the line! Slack off till I make it fast!"

In thirty seconds more we were safe. The second mate roused the watch, who had apparently taken refuge in the forecastle from the storm; the sloop was hauled up under the bark's stern; a second line was thrown to Bowsher, and one by one we were hoisted, in a sort of improvised breeches-buoy, to the *Onward's* quarter-deck. As I came aboard, coatless, hatless, and shivering from cold and excitement, the captain stared at me in amazement for a moment, and then exclaimed: "Good God! Mr. Kennan, is that you? What possessed you to come off to the ship such a night as this?"

"Well, Captain," I replied, trying to force a smile, "it didn't blow in this way when we started; and we had an accident—carried our mast away."

"But," he remonstrated, "it has been blowing great guns ever since dark. We've got two anchors down, and we've been dragging them both. I finally had them buoyed, and told the mate that if they dragged again we'd slip the cables and run out to sea. You might not have found us here at all, and then where would you have been?"

"Probably at the bottom of the gulf," I replied. "I haven't expected anything else for the last three hours."

The ill-fated sloop from which we made this narrow escape was so crushed in her collision with the bark that the sea battered her to pieces in the course of the night, and when I went on deck the next morning, a few ribs and shattered planks, floating awash at the end of the line astern, were all of her that remained.

CHARLES DARWIN

(1809–1882)

From *Voyage of the Beagle*

When Charles Darwin set out on his legendary journey around the world in 1831, he was an aimless youth of twenty-two, enamored with the natural world but contemplating a career in the church. He went along as a companion to Captain FitzRoy, whose primary purpose was to chart the coasts of Patagonia and Tierra del Fuego. But Darwin took every opportunity to be dropped off on shore, often traveling long distances to rendezvous with the Beagle *at the next port. When he returned to England five years later, he had amassed enough scientific observations and specimens to become an acknowledged expert in natural history and geology. More importantly, the journey aroused his curiosity and intellect and showed him his calling; in 1859 he published the immortal work,* On the Origin of Species by Means of Natural Selection.

Darwin's Voyage of the *Beagle, published in 1839 "as a sketch" for a general readership, reveals a young man in a near constant state of rapture, as if he can hardly believe his good fortune. In the pages to follow, Darwin describes his stay at Maldonado, on the east coast of Uruguay.*

There is real adventure—and humor—here as he rides horseback whirling a native bola and captures his own horse, and also in the thrilling journey he was making in his mind as he examined, questioned, collected, and recorded everything around him.

July 5th, 1832—In the morning we got under way, and stood out of the splendid harbour of Rio de Janeiro. In our passage to the Plata, we saw nothing particular, excepting on one day a great shoal of porpoises, many hundreds in number. The whole sea was in places furrowed by them; and a most extraordinary spectacle was presented, as hundreds, proceeding together by jumps, in which their whole bodies were exposed, thus cut the water. When the ship was running nine knots, these animals could cross and recross the bows with the greatest ease, and then dash away right ahead. As soon as we entered the estuary of the Plata, the weather was very unsettled. One dark night we were surrounded by numerous seals and penguins, which made such strange noises, that the officer on watch reported he could hear the cattle bellowing on shore. On a second night we witnessed a splendid scene of natural fireworks; the mast-head and yard-arm ends shone with St. Elmo's light; and the form of the vane could almost be traced, as if it had been rubbed with phosphorus. The sea was so highly luminous, that the tracks of the penguins were marked by a fiery wake, and lastly, the darkness of the sky was momentarily illuminated by the most vivid lightning.

When within the mouth of the river, I was interested by observing how slowly the waters of the sea and river mixed. The latter, muddy and discoloured, from its less specific gravity, floated on the surface of the salt water. This was curiously exhibited in the wake of the vessel, where a line of blue was seen mingling in little eddies, with the adjoining fluid.

July 26th—We anchored at Monte Video. The *Beagle* was employed in surveying the extreme southern and eastern coasts of America, south of the Plata, during the two succeeding years. To prevent useless repetitions, I will extract those parts of my journal which refer to the same districts, without always attending to the order in which we visited them.

. . .

Maldonado is situated on the northern bank of the Plata, and not very far from the mouth of the estuary. It is a most quiet, forlorn, little town; built, as is universally the case in these countries, with the streets running at right angles to each other, and having in the middle a large plaza or square, which, from its size, renders the scantiness of the population more evident and more unsociable. It possesses scarcely any trade; the exports being confined to a few hides and living cattle. The inhabitants are chiefly landowners, together with a few shopkeepers and the necessary tradesmen, such as blacksmiths and carpenters, who do nearly all the business for a circuit of 50 miles round. The town is separated from the river by a band of sand-hillocks, about a mile broad: it is surrounded on all other sides, by an open slightly undulating country, covered by one uniform layer of fine green turf, on which countless herds of cattle, sheep, and horses graze. There is very little land cultivated even close to the town. A few hedges, made of cacti and agave, mark out where some wheat or Indian corn has been planted. The features of the country are very similar along the whole northern bank of the Plata. The only difference is, that here the granitic hills are rather more boldly pronounced. The scenery is very uninteresting; there is scarcely a house, an enclosed piece of ground, or even a tree, to give it an air of cheerfulness. Yet, after being imprisoned for some time in a ship, there is a charm in the unconfined feeling of walking over boundless plains of turf. Moreover, if your view is limited to a small space, many objects possess beauty. Some of the smaller birds are brilliantly coloured; and the bright green sward, browsed short by the cattle, is ornamented by dwarf flowers, among which a plant, looking like the daisy, claimed the place of an old friend. What would a florist say to whole tracts so thickly covered by the *Verbena melindres,* as, even at a distance, to appear of the most gaudy scarlet?

I stayed ten weeks at Maldonado, in which time a nearly perfect collection of the animals, birds, and reptiles, was procured. Before making any observations respecting them, I will give an account of a little excursion I made as far as the river Polanco, which is about 70 miles distant, in a northerly direction. I may mention, as a proof how cheap every thing is in this country, that I paid only two dollars a day, or eight shillings, for two men, together with a troop of about a dozen riding-horses. My companions were well armed with pistols and sabres; a precaution which I thought rather unnecessary; but the first piece of news we heard was, that, the day before, a traveller from Monte Video had been found dead on the road, with his throat cut. This happened close to a cross, the record of a former murder.

On the first night we slept at a retired little country-house; and there I soon found out, that I possessed two or three articles, especially a pocket compass, which created unbounded astonishment. In every house I was asked to show the compass, and by its aid, together with a map, to point out the direction of various places. It excited the liveliest admiration that I, a perfect stranger, should know the road (for direction and road are synonymous in this open country) to places where I had never been. At one house a young woman, who was ill in bed, sent to entreat me to come and show her the compass. If their surprise was great, mine was greater, to find such ignorance among people who possessed their thousands of cattle, and *estancias* of great extent. It can only be accounted for by the circumstance that this retired part of the country is seldom visited by foreigners. I was asked whether the earth or sun moved; whether it was hotter or colder to the north; where Spain was, and many other such questions. The greater number of the inhabitants had an indistinct idea that England, London, and North America, were different names for the same place; but the better informed well knew that London and North America were separate countries close together, and that England was a large town in London! I carried with me some Promethean matches, which I ignited by biting; it was thought so wonderful that a man should strike fire with his teeth, that it was usual to collect the whole family to see it: I was once offered a dollar for a single one. Washing my face in the morning, caused much speculation at the village of Las Minas; a superior tradesman closely cross-questioned me about so singular a practice; and likewise why on board we wore our beards; for he had heard from my guide that we did so. He eyed me with much suspicion; perhaps he had heard of ablutions in the Mahomedan religion, and knowing me to be a heretic, probably he came to the conclusion that all heretics were Turks. It is the general custom in this country to ask for a night's lodging at the first convenient house. The astonishment at the compass, and my other feats in jugglery, was to a certain degree advantageous, as with that, and the long stories my guides told of my breaking stones, knowing venomous from harmless snakes, collecting insects, &c., I repaid them for their hospitality. . . .

The next day we rode to the village of Las Minas. The country was rather more hilly, but otherwise continued the same; an inhabitant of the Pampas no doubt would have considered it as truly Alpine. The country is so thinly inhabited, that during the whole day we scarcely met a single person. Las Minas is much smaller even than Maldonado. It is seated on a little plain, and is surrounded by low rocky mountains. It is of the usual symmetrical form; and with its whitewashed church standing in the centre, had rather a pretty appearance. The outskirting houses rose out of the plain like isolated beings, without the accompaniment of gardens or courtyards. This is generally the case in the country, and all the houses have, in consequence, an uncomfortable aspect. At night we stopped at a pulperia, or drinking-shop. During the evening a great number of Gauchos came in to drink spirits and smoke cigars: their appearance is very striking; they are generally tall and handsome, but with a proud and dissolute expression of countenance. They frequently wear their moustaches, and long black hair curling down their backs. With their brightly coloured garments, great spurs clanking about their heels, and knives stuck as daggers (and often so used) at their waists, they look a very different race of men from what might be expected from their name of Gauchos, or simple countrymen. Their politeness is excessive: they never drink their spirits without expecting you to taste it; but whilst making their exceedingly graceful bow, they seem quite as ready, if occasion offered, to cut your throat.

On the third day we pursued rather an irregular course, as I was employed in examining some beds of marble. On the fine plains of turf we saw many ostriches (*Struthio rhea*). Some of the flocks contained as many as twenty or thirty birds. These, when standing on any little eminence, and seen against the clear sky, presented a very noble appearance. I never met with such tame ostriches in any other part of the country: it was easy to gallop up within a short distance of them; but then, expanding their wings, they made all sail right before the wind, and soon left the horse astern.

At night we came to the house of Don Juan Fuentes, a rich landed proprietor, but not personally known to either of my companions. On approaching the house of a stranger, it is usual to follow several little pieces of etiquette: riding up slowly to the door, the salutation of Ave Maria is given, and until somebody comes out, and asks you to alight, it is not customary even to get off your horse. Having entered the house, some general conversation is kept up for a few minutes, till permission is asked to pass the night there. This is granted as a matter of course. The stranger then takes his meals with the family, and a room is assigned to him, where with the horsecloths belonging to his *recado* (or saddle of the Pampas) he makes his bed. It is curious how similar circumstances produce such similar results in manners. At the Cape of Good Hope the same hospitality, and very nearly the same points of etiquette, are universally observed. The difference, however, between the character of the Spaniard and that of the Dutch boor is shown, by the former never asking his guest a single question beyond the strictest rule of politeness, whilst the honest Dutchman demands where he has been, where he is going, what is his business, and even how many brothers, sisters, or children he may happen to have.

Shortly after our arrival at Don Juan's, one of the large herds of cattle was driven in towards the house, and three beasts were picked out to be slaughtered for the supply of the establishment. These half-wild cattle are very active; and knowing full well the fatal lazo, they led the horses a long and laborious chase. After witnessing the rude wealth displayed in the number of cattle, men, and horses, Don Juan's miserable house was quite curious. The floor consisted of hardened mud, and the windows were without glass; the furniture of the sitting-room boasted only of a few of the roughest chairs and stools, with a couple of tables. The supper, although several strangers were present, consisted of two huge piles, one of roast beef, the other of boiled, with some pieces of pumpkin: besides this latter there was no other vegetable, and not even a morsel of bread. For drinking, a large earthenware jug of water served the whole party. Yet this man was the owner of several square miles of land, of which nearly every acre would produce corn, and, with a little trouble, all the common vegetables. The evening was spent in smoking, with a little impromptu singing, accompanied by the guitar. The signoritas all sat together in one corner of the room, and did not sup with the men.

So many works have been written about these countries, that it is almost superfluous to describe either the lazo or the bolas. The former consists of a very strong, but thin, well-plaited rope, made of raw hide. One end is attached to the broad surcingle, which fastens together the complicated gear of the *recado,* or saddle used in the Pampas; the other is terminated by a small ring of iron or brass, by which a noose can be formed. The Gaucho, when he is going to use the lazo, keeps a small coil in his bridle hand, and in the other holds the running noose, which is made very large, generally having a diameter of about 8 feet. This he whirls round his head, and by the dexterous movement of his wrist keeps the noose open; then, throwing it, he causes it to fall on any particular spot he chooses. The lazo, when not used, is tied up in a small coil to the after part of the *recado.* The bolas, or balls, are of two kinds: the simplest, which is chiefly used for catching ostriches, consists of two round stones, covered with leather, and united by a thin plaited thong, about 8 feet long. The other kind differs only, in having three balls united by the thongs to a common centre. The Gaucho holds the smallest of the three in his hand, and whirls the other two round and round his head; then, taking aim, sends them like chain shot revolving through the air. The balls no sooner strike any object, than, winding round it, they cross each other, and become firmly hitched. The size and weight of the balls varies, according to the purpose for which they are made: when of stone, although not so large as a big apple, yet they are sent with such force as sometimes to break the leg even of a horse. I have seen the balls made of wood, and as large as a turnip, for the sake of catching these animals without injuring them. The balls are sometimes made of iron, and these can be hurled to the greatest distance. The main difficulty in using either lazo or bolas, is to ride so well, as to be able at full speed, and while suddenly turning about, to whirl them so steadily round the head, as to take aim: on foot any person would soon learn the art. One day, as I was amusing myself by galloping and whirling the balls round my head, by accident the free one struck a bush; and its revolving motion being thus destroyed, it immediately fell to the ground, and like magic caught one hind leg of my horse; the other ball was then jerked out of my hand, and the horse fairly secured. Luckily he was an old practised animal, and knew what it meant; otherwise he would probably have kicked till he had thrown himself down. The Gauchos roared with laughter; they cried they had seen every sort of animal caught, but had never before seen a man caught by himself.

. . .

During our stay at Maldonado I paid particular attention to the mammalia and birds. Of the latter I procured, within the distance of a morning's walk, no less than eighty species, of which many were exceedingly beautiful—I think even more so than those of Brazil. The other orders were not neglected. Reptiles were numerous, and nine different kinds of snakes were taken. Of the indigenous mammalia, the only one now left of any size, which is common, is the *Cervus Campestris*. This deer is exceedingly abundant throughout the countries bordering the Plata. It is found in Northern Patagonia as far south as the Rio Negro (lat. 41°); but further southward none were seen by the officers employed in surveying the coast. It appears to prefer a hilly country; I saw very many small herds, containing from five to seven animals each, near the Sierra Ventana, and among the hills north of Maldonado. If a person crawling close along the ground, slowly advances towards a herd, the deer frequently, out of curiosity, approach to reconnoitre him. I have by this means killed, from one spot, three out of the same herd. Although so tame and inquisitive, yet when approached on horseback, they are exceedingly wary. In this country nobody goes on foot, and the deer knows man as its enemy, only when he is mounted and armed with the bolas. At Bahia Blanca, a recent establishment in Northern Patagonia, I was surprised to find how little the deer cared for the noise of a gun: one day I fired ten times, from within 80 yards, at one animal; and it was much more startled at the ball cutting up the ground than at the report of the rifle. My powder being exhausted, I was obliged (to my shame as a sportsman be it spoken), to get up and halloo till the deer ran away.

The most curious fact with respect to this animal, is the overpoweringly strong and offensive odour which proceeds from the buck. It is quite indescribable: several times whilst skinning the specimen which is now mounted at the Zoological Museum, I was almost overcome by nausea. I tied up the skin in a silk pocket-handkerchief, and so carried it home: this handkerchief, after being well washed, I continually used, and it was, of course, as repeatedly washed; yet every time, for a space of one year and seven months, when first unfolded, I distinctly perceived the odour. This appears an astonishing instance of the permanence of some matter, which in its nature, nevertheless, must be most subtile and volatile. Frequently, when passing at the distance of half a mile to leeward of a herd, I have perceived the whole air tainted with the effluvium. I believe the smell from the buck is most powerful at the period when its horns are perfect, or free from the hairy skin. When in this state the meat is, of course, quite uneatable; but the Gauchos assert, that if buried for some time in fresh earth, the taint is removed. I have somewhere read that the islanders in the north of Scotland treat the rank carcasses of the fish-eating birds in the same manner.

The order Rodentia is here very numerous in species: of mice alone I obtained no less than eight kinds.[†] The largest gnawing animal in the world, the *Hydrocharus Capybara* (the water-hog), is here also common. One which I shot at Monte Video weighed 98 pounds: its length, from the end of the snout to the stump-like tail, was 3 feet 2 inches; and its girth, 3 feet 8. These great Rodents are generally called *carpinchos*: they occasionally frequent the islands in the mouth of the Plata, where the water is quite salt, but are far more abundant on the borders of fresh-water lakes and rivers. Near Maldonado three or four generally live together. In the daytime they either lie among the aquatic plants, or openly feed on the turf plain.[††] When viewed at a distance, from their manner of walking and colour, they resemble pigs: but when seated on their haunches, and attentively watching any object with one eye, they reassume the appearance of their congeners, the cavies.[1] Both the front and side view of their head has quite a ludicrous aspect, from the great depth of their jaw. These animals, at Maldonado, were very tame; by cautiously walking, I approached within 3 yards of four old ones. This tameness may probably be accounted for, by the Jaguar having been banished for some years, and by the Gaucho not thinking it worth his while to hunt them. As I approached nearer and nearer they frequently made their peculiar noise, which is a low abrupt grunt; not having much actual

---

[†] These have been named and described by Mr Waterhouse at the meetings of the Zoological Society. I must be allowed to take this opportunity of returning my cordial thanks to Mr Waterhouse, and to the other gentlemen attached to that Society, for their kind and most liberal assistance on all occasions.

[††] In the stomach and duodenum of a *carpincho* which I opened, I found a very large quantity of a thin yellowish fluid, in which scarcely a fibre could be distinguished. Mr Owen informs me that a part of the œsophagus is so constructed, that nothing much larger than a crowquill can be passed down. Certainly the broad teeth and strong jaws of this animal are well fitted to grind into pulp the aquatic plants on which it feeds.

---

[1] Meaning that they resemble their own kind, rodents of the family Caviidea, commonly called cavies or guinea pigs.

sound, but rather arising from the sudden expulsion of air: the only noise I know at all like it, is the first hoarse bark of a large dog. Having watched the four from almost within arm's length (and they me) for several minutes, they rushed into the water at full gallop, with the greatest impetuosity, and emitted, at the same time, their bark. After diving a short distance they came again to the surface, but only just showed the upper part of their heads. When the female is swimming in the water and has young ones, they are said to sit on her back. These animals are easily killed in numbers; but their skins are of trifling value, and the meat is very indifferent. I have never heard of the carpincho being found south of the Plata; but as I see in a map that there is a Laguna del Carpincho high up the Rio Salado, I suppose such must have occurred. On the islands in the Rio Parana they are exceedingly abundant, and afford the ordinary prey to the Jaguar.

The Tucutuco (*Ctenomys Braziliensis*) is a curious small animal, which may be briefly described as a Rodent, with the habits of a mole. It is extremely abundant in some parts of the country,[†] but is difficult to be procured, and still more difficult to be seen, when at liberty. It lives almost entirely under ground, and prefers a sandy soil with a gentle inclination. The burrows are said not to be deep, but of great length. They are seldom open; the earth being thrown up at the mouth into hillocks, not quite so large as those made by the mole. Considerable tracts of country are so completely undermined by these animals, that horses, in passing over, sink above their fetlocks. The tucutucos appear, to a certain degree, to be gregarious. The man who procured the specimens for me had caught six together, and he said this was a common occurrence. They are nocturnal in their habits; and their principal food is afforded by the roots of plants, which is the object of their extensive and superficial burrows. Azara says they are so difficult to be obtained, that he never saw more

---

[†] The wide plains north of the Rio Colorado are undermined by these animals; and near the Strait of Magellan, where Patagonia blends with Tierra del Fuego, the whole sandy country forms a great warren for the tucutuco.

than one. He states that they lay up magazines of food within their burrows. This animal is universally known by a very peculiar noise, which it
makes when beneath the ground. A person, the first time he hears it, is
much surprised; for it is not easy to tell whence it comes, nor is it possible to guess what kind of creature utters it. The noise consists in a short,
but not rough, nasal grunt, which is repeated about four times in quick
succession; the first grunt is not so loud, but a little longer, and more distinct than the three following: the musical time of the whole is constant,
as often as it is uttered.† The name tucutuco is given in imitation of the
sound. In all times of the day, where this animal is abundant, the noise
may be heard, and sometimes directly beneath one's feet. When kept in a
room, the tucutucos move both slowly and clumsily, which appears owing
to the outward action of their hind legs; and they are likewise quite incapable of jumping even the smallest vertical height. Mr Reid, who dissected a specimen which I brought home in spirits, informs me that the
socket of the thigh-bone is not attached by a ligamentum teres; and this
explains, in a satisfactory manner, the awkward movements of their hinder extremities. When eating, they rest on their hind legs and hold the
piece in their fore paws; they appeared also to wish to drag it into some
corner. They are very stupid in making any attempt to escape; when
angry or frightened, they uttered the tucu-tuco. Of those I kept alive,
several, even the first day, became quite tame, not attempting to bite or
to run away; others were a little wilder.

The man who caught them asserted that very many are invariably
found blind. A specimen which I preserved in spirits was in this state; Mr
Reid considers it to be the effect of inflammation in the nictitating mem-
brane. When the animal was alive I placed my finger within half an inch

---

† At the R. Negro, in Northern Patagonia, there is an animal of the same habits,
and probably a closely allied species, but which I never saw. Its noise is different from
the Maldonado kind; it is repeated only twice instead of three or four times, and is
more distinct and sonorous: when heard from a distance, it so closely resembles the
sound made in cutting down a small tree with an axe, that I have sometimes
remained in doubt concerning it.

of its head, and not the slightest notice was taken: it made its way, however, about the room nearly as well as the others. Considering the subterranean habits of the tucutuco, the blindness, though so frequent, cannot be a very serious evil; yet it appears strange that any animal should possess an organ constantly subject to injury. The mole, whose habits in nearly every respect, excepting in the kind of food, are so similar, has an extremely small and protected eye, which, although possessing a limited vision, at once seems adapted to its manner of life.

Birds of many kinds are extremely abundant on the undulating grassy plains around Maldonado. Several species, of the genus Cassicus, allied to our starlings in habits and structure, and of Tyrant-flycatchers, and a mocking-bird, from their numbers, give a character to the ornithology. Some of the Cassici are very beautiful, black and yellow being the prevailing colours; but *Oriolus ruber,* Gme., offers an exception, in having its head, shoulders, and thighs of the most splendid scarlet. This bird differs from its congeners in being solitary. It frequents marshes; and, seated on the summit of a low bush, with its mouth wide open, utters a plaintive agreeable cry, which can be heard at a long distance.

Another species,[†] of a purplish-black colour, with a metallic lustre, feeds on the plain in large flocks, mingled with other birds. Several may often be seen standing on the back of a cow or horse. While perched on a hedge, and pluming themselves in the sun, they sometimes attempt to sing, or rather to hiss: the noise is very peculiar; it resembles that of bubbles of air passing rapidly from a small orifice under water, so as to produce an acute sound. Azara states that this bird, like the cuckoo, deposits its eggs in other birds' nests. I was several times told by the country people, that there was some bird with this habit; and my assistant in collecting, who is a very accurate person, found a nest of the sparrow[††] of the country, with one egg in it larger than the others, and of

---

[†] Le Troupiale commun of Azara (vol. iii, p. 169)—a second species of Molothrus.
[††] A Zonotrichia;—the *chingolo* of Azara. The egg is rather less than that of the missel-thrush; it is of a nearly globular form, but with one end rather smaller than the

a different colour and shape. Mr Swainson[††] has remarked that with the exception of the *Molothrus pecoris*, the cuckoos are the only birds which can be called truly parasitical; namely, such as "fasten themselves, as it were, on another living animal, whose animal heat brings their young into life, whose food they alone live upon, and whose death would cause theirs during the period of infancy." The *Molothrus pecoris* is a North American bird, and is closely allied in general habits, even in such peculiarities as standing on the backs of cattle (as its name implies), and in appearance, with the species from the plains of La Plata; it only differs in being rather smaller and of a different colour, yet the two birds would be considered by every naturalist as distinct species. It is very interesting to see so close an agreement in structure, and in habits, between allied species coming from opposite parts of a great continent. It is also very remarkable, that the cuckoos and the molothri, although opposed to each other in almost every habit, should agree in the one strange one of their parasitical propagation. The molothrus, like our starling, is eminently sociable, and lives on the open plains without art or disguise: the cuckoo, as every one knows, is a singularly shy bird; it frequents the most retired thickets, and feeds on fruit and caterpillars. In structure these birds are likewise widely removed from each other.

---

other. The ground colour is a pale pinkish-white, with irregular spots and blotches of a pinkish-brown, and others less distinct of a grayish hue. The egg is now in the museum of the Zoological Society.

    [††] Magazine of Zoology and Botany, vol. i, p. 217.

ALFRED RUSSEL WALLACE

(1823–1913)

From *The Malay Archipelago*

In 1858, while laid up from his scientific explorations of Malaysia by a bout of tropical fever, Alfred Russel Wallace was struck by the theory of natural selection, at the very same time that Charles Darwin was com-ing to the same conclusion back in England. Wallace shared his ideas with Darwin in a letter, who less than a year later published The Ori-gin of Species *while Wallace was still abroad.*

Wallace returned from the South Sea islands in 1862 and published his classic book, still in print today, in 1869. Although he published papers on his scientific discoveries, The Malay Archipelago—*an absorbing mix of natural history, anthropology, geography, and personal travelogue—was intended for a general audience. A self-effacing, self-educated man, he had fewer opportunities to gain recognition than did his rival Darwin. Today he is considered one of the great unsung heroes of modern science, as well as one of the most daring thinkers and explorers of the nineteenth century.*

During his eight-year sojourn Wallace collected 125,600 specimens, traveled 14,000 miles within the archipelago—much of that distance

on foot or by native dug-out canoe—and acquired a tremendous knowl-
edge of the region's flora, fauna, and local tribes. Darwin wrote to Wal-
lace in 1869, "that you ever returned alive is wonderful after all your
risks from illness and sea voyages . . . your perseverance in the name of
science is nothing short of heroic." Both the trials Wallace endured and
the reverence with which he approached his work come through in the
following passages. In the first, of his exploration of the Aru Islands, we
get a glimpse into the mind of a nineteenth-century naturalist as he
struggles with the fact that he must kill that which he wants to share
with science—in this case the rare bird of paradise. The second passage
describes one of several disastrous voyages through the archipelago on a
native prau—in Wallace's words "an outlandish craft shaped something
like a Chinese junk," and clearly none too easy to sail.

[MARCH TO MAY 1857.]

My boat was at length ready, and having obtained two men besides
my own servants,[1] after an enormous amount of talk and trouble, we left
Dobbo on the morning of March 13th, for the mainland of Aru. By noon
we reached the mouth of a small river or creek, which we ascended,
winding among mangrove swamps, with here and there a glimpse of dry
land. In two hours we reached a house, or rather small shed, of the most
miserable description, which our steersman, the "Orang-kaya"[2] of
Wamma, said was the place we were to stay at, and where he had assured
me we could get every kind of bird and beast to be found in Aru. The
shed was occupied by about a dozen men, women, and children; two
cooking fires were burning in it, and there seemed little prospect of my
obtaining any accommodation. I however deferred inquiry till I had seen

[1] Wallace's servants were two local men he hired as guide and cook, and they traveled by native canoe.
[2] Village chief.

the neighbouring forest, and immediately started off with two men, net, and guns, along a path at the back of the house. In an hour's walk I saw enough to make me determine to give the place a trial, and on my return, finding the "Orang-kaya" was in a strong fever-fit and unable to do anything, I entered into negotiations with the owner of the house for the use of a slip at one end of it about five feet wide, for a week, and agreed to pay as rent one "parang," or chopping-knife. I then immediately got my boxes and bedding out of the boat, hung up a shelf for my bird-skins and insects, and got all ready for work next morning. My own boys slept in the boat to guard the remainder of my property; a cooking place sheltered by a few mats was arranged under a tree close by, and I felt that degree of satisfaction and enjoyment which I always experience when, after much trouble and delay, I am on the point of beginning work in a new locality.

One of my first objects was to inquire for the people who are accustomed to shoot the Paradise birds. They lived at some distance in the jungle, and a man was sent to call them. When they arrived, we had a talk by means of the "Orang-kaya" as interpreter, and they said they thought they could get some. They explained that they shoot the birds with a bow and arrow, the arrow having a conical wooden cap fitted to the end as large as a teacup, so as to kill the bird by the violence of the blow without making any wound or shedding any blood. The trees frequented by the birds are very lofty; it is therefore necessary to erect a small leafy covering or hut among the branches, to which the hunter mounts before daylight in the morning and remains the whole day, and whenever a bird alights they are almost sure of securing it. They returned to their homes the same evening, and I never saw anything more of them, owing, as I afterwards found, to its being too early to obtain birds in good plumage.

The first two or three days of our stay here were very wet, and I obtained but few insects or birds, but at length, when I was beginning to despair, my boy Baderoon returned one day with a specimen which repaid me for months of delay and expectation. It was a small bird, a little less than a thrush. The greater part of its plumage was of an intense

cinnabar red, with a gloss as of spun glass. On the head the feathers became short and velvety, and shaded into rich orange. Beneath, from the breast downwards, was pure white, with the softness and gloss of silk, and across the breast a band of deep metallic green separated this colour from the red of the throat. Above each eye was a round spot of the same metallic green; the bill was yellow, and the feet and legs were of a fine cobalt blue, strikingly contrasting with all the other parts of the body. Merely in arrangement of colours and texture of plumage this little bird was a gem of the first water, yet these comprised only half its strange beauty. Springing from each side of the breast, and ordinarily lying concealed under the wings, were little tufts of greyish feathers about two inches long, and each terminated by a broad band of intense emerald green. These plumes can be raised at the will of the bird, and spread out into a pair of elegant fans when the wings are elevated. But this is not the only ornament. The two middle feathers of the tail are in the form of slender wires about five inches long, and which diverge in a beautiful double curve. About half an inch of the end of this wire is webbed on the outer side only, and coloured of a fine metallic green, and being curled spirally inwards form a pair of elegant glittering buttons, hanging five inches below the body, and the same distance apart. These two ornaments, the breast fans and the spiral tipped tail wires, are altogether unique, not occurring on any other species of the eight thousand different birds that are known to exist upon the earth; and, combined with the most exquisite beauty of plumage, render this one of the most perfectly lovely of the many lovely productions of nature. My transports of admiration and delight quite amused my Aru hosts, who saw nothing more in the "Burong raja" than we do in the robin or the goldfinch.

Thus one of my objects in coming to the far East was accomplished. I had obtained a specimen of the King Bird of Paradise (*Paradisea regia*), which had been described by Linnæus from skins preserved in a mutilated state by the natives. I knew how few Europeans had ever beheld the perfect little organism. I now gazed upon, and how very imperfectly it was still known in Europe. The emotions excited in the minds of a naturalist, who has long desired to see the actual thing which he has hitherto known only by description, drawing, or badly-preserved external covering—especially when that thing is of surpassing rarity and beauty, require the poetic faculty fully to express them. The remote island in which I found myself situated, in an almost unvisited sea, far from the tracks of merchant fleets and navies; the wild luxuriant tropical forest, which stretched far away on every side; the rude uncultured savages who gathered round me,—all had their influence in determining the emotions with which I gazed upon this "thing of beauty." I thought of the long ages of the past, during which the successive generations of this little creature had run their course—year by year being born, and living and dying amid these dark and gloomy woods, with no intelligent eye to gaze upon their loveliness; to all appearance such a wanton waste of beauty. Such ideas excite a feeling of melancholy. It seems sad, that on the one hand such exquisite creatures should live out their lives and exhibit their charms only in these wild inhospitable regions, doomed for ages yet to come to hopeless barbarism; while on the other hand, should civilized man ever reach these distant lands, and bring moral, intellectual, and physical light into the recesses of these virgin forests, we may be sure that he will so disturb the nicely-balanced relations of organic and inorganic nature as to cause the disappearance, and finally the extinction, of these very beings whose wonderful structure and beauty he alone is fitted to appreciate and enjoy. This consideration must surely tell us that all living things were *not* made for man. Many of them have no relation to him. The cycle of their existence has gone on independently of his, and is disturbed or broken by every advance in man's intellectual development; and their happiness and enjoyments, their loves and hates, their struggles for existence, their vigorous life and early death, would seem to be immediately related to their own well-being and perpetuation alone, limited only by the equal well-being and perpetuation of the numberless other organisms with which each is more or less intimately connected.[3]

After the first king-bird was obtained, I went with my men into the for-

---

[3] A popular belief at the time was that all of nature had been created in relationship, and in servitude, of mankind. Although Wallace's opinion that Western cultures were more evolved than indigenous ones is entirely in keeping with his Victorian society, his suggestion that other species are not subordinate or in any way related to humans was radical for his day.

est, and we were not only rewarded with another in equally perfect plumage, but I was enabled to see a little of the habits of both it and the larger species. It frequents the lower trees of the less dense forests, and is very active, flying strongly with a whirring sound, and continually hopping or flying from branch to branch. It eats hard stone-bearing fruits as large as a gooseberry, and often flutters its wings after the manner of the South American manakins, at which time it elevates and expands the beautiful fans with which its breast is adorned. The natives of Aru call it "Goby-goby."

One day I got under a tree where a number of the Great Paradise birds were assembled, but they were high up in the thickest of the foliage, and flying and jumping about so continually that I could get no good view of them. At length I shot one, but it was a young specimen, and was entirely of a rich chocolate-brown colour, without either the metallic green throat or yellow plumes of the full-grown bird. All that I had yet seen resembled this, and the natives told me that it would be about two months before any would be found in full plumage. I still hoped, therefore, to get some. Their voice is most extraordinary. At early morn, before the sun has risen, we hear a loud cry of "Wawk—wawk—wawk, wŏk—wŏk—wŏk," which resounds through the forest, changing its direction continually. This is the Great Bird of Paradise going to seek his breakfast. Others soon follow his example; lories and parroquets cry shrilly, cockatoos scream, king-hunters croak and bark, and the various smaller birds chirp and whistle their morning song. As I lie listening to these interesting sounds, I realize my position as the first European who has ever lived for months together in the Aru islands, a place which I had hoped rather than expected ever to visit. I think how many besides myself have longed to reach these almost fairy realms, and to see with their own eyes the many wonderful and beautiful things which I am daily encountering. But now Ali and Baderoon are up and getting ready their guns and ammunition, and little Baso has his fire lighted and is boiling my coffee, and I remember that I had a black cockatoo brought in late last night, which I must skin immediately, and so I jump up and begin my day's work very happily.

. . .

I now take up my narrative at my departure from Wahai, with the intention of carrying various necessary stores to my assistant, Mr. Allen,[4] at Silinta, in Mysol, and then continuing my journey to Waigiou.[5] . . .

Between Ceram and Mysol there are sixty miles of open sea, and along this wide channel the east monsoon blows strongly; so that with native praus, which will not lay up to the wind, it requires some care in crossing. In order to give ourselves sufficient leeway, we sailed back from Wahai eastward, along the coast of Ceram, with the land-breeze; but in the morning (June 18th) had not gone nearly so far as I expected. My pilot, an old and experienced sailor, named Gurulampoko, assured me there was a current setting to the eastward, and that we could easily lay across to Silinta, in Mysol. As we got out from the land the wind increased, and there was a considerable sea, which made my short little vessel plunge and roll about violently. By sunset we had not got halfway across, but could see Mysol distinctly. All night we went along uneasily, and at daybreak, on looking out anxiously, I found that we had fallen much to the westward during the night, owing, no doubt, to the pilot being sleepy and not keeping the boat sufficiently close to the wind. We could see the mountains distinctly, but it was clear we should not reach Silinta, and should have some difficulty in getting to the extreme westward point of the island. The sea was now very boisterous, and our prau was continually beaten to leeward by the waves, and after another weary day we found we could not get to Mysol at all, but might perhaps reach the island called Pulo Kanary, about ten miles to the north-west. Thence we might await a favourable wind to reach Waigamma, on the north side of the island, and visit Allen by means of a small boat.

---

[4] Charles Allen, a young English naturalist who assisted Wallace on the voyage and had been collecting in other parts of the archipelago.

[5] Another island in the archipelago.

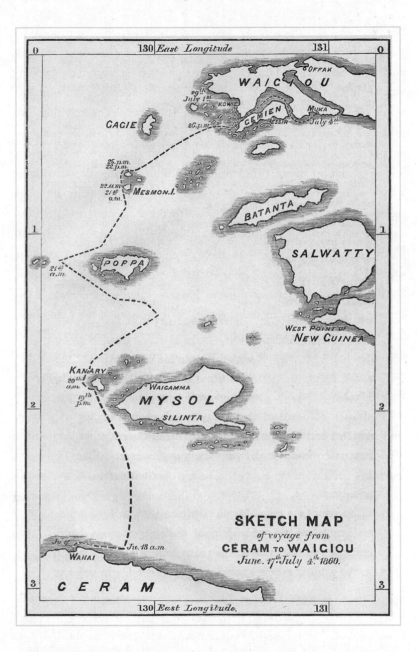

SKETCH MAP
of voyage from
CERAM TO WAIGIOU
June. 17ᵗʰ July 4ᵗʰ 1860.

About nine o'clock at night, greatly to my satisfaction, we got under the lee of this island, into quite smooth water—for I had been very sick and uncomfortable, and had eaten scarcely anything since the preceding morning. We were slowly nearing the shore, which the smooth dark water told us we could safely approach, and were congratulating ourselves on soon being at anchor, with the prospect of hot coffee, a good supper, and a sound sleep, when the wind completely dropped, and we had to get out the oars to row. We were not more than two hundred yards from the shore, when I noticed that we seemed to get no nearer although the men were rowing hard, but drifted to the westward; and the prau would not obey the helm, but continually fell off, and gave us much trouble to bring her up again. Soon a loud ripple of water told us we were seized by one of those treacherous currents which so frequently frustrate all the efforts of the voyager in these seas; the men threw down the oars in despair, and in a few minutes we drifted to leeward of the island fairly out to sea again, and lost our last chance of ever reaching Mysol! Hoisting our jib, we lay to, and in the morning found ourselves only a few miles from the island, but with such a steady wind blowing from its direction as to render it impossible for us to get back to it.

We now made sail to the northward, hoping soon to get a more southerly wind. Towards noon the sea was much smoother, and with a S.S.E. wind we were laying in the direction of Salwatty, which I hoped to reach, as I could there easily get a boat to take provisions and stores to my companion in Mysol. This wind did not, however, last long, but died away into a calm; and a light west wind springing up, with a dark bank of clouds, again gave us hopes of reaching Mysol. We were soon, however, again disappointed. The E.S.E. wind began to blow again with violence, and continued all night in irregular gusts, and with a short cross sea tossed us about unmercifully, and so continually took our sails aback, that we were at length forced to run before it with our jib only, to escape being swamped by our heavy mainsail. After another miserable and anxious night, we found that we had drifted westward of the island of Poppa, and the wind being again a little southerly, we made all sail in order to reach it. This we did not succeed in doing, passing to the north-west, when the wind again blew hard from the E.S.E., and our last hope of finding a refuge till better weather was frustrated. This was a very serious matter to me, as I could not tell how Charles Allen might act, if, after waiting in vain for me, he should return to Wahai, and find that I had left there long before, and had not since been heard of. Such an event as our missing an island forty miles long would hardly occur to him, and he would conclude either that our boat had foundered, or that my crew had murdered me and run away with her. However, as it was physically impossible now for me to reach him, the only thing to be done was to make the best of my way to Waigiou, and trust to our meeting some traders, who might convey to him the news of my safety.

Finding on my map a group of three small islands, twenty-five miles north of Poppa, I resolved, if possible, to rest there a day or two. We could lay our boat's head N.E. by N.; but a heavy sea from the eastward so continually beat us off our course, and we made so much leeway, that I found it would be as much as we could do to reach them. It was a delicate point to keep our head in the best direction, neither so close to the wind as to stop our way, or so free as to carry us too far to leeward. I continually directed the steersman myself, and by incessant vigilance succeeded, just at sunset, in bringing our boat to an anchor under the lee of the southern point of one of the islands. The anchorage was, however, by no means good, there being a fringing coral reef, dry at low water, beyond which, on a bottom strewn with masses of coral, we were obliged to anchor. We had now been incessantly tossing about for four days in our small undecked boat, with constant disappointments and anxiety, and it was a great comfort to have a night of quiet and comparative safety. My old pilot had never left the helm for more than an hour at a time, when one of the others would relieve him for a little sleep; so I determined the next morning to look out for a secure and convenient harbour, and rest on shore for a day.

In the morning, finding it would be necessary for us to get round a rocky point, I wanted my men to go on shore and cut jungle-rope, by which to secure us from being again drifted away, as the wind was directly off shore. I unfortunately, however, allowed myself to be over-ruled by the pilot and crew, who all declared that it was the easiest thing possible, and that they would row the boat round the point in a few min-utes. They accordingly got up the anchor, set the jib, and began rowing; but, just as I had feared, we drifted rapidly off shore, and had to drop anchor again in deeper water, and much farther off. The two best men, a Papuan and a Malay, now swam on shore, each carrying a hatchet, and went into the jungle to seek creepers for rope. After about an hour our anchor loosed hold, and began to drag. This alarmed me greatly, and we let go our spare anchor, and, by running out all our cable, appeared toler-ably secure again. We were now most anxious for the return of the men, and were going to fire our muskets to recall them, when we observed them on the beach, some way off, and almost immediately our anchors again slipped, and we drifted slowly away into deep water. We instantly seized the oars, but found we could not counteract the wind and current, and our frantic cries to the men were not heard till we had got a long way off, as they seemed to be hunting for shell-fish on the beach. Very soon, however, they stared at us, and in a few minutes seemed to comprehend their situation; for they rushed down into the water, as if to swim off, but again returned on shore, as if afraid to make the attempt. We had drawn up our anchors at first not to check our rowing; but now, finding we could do nothing, we let them both hang down by the full length of the cables. This stopped our way very much, and we drifted from shore very slowly, and hoped the men would hastily form a raft, or cut down a soft-wood tree, and paddle out to us, as we were still not more than a third of a mile from shore. They seemed, however, to have half lost their senses, gesticulating wildly to us, running along the beach, then going into the forest; and just when we thought they had prepared some mode of mak-ing an attempt to reach us, we saw the smoke of a fire they had made to cook their shell-fish! They had evidently given up all idea of coming after us, and we were obliged to look to our own position.

We were now about a mile from shore, and midway between two of the islands, but we were slowly drifting out to sea to the westward, and our only chance of yet saving the men was to reach the opposite shore. We therefore set our jib and rowed hard; but the wind failed, and we drifted out so rapidly that we had some difficulty in reaching the extreme westerly point of the island. Our only sailor left, then swam ashore with a rope, and helped to tow us round the point into a tolerably safe and secure anchorage, well sheltered from the wind, but exposed to a little swell which jerked our anchor and made us rather uneasy. We were now in a sad plight, having lost our two best men, and being doubtful if we had strength left to hoist our mainsail. We had only two days' water on board, and the small, rocky, volcanic island did not promise us much chance of finding any. The conduct of the men on shore was such as to render it doubtful if they would make any serious attempt to reach us, though they might easily do so, having two good choppers, with which in a day they could make a small outrigger raft on which they could safely cross the two miles of smooth sea with the wind right aft, if they started from the east end of the island, so as to allow for the current. I could only hope they would be sensible enough to make the attempt, and determined to stay as long as I could to give them the chance.

We passed an anxious night, fearful of again breaking our anchor or rattan cable. In the morning (23d), finding all secure, I waded on shore with my two men, leaving the old steersman and the cook on board, with a loaded musket to recall us if needed. We first walked along the beach, till stopped by the vertical cliffs at the east end of the island, finding a place where meat had been smoked, a turtle-shell still greasy, and some cut wood, the leaves of which were still green,—showing that some boat had been here very recently. We then entered the jungle, cutting our way up to the top of the hill, but when we got there could see nothing, owing to the thickness of the forest. Returning, we cut some bamboos, and sharpened them to dig for water in a low spot where some sago-trees were growing; when, just as we were going to begin, Hoi, the Wahai man, called out to say he had found water. It was a deep hole among the sago-trees, in stiff black clay, full of water, which was fresh, but smelt horribly from the quantity of dead leaves and sago refuse that had fallen in. Hastily concluding that it was a spring, or that the water had filtered in, we baled it all out as well as a dozen or twenty buckets of mud and rubbish, hoping by night to have a good supply of clean water. I then went on board to breakfast, leaving my two men to make a bamboo raft to carry us on shore and back without wading. I had scarcely finished when our cable broke, and we bumped against the rocks. Luckily it was smooth and calm, and no damage was done. We searched for and got up our anchor, and found that the cable had been cut by grating all night upon the coral. Had it given way in the night, we might have drifted out to sea without our anchor, or been seriously damaged. In the evening we went to fetch water from the well, when, greatly to our dismay, we found nothing but a little liquid mud at the bottom, and it then became evident that the hole was one which had been made to collect rain water, and would never fill again as long as the present drought continued. As we did not know what we might suffer for want of water, we filled our jar with this muddy stuff so that it might settle. In the afternoon I crossed over to the other side of the island, and made a large fire, in order that our men might see we were still there.

The next day (24th) I determined to have another search for water; and when the tide was out rounded a rocky point and went to the extremity of the island without finding any sign of the smallest stream. On our way back, noticing a very small dry bed of a watercourse, I went up it to explore, although everything was so dry that my men loudly declared it was useless to expect water there; but a little way up I was rewarded by finding a few pints in a small pool. We searched higher up in every hole and channel where water marks appeared, but could find not a drop more. Sending one of my men for a large jar and teacup, we searched along the beach till we found signs of another dry watercourse, and on ascending this were so fortunate as to discover two deep sheltered rock-holes containing several gallons of water, enough to fill all our jars. When the cup came we enjoyed a good drink of the cool pure water, and before we left had carried away, I believe, every drop on the island.

In the evening a good-sized prau appeared in sight, making apparently for the island where our men were left, and we had some hopes they might be seen and picked up, but it passed along mid-channel, and did not notice the signals we tried to make. I was now, however, pretty easy as to the fate of the men. There was plenty of sago on our rocky island, and there would probably be some on the flat one they were left on. They had choppers, and could cut down a tree and make sago,[6] and would most likely find sufficient water by digging. Shell-fish were abundant, and they would be able to manage very well till some boat should touch there, or till I could send and fetch them. The next day we devoted to cutting wood, filling up our jars with all the water we could find, and making ready to sail in the evening. I shot a small lory closely resembling a common species at Ternate, and a glossy starling which differed from the allied birds of Ceram and Matabello. Large wood-pigeons, and crows were the only other birds I saw, but I did not obtain specimens.

About eight in the evening of June 25th we started, and found that with all hands at work we could just haul up our mainsail. We had a fair wind during the night and sailed north-east, finding ourselves in the morning about twenty miles west of the extremity of Waigiou with a number of islands intervening. About ten o'clock we ran full on to a coral reef, which alarmed us a good deal, but luckily got safe off again. About two in the afternoon we reached an extensive coral reef, and were sailing close alongside of it, when the wind suddenly dropped, and we drifted on to it before we could get in our heavy mainsail, which we were obliged to let run down and fall partly overboard. We had much difficulty in getting off, but at last got into deep water again, though with reefs and islands all around us. At night we did not know what to do, as no one on board could tell where we were or what dangers might surround us, the only one of our crew who was acquainted with the coast of Waigiou having been left on the island. We therefore took in all sail and allowed ourselves to drift, as we were some miles from the nearest land. A light

---

[6] A native food made out of the fermented pulp of the sago-tree.

breeze, however, sprang up, and about midnight we found ourselves again bumping over a coral reef. As it was very dark, and we knew nothing of our position, we could only guess how to get off again, and had there been a little more wind we might have been knocked to pieces. However, in about half an hour we did get off, and then thought it best to anchor on the edge of the reef till morning. Soon after daylight on the 27th, finding our prau had received no damage, we sailed on with uncertain winds and squalls, threading our way among islands and reefs, and guided only by a small map, which was very incorrect and quite useless, and by a general notion of the direction we ought to take. In the afternoon we found a tolerable anchorage under a small island and stayed for the night, and I shot a large fruit-pigeon new to me, which I have since named *Carpophaga tumida*. I also saw and shot at the rare white-headed kingfisher (*Halcyon saurophaga*), but did not kill it. The next morning we sailed on, and having a fair wind reached the shores of the large island of Waigiou. On rounding a point we again ran full on to a coral reef with our mainsail up, but luckily the wind had almost died away, and with a good deal of exertion we managed to get safely off.

We now had to search for the narrow channel among the islands, which we knew was somewhere hereabouts, and which leads to the villages on the south side of Waigiou. Entering a deep bay which looked promising, we got to the end of it, but it was then dusk, so we anchored for the night, and having just finished all our water could cook no rice for supper. Next morning early (29th) we went on shore among the mangroves, and a little way inland found some water, which relieved our anxiety considerably, and left us free to go along the coast in search of the opening, or of some one who could direct us to it. During the three days we had now been among the reefs and islands, we had only seen a single small canoe, which had approached pretty near to us, and then, notwithstanding our signals, went off in another direction. The shores seemed all desert; not a house, or boat, or human being, or a puff of smoke was to be seen; and as we could only go on the course that the ever-changing wind would allow us (our hands being too few to row any distance), our prospects of getting to our destination seemed rather remote and precarious. Having gone to the eastward extremity of the deep bay we had entered, without finding any sign of an opening, we turned westward; and towards evening were so fortunate as to find a small village of seven miserable houses built on piles in the water. Luckily the Orang-kaya, or head man, could speak a little Malay, and informed us that the entrance to the strait was really in the bay we had examined, but that it was not to be seen except when close in-shore. He said the strait was often very narrow, and wound among lakes and rocks and islands, and that it would take two days to reach the large village of Muka, and three more to get to Waigiou. I succeeded in hiring two men to go with us to Muka, bringing a small boat in which to return; but we had to wait a day for our guides, so I took my gun and made a little excursion into the forest. The day was wet and drizzly, and I only succeeded in shooting two small birds, but I saw the great black cockatoo, and had a glimpse of one or two Birds of Paradise, whose loud screams we had heard on first approaching the coast.

Leaving the village the next morning (July 1st) with a light wind, it took us all day to reach the entrance to the channel, which resembled a small river, and was concealed by a projecting point, so that it was no wonder we did not discover it amid the dense forest vegetation which everywhere covers these islands to the water's edge. A little way inside it becomes bounded by precipitous rocks, after winding among which for about two miles, we emerged into what seemed a lake, but which was in fact a deep gulf having a narrow entrance on the south coast. This gulf was studded along its shores with numbers of rocky islets, mostly mushroom shaped, from the water having worn away the lower part of the soluble coralline limestone, leaving them overhanging from ten to twenty feet. Every islet was covered with strange-looking shrubs and trees, and was generally crowned by lofty and elegant palms, which also studded the ridges of the mountainous shores, forming one of the most singular and picturesque landscapes I have ever seen. The current which had brought us through the narrow strait now ceased, and we were obliged to row, which with our short and heavy prau was slow work. I went on shore several times, but the rocks were so precipitous, sharp, and honey-combed, that I found it impossible to get through the tangled thickets with which they were everywhere clothed. It took us three days to get to the entrance of the gulf, and then the wind was such as to prevent our going any further, and we might have had to wait for days or weeks, when, much to my surprise and gratification, a boat arrived from Muka with one of the head men, who had in some mysterious manner heard I was on my way, and had come to my assistance, bringing a present of cocoa-nuts and vegetables. Being thoroughly acquainted with the coast, and having several extra men to assist us, he managed to get the prau along by rowing, poling, or sailing, and by night had brought us safely into harbour, a great relief after our tedious and unhappy voyage. We had been already eight days among the reefs and islands of Waigiou, coming a distance of about fifty miles, and it was just forty days since we had sailed from Goram.

Immediately on our arrival at Muka, I engaged a small boat and three natives to go in search of my lost men, and sent one of my own men with them to make sure of their going to the right island. In ten days they returned, but to my great regret and disappointment, without the men. The weather had been very bad, and though they had reached an island within sight of that in which the men were, they could get no further. They had waited there six days for better weather, and then, having no more provisions, and the man I had sent with them being very ill and not expected to live, they returned. As they now knew the island, I was deter-mined they should make another trial, and (by a liberal payment of knives, handkerchiefs, and tobacco, with plenty of provisions) persuaded them to start back immediately, and make another attempt. They did not return again till the 29th of July, having stayed a few days at their own vil-lage of Bessir on the way; but this time they had succeeded and brought with them my two lost men, in tolerable health, though thin and weak. They had lived exactly a month on the island; had found water, and had subsisted on the roots and tender flower-stalks of a species of Bromelia, on shell-fish, and on a few turtles' eggs. Having swum to the island, they had only a pair of trousers and a shirt between them, but had made a hut of palm-leaves, and had altogether got on very well. They saw that I waited for them three days at the opposite island, but had been afraid to cross, lest the current should have carried them out to sea, when they would have been inevitably lost. They had felt sure I would send for them on the first opportunity, and appeared more grateful than natives usually are for my having done so; while I felt much relieved that my voyage, though sufficiently unfortunate, had not involved loss of life.

HENRY MORTON STANLEY

(1841–1904)

From *Through the Dark Continent*

In 1869, as a young journalist working for an American paper (he was
Welsh by birth), Stanley ventured deep into Africa in search of a good
story. He went to look for explorer and national hero Dr. David Livingstone, who left England four years earlier on a mission to trace the
headwaters of the Nile and whose whereabouts were a complete mystery. Stanley found the man, a dramatic story, and rather unexpectedly,
his fate. He soon became a huge player in the most complex and hotly
debated geographical question of the day: the source of the mighty
White Nile.

A few months after his singularly sensational encounter with Stanley, Livingstone, whose health had been broken for some time, died in
central Africa without having answered the great question. Was Lake
Victoria the source of the Nile, as John Hanning Speke thought, or was
Lake Tanganyika, as Sir Richard Francis Burton believed? Finally, did
a river that Livingstone called the Lualaba (and Stanley calls the Livingstone) flow into the Nile and was therefore the true source? Greatly
moved by his mentor's death, Stanley went back with an official British

expedition in 1874 to finish Livingstone's work. He circumnavigated Lakes Victoria and Tanganyika, then followed the Lualaba to see if it led west into the Congo or north to the Nile.

Never was there a more challenging or prolonged journey. Stanley's descent of the Lualaba was one of "unrelieved horror." For many months he had no idea where the river was taking him. It plunged him through countless cataracts, all but the worst of which he had little choice but to face head-on, given that the banks of the river were often thick with cannibals and impenetrable jungle. The trip took three years. Along the way many men died of sickness, drowning, or injury, but in the end Stanley succeeded in establishing the source of the Nile as Lake Victoria and in mapping the continent's other great river, the Congo, into which the Lualaba flows.

Stanley emerges from his fine book and from history as a man of unparalleled courage, tenacity, and diplomacy. In the excerpt that follows we find him at one of many near breaking points on the turbulent river. He has to find his way past two dangerous drops, one of which becomes the scene of a hair-raising rescue of several of his men. Soon thereafter, out of food, Stanley is forced to approach a hostile tribal chief to beg for help, and there he learns the river's true name, and hence, his direction.

Early on the morning of the 6th[1] I began to explore the First Cataract of the Stanley Falls. I found a small stream about two hundred yards wide, separated by a lateral dyke of igneous rocks from the main stream, which took the boat safely down for a couple of miles. Then presently other dykes appeared, some mere low narrow ridges of rock and others, much larger and producing tall trees, inhabited by the Baswa tribe. Among these islets the left stream rushed down in cascades or foamy sheets, over low terraces, with a fall of from one foot to ten feet.

[1] 6th of January, 1877.

The Baswas, no doubt, have recently fled to these islets to seek refuge from some powerful tribe situated inland west of the river.

The main stream, 900 yards wide, rushed towards the east-north-east, and, after a mile of rapids, tilted itself against a hilly ridge that lay north and south, the crest of which was probably 300 feet above the river. With my glass, from the fork of a tree 20 feet above the ground, I saw at once that a descent by the right side was an impossibility, as the waves were enormous, and the slope so great that the river's face was all a foam; and that at the base of the hilly ridge which obstructed its course the river seemed piling itself into a watery bank, whence it escaped into a scene of indescribable confusion down to the horror of whirling pools, and a mad confluence of tumbling, rushing waters. It was now quite easy to under-stand why our friends the Kankoré people, in attempting to illustrate the scene at the First Cataract, placed one hand overlapping the other—they meant to say that the water, driven with impetuosity against the hill, rose up and overlapped the constant flow from the steep slope.

I decided, therefore, to go down along the left stream, overland, and to ascertain the best route I took eight men with me, leaving five to guard the boat. Within two hours we had explored the jungle, and "blazed" a path below the falls—a distance of two miles.

Then returning to camp I sent Frank[2] off with a detachment of fifty men with axes, to clear the path, and a musket-armed guard of fifteen men, to be stationed in the woods parallel with the projected land route, and, leaving a guard of twenty men to protect the camp, I myself rowed up river along the left bank, a distance of three miles. Within a bend, a mile above our camp, I discovered a small black-water river, about forty yards wide, issuing from the southwest, which I named Black River, from the colour of its water. Two miles above this, the affluent Lumami, which Livingstone calls "Young's River," entered the great stream, by a mouth 600 yards wide, between low banks densely covered with trees. At noon I took an observation of the sun—the declination of which being south

---

[2] Frank Pocock, one of three Englishmen who accompanied Stanley on his expedition, and the last to die along the way.

gave me a clear water horizon—and ascertained it to be south latitude 0° 32' 0.

By noon of the 7th, having descended with the canoes as near as prudence would permit to the first fall of the left stream, we were ready for hauling the canoes overland. A road, 15 feet in width, had been cut through the tangle of rattan, palms, vines, creepers, and brushwood, tolerably straight except where great forest monarchs stood untouched, and whatever brushwood had been cut from the jungle had been laid across the road in thick piles. A rude camp had also been constructed half-way on the river side of the road, into which everything was conveyed. By 8 P.M. we had hauled the canoes over one mile of ground.

The next day, while the people were still fresh, we buckled on to the canoes, and by 3 P.M. of the 8th had passed the falls and rapids of the First Cataract, and were afloat in a calm creek between Baswa Island and the left bank!

Not wishing to stay in such a dangerous locality longer than was absolutely necessary, we re-embarked, and descending cautiously down the creek, came, in a short time to the great river, with every prospect of a good stretch of serene water. But soon we heard the roar of another cataract, and had to hug the left bank closely. Then we entered other creeks, which wound lazily by jungle-covered islets, and after two miles of meanderings among most dismal islands and banks, emerged in view of the great river, with the cataract's roar sounding solemnly and terribly near. As it was near evening, and our position was extremely unpleasant, we resolved to camp for the night at an island which lay in mid-stream. Meanwhile, we heard drums and war-horns sounding on the left bank, and though the islanders also responded to them, of the two evils it was preferable to risk an encounter with the people of the island rather than with those of the main, until we could discover our whereabouts. We had no time for consultation, or even thought—the current was swift, and the hoarse roar of the Second Cataract was more sonorous than that of the first, thundering into our affrighted ears that, if we were swept over, destruction, sudden and utter, awaited us.

The islanders were hostilely alert and ready, but spurred on by our terror of the falls, we drove our vessels straight on to the bank, about 500
feet above the falling water. In fifteen minutes we had formed a rude
camp, and enclosed it by a slight brushwood fence, while the islanders,
deserting the island, crossed over to their howling, yelling friends on the
left bank. In a small village close to our camp we found an old lady, of
perhaps sixty-five years of age, who was troubled with a large ulcer in her
foot, and had therefore been unable to escape. She was a very decent
creature, and we carried her to our camp, where by dressing her foot and
paying her kind attentions we succeeded in making her very communica-
tive. But Katembo[3] could understand only very few words of her speech,
which proved to me that we were rapidly approaching lands where no
dialect that we knew would be available.

We managed to learn, however, that the name of the island was Cheandoah, or Kewandoah, of the Baswa, tribe; that the howling savages on
the left bank were the renowned Bakumu—cannibals, and most warlike;
that the Bakumu used bows and arrows, and were the tribe that had
driven the Baswa long ago to seek refuge on these islands. When we
asked her the name of the river she said Lumami was the name of the
left branch, and the Lowwa of the right branch. She gave the word
Kukeya as indicating the left bank, and Ngyeyeh for the right bank.
Waki-biano, she said, was the name of the large island which we had
passed when we saw the villages of the Baswa below the first cataract.
The words Ubi, or Eybiteri, we understood her to employ for the Falls as
being utterly impassable.

During the morning of the 9th we explored the island of Cheandoah,
which was much longer than we at first supposed. It was extremely popu-
lous, and contained five villages. We discovered an abundance of spears
here and iron-ware of all kinds used by the natives, such as knives, hammers, hatchets, tweezers, anvils of iron, or, in other words, inverted
hammers, borers, pole-burners, fish-hooks, darts, iron rods; all the spears

---

[3] Stanley's friend and interpreter.

possessed broad points, and were the first of this style I had seen. Almost all the knives, large and small, were encased in sheaths of wood covered with goat-skin, and ornamented with polished iron bands. They varied in size, from a butcher's cleaver to a lady's dirk, and belts of undressed goat-skin, of red buffalo or antelope hide, were attached to them for suspension from the shoulders. There were also seen here iron bells, like our cow and goat bells, curiously carved whistles, fetishes or idols of wood, uncouth and rudely cut figures of human beings, brightly painted in vermilion, alternating with black; baskets made of palm fibre, large wooden and dark clay pipes, iron rings for arms and legs, numerous treasures of necklaces of the *Achatina monetaria,* the black seeds of a species of plantain, and the crimson berries of the *Abrus precatorius*; copper, iron, and wooden pellets. The houses were all of the gable-roofed pattern which we had first noticed on the summit of the hills on which Riba-Riba, Manyema, is situate; the shields of the Baswa were also after the same type.

The vegetation of the island consisted of almost every variety of plant and tree found in this region, and the banana, plantain, castor-oil, sugar-cane, cassava, and maize flourished; nor must the oil-palm be forgotten, for there were great jars of its dark-red butter in many houses.

The grand problem now before me was how to steer clear of the Bakumu savages of the left bank, whose shouts and fierce yells came pealing to our ears, and were heard even above the roar and tremendous crash of the cataract. As I travelled round the island, many desperate ideas suggested themselves to me, and if I had been followed by a hundred practised and daring men it might have been possible to have dragged the canoes the length of the island past the first terrace of the cataract, and, after dashing across to Ntunduru Island, to have dragged them through its jungle and risked the falls by Asama Island; but there were not thirty men in the entire Expedition capable of listening to orders and implicitly obeying instructions.[4]

---

[4] The expedition started out with 356 men, nearly all of them from local tribes. Only 114 survived the journey.

To the east of Cheandoah the right branch was again forked by another island, and the whole face of the river was wild beyond description, and the din of its furious waves stunning; while the western branch, such was its force, went rushing down a terrace, and then swept round in an extensive whirlpool, with a central depression quite eighteen inches below the outer rim. We pushed a rotten and condemned canoe above the fall, watched it shoot down like an arrow, and circle round that terrible whirling pool and the next instant saw it drawn in by that dreadful suction and presently ejected stern foremost 30 yards below. Close to the bank were nooks and basin-like formations in the trap rocks in which every now and again the water became strongly agitated, and receding about twelve inches, would have upwards with a rushing and gurgling that was awful.

There was only one way to resolve the problem, and that was to meet the Bakumu and dare their worst, and then to drag the canoes through the dense forest on the left bank. Accordingly, we prepared for what we felt assured would be a stubborn contest. At early dawn of the 10th January, with quick throbbing pulses, we stole up river for about a mile, and then with desperate haste dashed across to the shore, where we became immediately engaged. We floated down to the bend just above the cataract, and there secured our boats and canoes out of the influence of the stream. Leaving Frank with eight musketeers and sixty axes to form a stockade, I led thirty-six men in a line through the bushes, and drove the united Baswa and Bakumu backward to their villages, the first of which were situated a mile from the river. Here a most determined stand was made by them, for they had piled up heaps of brushwood, and cut down great trees to form defences, leaving only a few men in front. We crept through the jungle on the south side and succeeded in forcing an entrance, and driving them out. We had thus won peace for this day, and retreated to our camp. We then divided the Expedition into two parties, or relays, one to work by night, the other by day, after which I took a picked body of pioneers with axes and guns and cut a narrow path three miles in length, which brought us opposite Ntunduru Island, blazing the trees as a guide, and forming rude camps at intervals of half a mile. Material—dried palm branches and bundles of cane smeared over with gum frankincense—was also brought from the village to form lights for the working parties at night: these were to be fastened at elevated positions on trees to illuminate the jungle.

We were not further disturbed during this day. In the evening Frank began his work with fifty axemen, and ten men as scouts, deployed in the bushes in front of the working parties. Before dawn we were all awakened, and, making a rush with the canoes, succeeded in safely reaching our first camp by 9 A.M. with all canoes and baggage. During the passage of the rear-guard the Bakumu made their presence known to us by a startling and sudden outburst of cries; but the scouts immediately replied to them with their rifles, and maintained their position until they were supported by the other armed men, who were now led forward as on the day before. We chased the savages two miles inland, to other villages which we had not hitherto seen, and these also we compelled them to abandon.

In the evening, Frank, who had enjoyed but a short rest during the day, manfully set to work again, and by dawn had prepared another three-quarters of a mile of road. At 10 A.M. of the 12th, by another rush forward, we were in our second camp. During this day also there was a slight interchange of hostilities, but, being soon released from the savages, the day party was able to prepare half a mile of good road, which Frank during the night was able to extend to a mile and a quarter. By 5 P.M. of the 13th therefore we were safe in our third camp. Excepting Kachéché and a few men detailed as sentries, we all rested for this night, but in the morning, refreshed from our labours, made the fourth and final rush, and thus, after seventy-eight hours' terrific exertion, succeeded in reaching the welcome river and launching our canoes.

The Bakumu, utterly disheartened by their successive punishments and bad success, left us alone to try our hands at the river, which, though dangerous, promised greater progress than on land.

. . .

January 14.—As soon as we reached the river we began to float the canoes down a two-mile stretch of rapids to a camp opposite the south end of Ntunduru Island. Six canoes were taken safely down by the gallant boat's crew. The seventh canoe was manned by Muscati, Uledi Muscati, and Zaidi, a chief. Muscati, the steersman, lost his presence of mind, and soon upset his canoe in a piece of bad water. Muscati and his friend Uledi swam down the furious stream to Ntunduru Island, whence they were saved by the eighth canoe, manned by stout-hearted Manwa Sera and Uledi, the coxswain of the Lady Alice; but poor Zaidi, the chief, paralysed by the roar of the stream, unfortunately thought his safety was assured by clinging to his canoe, which was soon swept past our new camp, in full view of those who had been deputed with Frank to form it, to what seemed inevitable death. But a kindly Providence, which he has himself gratefully acknowledged, saved him even on the brink of eternity. The great fall at the north end of Ntunduru Island happens to be disparted by a single pointed rock, and on this the canoe was driven, and, borne down by the weight of the waters, was soon split in two, one side of which got jammed below, and the other was tilted upward. To this the almost drowned man clung, while perched on the rocky point, with his ankles washed by the stream. To his left, as he faced up-stream, there was a stretch of 50 yards of falling water; to his right were nearly fifty yards of leaping brown waves, while, close behind him the water fell down sheer six to eight feet, through a gap 10 yards wide, between the rocky point on which he was perched and a rocky islet 30 yards long.

When called to the scene by his weeping friends, from my labours up-river, I could scarcely believe my eyes, or realise the strange chance which placed him there, and, certainly, a more critical position than the poor fellow was in cannot be imagined. The words "there is only a step between me and the grave" would have been very appropriate coming from him. But the solitary man on that narrow-pointed rock, whose knees were sometimes washed by rising waves, was apparently calmer than any of us; though we could approach him within fifty yards he could not hear a word we said; he could see us, and feel assured that we sympathised with him in his terrible position.

We then, after collecting our faculties, began to prepare means to save him. After sending men to collect rattans, we formed a cable, by which we attempted to lower a small canoe, but the instant it seemed to reach him the force of the current hurrying to the fall was so great that the cable snapped like pack-thread, and the canoe swept by him like an arrow, and was engulfed, shattered, split, and pounded into fragments. Then we endeavoured to toss towards him poles tied to creepers, but the vagaries of the current and its convulsive heaving made it impossible to reach him with them, while the man dared not move a hand, but sat silent, watching our futile efforts, while the conviction gradually settled on our minds that his doom, though protracted, was certain.

Then, after anxious deliberation with myself, I called for another canoe, and lashed to the bow of it a cable consisting of three one-inch rattans twisted together and strengthened by all the tent ropes. A similar cable was lashed to the side, and a third was fastened to the stern, each of these cables being 90 yards in length. A shorter cable, 30 yards long, was lashed to the stern of the canoe, which was to be guided within reach of him by a man in the canoe.

Two volunteers were called for. No one would step forward. I offered rewards. Still no one would respond. But when I began to speak to them, asking them how they would like to be in such a position without a single friend offering to assist in saving them, Uledi, the coxswain, came forward and said, "Enough, master, I will go. Mambu Kwa Mungu"—"My fate is in the hands of God"—and immediately began preparing himself, by binding his loin-cloth firmly about his waist. Then Marzouk, a boatboy, said, "Since Uledi goes, I will go too." Other boat-boys, young Shumari and Saywa, offered their services, but I checked them, and said, "You surely are not tired of me, are you, that you all wish to die? If all my brave boat-boys are lost, what shall we do?"

Uledi and his friend Marzouk stepped into the canoe with the air of gladiators, and we applauded them heartily, but enjoined on them to be careful. Then I turned to the crowd on the shore who were manning the cables, and bade them beware of the least carelessness, as the lives of the three young men depended on their attention to the orders that would be given.

The two young volunteers were requested to paddle across river, so that the stern might be guided by those on shore. The bow and side cables were slackened until the canoe was within twenty yards of the roaring falls, and Uledi endeavoured to guide the cable to Zaidi, but the convulsive heaving of the river swept the canoe instantly to one side, where it hovered over the steep slope and brown waves of the left branch, from the swirl of which we were compelled to draw it. Five times the attempt was made, but at last, the sixth time, encouraged by the safety of the cables, we lowered the canoe until it was within ten yards of Zaidi, and Uledi lifted the short cable and threw it over to him and struck his arm. He had just time to grasp it before he was carried over into the chasm below. For thirty seconds we saw nothing of him, and thought him lost, when his head rose above the edge of the falling waters. Instantly the word was given to "haul away," but at the first pull the bow and side cables parted, and the canoe began to glide down the left branch with my two boat-boys on board! The stern cable next parted, and, horrified at the result, we stood muttering "La il Allah, il Allah," watching the canoe sev-

ered from us drifting to certain destruction, when we suddenly observed
it halted. Zaidi in the chasm clinging to his cable was acting as a kedge-
anchor, which swept the canoe against the rocky islet. Uledi and Marzouk sprang out of the canoe, and leaning over assisted Zaidi out of the
falls, and the three, working with desperate energy, succeeded in securing the canoe on the islet.

But though we hurrahed and were exceedingly rejoiced, their position
was still but a short reprieve from death. There were fifty yards of wild
waves, and a resistless rush of water, between them and safety, and to the
right of them was a fall 300 yards in width, and below was a mile of falls
and rapids, and great whirlpools, and waves rising like little hills in the
middle of the terrible stream, and below these were the fell cannibals of
Wane-Mukwa and Asama.

How to reach the islet was a question which now perplexed me. We
tied a stone to about a hundred yards of whipcord, and after the twentieth attempt they managed to catch it. To the end of the whipcord they
tied the tent rope which had parted before, and drawing it to our side we
tied the stout rattan creeper, which they drew across taut, and fastened
to a rock, by which we thought we had begun to bridge the stream. But
night drawing nigh, we said to them that we would defer further experiment until morning.

Meantime the ninth canoe, whose steersman was a supernumerary of
the boat, had likewise got upset, and he out of six men was drowned, to
our great regret, but the canoe was saved. All other vessels were brought
down safely, but so long as my poor faithful Uledi and his friends are on
the islet, and still in the arms of death, the night finds us gloomy, sorrow-
ing, and anxious.

January 15.—My first duty this morning was to send greetings to the
three brave lads on the islet, and to assure them that they should be
saved before they were many hours older. Thirty men with guns were
sent to protect thirty other men searching for rattans in the forest, and by
nine o'clock we possessed over sixty strong canes, besides other long

climbers, and as fast as we were able to twist them together they were drawn across by Uledi and his friends. Besides, we sent light cables to be lashed round the waist of each man, after which we felt trebly assured that all accidents were guarded against. Then hailing them I motioned to Uledi to begin, while ten men seized the cable, one end of which he had fastened round his waist. Uledi was seen to lift his hands up to heaven, and waving his hand to us he leaped into the wild flood, seizing the bridge cable as he fell into the depths. Soon he rose, hauling himself hand over hand, the waves brushing his face, and sometimes rising over his head, until it seemed as if he scarcely would be able to breathe; but by jerking his body occasionally upward with a desperate effort, he so managed to survive the waves and to approach us, where a dozen willing hands were stretched out to snatch the half-smothered man. Zaidi next followed, but after the tremendous proofs he had given of his courage and tenacious hold we did not much fear for his safety, and he also landed, to be warmly congratulated for his double escape from death. Marzouk, the youngest, was the last, and we held our breaths while the gallant boy was struggling out of the fierce grasp of death. While yet mid-way the pressure of water was so great that he lost his hold of two cables, at which the men screamed in terror lest he should relax his hold alto-gether from despair, but I shouted harshly to him, "Pull away, you fool. Be a man," at which with three hauls he approached within reach of our willing hands, to be embraced and applauded by all. The cheers we gave were so loud and hearty that the cannibal Wane-Mukwa must have known, despite the roar of the waters, that we had passed through a great and thrilling scene.

February 3.— . . . Livingstone called floating down the Lualaba a fool-hardy feat. So it has proved, indeed, and I pen these lines with half a feeling that they will never be read by any man; still, as we persist in floating down according to our destiny, I persist in writing, leaving events to an all-gracious Providence. Day and night we are stunned with the dreadful drumming which announces our arrival and presence on their waters. Either bank is equally powerful. To go from the right bank to the left bank is like jumping from the frying-pan into the fire. As we row down amongst these islands, between the savage countries on either side of us, it may well be said that we are "running the gauntlet." . . .

February 6.—A little before we sought our camp amid the islands, the river for the first time deflected west. All this morning its course was from west half south to west by north. Our observations at noon showed we had not made quite a mile of nothing, for our north latitude was 1° 51′ 59″. The Livingstone is now from four to seven miles across from bank to bank. So far as we can see through a glass, the banks are very low, from 6 to 10 feet high, capped with woods. The islands are also densely wooded.

We have had in this extraordinary journey by river all the terrors as well as pleasures of river life. We now glide down narrow streams, between palmy and spicy islands, whose sweet fragrance and vernal colour causes us to forget at moments our dangerous life. We have before us the winding shores of islands crowned with eternal spring-life and verdure. Teak and cotton wood, the hyphene, borassus, wild date, and Guinea oil-palms, the tall serpent-like rattan, with its pretty, drooping feathery leaves; the bushy and many-rooted mangrove, the towering gum, the shea-butter tree, the *Ficus Kotschyana,* the branchy *Tamar Indica,* with an undergrowth of extraordinary variety. Along the banks, especially wherever there is a quiet nook, thrive dense growths of the *Arundo phragmites* grass, whose long, bright green leaves we hear rustle as we glide by before the breeze blowing up river . . .

In the undergrowth, where the giant trees are wanting, we find the amoma flourish best, their clusters of crimson fruit, growing at the base of the stalk, serving me for a tartish dessert, and their grains, commonly called "grains of paradise" being sought after by the bhang smokers of my Expedition to sweeten their breath and increase saliva. The leaves are always of a fresh green, and give one a true idea of a tropical forest and moist, warm climate. Not far off from these is the *Phrynium ramosissi-*

mum, whose broad and long fronds serve to thatch the natives' huts and fishers' sheds, or to fold their cassava bread, or for platters and salt-baskets, or for storing the minnows or whitebait for market. You may also see here the *Strelitza vagina,* or the wild banana, or the violet-tree, and the oil-berry tree, the black ivory nut-tree, which might be made a valuable article of commerce; the *Semicarbus anacardium,* commonly called the marking-ink plant, the *Encephastos Aldensteini,* the ginger plant, the dragon's-blood tree, various species of the Verbenacæ, such as the *Vitex umbrosa,* the physic nut-tree (*Jutrophe purgans*) . . .

Some other pleasures we have are in watching a sunny bank, where we may rest assured the crocodile lies dreaming of fish banquets, and whence he will rise and plunge with a startling splash; or in watching the tricks of some suspicious and watchful behemoth, whose roar has its volume redoubled as it is reverberated from shore to shore in these eerie wilds.

Our terrors are numerous. First, the rocks and rapids, the plunging cataract and whirling pool, which fortunately are past, and which we pray we shall not have to encounter again. Then the sudden storm, which now blows each day up river, and, first wrinkling the face of the river, soon raises heavy brown waves, like those of a lake, which, having already suffered from, we are careful to avoid; but the greatest danger, an ever-recurring one, is that which we have to encounter each time the wild howling cannibal aborigines observe us. Indeed, the sense of security is short-lived, our pleasure evanescent; but the sense of danger is always present and pervades our minds whether in our sleeping or our waking hours.

February 7.—Obtained no latitude. It has been a tempestuous day. Great heavy swells rolled up river in our front, and the wind howled and shrieked so through the dismal glades that we became quite gloomy. To add to our troubles, our food is finished; we have no more, and to attempt to obtain it will cost human life. Empty stomachs serve to render the prospects in unknown and wild regions still darker. We have three asses with us; but then my people have grown to look at them as fellow-members of the Expedition. They say they will die first, but the faithful asses which have accompanied us so far the people say shall not be touched. So far so good; but what are we to do? Late at night the chiefs came to me and declared they must have food to-morrow. I told them they should have it, that from the first village we saw we should go and demand it.

February 8.—Thank God! An anxious day has terminated with tranquillity to long-disturbed minds. . . . Our course yesterday was west by south, and to-day west-south-west. We embarked at 7 A.M., and rowed past a very long wooded island, which lay on our left. At 8 A.M. we began to observe on the right bank a long hilly ridge, with cultivated slopes, and a dense population, which we later learned was called Upoto—or Mbapoto, as one man called it. I solemnly addressed my people, and, while telling them to prepare every weapon, gun, spear, axe, and knife, reminded them that it was an awful thing to commence hostilities, whether for food or anything else. They groaned in spirit, and asked me what they should do when their bowels yearned for something to satisfy its cravings; and though there was an abundance of copper, brass, iron, shells, beads, and cloth, nobody would sell even a small piece of cassava to them, or even look at them without manifesting a thirst for their blood.

I had prepared the brightest and most showy wares close by me, and resolved to be as cunning and patient as a serpent in this intercourse. At 11 A.M. we sighted the village of Rubunga, and, giving instructions to Frank not to approach nearer to me than a quarter of a mile with the canoes, we rowed steadily down until within a few hundred yards of it, when we lay-to on our oars. Presently three canoes advanced to meet us without the usual savage demonstrations. Not even a drum was beaten, a horn blown, or a cry uttered. This was promising. We tried the words "Sen-nen-neh!" "Cha-re-reh!" in soft, mild, melodious strains. They ran away. Things appeared gloomy again. However, patience!

We had reserved one banana and a piece of cassava. We had our mouths and our stomachs with us. An appropriate gesture with the banana to the mouth, and a gentle fondling with a puckered stomach, would, we thought, be a manner of expressing extreme want, eloquent enough to penetrate the armoured body of a crocodile. We came opposite the village at 30 yards' distance, and dropped our stone anchor, and I stood up with my ragged old helmet pushed back far, that they might scrutinise my face, and the lines of suasion be properly seen. With the banana in one hand, and a gleaming armlet of copper and beads of various colours in the other, I began the pantomime. I once knew an idiot in Brusa, Asia Minor, who entreated me for a para in much the same dumb strain that I implored the assembled hundreds of Rubunga to relax that sullen sternness, that uncompromising aspect, that savage front, and yield to the captivating influence of fair and honest barter. I clashed the copper bracelets together, lovingly handled the bright gold-brown of the shining armlet, exposed with all my best grace of manner long necklaces of bright and clean *Cyprœa monela,* and allured their attention with beads of the brightest colours. Nor were the polished folds of yellow brass wire omitted; and again the banana was lifted to my open mouth. Then what suspense, what patience, what a saint-like air of resignation! Ah, yes! but I think I may be pardoned for all that degrading pantomime. I had a number of hungry, half wild children; and through a cannibal world we had ploughed to reach these unsophisticated children of nature.

We waited, and at length an old chief came down the high bank to the lower landing near some rocks. Other elders of the people in head-dresses of leopard and civet skin joined him soon, and then all sat down. The old chief nodded with his head. We raised our anchor, and with two strokes of the oars had run our boat ashore, and, snatching a string or two of cowries, I sprang on land, followed by the coxswain Uledi, and in a second I had seized the skinny hand of the old chief, and was pressing it hard for joy. Warm-hearted Uledi, who the moment before was breathing furious hate of all savages, and of the procrastinating old chief in particular, embraced him with a filial warmth. Young Saywa, and Murabo, and Shumari, prompt as tinder upon all occasions, grasped the lesser chiefs' hands, and devoted themselves with smiles and jovial frank bearing to conquer the last remnants of savage sullenness, and succeeded so well that in an incredibly short time the blood-brotherhood ceremony between the suddenly formed friends was solemnly entered into, and the irrevocable pact of peace and goodwill had been accomplished!

The old chief pointed with his finger to the face of Frank, which shone white amongst the dusky bodies of his comrades, and I beckoned to him. The canoes were all to anchor 100 yards off shore, but Frank was required to respond to the chief of Rubunga's wish for friendship. We distributed presents to each native, and in return we received great bunches of mellow, ripe, and green bananas, as well as of fish. It was agreed between us that we should encamp on this little islet, on which we find ourselves to-night, with a feeling as though we were approaching home.

Before leaving the chief of Rubunga's presence, I asked him the name of the river, in a mongrel mixture of Ki-swahili, Kinyamwezi, Kijiji, Ki-regga, and Ki-Kusu. He understood after a while, and replied it was "Ibari." But after he had quite comprehended the drift of the question, he replied in a sonorous voice, *"Ikutu ya Kongo!"*

There had really been no doubt in my mind since we had left the Stanley Falls that the terrible river would prove eventually to be the river of Congo-land, but it was very agreeable to be told so.

WILLIAM JOHN WILLS

(1834–1861)

From *An Account of the Crossing of the Continent of Australia*

In 1861, Robert O'Hara Burke, William Wills, and John King reached
the Gulf of Carpentaria, having made the first transcontinental crossing of Australia. Many imperialists surmised that the interior contained
a vast inland sea, precious minerals, or at least prime sheep country.
For the most part the men found only searing desert, but their crossing
was heralded a brave achievement, if only because others had tried
before them and turned back. But, like Lewis and Clark when they
reached the Pacific, the men's historic moment was made less jubilant
by the knowledge of an arduous return trip yet to come. And for Burke,
Wills, and King it would be a journey of Shakespearian proportions—
of desperate hardship, cruel irony, and tragedy.

   This excerpt from Wills's journal begins as the men reach Cooper's
Creek in central Australia in an already severely weakened state. They
arrive there expecting to find a critically important support party with
food and supplies. They are just eight hours too late. Their compatriots
had given up on them and turned back. Knowing that they are too
exhausted to overtake their rescuers (who happened to be only fourteen

miles away), Wills and his mates start down Cooper's Creek, hoping
that they have the strength to reach an outpost of civilization at the
prophetically named Mount Hopeless. At first they find food, but soon
are too weak to forage. In Wills's last letter, he wrote to his father with
resigned calm that he thought he had but four or five days to live: "We
are on the point of starvation. . . . We got back here in four months and
four days and found that the others had left the creek the same day. We
were not in a fit state to follow them." His journal is a chronicle of that
slow ebb of his confidence, strength, and life.

Only King survived, and several months later he was found living
among the aborigines who saved him.

S*unday, April 21* [1861] Arrived at the depôt this evening, just in
time to find it deserted. A note left in the plant by Brahe communicates
the pleasing information that they have started today for the Darling; their
camels and horses all well and in good condition. We and our camels
being just done up, and scarcely able to reach the depôt, have very little
chance of overtaking them. Brahe[1] has fortunately left us ample provisions to take us to the bounds of civilization. These provisions, together
with a few horse-shoes and nails and some odds and ends, constitute all
the articles left, and place us in a very awkward position in respect to
clothing. Our disappointment at finding the depôt deserted may easily be
imagined;—returning in an exhausted state, after four months of the
severest travelling and privation, our legs almost paralyzed, so that each of
us found it a most trying task only to walk a few yards. Such a leg-bound
feeling I never before experienced, and hope I never shall again. The
exertion required to get up a slight piece of rising ground, even without
any load, induces an indescribable sensation of pain and helplessness,
and the general lassitude makes one unfit for anything. Poor Gray[2] must

[1] Brahe was in the relief party.
[2] Gray died of starvation on the march, the first of the four to perish.

have suffered very much many times when we thought him shamming. It is most fortunate for us that these symptoms, which so early affected him, did not come on us until we were reduced to an exclusively animal diet of such an inferior description as that offered by the flesh of a worn out and exhausted horse. We were not long in getting out the grub that Brahe had left, and we made a good supper off some oatmeal porridge and sugar. This, together with the excitement of finding ourselves in such a peculiar and almost unexpected position, had a wonderful effect in removing the stiffness from our legs. Whether it is possible that the vegetables can so have affected us, I know not; but both Mr. Burke and I remarked a most decided relief and a strength in the legs greater than we had had for several days. I am inclined to think that but for the abundance of portulac[3] that we obtained on the journey, we should scarcely have returned to Cooper's Creek at all.

Tuesday, April 23 From Depôt.—Having collected together all the odds and the ends that seemed likely to be of use to us, in addition to provisions left in the plant, we started at a quarter past nine a.m., keeping down the southern bank of the creek. We only went about five miles, and camped at half past eleven on a billibong,[4] where the feed was pretty good. We find the change of diet already making a great improvement in our spirits and strength.

Wednesday, April 24 From Camp No. 1 —As we were about to start this morning some blacks came by, from whom we were fortunate enough to get about twelve pounds of fish for a few pieces of straps and some matches,&c. This is a great treat for us, as well as a valuable addition to our rations. We started at a quarter past eight p.m. on our way down the creek, the blacks going in the opposite direction—little thinking that in a

---

[3] Probably portulaca, a tropical hero with succulent leaves.
[4] Watering hole.

few miles they would be able to get lots of pieces for nothing, better than those they had obtained from us. To Camp No.2.

Thursday, April 25 From Camp No.2.—Awoke at five o'clock, after a most refreshing night's rest. The sky was beautifully clear and the air rather chilly. We had scarcely finished breakfast when our friends the blacks, from whom we obtained the fish, made their appearance with a few more, and seemed inclined to go with us and keep up the supply. We gave them some sugar, with which they were greatly pleased. They are by far the most well-behaved blacks we have seen on Copper's Creek. We did not get away from the camp until half-past nine a.m., continuing our course down the most southern branch of the creek, which keeps a general S.W. course. We passed across the stony point which abuts on one of the largest waterholes in the creek, and camped at half-past twelve about a mile below the most dangerous part of the rocky path. At this latter place we had an accident that might have resulted badly for us. One of the camels fell while crossing the worst part, but we fortunately got him out with only a few cuts and bruises. The waterhole at this camp is a very fine one, being several miles long.

Friday, April 26 From Camp No.3.—Last night was beautifully calm, and comparatively warm, although the sky was very clear. Reloaded the camels by moonlight this morning, and started at a quarter to six. Striking off to the south of the creek, we soon got on a native path, which leaves the creek just below the stony ground, and takes a course nearly west across a piece of open country, bounded on the south by sand-ridges, and on the north by the scrubby ground which flanks the bank of the creek at this part of its course. Leaving the path on the right at a distance of three miles, we turned up a small creek which passes down between some sand-hills; and finding a nice patch of feed for the camels at a waterhole, we halted at fifteen minutes past seven for breakfast. We started again at fifty minutes past nine a.m. Continuing our westerly course along the path we crossed to the S. of the watercourse above the water, and proceeded over the most splendid saltbush country that one could wish to see, bounded on the left by sand-hills, whilst to the right the peculiar-looking flat-topped sandstone ranges form an extensive amphitheatre, through the far side of the arena of which may be traced the dark line of creek timber. At twelve o'clock we camped in the bed of the creek. This comparative rest, and the change in diet, have also worked wonders, however; the leg-tied feeling is now entirely gone, and I believe that in less than a week we shall be fit to undergo any fatigue whatever. The camels are improving, and seem capable of doing all that we are likely to require of them. To Camp No. 4.

Saturday, April 27 We started at six o'clock, and, following the native path, which at about a mile from our camp takes a southerly direction, we soon came to the high sandy alluvial deposit, which separates the creek at this point from the stony rises. Here we struck off from the path, keeping well to the S. of the creek, in order that we might mess in a branch of it that took a southerly direction. At twenty minutes past nine we came in on the creek again where it runs due south, and halted for breakfast at a fine waterhole, with fine fresh feed for the camels. Here we remained until noon, when we moved on again, and camped at one o'clock on a general course; having been throughout the morning S.W. eight miles. The weather is most agreeable and pleasant; nothing could be more favourable for us up to the present time. To Camp No. 5.

Sunday, April 28 From Camp No. 5.—Morning fine and calm, but rather chilly. Started at a quarter to five a.m., following down the bed of a creek in a westerly direction, by moonlight. Our stage was, however, very short, for about a mile one of the camels (Landa) got bogged by the side of a waterhole, and although we tried every means in our power, we found it impossible to get him out. All the ground beneath the surface was a bottomless quicksand, through which the beast sank too rapidly for us to get bushes or timber fairly beneath him, and being of a very sluggish stupid nature, he could never be got to make sufficiently strenuous efforts towards extricating himself. In the evening, as a last chance, we let the water in from the creek, so as to buoy him up and at the same time soften the ground about his legs, but it was of no avail. The brute lay quietly in it as if he quite enjoyed his position. To Camp No.6.

Monday, April 29—From Camp No. 6.—Finding Landa still in the hole, we made a few attempts at extricating him, and then shot him; and after breakfast commenced cutting off what flesh we could get at, for jerking.

Tuesday, April 30 Camp No. 6.—Remained here to-day for the purpose of drying the meat, for which process the weather is not very favourable.

Wednesday, May 1 From Camp No. 6.—Started at twenty minutes to nine, having loaded our only camel, Rajah, with the most necessary and useful articles, and packed up a small swag each of bedding and clothing for our own shoulders. We kept on the right bank of the creek for about a mile, and then crossed over at a native camp to the left, where we got on a path running due west, the creek having turned to the N. Following the path, we crossed an open plain, and then sand-ridges, whence we saw the creek straight ahead of us, running nearly S. again. The path took us to the southernmost point of the bend, in a distance of about two and a-half miles from where we had crossed the creek, thereby saving us from three to four miles, as it cannot be less than six miles round by the creek. To Camp No. 7.

Thursday, May 2 Camp No. 7.—Breakfasted by moonlight, and started at half-past six. Following down the left bank of the creek in a westerly direction, we came, at a distance of six miles, on a lot of natives, who were camped on the bed of a creek. They seemed to have just breakfasted, and were most liberal in the presentations of fish and cake. We could only return the compliment by some fish-hooks and sugar. About a mile further on, we came to a separation of the creek, where what looked like the main branch looked towards the south. This channel we fol-lowed, not, however, without some misgivings as to its character, which were soon increased by the small and unfavourable appearance that the creek assumed. On our continuing along it a little further, it began to improve, and widened out, with fine waterholes of considerable depth. The banks were very steep, and a belt of scrub lined it on either side. This made it very inconvenient for travelling, especially as the bed of the creek was full of water for considerable distances. At eleven a.m., we halted until half past one p.m., and then moved on again, taking a S.S.W. course for about two miles, when, at the end of a very long waterhole, it breaks into billibongs, which continue splitting into sandy channels until they are all lost in the earthy soil of a box forest. Seeing little chance of water ahead, we turned back to the end of the long waterhole, and camped for the night. On our way back, Rajah showed signs of being done up. He had been trembling greatly all the morning. On this account his load was further lightened to the amount of a few pounds, by the doing away with the sugar, ginger, tea, cocoa, and two or three tin-plates. To camp No. 8.

Friday, May 3 Camp No. 8.—Started at seven a.m., striking off in a northerly direction for the main creek. At a mile and a-half came to a branch which (left unfinished.) To camp No. 9.

Saturday, May 4 Junction from Camp No. 9.—Night and morning very cold. Sky clear, almost calm; occasionally a light breath of air from south. Rajah appears to feel the cold very much. He was so stiff this morning as to be scarcely able to get up with his load. Started to return down the creek at 6.45, and halted for breakfast at nine a.m., at the same spot as we breakfasted at yesterday. Proceeding from there down the creek, we soon found a repetition of the features that were exhibited by the creek examined on Thursday. At a mile and a-half we came to the last water-hole, and below that the channel became more sandy and shallow, and continued to send off billibongs to the south and west, slightly changing its course each time until it disappeared altogether in a north-westerly direction. Leaving King with the camel, we went on a mile or two to see if we could find water, and being unsuccessful, we were obliged to return to where we had breakfasted, as being the best place for feed and water.

Sunday, May 5 To Camp No. 10.—Started by myself to reconnoitre the country in a southerly direction, leaving Mr. Burke and King with the camel at Camp No. 10. Travelled S. W. by S. for two hours, following the course of the most southerly billibongs. Found the earthy soil becoming more loose and cracked up, and the box-track gradually disappearing. Changed course to west, for a high sand ridge, which I reached in one hour and a half, and continuing in the same direction to one still higher, obtained from it a good view of the surrounding country. To the north were the extensive box forests bounding the creek on either side. To the east earthy plains intersected by water-courses and lines of timber, and bounded in the distance by sand-ridges. To the south the projection of the sand-ridge partially intercepted the view; the rest was composed of earthy plains, apparently clothed with chrysanthemums. To the westward, another but smaller plain was bounded also by high sand-ridges, running nearly parallel with the one on which I was standing. This dreary prospect offering no encouragement for me to proceed, I returned to Camp 10 by a more direct and better route than I had come, passing over some good saltbush land, which borders on the billibongs to the westward.

Monday, May 6 From Camp No. 10 back to Camp No. 9.—Moved up the creek again to Camp No. 9, at the junction, to breakfast, and remained the day there. The present state of things is not calculated to raise our spirits much. The rations are rapidly diminishing; our clothing especially the boots, are all going to pieces, and we have not the materials for repairing them properly; the camel is completely done up, and can scarcely get along, although he has the best of feed, and is resting half his time. I suppose this will end in our having to live like the blacks for a few months.

Tuesday, May 7 Camp No. 9.—Breakfasted at daylight, but when about to start, found that the camel would not rise, even without any load on his back. After making every attempt to get him up, we were obliged to leave him to himself. Mr. Burke and I started down the creek to reconnoitre. At about eleven miles we came to some blacks fishing. They gave us some half-a-dozen fish each for luncheon, and intimated that if we would go to their camp, we should have some more, and some bread. I tore in two a piece of macintosh stuff that I had, and Mr. Burke gave one piece, and I the other. We then went on to their camp, about three miles further. They had caught a considerable quantity of fish, but most of them were small.

On our arrival at the camp, they led us to a spot to camp on, and soon afterwards brought a lot of fish and bread, which they call nardoo.[5] The lighting a fire with matches delights them, but they do not care about having them. In the evening, various members of the tribe came down with lumps of nardoo and handfuls of fish, until we were positively unable to eat any more. They also gave us some stuff they call bedgery, or pedgery. It has a highly intoxicating effect, when chewed even in small quantities. It appears to be the dried stems and leaves of some shrub.

Wednesday, May 8 Left the blacks' camp at half-past seven, Mr. Burke returning to the junction, whilst I proceeded to trace down the creek. This I found a shorter task than I had expected, for it soon showed signs of running out, and at the same time kept considerably to the north of west. There were several fine waterholes within about four miles of the camp I had left, but not a drop all the way beyond that, a distance of seven miles. Finding that the creek turned greatly towards the north, I returned to the blacks' encampment; and, as I was about to pass, they invited me to stay. So I did so, and was even more hospitably entertained than before, being on this occasion offered a share of a gunyah,[6] and sup-

[5] A plant whose seed is a staple carbohydrate for the aborigines.
[6] Shelter.

plied with plenty of fish and nardoo, as well as a couple of nice fat rats. The latter I found most delicious. They were baked in the skins. Last night was clear and calm, but unusually warm. We slept by a fire, just in front of the blacks' camp. They were very attentive in bringing us firewood, and keeping the fire up during the night.

Thursday, May 9 Parted from my friends, the blacks, at half-past seven, and started for Camp No.9.

Friday, May 10 Camp No.9.—Mr. Burke and King employed in jerking the camel's flesh, whilst I went out to look for the nardoo seed, for making bread. In this I was unsuccessful, not being able to find a single tree of it in the neighbourhood of the camp. I however tried boiling the large kind of bean which the blacks call padlu; they boil easily, and when shelled are very sweet, much resembling in taste the French chesnut. They are to be found in large quantities nearly everywhere.

Saturday, May 11 Camp No.9.—To-day Mr. Burke and King started down the creek for the blacks' camp, determined to ascertain all particulars about the nardoo. I have now my turn at the meat jerking, and must divise some means for trapping the birds and rats, which is a pleasant prospect after our dashing trip to Carpentaria, having to hang about Cooper's Creek, living like the blacks.

Sunday, May 12 Mr. Burke and King returned this morning, having been unsuccessful in their search for the blacks, who, it seems, have moved over to the other branch of the creek. Decided on moving out on the main creek tomorrow, and then trying to find the natives of the creek.

Monday, May 13 Shifted some of the things, and brought them back again, Mr. Burke thinking it better for one to remain here with them for a few days, so as to eat the remains of the fresh meat, whilst the others went in search of the blacks and nardoo.

Tuesday, May 14 Mr. Burke and King gone up the creek to look for blacks, with four days' provisions. Self employed in preparing for a final start on their return. This evening Mr. Burke and King returned, having been some considerable distance up the creek, and found no blacks. It is now settled that we plant the things,[7] and all start together the day after tomorrow. The weather continues very fine; the nights calm, clear, and cold, and the days clear, with a breeze generally from S., but to-day from E., for a change. This makes the first part of the day rather cold. When clouds appear they invariably move from W. to E.

Wednesday, May 15 Camp 9.—Planting the things, and preparing to leave the creek for Mount Hopeless.

Thursday, May 16 Having completed our planting, & c., started up the creek to the second blacks' camp, a distance of about eight miles. Finding our loads rather too heavy, we made a small plant here of such articles as could best be spared.

Friday, May 17 Nardoo.—Started this morning on a blacks' path, leaving the creek on our left, our intention being to keep a south-easterly direction until we should cut some likely-looking creek, and then to follow it down. On approaching the foot of the first sand-hill King caught sight in the flat of some nardoo seeds, and we soon found that the flat was covered with them. This discovery caused somewhat of a revolution in our feelings, for we considered that with the knowledge of this plant we were in a position to support ourselves, even if we were destined to remain on the creek and wait for assistance from town. Crossing some sand-ridges running N. and S., we struck into a creek which runs out of Cooper's Creek, and followed it down. At about five miles we came to a large waterhole, beyond which the watercourse runs out on extensive flats and

---

[7] They leave a depot of belongings, to lighten their loads, and to return if they need to. At this point one begins to think that they are lost, or that the disorienting effects of starvation are beginning to affect their ability to plan a route out.

earthy plains. Calm night; sky cleared towards morning, and it became very cold. A slight easterly breeze sprang up at sunrise, but soon died away again. The sky again became overcast, and remained so throughout the day. There was occasionally a light breeze from south, but during the greater portion of the day it was quite calm. Fine halo around the sun in the afternoon.

Saturday, May 18 Camp No. 16. Calm night, sky sometimes clear and sometimes partially overcast with veil clouds.

Tuesday, May 21 Creek.

Wednesday, May 22 Cooper's Creek.

Friday, May 24 Started with King to celebrate the Queen's birthday by fetching from Nardoo Creek what is now to us the staff of life. Returned at a little after two p.m., with a fair supply, but find the collecting of the seed a slower and more troublesome process than could be desired. Whilst picking the seed, about eleven o'clock a.m., both of us heard distinctly the noise of an explosion, as if of a gun, at some considerable distance. We supposed it to have been a shot fired by Mr. Burke; but on returning to the camp found that he had not fired nor had heard the noise. The sky was partially overcast with high cum. str. clouds, and a light breeze blew from the east, but nothing to indicate a thunderstorm in any direction.

Monday, May 27 Started up the creek this morning for the depôt, in order to deposit journals and a record of the state of affairs here. On reaching the sand-hills below where Landa was bogged I passed some blacks on a flat collecting nardoo seed. Never saw such an abundance of the seed before. The ground in some parts was quite black with it. There were only two or three gins[8] and children, and they directed me on, as if to their

8 Aboriginal women.

camp, in the direction I was before going; but I had not gone far over the first sand-hill when I was overtaken by about twenty blacks, bent on taking me back to their camp, and promising any quantity of nardoo and fish. On my going with them, one carried the shovel, and another insisted on taking my swag, in such a friendly manner that I could not refuse them. They were greatly amused with the various little things I had with me. In the evening they supplied me with abundance of nardoo and fish; and one of the old men, Poko Tinnamira, shared his gunyah with me . . . The night was very cold, but, by the help of several fires—

Tuesday, May 28 Left the blacks' camp, and proceeded up the creek. Obtained some mussels near where Landa died, and halted for breakfast. Still feel very unwell from the effects of the constipation of the bowels. The stools are exceedingly painful. After breakfast, travelled on to our third camp coming down.

Wednesday, May 29 Started at seven o'clock, and went on to the duck-holes, where we breakfasted coming down. Halted there at thirty minutes past nine for a feed, and then moved on. At the stones saw a lot of crows quarrelling about something near the water. Found it to be a large fish, of which they had eaten a considerable portion. Finding it quite fresh and good, I decided the quarrel by taking it with me. It proved a most valuable addition to my otherwise scanty supper of nardoo porridge. This evening I camped very comfortably in a mia-mia[9] about eleven miles from the depôt. The night was very cold, although not entirely cloudless. A brisk easterly breeze sprang up in the morning, and blew freshly all day. In the evening the sky clouded in, and there were one or two slight showers, but nothing to wet the ground.

Thursday, May 30 Reached the depôt this morning, at eleven o'clock. No traces of any one except blacks having been here since we left. Deposited

---

[9] Deserted hut.

some journals, and a notice of our present condition. Started back in the afternoon, and camped at the first waterhole. Last night being cloudy, was unusually warm and pleasant.

Friday, May 31 Decamped at thirty minutes past seven, having first breakfasted. Passed between the sand-hills at nine, and reached the blanket mi-mias at twenty minutes to eleven; from there proceeded on to the rocks, where I arrived at half-past one, having delayed about half-an-hour on the road in gathering some portuloc. It had been a fine morning, but the sky now became overcast, and threatened to set in for a steady rain; and as I felt very weak and tired I only moved on about a mile further, and camped in a sheltered gully, under some bushes. Night clear and very cold.

Saturday, June 1 Started at a quarter to eight a.m. Passed the duck-holes at ten a.m., and my second camp up at two p.m., having rested in the meantime about forty-five minutes. Thought to have reached the blacks' camp, or at least where Landa was bogged, but found myself altogether too weak and exhausted; in fact, had extreme difficulty in getting across the numerous little gullies, and was at last obliged to camp, from sheer fatigue. Night ultimately clear and cloudy, with occasional showers.

Sunday, June 2 Started at half-past six, thinking to breakfast at the blacks' camp, below Landa's grave; found myself very much fagged, and did not arrive at their camp until ten a.m., and then found myself disappointed as to a good breakfast, the camp being deserted. Having rested awhile, and eaten a few fish-bones, I moved down the creek, hoping by a late march to be able to reach our own camp, but I soon found, from my extreme weakness, that that would be out of the question. A certain amount of good luck, however, still stuck to me, for, on going along by a large waterhole, I was so fortunate as to find a large fish, about a pound and a-half in weight, which was just being choked by another which it had tried to swallow, but which had stuck in its throat. I soon had a fire lit, and both of the fish cooked and eaten. The large one was in good condition. Moving on again after my late breakfast, I passed Camp 67 of the journey to Carpentaria, and camped for the night under some polygonum bushes.

Monday, June 3 Started at seven o'clock, and, keeping on the south bank of the creek, was rather encouraged, at about three miles, by the sound of numerous crows a-head; presently fancied I could see smoke, and was shortly afterwards set at my ease by hearing a cooey from Pitchery,[10] who stood on the opposite bank, and directed me around the lower end of the waterhole, continually repeating his assurance of abundance of fish and bread. Having with some considerable difficulty managed to ascend the sandy path that led to the camp, I was conducted by the chief to a fire, where a large pile of fish were just being cooked in the most approved style. These I imagined to be for the general consumption of the half a dozen natives gathered around, but it turned out that they had already had their breakfast. I was expected to dispose of this lot—a task which, to my own astonishment, I soon accomplished, keeping two or three blacks pretty steadily at work extracting the bones for me. The fish being disposed of, next came a supply of nardoo cake and water, until I was so full as to be unable to eat any more, when Pitchery allowing me a short time to recover myself, fetched a large bowl of the raw nardoo flour, mixed to a thin paste—a most insinuating article, and one that they appear to esteem a great delicacy. I was then invited to stop the night there, but this I declined, and proceeded on my way home.

Tuesday, June 4 Started for the blacks' camp, intending to test the practicability of living with them, and to see what I could learn as to their ways and manners.

Wednesday, June 5 Remained with the blacks. Light rain during the greater part of the night, and more or less throughout the day, in showers. Wind blowing in squalls from S.

[10] Aborigine Wills had met earlier.

Thursday, June 6 Returned to our own camp, found that Mr. Burke and King had been well supplied with fish by the blacks. Made preparation for shifting our camp nearer to their's on the morrow.

Friday, June 7 Started in the afternoon for the blacks' camp with such things as we could take; found ourselves all very weak, in spite of the abundant supply of fish that we have lately had. I myself could scarcely get along, although carrying the lightest swag—only about thirty pounds. Found that the blacks had decamped, so determined on proceeding to-morrow up to the next camp, near the nardoo field.

Saturday, June 8 With the greatest fatigue and difficulty we reached the nardoo camp. No blacks, greatly to our disappointment. Took possession of their best mia mia, and rested for the remainder of the day.

Sunday, June 9 King and I proceeded to collect nardoo, leaving Mr. Burke at home.

Monday, June 10 Mr. Burke and King collecting nardoo; self at home, too weak to go out. Was fortunate enough to shoot a crow.

Tuesday, June 11 King out for nardoo. Mr. Burke up the creek to look for the blacks.

Wednesday, June 12 King out collecting nardoo. Mr. Burke and I at home, pounding and cleaning. I still feel myself, if anything, weaker in the legs, although the nardoo appears to be more thoroughly (?) digested.

Thursday, June 13 Last night the sky was pretty clear, and the air rather cold, but nearly calm. Mr. Burke and King out for nardoo. Self weaker than ever, scarcely able to go to the water hole for water.

Friday, June 14 Night alternately clear and cloudy, no wind, beautifully mild for the time of year; in the morning some heavy clouds on the horizon. King out for nardoo; brought in a good supply. Mr. Burke and I at home, pounding and cleaning seed. I feel weaker than ever, and both Mr. B. and King are beginning to feel very unsteady in the legs.

Saturday, June 15 Night clear, calm, and cold; morning very fine, with a light breath of air from N.E. King out for nardoo; brought in a fine supply. Mr. Burke and I pounding and cleaning. He finds himself getting very weak, and I am not a bit stronger. I have determined on beginning to chew tobacco and eat less nardoo, in hopes that it may induce some change in the system. I have never yet recovered from the effects of the constipation, and the passage of the stools is always exceedingly painful.

Sunday, June 16 Wind shifted to N., clouds moving from W. to E.; thunder audible two or three times to the southward; sky becoming densely overcast, with an occasional shower about nine a.m. We finished up the remains of the Rajah for dinner yesterday. King was fortunate enough to shoot a crow this morning. The rain kept all hands in pounding and cleaning seed during the morning. The weather cleared up towards the middle of the day, and a brisk breeze sprang up in the south, lasting till near sunset, but rather irregular in its force. Distant thunder was audible to westward and southward frequently during the afternoon.

Monday, June 17 Night very boisterous and stormy. Northerly wind blowing in squalls, and heavy showers of rain, with thunder in the north and west. Heavy clouds moving rapidly from north to south; gradually clearing up during the morning, the wind continuing equally during the day from W. and N. W. King out in the afternoon for nardoo.

Tuesday, June 18 Exceedingly cold night. Sky clear, slight breeze, very chilly, and changeable; very heavy dew.

Wednesday, June 19 Night calm; sky during first part overcast most of which cleared away towards morning, leaving the air much colder, but the sky remained more or less hazy all night, and it was not nearly as cold as last night. About eight o'clock a strong southerly wind sprung up, which enabled King to blow the dust out of our nardoo seeds, but made me too weak to render him any assistance.

Thursday, June 20 Night and morning very cold, sky clear. I am completely reduced by the effects of the cold and starvation. King gone out for nardoo. Mr. Burke at home pounding seed; he finds himself getting very weak in the legs. King holds out by far the best; the food seems to agree with him pretty well. Finding the sun come out pretty warm towards noon, I took a sponging all over, but it seemed to do little good beyond the cleaning effects, for my weakness is so great that I could not do it with proper expedition. I cannot understand this nardoo at all; it certainly will not agree with me in any form. We are now reduced to it alone, and we manage to get from four to five pounds per day between us. The stools it causes are enormous, and seem greatly to exceed the quantity of bread consumed, and is very slightly altered in appearance from what it was when eaten.

Friday, June 21 Last night was cold and clear, winding up with a strong wind from N.E. in the morning. I feel much weaker than ever, and can scarcely crawl out of the mia-mia. Unless relief comes in some form or other, I cannot possibly last more than a fortnight. It is a great consolation, at least, in this position of ours, to know that we have done all we could, and that our deaths will rather be the result of the mismanagement of others than of any rash acts of our own. Had we come to grief elsewhere, we could only have blamed ourselves; but here we are, returned to Cooper's Creek, where we had every reason to look for provisions and clothing; and yet we have to die of starvation, in spite of the explicit instructions given by Mr. Burke, that the depôt party should await our return, and the strong recommendation to the committee that we should be followed up by a party from Menindie.

Saturday, June 22 Night cloudy and warm. Every appearance of rain. Thunder once or twice during the night. Clouds moving in an easterly direction. Lower atmosphere perfectly calm. There were a few drops of rain during the night, and in the morning, about nine a.m., there was every prospect of more rain until towards noon, when the sky cleared up for a time. Mr. Burke and King out for nardoo. The former returned much fatigued. I am so weak to-day as to be unable to get on my feet.

Sunday, June 23 All hands at home. I am so weak as to be incapable of crawling out of the mia-mia. King holds out well, but Mr. Burke finds himself weaker every day.

Monday, June 24 A fearful night. At about an hour before sunset, a southerly gale sprang up and continued throughout the greater portion of the night; the cold was intense, and it seemed as if one would be shrivelled up. Towards morning, it fortunately lulled a little, but a strong cold breeze continued till near sunset, after which it became perfectly calm. King went out for nardoo, in spite of the wind, and came in with a good load, but he himself terribly cut up. He says that he can no longer keep up the work, and as he and Mr. Burke are both getting rapidly weaker, we have but a slight chance of anything but starvation, unless we can get hold of some blacks.

Tuesday, June 23 (sic) Night calm, clear, and intensely cold, especially towards morning. Near daybreak, King reported seeing a moon in the E., with a haze of light stretching up from it, he declared it to be quite as large as the moon, and not dim at the edges. I am so weak that any attempt to get a sight of it was out of the question; but I think it must have been Venus in the zodiacal light that he saw, with a corona around her. Mr. Burke and King remain at home cleaning and pounding seed. They are both getting weaker every day. The cold plays the deuce with us, from the small amount of clothing we have. My wardrobe consists of a wide-a-awake, a merino shirt, a regatta shirt without sleeves, the remains of a pair of flannel trousers, two pairs of socks in rags, and a waistcoat of which I have managed to keep the pockets together. The others are no better off. Besides these we have between us for bedding, two small camel pads, some horsehair, two or three little bits of a rag, and pieces of oilcloth saved from the fire. The day turned out nice and warm.

Wednesday, June 24 (sic) Calm night; sky overcast with hazy clouds. An easterly breeze sprang up towards morning, making the air much colder. Mr. Burke and King are preparing to go up the creek in search of the blacks. They will leave me some nardoo, wood and water, with which I must do the best I can until they return. I think this is almost our only chance. I feel myself, if anything, rather better, but I cannot say stronger. The nardoo is beginning to agree better with me; but without some change I see little chance for any of us. They have both shown great hesitation and reluctance with regard to leaving me, and have repeatedly desired my candid opinion in the matter. I could only repeat, however, that I considered it our only chance, for I could not last long on the nardoo, even if a supply could be kept up.

Thursday, June 25 (sic) Cloudy, calm, and comparatively warm night, clouds almost stationary. In the morning a gentle breeze from east. Sky partially cleared up during the day, making it pleasantly warm and bright, it remained clear during the afternoon and evening, offering every prospect of a clear cold night.

Friday, June 26 (sic) Clear cold night, slight breeze from the E., day beautifully warm and pleasant. Mr. Burke suffers greatly from the cold, and is getting extremely weak; he and King start to-morrow up the creek, to look for the blacks—it is the only chance we have of being saved from starvation. I am weaker than ever although I have a good appetite, and relish the nardoo much, but it seems to give us no nutriment, and the birds here are so shy as not to be got at. Even if we got a good supply of fish, I doubt whether we could do much work on them and the nardoo alone.

Nothing now but the greatest good luck can now save any of us; and as for myself, I may live four or five days if the weather continues warm. My pulse are at forty-eight, and very weak, and my legs and arms are nearly skin and bone. I can only look out, like Mr. Micawber, "for something to turn up;" but starvation on nardoo is by no means very unpleasant, but for the weakness one feels, and the utter inability to move oneself, for as far as appetite is concerned, it gives me the greatest satisfaction. Certainly, fat and sugar would be more to one's taste, in fact, those seem to me to be the great stand by for one in this extraordinary continent; not that I mean to depreciate the farinacious food, but the want of sugar and fat in all substances obtainable here is so great that they become almost valueless to us as articles of food, without the addition of something else.

PART II

Personal Odysseys

"How far does the desert reach to the north, from the point where the river ends," I asked. And Mohammed Bai replied: "To the end of the world. And it takes three months to get there."

—SVEN HEDIN

CAPTAIN JOSHUA SLOCUM

(1844–c. 1909)

From *Voyage of the* Liberdade

Joshua Slocum earned hero status when in the last decade of the century he became the first person to sail solo around the globe. His 1899 account of his experiences aboard the thirty-five-foot boat Spray, Sailing Alone Around the World, *stands as one of the seminal adventure stories of our time. Not only did Slocum make history, but his captivating book inspired countless other personal odysseys in small boats; like all the best explorers, he expanded the realm of what was previously thought possible.*

Much less well known is Slocum's delightful short piece Voyage of the Liberdade, *published in 1894. Although no firsts were established on this earlier voyage (1888), its genesis could hardly be more romantic. Slocum, his wife, and two sons found themselves shipwrecked in Uruguay during a cholera epidemic, the trading vessel they sailed in from America, the* Aquidneck, *having been confiscated and sold to wreckers. In his typically unstoppable, exuberant fashion, Slocum decides that rather than wait for a passage home, he will design a boat after local fishing craft (he often calls the* Liberdade *"the canoe," refer-*

ring to its origins), build it himself with a handful of crude tools, and sail his family home to Boston. And so he does, covering over 5,000 miles in 53 days in a sturdy little boat that his six-year-old son Garfield, trying to kneel beside his bunk at night, complained "wasn't big enough to pray in."

Slocum, utterly in love with the sea and all things nautical, had a way of facing any adversity with glee, and yet all indications are that this was an idyllic Swiss Family Robinson–type journey. They run into storms and are nearly upset by a whale passing underneath the small craft, but even in those passages the book possesses a breathless, awestruck quality. "For all the vicissitudes, I love a life on the broad, free ocean," Slocum concludes, and we believe him. This passage covers the main events of the first half of the voyage.

The efficiency of our canoe was soon discovered: On the 24th of June, after having sailed about the bay some few days to temper our feelings to the new craft, and shake things into place, we crossed the bar and stood out to sea, while six vessels lay inside "barbound," that is to say by their pilots it was thought too rough to venture out, and they, the pilots, stood on the point as we put out to sea, crossing themselves in our behalf, and shouting that the bar was *crudo*. But the *Liberdade* stood on her course, the crew never regretting it.

The wind from the sou'west at the time was the moderating side of a *pampiero*[1] which had brought in a heavy swell from the ocean, that broke and thundered on the bar with deafening roar and grand display of majestic effort.

But our little ship bounded through the breakers like a fish—as natural to the elements, and as free!

Of all the seas that broke furiously about her that day, often standing

---

[1] A strong cold wind that blows from the southwest over the plains east of the Andes.

her on end, not one swept over or even boarded her, and she finally came through the storm of breakers in triumph. Then squaring away before the wind she spread her willing sails, and flew onward like a bird.

It required confidence and some courage to face the first storm in so small a bark, after having been years in large ships; but it would have required more courage than was possessed by any of us to turn back, since thoughts of home had taken hold on our minds.

Then, too, the old boating trick came back fresh to me, the love of the thing itself gaining on me as the little ship stood out: and my crew with one voice said: "Go on." The heavy South Atlantic swell rolling in upon the coast, as we sped along, toppled over when it reached the ten fathom line, and broke into roaring combers, which forbade our nearer approach to the land.

Evidently, our safest course was away from the shore, and out where the swelling seas, though grand, were regular, and raced under our little craft that danced like a mite on the ocean as she drove forward. In twenty-four hours from the time Paranagua bar was crossed we were up with Santos Heads, a run of 150 miles.

A squall of wind burst on us through a gulch, as we swept round the Heads, tearing our sails into shreds, and sending us into Santos under bare poles.

Chancing then upon an old friend, the mail steamship *Finance,* Capt. Baker, about to sail for Rio, the end of a friendly line was extended to us, and we were towed by the stout steamer toward Rio, the next day, as fast as we could wish to go. My wife and youngest sailor took passage on the steamer, while Victor[2] remained in the canoe with me, and stood by with axe in hand, to cut the tow-line, if the case should require it—and I steered.

"Look out," said Baker, as the steamer began to move ahead, "look out that I don't snake that canoe out from under you."

"Go on with your mails, Baker," was all I could say, "don't blow up your ship with my wife and son on board, and I will look out for the packet on the other end of the rope."

Baker opened her up to thirteen knots, but the *Liberdade* held on!

The line that we towed with was 1 1/3 inches in diameter, by ninety fathoms long. This, at times when the steamer surged over seas, leaving the canoe on the opposite side of a wave astern, would become as taut as a harp-string. At other times it would slacken and sink limp in a bight, under the forefoot, but only for a moment, however, when the steamer's next great plunge ahead would snap it taut again, pulling us along with a heavy, trembling jerk. Under the circumstances, straight steering was imperative, for a sheer to port or starboard would have finished the career of the *Liberdade,* by sending her under the sea. Therefore, the trick of twenty hours fell to me—the oldest and most experienced helmsman. But I was all right and not over-fatigued until Baker cast oil upon the "troubled waters." I soon got tired of that.

Victor was under the canvas covering, with the axe still in hand, ready to cut the line which was so arranged that he could reach it from within, and cut instantly, if by mischance the canoe should take a sheer.

I was afraid that the lad would become sleepy, and putting his head

2 Captain Slocum's first son; "youngest sailor" refers to his second son, Garfield.

"under his wing" for a nap, would forget his post, but my frequent cry, "Stand by there, Victor," found him always on hand, though complaining somewhat of the dizzy motion.

Heavy sprays dashed over me at the helm, which, however, seeming to wash away the sulphur and brimstone smoke of many a quarantine, brought enjoyment to my mind.

Confused waves rose about us, high and dangerous—often high above the gunwale of the canoe—but her shapely curves balanced her well, and she rode over them all in safety.

This canoe ride was thrilling and satisfactory to us all. It proved beyond a doubt that we had in this little craft a most extraordinary sea-boat, for the tow was a thorough test of her seaworthiness.

The captain of the steamer ordered oil cast over from time to time, relieving us of much spray and sloppy motion, but adding to discomforts of taste to me at the helm, for much of the oil blew over me and in my face. Said the captain to one of his mates (an old whaler by the way, and whalers for some unaccountable reason have never too much regard for a poor merchantman), "Mr. Smith."

"Aye, aye, sir," answered old Smith.

"Mr. Smith, hoist out that oil."

"Aye, aye, sir," said the old "blubberhunter," in high glee, as he went about it with alacrity, and in less than five minutes from the time the order was given, I was smothering in grease and our boat was oiled from keel to truck.

"She's all right now," said Smith.

"That's all right," said Baker, but I thought it all wrong. The wind, meanwhile, was in our teeth and before we crossed Rio bar I had swallowed enough oil to cure any amount of consumption.

Baker, I have heard, said he wouldn't care much if he should "drown Slocum." But I was all right so long as the canoe didn't sheer, and we arrived at Rio safe and sound after the most exciting boat-ride of my life. I was bound not to cut the line that towed us so well; and I knew that Baker wouldn't let it go, for it was his rope.

. . .

July 23rd, 1888, was the day, as I have said, on which we sailed from Rio de Janeiro.

Meeting with head winds and light withal, through the day we made but little progress; and finally, when night came on, we anchored twenty miles east of Rio Heads, near the shore. Long, rolling seas rocked us as they raced by, then, dashing their great bodies against defying rocks, made music by which we slept that night. But a trouble unthought of before came up in Garfield's mind before going to his bunk; "Mamma," cried he, as our little bark rose and fell on the heavy waves, tumbling the young sailor about from side to side in the small quarters while he knelt seriously at his evening devotion, "mamma, this boat isn't big enough to pray in!" But this difficulty was gotten over in time, and Garfield learned to watch as well as to pray on the voyage, and full of faith that all would be well, laid him down nights and slept as restfully as any Christian on sea or land.

By daylight of the second day we were again underweigh, beating to the eastward against the old head wind and head sea. On the following night we kept her at it, and the next day made Cape Frio where we anchored near the entrance to a good harbour.

Time from Rio, two days; distance, 70 miles.

The wind and tide being adverse, compelled us to wait outside for a favourable change. While comfortably anchored at this place, a huge whale, nosing about, came up under the canoe, giving us a toss and a great scare. We were at dinner when it happened. The meal, it is needless to say, was finished without dessert. The great sea animal—fifty to sixty feet long—circling around our small craft, looked terribly big. He was so close to me twice, as he swam round and round the canoe, that I could have touched him either time with a paddle. His flukes stirring the water like a steamer propeller appeared alarmingly close and powerful!— and what an ugly mouth the monster had! Well, we expected instant annihilation. The fate of the stout whale-ship *Essex* came vividly before me. The voyage of the *Liberdade,* I thought, was about ended, and I looked about for pieces of bamboo on which to land my wife and family. Just then, however, to the infinite relief of all of us, the leviathan moved off, without doing us much harm, having felt satisfied, perhaps, that we had no Jonah on board.

We lost an anchor through the incident, and received some small damage to the keel, but no other injury was done—even this, I believe, upon second thought, was unintentional—done in playfulness only! "A shark can take a joke," it is said, and crack one too, but for broad, rippling humour the whale has no equal.

"If this be a sample of our adventures in the beginning," thought I, "we shall have enough and to spare by the end of the voyage." A visit from this quarter had not been counted on; but Sancho Panza says, "When least aware starts the hare," which in our case, by the by, was a great whale!

When our breath came back and the hair on our heads settled to a normal level, we set sail, and dodged about under the lee of the cape till a cove, with a very enticing sand beach at the head of it, opened before us, some three miles northwest of where we lost the anchor in the remarkable adventure with the whale. The "spare bower" was soon bent to the cable. Then we stood in and anchored near a cliff, over which was a goat-path leading in the direction of a small fishing village, about a mile away. Sheering the boat in to the rocky side of the cove which was steep to, we leaped out, warp in hand, and made fast to a boulder above the tidal flow, then, scrambling over the cliff, we repaired to the village, first improvising a spare anchor from three sticks and a stone which answered the purpose quite well.

Judging at once that we were strangers the villagers came out to meet us, and made a stir at home to entertain us in the most hospitable manner, after the custom of the country, and with the villagers was a gentleman from Canada, a Mr. Newkirk, who, as we learned, was engaged, when the sea was smooth, in recovering treasure that was lost near the cape in the British warship *Thetis,* which was wrecked there in 1830. The treasure, some millions in silver coins and gold in bars, from Peru for England, was dumped in the cove, which has since taken the name of the ship that bore it there and, as I have said, came to grief in that place which is on the west shore near the end of the cape.

Some of the coins were given to us to be treasured as souvenirs of the pleasant visit. We found in Mr. Newkirk a versatile, roving genius; he had been a schoolmaster at home, captain of a lake schooner once, had practised medicine, and preached some, I think; and what else I do not know. He had tried many things for a living, but, like the proverbial moving stone had failed to accumulate. "Matters," said the Canadian, "were getting worse and worse even, till finally to keep my head above water I was forced to go under the sea," and he had struck it rich, it would seem, if gold being brought in by the boat-load was any sign. This man of many adventures still spoke like a youngster; no one had told him that he was growing old. He talked of going home, as soon as the balance of the treasure was secured, "just to see his dear old mother," who, by the way, was seventy-four years old when he left home, some twenty years before. Since his last news from home, nearly two decades had gone by. He was "the youngest of a family of eighteen children, all living," he said, "though," added he, "our family came near being made one less yesterday, by a whale which I thought would eat my boat, diving-bell, crew, money and all, as he came toward us, with open mouth. By a back stroke of the oars, however, we managed to cheat him out of his dinner, if that was what he was after, and I think it was, but here I am!" he cried, "all right!" and might have added, "wealthy after all."

After hearing the diver's story, I related in Portuguese our own adventure of the same day, and probably with the same whale, the monster having gone in the direction of the diver's boat. The astonishment of the listeners was great; but when they learned of our intended voyage to *America do Norte*, they crossed themselves and asked God to lend us grace!

"Is North America near New York?" asked the village merchant, who owned all the boats and nets of the place.

"Why, America is *in* New York," answered the ex-schoolmaster.

"I thought so," said the self-satisfied merchant. And no doubt he thought some of us very stupid, or rude, or both, but in spite of manners I had to smile at the assuring air of the Canadian.

"Why did you not answer him correctly?" I asked of the ex-school-master.

"I answered him," said Newkirk, "according to his folly. Had I corrected his rusty geography before these simple, impoverished fishermen, he would not soon forgive me; and as for the rest of the poor souls here, the knowledge would do them but little good."

I may mention that in this out-of-the-way place there were no schools, and except the little knowledge gained in their church, from the catechism, and from the fumbling of beads, they were the most innocent of this world's scheme, of any people I ever met. But they seemed to know all about heaven, and were, no doubt, happy.

After the brief, friendly chat that we had, coffee was passed around, the probabilities of the *Liberdade*'s voyage discussed, and the crew cautioned against the dangers of the *balaena* (whale), which were numerous along the coast, and vicious at that season of the year, having their young to protect.

I realized very often the startling sensation alone of a night at the helm, of having a painful stillness broken by these leviathans bursting the surface of the water with a noise like the roar of a great sea, uncomfortably near, reminding me of the Cape Frio adventure; and my crew, I am sure, were not less sensitive to the same feeling of an awful danger, however imaginary. One night in particular, dark and foggy I remember, Victor called me excitedly, saying that something dreadful ahead and drawing rapidly near had frightened him.

It proved to be a whale, for some reason that I could only guess at, threshing the sea with its huge body, and surging about in all directions, so that it puzzled me to know which way to steer to go clear. I thought at first, from the rumpus made, that a fight was going on, such as we had once witnessed from the deck of the *Aquidneck,* not far from this place. Our course was changed as soon as we could decide which way to avoid, if possible, all marine disturbers of the peace. We wished especially to keep away from infuriated swordfish, which I feared might be darting about, and be apt to give us a blind thrust. Knowing that they sometimes

pierce stout ships through with their formidable weapons, I began to feel
ticklish about the ribs myself, I confess, and the little watch below, too,
got uneasy and sleepless; for one of these swords, they knew well, would
reach through and through our little boat, from keel to deck. Large ships
have occasionally been sent into port leaky from the stab of a sword, but
what I most dreaded was the possibility of one of us being ourselves
pinned in the boat.

A swordfish once pierced a whale-ship through the planking, and
through the solid frame timber and the thick ceiling, with his sword,
leaving it there, a valuable plug indeed, with the point, it was found upon
unshipping her cargo at New Bedford, even piercing through a cask in
the hold.

. . .

July 30th, early in the day, and after a pleasant visit at the cape, we sailed
for the north, securing first a few sea shells to be cherished, with the
Thetis relics, in remembrance of a most enjoyable visit to the hospitable
shores of Cape Frio.

Having now doubled Cape Frio, a prominent point in our voyage, and
having had the seaworthiness of our little ship thoroughly tested, as
already told; and seeing, moreover, that we had nothing to fear from common small fry of the sea (one of its greatest monsters having failed to
capsize us), we stood on with greater confidence than ever, but watchful,
nevertheless, for any strange event that might happen.

A fresh polar wind hurried us on, under shortened sail, toward the
softer "trades" of the tropics, but, veering to the eastward by midnight, it
brought us well in with the land. Then, "Larboard watch, ahoy! all hands
on deck and turn out reefs," was the cry. To weather Cape St. Thome we
must lug on all sail. And we go over the shoals with a boiling sea and current in our favour. In twenty-four hours from Cape Frio, we had lowered
the Southern Cross three degrees—180 miles.

Sweeping by the cape, the canoe sometimes standing on end, and
sometimes buried in the deep hollow of the sea, we sunk the light on St.
Thome soon out of sight, and stood on with flowing sheet. The wind on

the following day settled into regular south-east "trades," and our cedar canoe skipped briskly along, over friendly seas that were leaping toward home, doffing their crests onward and forward, but never back, and the splashing waves against her sides, then rippling along the thin cedar planks between the crew and eternity, vibrated enchanting music to the ear, while confidence grew in the bark that was HOMEWARD BOUND.

But coming upon coral reefs, of a dark night, while we listened to the dismal tune of the seas breaking over them with an eternal roar, how intensely lonesome they were! no sign of any living thing in sight, except, perhaps, the phosphorescent streaks of a hungry shark, which told of bad company in our wake, and made the gloom of the place more dismal still.

One night we made shelter under the lee of the extensive reefs called the Paredes (walls), without seeing the breakers at all in the dark, although they were not far in the distance. At another time, dragging on sail to clear a lee shore, of a dark and stormy night, we came suddenly into smooth water, where we cast anchor and furled our sails, lying in a magic harbour till daylight the next morning, when we found ourselves among a maze of ugly reefs, with high seas breaking over them, as far as the eye could reach, on all sides, except at the small entrance to the place that we had stumbled into in the night. The position of this future harbour is South Lat. 16° 48′, and West Long. from Greenwich 39° 30′. We named the place "PORT LIBERDADE."

The next places sighted were the treacherous Abrohles, and the village of Caravellas back of the reef where, upon refitting, I found that a chicken cost a thousand reis, a bunch of bananas four hundred reis; but where a dozen limes cost only twenty reis—one cent. Much whaling gear lay strewn about the place, and on the beach was the carcass of a whale about nine days slain. Also leaning against a smart-looking boat was a grey-haired fisherman, boat and man relics of New Bedford, employed at this station in their familiar industry. The old man was bare-footed and thinly clad, after the custom in this climate. Still, I recognized the fisherman and sailor in the set and rig of the few duds he had on, and the ample straw hat (donkey's breakfast) that he wore, and doffed in a seaman-like manner, upon our first salute. *"Filio do Mar do Nord Americano,"* said an affable native close by, pointing at the same time to that "son of the sea of North America," by way of introduction, as soon as it was learned that we, too, were of that country. I tried to learn from this ancient mariner the cause of his being stranded in this strange land. He may have been cast up there by the whale for aught I could learn to the contrary.

Choosing a berth well to windward of the dead whale—the one that landed "the old man of the sea" there, maybe!—we anchored for the night, put a light in the rigging and turned in. Next morning, the village was astir betimes; canoes were being put afloat, and the rattle of poles, paddles, bait boxes, and many more things for the daily trip that were being hastily put into each canoe, echoed back from the tall palm groves notes of busy life, telling us that it was time to weigh anchor and be sailing. To this cheerful tune we lent ear and, hastening to be underweigh, were soon clear of the port. Then, skimming along near the beach in the early morning, our sails spread to a land breeze, laden with fragrance from the tropic forest and the music of many songsters, we sailed in great felicity, dreading no dangers from the sea, for there were none now to dread or fear.

Proceeding forward through this belt of moderate winds, fanned by alternating land and sea breezes, we drew on toward a region of high trade-winds that reach sometimes the dignity of a gale. It was no surprise, therefore, after days of fine-weather sailing, to be met by a storm, which so happened as to drive us into the indifferent anchorage of St. Paulo, thirty miles from Bahia, where we remained two days for shelter.

Time, three days from Caravellas; distance sailed, 270 miles.

A few fishermen lounged about the place, living, apparently, in wretched poverty, spending their time between waiting for the tide to go out, when it was in, and waiting for it to come in, when it was out, to float a canoe or bring fish to their shiftless nets. This, indeed, seemed their only concern in life; while their ill-thatched houses, forsaken of the adobe that once clung to the wicker walls, stood grinning in rows, like emblems of our mortality.

We found at this St. Paulo anything but saints. The wretched place should be avoided by strangers, unless driven there for shelter, as we ourselves were, by stress of weather. We left the place on the first lull of the wind, having been threatened by an attack from a gang of rough, half-drunken fellows, who rudely came on board, jostling about, and jabbering in a dialect which, however, I happened to understand. I got rid of them by the use of my broken Portuguese, and once away I was resolved that they should stay away. I was not mistaken in my suspicions that they would return and try to come aboard, which shortly afterward they did, but my resolution to keep them off was not shaken. I let them know, in their own jargon this time, that I was well armed. They finally paddled back to the shore, and all visiting was then ended. We stood a good watch that night, and by daylight next morning, Aug. 12th, put to sea, standing out in a heavy swell, the character of which I knew better, and could trust to more confidently than a harbour among treacherous natives.

Early in the same day, we arrived at *Bahia do todos Santos* (All Saints' Bay), a charming port, with a rich surrounding country. It was from this port, by the way, that Robinson Crusoe sailed for Africa to procure slaves for his plantation and that of his friend, so fiction relates.

. . .

From Bahia to Pernambuco our course lay along that part of the Brazilian coast fanned by constant tradewinds. Nothing unusual occurred to disturb our peace or daily course, and we pressed forward night and day, as was our wont from the first.

Victor and I stood watch and watch at sea, usually four hours each.

The most difficult of our experiences in fine weather was the intense drowsiness brought on by constantly watching the oscillating compass at night: even in the daytime this motion would make one sleepy.

We soon found it necessary to arrange a code of signals which would communicate between the tiller and the "man forward." This was accomplished by means of a line or messenger extending from one to the other, which was understood by the number of pulls given by it; three pulls, for instance, meant "Turn out," one in response, "Aye, aye, I am awake, and what is it that is wanted?" one pull in return signified that it was "Eight bells," and so on. But three quick jerks meant "Tumble out and shorten sail."

Victor, it was understood, would tie the line to his arm or leg when he turned in, so that by pulling I would be sure to arouse him, or bring him somewhat unceremoniously out of his bunk. Once, however, the messenger failed to accomplish its purpose. A boot came out on the line in answer to my call, so easily, too, that I suspected a trick. It was evidently a preconceived plan by which to gain a moment more of sleep. It was a clear imposition on the man at the wheel!

We had also a sign in this system of telegraphing that told of flying-fish on board—manna of the sea—to be gathered up for the *cuisine* whenever they happened to alight or fall on deck, which was often, and as often they found a warm welcome.

The watch was never called to make sail. As for myself, I had never to be called, having thoughts of the voyage and its safe completion on my mind to keep me always on the alert. I can truly say that I never, on the voyage, slept so sound as to forget where I was, but whenever I fell into a doze at all it would be to dream of the boat and the voyage.

Press on! press on! was the watchword while at sea, but in port we enjoyed ourselves and gave up care for rest and pleasure, carrying a supply, as it were, to sea with us, where sail was again carried on.

Though a mast should break, it would be no matter of serious concern, for we would be at no loss to mend and rig up spars for this craft at short notice, most anywhere.

The third day out from Bahia was set fine weather. A few flying-fish made fruitless attempts to rise from the surface of the sea, attracting but little attention from the sea-gulls which sat looking wistfully across the unbroken deep with folded wings.

And the *Liberdade,* doing her utmost to get along through the common quiet, made but little progress on her way. A dainty fish played in her light wake, till tempted by an evil appetite for flies, it landed in the cockpit upon a hook, thence into the pan, where many a one had brought up before. Breakfast was cleared away at an early hour; then day of good things happened—"the meeting of the ships."

> When o'er the silent sea alone
>   For days and nights we've cheerless gone,
> Oh they who've felt it know how sweet,
>   Some sunny morn a sail to meet.

> Sparkling at once is every eye,
>   "Ship ahoy! ship ahoy!" our joyful cry
> While answering back the sound we hear,
>   "Ship ahoy! ship ahoy! what cheer, what cheer."

> Then sails are backed, we nearer come,
>   Kind words are said of friends and home,
> And soon, too soon, we part with pain,
>   To sail o'er silent seas again.

On the clear horizon could be seen a ship, which proved to be our staunch old friend, the *Finance*, on her way out to Brazil, heading nearly for us. Our course was at once changed, so as to cross her bows. She rose rapidly, hull up, showing her lines of unmistakable beauty, the Stars and Stripes waving over all. They on board the great ship soon descried our little boat, and gave sign by a deep whistle that came rumbling over the sea, telling us that we were recognized. A few moments later and the engines stopped. Then came the hearty hail, "Do you want assistance?" Our answer, "No" brought cheer on cheer from the steamer's deck, while the *Liberdade* bowed and courtesied to her old acquaintance, the superior ship. Captain Baker, meanwhile, not forgetting a sailor's most highly prized luxury, had ordered in the slings a barrel of potatoes—new from home! Then dump they came, in a jiffy, into the canoe, giving her a settle in the water of some inches. Other fresh provisions were handed us, also some books and late papers. J. Aspinwill Hodge, D.D., on a tour of inspection in the interest of the Presbyterian Mission in Brazil—on deck here with his camera—got an excellent photograph of the canoe.†

One gentleman passed us a bottle of wine, on the label of which was written the name of an old acquaintance, a merchant of Rio. We pledged Mr. Gudgeon and all his fellow passengers in that wine, and had some left long after, to the health of the captain of the ship, and his crew. There was but little time for words, so the compliments passed were brief. The ample plates in the sides of the *Finance,* inspiring confidence in American thoroughness and build, we had hardly time to scan, when her shrill whistle said "good-bye," and moving proudly on, the great ship was soon out of sight, while the little boat, filling away on the starboard tack, sailed on toward home, perfumed with the interchange of a friendly greeting, tinged though with a palpable lonesomeness. Two days after this pleasant meeting, the Port of Pernambuco was reached.

Tumbling in before a fresh "trade" wind that in the evening had sprung up, accompanied with long, rolling seas, our canoe came nicely round the point between lighted reef and painted buoy. Spray from the break-ers on the reef opportunely wetting her sails gave them a flat surface to the wind as we came close haul.

The channel leading up the harbour was not strange to us, so we sailed confidently along the lee of the wonderful wall made by worms, to which alone Pernambuco is indebted for its excellent harbour; which, extending also along a great stretch of the coast, protects Brazil from the encroach-ment of the sea.

At 8 p.m. we came to in a snug berth near the *Alfandega,* and early next morning received the official visit from the polite port officers.

Time from Bahia, five days; distance sailed, 390 miles.

Pernambuco, the principal town of a large and wealthy province of the

---

† We had the pleasure of meeting this gentleman again on the voyage at Barbadoes, again at New London, and finally with delight we heard him lecture on his travels, at Newport, and saw there produced on the wall the very picture of the *Liberdade* taken by the doctor on the great ocean.

same name, is a thriving place, sending out valuable cargoes, principally of sugar and cotton. I had loaded costly cargoes here, times gone by. I met my old merchant again this time, but could not carry his goods on the *Liberdade*. However, fruits from his orchards and a run among the trees refreshed my crew, and prepared them for the coming voyage to Barbadoes, which was made with expedition.

From Pernambuco we experienced a strong current in our favour, with, sometimes, a confused cross sea that washed over us considerably. But the swift current sweeping along through it all made compensation for discomforts of motion, though our "ups and downs" were many. Along this part of the coast (from Pernambuco to the Amazon), if one day should be fine, three stormy ones would follow, but the gale was always fair, carrying us forward at a goodly rate.

Along about half way from Cape St. Roque to the Amazon, the wind which had been blowing hard for two days, from E.S.E., and raising lively waves all about, increased to a gale that knocked up seas, washing over the little craft more than ever. The thing was becoming monotonous and tiresome; for a change, therefore, I ran in toward the land, so as to avoid the ugly cross sea farther out in the current. This course was a mistaken one; we had not sailed far on it when a sudden rise of the canoe, followed by an unusually long run down on the slope of a roller, told us of a danger that we hardly dared to think of, then a mighty comber broke, but, as Providence willed, broke short of the canoe, which under shortened sail was then scudding very fast.

We were on a shoal, and the sea was breaking from the bottom! The second great roller came on, towering up, up, up, until nothing longer could support the mountain of water, and it seemed only to pause before its fall to take aim and surely gather us up in its sweeping fury.

I put the helm a-lee; there was nothing else to do but this, and say prayers. The helm hard down, brought the canoe round, bows to the danger, while in breathless anxiety we prepared to meet the result as best we could. Before we could say "Save us, or we perish," the sea broke over with terrific force and passed on, leaving us trembling in His hand, more palpably helpless than ever before. Other great waves came madly on, leaping toward destruction; how they bellowed over the shoal! I could smell the slimy bottom of the sea, when they broke! I could tast the salty sand!

In this perilous situation, buried sometimes in the foaming breakers, and at times tossed like a reed on the crest of the waves, we struggled with might and main at the helm and the sheets, easing her up or forcing her ahead with care, gaining little by little toward deep water, till at last she came out of the danger, shook her feathers like a sea-bird, and rode on waves less perilous. Then we had time and courage to look back, but not till then.

And what a sight we beheld! The horizon was illumined with phosphorescent light from the breakers just passed through. The rainstorm which had obscured the coast was so cleared away now that we could see the whole field of danger behind us. One spot in particular, the place where the breakers dashed over a rock which appeared awash, in the glare flashed up a shaft of light that reached to the heavens.

This was the greatest danger we had yet encountered. The elasticity of our canoe, not its bulk, saved it from destruction. Her light, springy timbers and buoyant bamboo guards brought her upright again and again through the fierce breakers. We were astonished at the feats of wonder of our brave little craft.

Fatigued and worn with anxiety, when clear of the shoal we hauled to under close reefs, heading off shore, and all hands lay down to rest till daylight. Then, squaring away again, we set what sail the canoe could carry, scudding before it, for the wind was still in our favour, though blowing very hard. Nevertheless the weather seemed fine and pleasant at this stage of our own pleased feelings. Any weather that one's craft can live in, after escaping a lee shore, is pleasant weather—though some may be pleasanter than other.

What we most wished for, after this thrilling experience, was sea room, fair wind, and plenty of it. That these without stint would suit us best, was agreed on all hands. Accordingly then I shaped the course seaward, clearing well all the dangers of the land.

The fierce tropical storm of the last few days turned gradually into mild trade-winds, and our cedar canoe skipped nimbly once more over tranquil seas. Our own agitation, too, had gone down and we sailed on unruffled by care. Gentle winds carried us on over kindly waves, and we were fain to count fair days ahead, leaving all thoughts of stormy ones behind. In this hopeful mood we sailed for many days, our spirits never lowering, but often rising higher out of the miserable condition which we had fallen into through misfortunes on the foreign shore. When a star came out, it came as a friend, and one that had been seen by friends of old. When all the stars shone out, the hour at sea was cheerful, bright, and joyous. Welby saw, or had in the mind's-eye, a day like many that we experienced in the soft, clear "trades" on this voyage, when writing the pretty lines:—

> The twilight hours like birds flew by,
>   As lightly and as free,
> Ten thousand stars were in the sky,
>   Ten thousand on the sea.
>
> For every rippling, dancing wave,
>   That leaped upon the air,
> Had caught a star in its embrace,
>   And held it trembling there.

"The days pass, and our ship flies fast upon her way."

For several days while sailing near the line we saw the constellations of both hemispheres, but heading north, we left those of the south at last, with the Southern Cross—most beautiful in all the heavens—to watch over a friend.

Leaving these familiar southern stars and sailing toward constellations in the north, we hoist all sail to the cheery breeze which carries us on.

In this pleasant state of sailing with our friends all about us, we stood on and on, never doubting once our pilot or our ship.

A phantom of the stately *Aquidneck*[3] appeared one night, sweeping by with crowning skysails set, that fairly brushed the stars. No apparition could have affected us more than the sight of this floating beauty, so like the *Aquidneck,* gliding swiftly and quietly by, from her mission to some foreign land—she, too, was homeward bound!

This incident of the *Aquidneck's* ghost, as it appeared to us, passing at midnight on the sea, left a pang of lonesomeness for a while.

But a carrier dove came next day, and perched upon the mast, as if to tell that we had yet a friend! Welcome harbinger of good! you bring us thoughts of angels.

The lovely visitor remained with us two days, off and on, but left for good on the third, when we reached away from Avis Island, to which, maybe, it was bound. Coming as it did from the east, and flying west toward the island when it left, bore out the idea of the lay of sweet singer Kingsley's "Last Buccaneer."

> If I might but be a sea dove, I'd fly across the main
> To the pleasant Isle of Avis, to look at it once again.

The old Buccaneer, it may have been, but we regarded it as the little bird, which most likely it was, that sits up aloft to look out for poor "Jack."†

A moth, blown to our boat on the ocean, found shelter and a welcome there. The dove we secretly worshipped.

With utmost confidence in our little craft, inspired by many thrilling events, we now carried sail, blow high, blow low, till at times she reeled along with a bone in her mouth quite to the mind of her mariners. Think-

---

† There's a sweet little cherub that sits up aloft,
  To look out for a berth for poor Jack.
                    —*Dibdin's Poems.*

---

[3] The boat the Slocums sailed down to South America, and which was wrecked there.

ing one day that she might carry more sail on the mast already bending hopefully forward, and acting upon the liberal thought of sail, we made a wide mistake, for the mainmast went by the board, under the extra press and the foremast tripped over the bows. Then spars, booms, and sails swung alongside like the broken wings of a bird, but were grappled, however, and brought aboard without much loss of time. The broken mast was then secured and strengthened by "fishes" or splints after the manner in which doctors fish a broken limb.

Both of the masts were very soon refitted and again made to carry sail, all they could stand; and we were again bowling along as before. We made that day a hundred and seventy-five miles, one of our best days' work.

I protest here that my wife should not have cried "More sail! more sail!" when as it has been seen the canoe had on all the sail that she could carry. Nothing further happened to change the usual daily events until we reached Barbadoes. Flying-fish on the wing striking our sails, at night, often fell on deck, affording us many a toothsome fry. This happened daily, while sailing throughout the trade-wind regions. To be hit by one of these fish on the wing, which sometimes occurs, is no light matter, especially if the blow be on the face, as it may cause a bad bruise or even a black eye. The head of the flying-fish being rather hard makes it in fact a might slugger to be dreaded. They never come aboard in the daylight. The swift darting bill-fish, too, is a danger to be avoided in the tropics at night. They are met with mostly in the Pacific Ocean; therefore South Sea Islanders are loath to voyage during the "bill-fish season."

As to the flight of these fishes, I would estimate that of the flying-fish as not exceeding fifteen feet in height, or five hundred yards of distance, often not half so much.

Bill-fish, darting like an arrow from a bow, have, fortunately for sailors, not the power or do not rise much above the level of the waves, and cannot dart further, say, than two hundred and fifty feet, according to the day for jumping. Of the many swift fish in the sea, the dolphin, perhaps, is the most marvellous. Its oft-told beauty, too, is indeed remarkable. A few of these fleet racers were captured, on the voyage, but were found tough and rank; notwithstanding some eulogy on them by other epicures, we threw the mess away. Those hooked by my crew were perhaps the tyrrhena pirates "turned into dolphins" in the days of yore.

On the 19th day from Pernambuco, early in the morning, we made Barbadoes away in the West. First, the blue, fertile hills, then green fields came into view, studded with many white buildings between sentries of giant wind-mills as old nearly as the hills. Barbadoes is the most pleasant island in the Antilles; to sail round its green fringe of coral sea is simply charming. We stood in to the coast, well to windward, sailing close in with the breakers so as to take in a view of the whole delightful panorama as we sailed along. By noon we rounded the south point of the island and shot into Carlysle Bay, completing the run from Pernambuco exactly in nineteen days. This was considerably more than a hundred miles a day. . . .

RICHARD HENRY DANA, JR.

(1815–1882)

From *Two Years Before the Mast*

As a young man at Harvard, Dana was afflicted with measles so badly that it affected his sight and he was forced to drop out of school. The son of a poet and literary critic who founded the North American Review, Dana came from a long line of New England intellectuals, and he was at university to become a lawyer. When in the hopes of curing his illness he impulsively signed up with the crew of a merchant vessel, he had no experience whatsoever of the sea or of adventure. The Pilgrim set sail from Boston on August 14, 1834, bound for California via Cape Horn. The two-year voyage turned out to be the most dramatic and defining chapter of Dana's life.

Life aboard the Pilgrim would prove to be a tough initiation to seamanship. The crew set anchor for the first time 103 days into the journey, having sailed day and night from New England to Chile. Their captain was a demonic figure who enjoyed flogging and "hazing" his men regularly and at random. In fact, Dana was so appalled by the injustice of Captain Thompson's actions that he made a vow to return home and continue his study of law so that he could try and relieve the

harsh conditions on board American ships. Two Years Before the Mast
*was published in part as an exposé, and yet it is consistently lyrical and
entertaining, rich with detailed observations about sailing and life at
sea. An instant success when it was first published, the book has
remained one of the finest examples of nautical literature for well over a
century.*

The following has the Pilgrim *rounding Cape Horn on the return
voyage and coming in full contact with the Cape's notorious weather.*

In our first attempt to double the Cape, when we came up to the latitude of it, we were nearly seventeen hundred miles to the westward, but,
in running for the Straits of Magellan, we stood so far to the eastward
that we made our second attempt at a distance of not more than four or
five hundred miles; and we had great hopes, by this means, to run clear
of the ice; thinking that the easterly gales, which had prevailed for a long
time, would have driven it to the westward. With the wind about two
points free, the yards braced in a little, and two close-reefed topsails and a
reefed foresail on the ship, we made great way toward the southward;
and almost every watch, when we came on deck, the air seemed to grow
colder, and the sea to run higher. Still we saw no ice, and had great hopes
of going clear of it altogether, when, one afternoon, about three o'clock,
while we were taking a *siesta* during our watch below, "All hands!" was
called in a loud and fearful voice. "Tumble up here, men!—tumble up!—
don't stop for your clothes—before we're upon it!" We sprang out of our
berths and hurried upon deck. The loud, sharp voice of the captain was
heard giving orders, as though for life or death, and we ran aft to the
braces, not waiting to look ahead, for not a moment was to be lost. The
helm was hard up, the after yards shaking, and the ship in the act of
wearing. Slowly, with the stiff ropes and iced rigging, we swung the yards
round, everything coming hard and with a creaking and rending sound,
like pulling up a plank which has been frozen into the ice. The ship wore
round fairly, the yards were steadied, and we stood off on the other tack,

leaving behind us, directly under our larboard quarter, a large ice island, peering out of the mist, and reaching high above our tops; while astern, and on either side of the island, large tracts of field-ice were dimly seen, heaving and rolling in the sea. We were now safe, and standing to the northward; but, in a few minutes more, had it not been for the sharp lookout of the watch, we should have been fairly upon the ice, and left our ship's old bones adrift in the Southern Ocean. After standing to the northward a few hours, we wore ship, and, the wind having hauled, we stood to the southward and eastward. All night long a bright lookout was kept from every part of the deck; and whenever ice was seen on the one bow or the other the helm was shifted and the yards braced, and, by quick working of the ship, she was kept clear. The accustomed cry of "Ice ahead!"—"Ice on the lee bow!"—"Another island!" in the same tones, and with the same orders following them, seemed to bring us directly back to our old position of the week before. During our watch on deck, which was from twelve to four, the wind came out ahead, with a pelting storm of hail and sleet, and we lay hove-to, under a close-reefed fore topsail, the whole watch. During the next watch it fell calm with a drenching rain until day-break, when the wind came out to the westward, and the weather cleared up, and showed us the whole ocean, in the course which we should have steered, had it not been for the head wind and calm, completely blocked up with ice. Here, then, our progress was stopped, and we wore ship, and once more stood to the northward and eastward; not for the Straits of Magellan, but to make another attempt to double the Cape, still farther to the eastward; for the captain was determined to get round if perseverance could do it, and the third time, he said, never failed.

With a fair wind we soon ran clear of the field-ice, and by noon had only the stray islands floating far and near upon the ocean. The sun was out bright, the sea of a deep blue, fringed with the white foam of the waves, which ran high before a strong southwester; our solitary ship tore on through the open water as though glad to be out of her confinement; and the ice islands lay scattered here and there, of various sizes and shapes, reflecting the bright rays of the sun, and drifting slowly north-ward before the gale. It was a contrast to much that we had lately seen, and a spectacle not only of beauty, but of life; for it required but little fancy to imagine these islands to be animate masses which had broken loose from the "thrilling regions of thick-ribbed ice," and were working their way, by wind and current, some alone, and some in fleets, to milder climes. No pencil has ever yet given anything like the true effect of an iceberg. In a picture, they are huge, uncouth masses, stuck in the sea, while their chief beauty and grandeur—their slow, stately motion, the whirling of the snow about their summits, and the fearful groaning and cracking of their parts—the picture cannot give. This is the large ice-berg,—while the small and distant islands, floating on the smooth sea, in the light of a clear dáy, look like little floating fairy isles of sapphire.

From a northeast course we gradually hauled to the eastward, and after sailing about two hundred miles, which brought us as near to the western coast of Terra del Fuego as was safe, and having lost sight of the ice altogether,—for the third time we put the ship's head to the southward, to try the passage of the Cape. The weather continued clear and cold, with a strong gale from the westward; and we were fast getting up with the latitude of the Cape, with a prospect of soon being round. One fine afternoon, a man who had gone into the fore-top to shift the rolling tackles sung out at the top of his voice, and with evident glee, "Sail ho!" Neither land nor sail had we seen since leaving San Diego; and only those who have traversed the length of a whole ocean alone can imagine what an excitement such an announcement produced on board. "Sail ho!" shouted the cook, jumping out of his galley; "Sail ho!" shouted a man, throwing back the slide of the scuttle, to the watch below, who were soon out of their berths and on deck; and "Sail ho!" shouted the captain down the companion-way to the passenger in the cabin. Beside the pleasure of seeing a ship and human beings in so desolate a place, it was important for us to speak a vessel, to learn whether there was ice to the eastward, and to ascertain the longitude; for we had no chronometer, and had been drifting about so long that we had nearly lost our reckoning; and opportunities for lunar observations are not frequent or sure in such a place as Cape Horn. For these various reasons the excitement in our little community was running high, and conjectures were made, and everything thought of for which the captain would hail, when the man aloft sung out—"Another sail, large on the weather bow!" This was a little odd, but so much the better, and did not shake our faith in their being sails. At length the man in the top hailed, and said he believed it was land, after all. "Land in your eye!" said the mate, who was looking through the telescope; "they are ice islands, if I can see a hole through a ladder"; and a few moments showed the mate to be right; and all our expectations fled; and instead of what we most wished to see we had what we most dreaded, and what we hoped we had seen the last of. We soon, however, left these astern, having passed within about two miles of them, and at sundown the horizon was clear in all directions.

Having a fine wind, we were soon up with and passed the latitude of the Cape, and, having stood far enough to the southward to give it a wide berth, we began to stand to the eastward, with a good prospect of being round and steering to the northward, on the other side, in a very few days. But ill luck seemed to have lighted upon us. Not four hours had we been standing on in this course before it fell dead calm, and in half an hour it clouded up, a few straggling blasts, with spits of snow and sleet, came from the eastward, and in an hour more we lay hove-to under a close-reefed main topsail, drifting bodily off to leeward before the fiercest storm that we had yet felt, blowing dead ahead, from the eastward. It seemed as though the genius of the place had been roused at finding that we had nearly slipped through his fingers, and had come down upon us with tenfold fury. The sailors said that every blast, as it shook the shrouds, and whistled through the rigging, said to the old ship, "No, you don't!"—"No, you don't!"

For eight days we lay drifting about in this manner. Sometimes—generally towards noon—it fell calm; once or twice a round copper ball showed itself for a few moments in the place where the sun ought to have been, and a puff or two came from the westward, giving some hope that a fair wind had come at last. During the first two days we made sail for these puffs, shaking the reefs out of the topsails and boarding the tacks of the courses; but finding that it only made work for us when the gale set in again, it was soon given up, and we lay-to under our close-reefs. We had less snow and hail than when we were farther to the westward, but we had an abundance of what is worse to a sailor in cold weather,—drenching rain. Snow is blinding, and very bad when coming upon a coast, but, for genuine discomfort, give me rain with freezing weather. A snowstorm is exciting, and it does not wet through the clothes (a fact important to a sailor); but a constant rain there is no escaping from. It wets to the skin, and makes all protection vain. We had long ago run through all our dry clothes, and as sailors have no other way of drying them than by the sun, we had nothing to do but to put on those which were the least wet. At the end of each watch, when we came below, we took off our clothes and wrung them out; two taking hold of a pair of trousers, one at each end,—and jackets in the same way. Stockings, mittens, and all, were wrung out also, and then hung up to drain and chafe dry against the bulk-heads. Then, feeling of all our clothes, we picked out those which were the least wet, and put them on, so as to be ready for a call, and turned-in, covered ourselves up with blankets, and slept until three knocks on the scuttle and the dismal sound of "All Starbowlines ahoy! Eight bells, there below! Do you hear the news?" drawled out from on deck, and the sulky answer of "Aye, aye!" from below, sent us up again.

On deck all was dark, and either a dead calm, with the rain pouring steadily down, or, more generally, a violent gale dead ahead, with rain pelting horizontally, and occasional variations of hail and sleet; decks afloat with water swashing from side to side, and constantly wet feet, for boots could not be wrung out like drawers, and no composition could stand the constant soaking. In fact, wet and cold feet are inevitable in such weather, and are not the least of those items which go to make up the grand total of the discomforts of a winter passage round Cape Horn. Few words were spoken between the watches as they shifted; the wheel was relieved, the mate took his place on the quarter-deck, the lookouts in the bows; and each man had his narrow space to walk fore and aft in, or rather to swing himself forward and back in, from one belaying-pin to another, for the decks were too slippery with ice and water to allow of much walking. To make a walk, which is absolutely necessary to pass away the time, one of us hit upon the expedient of sanding the decks; and afterwards, whenever the rain was not so violent as to wash it off, the weather-side of the quarter-deck, and a part of the waist and forecastle were sprinkled with the sand which we had on board for holystoning,[1] and thus we made a good promenade, where we walked fore and aft, two and two, hour after hour, in our long, dull, and comfortless watches. The bells seemed to be an hour or two apart, instead of half an hour, and an age to elapse before the

---

[1] Scrubbing the decks with holystone, a soft sandstone.

welcome sound of eight bells. The sole object was to make the time pass on. Any change was sought for which would break the monotony of the time; and even the two hours' trick at the wheel, which came round to us in turn, once in every other watch, was looked upon as a relief. The never-failing resource of long yarns, which eke out many a watch, seemed to have failed us now; for we had been so long together that we had heard each other's stories told over and over again till we had them by heart; each one knew the whole history of each of the others, and we were fairly and literally talked out. Singing and joking we were in no humor for; and, in fact, any sound of mirth or laughter would have struck strangely upon our ears, and would not have been tolerated any more than whistling or a wind instrument. The last resort, that of speculating upon the future, seemed now to fail us; for our discouraging situation, and the danger we were really in (as we expected every day to find ourselves drifted back among the ice), "clapped a stopper" upon all that. From saying "*when* we get home," we began insensibly to alter it to "*if* we get home," and at last the subject was dropped by a tacit consent.

In this state of things, a new light was struck out, and a new field opened, by a change in the watch. One of our watch was laid up for two or three days by a bad hand (for in cold weather the least cut or bruise ripens into a sore), and his place was supplied by the carpenter. This was a windfall, and there was a contest who should have the carpenter to walk with him. As "Chips" was a man of some little education, and he and I had had a good deal of intercourse with each other, he fell in with me in my walk. He was a Fin, but spoke English well, and gave me long accounts of his country,—the customs, the trade, the towns, what little he knew of the government (I found he was no friend of Russia), his voyages, his first arrival in America, his marriage and courtship; he had married a country-woman of his, a dress-maker, whom he met with in Boston. I had very little to tell him of my quiet, sedentary life at home; and in spite of our best efforts, which had protracted these yarns through five or six watches, we fairly talked each other out, and I turned him over to another man in the watch, and put myself upon my own resources.

I commenced a deliberate system of time-killing, which united some profit with a cheering up of the heavy hours. As soon as I came on deck, and took my place and regular walk, I began with repeating over to myself in regular order a string of matters which I had in my memory,— the multiplication table and the tables of weights and measures; the Kanaka numerals; then the States of the Union, with their capitals; the counties of England, with their shire towns, and the kings of England in their order, and other things. This carried me through my facts, and, being repeated deliberately, with long intervals, often eked out the first two bells. Then came the Ten Commandments, the thirty-ninth chapter of Job, and a few other passages from Scripture. The next in the order, which I seldom varied from, came Cowper's Castaway, which was a great favorite with me; its solemn measure and gloomy character, as well as the incident it was founded upon, making it well suited to a lonely watch at sea. Then his lines to Mary, his address to the Jackdaw, and a short extract from Table Talk (I abounded in Cowper, for I happened to have a volume of his poems in my chest); "Ille et nefasto" from Horace, and Goethe's Erl König. After I had got through these, I allowed myself a more general range among everything that I could remember, both in prose and verse. In this way, with an occasional break by relieving the wheel, heaving the log, and going to the scuttle-butt for a drink of water, the longest watch was passed away; and I was so regular in my silent recitations that, if there was no interruption by ship's duty, I could tell very nearly the number of bells by my progress.

Our watches below were no more varied than the watch on deck. All washing, sewing, and reading was given up, and we did nothing but eat, sleep, and stand our watch, leading what might be called a Cape Horn life. The forecastle was too uncomfortable to sit up in; and whenever we were below, we were in our berths. To prevent the rain and the sea-water which broke over the bows from washing down, we were obliged to keep the scuttle closed, so that the forecastle was nearly air-tight. In this little, wet, leaky hole, we were all quartered, in an atmosphere so bad that our lamp, which swung in the middle from the beams, sometimes actually burned blue, with a large circle of foul air about it. Still, I was never in better health than after three weeks of this life. I gained a great deal of flesh, and we all ate like horses. At every watch when we came below, before turning in, the bread barge and beef kid were overhauled. Each man drank his quart of hot tea night and morning, and glad enough we were to get it; for no nectar and ambrosia were sweeter to the lazy immortals than was a pot of hot tea, a hard biscuit, and a slice of cold salt beef to us after a watch on deck. To be sure, we were mere animals, and, had this life lasted a year instead of a month, we should have been little better than the ropes in the ship. Not a razor, nor a brush, nor a drop of water, except the rain and the spray, had come near us all the time; for we were on an allowance of fresh water; and who would strip and wash himself in salt water on deck, in the snow and ice, with the thermometer at zero?

After about eight days of constant easterly gales, the wind hauled occasionally a little to the southward, and blew hard, which, as we were well to the southward, allowed us to brace in a little, and stand on under all the sail we could carry. These turns lasted but a short while, and sooner or later it set in again from the old quarter; yet at each time we made something, and were gradually edging along to the eastward. One night, after one of these shifts of the wind, and when all hands had been up a great part of the time, our watch was left on deck, with the mainsail hanging in the buntlines, ready to be set if necessary. It came on to blow worse and worse, with hail and snow beating like so many furies upon the ship, it being as dark and thick as night could make it. The mainsail was blowing and slatting with a noise like thunder, when the captain came on deck and ordered it to be furled. The mate was about to call all hands, when the captain stopped him, and said that the men would be beaten out if they were called up so often; that, as our watch must stay on deck, it might as well be doing that as anything else. Accordingly, we went upon the yard; and never shall I forget that piece of work. Our watch had been so reduced by sickness, and by some having been left in California, that, with one man at the wheel, we had only the third mate and three beside myself to go aloft; so that at most we could only attempt to furl one yard-arm at a time. We manned the weather yard-arm, and set to work to make a furl of it. Our lower masts being short, and our yards very square, the sail had a head of nearly fifty feet, and a short leech, made still shorter by the deep reef which was in it, which brought the clew away out on the quarters of the yard, and made a bunt nearly as square as the mizzen royal yard. Beside this difficulty, the yard over which we lay was cased with ice, the gaskets and rope of the foot and leech of the sail as stiff and hard as a piece of leather hose, and the sail itself about as pliable as though it had been made of sheets of sheathing copper. It blew a perfect hurricane, with alternate blasts of snow, hail, and rain. We had no *fist* the sail with bare hands. No one could trust himself to mittens, for if he slipped he was a gone man. All the boats were hoisted in on deck, and there was nothing to be lowered for him. We had need of every finger God had given us. Several times we got the sail upon the yard, but it blew away again before we could secure it. It required men to lie over the yard to pass each turn of the gaskets, and when they were passed it was almost impossible to knot them so that they would hold. Frequently we were obliged to leave off altogether and take to beating our hands upon the sail to keep them from freezing. After some time—which seemed forever—we got the weather side stowed after a fashion, and went over to leeward for another trial. This was still worse, for the body of the sail had been blown over to leeward, and, as the yard was a-cock-bill by the lying over of the vessel, we had to light it all up to windward. When the yard-arms were furled, the bunt was all adrift again, which made more work for us. We got all secure at last, but we had been nearly an hour and a half upon the yard, and it seemed an age. It had just struck five bells when we went up, and eight were struck soon after we came down. This may seem slow work; but considering the state of everything, and that we had only five men to a sail with just half as many square yards of canvas in it as the mainsail of the *Independence,* sixty-gun ship, which musters seven hundred men at her quarters, it is not wonderful that we were no quicker about it. We were glad enough to get on deck, and still more to go below. The oldest sailor in the watch said, as he went down, "I shall never forget that main yard; it beats all my going a-fishing. Fun is fun, but furling one yard-arm of a course at a time, off Cape Horn, is no better than man-killing."

During the greater part of the next two days, the wind was pretty steady from the southward. We had evidently made great progress, and had good hope of being soon up with the Cape, if we were not there already. We could put but little confidence in our reckoning, as there had been no opportunities for an observation, and we had drifted too much to allow of our dead reckoning being anywhere near the mark. If it would clear off enough to give a chance for an observation, or if we could make land, we should know where we were; and upon these, and the chances of falling in with a sail from the eastward, we depended almost entirely.

Friday, July 22d. This day we had a steady gale from the southward, and stood on under close sail, with the yards eased a little by the weather braces, the clouds lifting a little, and showing signs of breaking away. In the afternoon, I was below with Mr. Hatch, the third mate, and two others, filling the bread locker in the steerage from the casks, when a bright gleam of sunshine broke out and shone down the companionway, and through the skylight, lighting up everything below, and sending a warm glow through the hearts of all. It was a sight we had not seen for weeks,—an omen, a godsend. Even the roughest and hardest face acknowledged its influence. Just at that moment we heard a loud shout from all parts of the deck, and the mate called out down the companionway to the captain, who was sitting in the cabin. What he said we could not distinguish, but the captain kicked over his chair, and was on deck at one jump. We could not tell what it was; and, anxious as we were to know, the discipline of the ship would not allow of our leaving our places. Yet, as we were not called, we knew there was no danger. We hurried to get through with our job, when, seeing the steward's black face peering out of the pantry, Mr. Hatch hailed him to know what was the matter. "Lan' o, to be sure, sir! No you hear 'em sing out, 'Lan' o?' De cap'em say 'im Cape Horn!"

This gave us a new start, and we were soon through our work and on deck; and there lay the land, fair upon the larboard beam, and slowly edging away upon the quarter. All hands were busy looking at it,—the captain and mates from the quarter-deck, the cook from his galley, and the sailors from the forecastle; and even Mr. Nuttall, the passenger, who had kept in his shell for nearly a month, and hardly been seen by anybody, and whom we had almost forgotten was on board, came out like a butterfly, and was hopping round as bright as a bird.

The land was the island of Staten Land, just to the eastward of Cape Horn; and a more desolate-looking spot I never wish to set eyes upon,—bare, broken, and girt with rocks and ice, with here and there, between the rocks and broken hillocks, a little stunted vegetation of shrubs. It was a place well suited to stand at the junction of the two oceans, beyond the reach of human cultivation, and encounter the blasts and snows of a perpetual winter. Yet, dismal as it was, it was a pleasant sight to us; not only as being the first land we had seen, but because it told us that we had passed the Cape,—were in the Atlantic,—and that, with twenty-four hours of this breeze, we might bid defiance to the Southern Ocean. It told us, too, our latitude and longitude better than any observation; and the captain now knew where we were, as well as if we were off the end of Long Wharf.

In the general joy, Mr. Nuttall said he should like to go ashore upon the island and examine a spot which probably no human being had ever set foot upon; but the captain intimated that he would see the island, specimens and all, in—another place, before he would get out a boat or delay the ship one moment for him.

We left the land gradually astern; and at sundown had the Atlantic Ocean clear before us.

IT IS USUAL, in voyages round the Cape from the Pacific, to keep to the eastward of the Falkland Islands; but as there had now set in a strong, steady, and clear southwester, with every prospect of its lasting, and we had had enough of high latitudes, the captain determined to stand immediately to the northward, running inside the Falkland Islands. Accordingly, when the wheel was relieved at eight o'clock, the order was given to keep her due north, and all hands were turned up to square away the yards and make sail. In a moment the news ran through the ship that the captain was keeping her off, with her nose straight for Boston, and Cape Horn over her taffrail. It was a moment of enthusiasm. Every one was on the alert, and even the two sick men turned out to lend a hand at the halyards. The wind was now due southwest, and blowing a gale to which a vessel close hauled could have shown no more than a single close-reefed sail; but as we were going before it, we could carry on. Accordingly, hands were sent aloft, and a reef shaken out of the topsails, and the reefed foresail set. When we came to mast-head the topsail yards, with all hands at the halyards, we struck up "Cheerly, men," with a chorus which might have been heard half-way to Staten Land. Under her increased sail, the ship drove on through the water. Yet she could bear it well; and the captain sang out from the quarter-deck, "Another reef out of that fore topsail, and give it to her!" Two hands sprang aloft; the frozen reef-points and earings were cast adrift, the halyards manned, and the sail gave out her increased canvas to the gale. All hands were kept on deck to watch the effect of the change. It was as much as she could well carry, and with a heavy sea astern it took two men at the wheel to steer her. She flung the foam from her bows, the spray breaking aft as far as the gangway. She was going at a prodigious rate. Still everything held. Preventer braces were reeved and hauled taut, tackles got upon the back-stays, and everything done to keep all snug and strong. The captain walked the deck at a rapid stride, looked aloft at the sails, and then to windward; the mate stood in the gangway, rubbing his hands, and talking aloud to the ship, "Hurrah, old bucket! the Boston girls have got hold of the tow-rope!" and the like; and we were on the forecastle, looking to see how the spars stood it, and guessing the rate at which she was going, when the captain called out "Mr. Brown, get up the topmast studding-sail! What she can't carry she may drag!" The mate looked a moment; but he would let no one be before him in daring. He sprang forward. "Hurrah, men! rig out the topmast studding-sail boom! Lay aloft, and I'll send the rigging up to you!" We sprang aloft into the top; lowered a girt-line down, by which we hauled up the rigging; rove the tacks and halyards;

ran out the boom and lashed it fast, and sent down the lower halyards as a preventer. It was a clear starlight night, cold and blowing; but everybody worked with a will. Some, indeed, looked as though they thought the "old man" was mad, but no one said a word. We had had a new topmast studding-sail made with a reef in it,—a thing hardly ever heard of, and which the sailors had ridiculed a good deal, saying that when it was time to reef a studding-sail it was time to take it in. But we found a use for it now; for, there being a reef in the topsail, the studding-sail could not be set without one in it also. To be sure, a studding-sail with reefed topsails was rather a novelty; yet there was some reason in it, for if we carried that away we should lose only a sail and a boom; but a whole topsail might have carried away the mast and all.

While we were aloft the sail had been got out, bent to the yard, reefed, and ready for hoisting. Waiting for a good opportunity, the halyards were manned and the yard hoisted fairly up to the block; but when the mate came to shake the catspaw out of the downhaul, and we began to boom-end the sail, it shook the ship to her centre. The boom buckled up and bent like a whip-stick, and we looked every moment to see something go; but, being of the short, tough upland spruce, it bent like whalebone, and nothing could break it. The carpenter said it was the best stick he had ever seen. The strength of all hands soon brought the tack to the boom-end, and the sheet was trimmed down, and the preventer and the weather brace hauled taut to take off the strain. Every rope-yarn seemed stretched to the utmost, and every thread of canvas; and with this sail added to her, the ship sprang through the water like a thing possessed. The sail being nearly all forward, it lifted her out of the water, and she seemed actually to jump from sea to sea. From the time her keel was laid, she had never been so driven; and had it been life or death with every one of us, she could not have borne another stitch of canvas.

Finding that she would bear the sail, the hands were sent below, and our watch remained on deck. Two men at the wheel had as much as they could do to keep her within three points of her course, for she steered as wild as a young colt. The mate walked the deck, looking at the sails, and then over the side to see the foam fly by her,—slapping his hands upon his thighs and talking to the ship,—"Hurrah, you jade; you've got the scent!—you know where you're going!" And when she leaped over the seas, and almost out of the water, and trembled to her very keel, the spars and masts snapping and creaking,—"There she goes!—There she goes,— handsomely?—As long as she cracks she holds!"—while we stood with the rigging laid down fair for letting go, and ready to take in sail and clear away, if anything went. At four bells we hove the log, and she was going eleven knots fairly; and had it not been for the sea from aft which sent the chip home, and threw her continually off her course, the log would have shown her to have been going somewhat faster. I went to the wheel with a young fellow from the Kennebec, Jack Stewart, who was a good helmsman, and for two hours we had our hands full. A few minutes showed us that our monkey-jackets must come off; and, cold as it was, we stood in our shirt-sleeves in a perspiration, and were glad enough to have it eight bells, and the wheel relieved. We turned-in and slept as well as we could, though the sea made a constant roar under her bows, and washed over the forecastle like a small cataract.

At four o'clock we were called again. The same sail was still on the vessel, and the gale, if there was any change, had increased a little. No attempt was made to take the studding-sail in; and, indeed, it was too late now. If we had started anything toward taking it in, either tack or halyards, it would have blown to pieces, and carried something away with it. The only way now was to let everything stand, and if the gale went down, well and good; if not, something must go,—the weakest stick or rope first,—and then we could get it in. For more than an hour she was driven on at such a rate that she seemed to crowd the sea into a heap before her; and the water poured over the spritsail yard as it would over a dam. Toward daybreak the gale abated a little, and she was just beginning to go more easily along, relieved of the pressure, when Mr. Brown, determined to give her no respite, and depending upon the wind's subsiding as the sun rose, told us to get along the lower studding-sail. This was an immense sail, and held wind enough to last a Dutchman a week,—hove-to. It was soon ready, the boom topped up, preventer guys rove, and the idlers called up to man the halyards; yet such was still the force of the gale that we were nearly an hour setting the sail; carried away the out-haul in doing it, and came very near snapping off the swinging boom. No sooner was it set than the ship tore on again like one mad, and began to steer wilder than ever. The men at the wheel were puffing and blowing at their work, and the helm was going hard up and hard down, constantly. Add to this, the gale did not lessen as the day came on, but the sun rose in clouds. A sudden lurch threw the man from the weather wheel across the deck and against the side. The mate sprang to the wheel, and the man, regaining his feet, seized the spokes, and they hove the wheel up just in time to save the ship from broaching to, though as she came up the studding-sail boom stood at an angle of forty-five degrees. She had evidently more on her than she could bear; yet it was in vain to try to take it in,—the clew-line was not strong enough, and they were thinking of cutting away, when another wide yaw and a come-to snapped the guys, and the swinging boom came in with a crash against the lower rigging. The outhaul block gave way, and the topmast studding sail boom bent in a manner which I never before supposed a stick could bend. I had my eye on it when the guys parted, and it made one spring and buckled up so as to form nearly a half-circle, and sprang out again to its shape. The clew-line gave way at the first pull; the cleat to which the halyards were belayed was wrenched off, and the sail blew round the spritsail yard and head guys, which gave us a bad job to get it in. A half-hour served to clear all away, and she was suffered to drive on with her topmast studding-sail set, it being as much as she could stagger under.

During all this day and the next night we went on under the same sail, the gale blowing with undiminished violence; two men at the wheel all the time; watch and watch, and nothing to do but to steer and look out for the ship, and be blown along;—until the noon of the next day,—

Sunday, July 24th, when we were in lat. 50° 27' S., lon. 62° 13' W., hav-ing made four degrees of latitude in the last twenty-four hours. Being now to the northward of the Falkland Islands, the ship was kept off, northeast, for the equator; and with her head for the equator, and Cape Horn over her taffrail, she went gloriously on; every heave of the sea leaving the Cape astern, and every hour bringing us nearer to home and to warm weather. Many a time, when blocked up in the ice, with everything dismal and discouraging about us, had we said, if we were only fairly round, and standing north on the other side, we should ask for no more; and now we had it all, with a clear sea and as much wind as a sailor could pray for. If the best part of a voyage is the last part, surely we had all now that we could wish. Every one was in the highest spirits, and the ship seemed as glad as any of us at getting out of her confinement. At each change of the watch, those coming on deck asked those going below, "How does she go along?" and got, for answer, the rate, and the customary addition, "Aye! and the Boston girls have had hold of the tow-rope all the watch." Every day the sun rose higher in the horizon, and the nights grew shorter; and at coming on deck each morning there was a sensible change in the temperature. The ice, too, began to melt from off the rigging and spars, and, except a little which remained in the tops and round the hounds of the lower masts, was soon gone. As we left the gale behind us, the reefs were shaken out of the topsails, and sail made as fast as she could bear it; and every time all hands were sent to the halyards a song was called for, and we hoisted away with a will.

Sail after sail was added, as we drew into fine weather; and in one week after leaving Cape Horn, the long top-gallant-masts were got up, top-gallant and royal yards crossed, and the ship restored to her fair proportions.

The Southern Cross and the Magellan Clouds settled lower and lower in the horizon; and so great was our change of latitude that each succeeding night we sank some constellation in the south, and raised another in the northern horizon.

Sunday, July 31st. At noon we were in lat. 36° 41′ S., lon. 38° 08′ W.; having traversed the distance of two thousand miles, allowing for changes of course, in nine days. A thousand miles in four days and a half! This is equal to steam.

Soon after eight o'clock the appearance of the ship gave evidence that this was the first Sunday we had yet had in fine weather. As the sun came up clear, with the promise of a fair, warm day, and, as usual on Sunday, there was no work going on, all hands turned-to upon clearing out the forecastle. The wet and soiled clothes which had accumulated there during the past month were brought up on deck; the chests moved; brooms, buckets of water, swabs, scrubbing-brushes, and scrapers carried down and applied, until the forecastle floor was as white as chalk, and everything neat and in order. The bedding from the berths was then spread on deck, and dried and aired; the deck-tub filled with water; and a grand washing begun of all the clothes which were brought up. Shirts, frocks, drawers, trousers, jackets, stockings, of every shape and color, wet and dirty,—many of them mouldy from having been lying a long time wet in a foul corner,—these were all washed and scrubbed out, and finally towed overboard for half an hour; and then made fast in the rigging to dry. Wet boots and shoes were spread out to dry in sunny places on deck; and the whole ship looked like a back yard on a washing-day. After we had done with our clothes, we began upon our persons. A little fresh water, which we had saved from our allowance, was put in buckets, and, with soap and towels, we had what sailors call a fresh-water wash. The same bucket, to be sure, had to go through several hands, and was spoken for by one after another, but as we rinsed off in salt water, pure from the ocean, and the fresh was used only to start the accumulated grime and blackness of five weeks, it was held of little consequence. We soaped down and scrubbed one another with towels and pieces of canvas, stripping to it; and then, getting into the head, threw buckets of water upon each other. After this came shaving, and combing, and brushing; and when, having spent the first part of the day in this way we sat down on the forecastle, in the afternoon, with clean duck trousers and shirts on, washed, shaved, and combed, and looking a dozen shades lighter for it, reading, sewing, and talking at our ease, with a clear sky and warm sun over our heads, a steady breeze over the larboard quarter, studding-sails out alow and aloft, and all the flying kites abroad,—we felt that we had got back into the pleasantest part of a sailor's life. At sunset the clothes were all taken down from the rigging,—clean and dry,—and stowed neatly away in our chests; and our southwesters, thick boots, Guernsey frocks, and other accompaniments of bad weather, put out of the way, we hoped, for the rest of the voyage, as we expected to come upon the coast early in the autumn.

Notwithstanding all that has been said about the beauty of a ship under full sail, there are very few who have ever seen a ship, literally, under all her sail. A ship coming in or going out of port, with her ordinary sails, and perhaps two or three studding-sails, is commonly said to be under full sail; but a ship never has all her sail upon her, except when she has a light, steady breeze, very nearly, but not quite, dead aft, and so regular that it can be trusted, and is likely to last for some time. Then, with all her sails, light and heavy, and studding-sails, on each side, alow and aloft, she is the most glorious moving object in the world. Such a sight very few, even some who have been at sea a good deal, have ever beheld; for from the deck of your own vessel you cannot see her, as you would a separate object.

One night, while we were in these tropics, I went out to the end of the flying-jib-boom upon some duty, and, having finished it, turned round, and lay over the boom for a long time, admiring the beauty of the sight before me. Being so far out from the deck, I could look at the ship as at a separate vessel; and there rose up from the water, supported only by the small black hull, a pyramid of canvas, spreading out far beyond the hull, and towering up almost, as it seemed in the indistinct night air, to the clouds. The sea was as still as an inland lake; the light trade-wind was gently and steadily breathing from astern; the dark blue sky was studded with the tropical stars; there was no sound but the rippling of the water under the stem; and the sails were spread out, wide and high,—the two lower studding-sails stretching on each side far beyond the deck; the top-mast studding-sails like wings to the topsails; the top-gallant studding-

sails spreading fearlessly out above them; still higher, the two royal stud-ding-sails, looking like two kites flying from the same string; and, highest of all, the little skysail, the apex of the pyramid, seeming actually to touch the stars, and to be out of reach of human hand. So quiet, too, was the sea, and so steady the breeze, that if these sails had been sculptured marble they could not have been more motionless. Not a ripple upon the surface of the canvas; not even a quivering of the extreme edges of the sail, so perfectly were they distended by the breeze. I was so lost in the sight that I forgot the presence of the man who came out with me, until he said (for he, too, rough old man-of-war's-man as he was, had been gazing at the show), half to himself, still looking at the marble sails,—"How quietly they do their work!"

FRANK THOMAS BULLEN

(1857–1915)

From *The Cruise of the* Cachalot

In 1876, out of work and kicking around coastal Massachusetts looking for his next post, nineteen-year-old Bullen—a Brit who ran away
to sea at the age of twelve—signed up with a captain whose details
about his business were hazy. Once on board, Bullen found himself
"booked for the sailor's horror—a cruise in a whaler." Although whaling's heyday had passed and conditions on board its vessels had
improved slightly, it still had a notorious reputation for its life of
extreme danger and brutal, messy toil. The Cachalot (an old word for
sperm whale) plied the seas for two years, coming back to Nantucket
with 300,000 barrels of oil and more than its share of stories: enraged
whales had splintered the tiny whaling boats with their jaws or tails,
the tyrannical captain was murdered by one of the crew, and several
men had drowned.

The Cruise of the Cachalot is an outrageous, captivating tale—one
of the all-time great reads of the era—which comes over more like fiction than fact. Bullen is the young kid who notices and comments
vividly on everything: the greenhorn crew and their harsh treatment by

Captain Slocum ("the debbil himself"), the hair-raising chases in tiny boats to spear the sperm whales, the ports of call, the light and moods and life of the sea. And though he had no education, his style combines a true storyteller's verve with the literary intellect of one who took with him an entire collection of Shakespeare, the only books on board besides the Bible.

Although he would be promoted to the prestigious position of spearsman later in the voyage, here Bullen describes his fear and innocence in his first encounter with a whale, as well as the gruesome work of cutting it up once killed.

Simultaneous ideas occurring to several people, or thought transference, whatever one likes to call the phenomenon, is too frequent an occurrence in most of our experience to occasion much surprise. Yet on the occasion to which I am about to refer, the matter was so very marked that few of us who took part in the day's proceedings are ever likely to forget it.

We were all gathered about the fo'lk'sle scuttle one evening, a few days after the gale referred to in the previous chapter, and the question of whale-fishing came up for discussion. Until that time, strange as it may seem, no word of this, the central idea of all our minds, had been mooted. Every man seemed to shun the subject, although we were in daily expectation of being called upon to take an active part in whale-fighting. Once the ice was broken, nearly all had something to say about it, and very nearly as many addle-headed opinions were ventilated as at a Colney Hatch debating society. For we none of us *knew* anything about it. I was appealed to continually to support this or that theory, but as far as whaling went I could only, like the rest of them, draw upon my imagination for details. How did a whale act, what were the first steps taken, what chance was there of being saved if your boat got smashed, and so on unto infinity. At last, getting very tired of this "Portugee Parliament" of all talkers and no listeners, I went aft to get a drink of water before turn-

ing in. The harpooners and other petty officers were grouped in the waist, earnestly discussing the pros and cons of attack upon whales. As I passed I heard the mate's harpooner say, "Feels like whale about. I bet a plug (of tobacco) we raise sperm whale to-morrow." Nobody took his bet, for it appeared that they were mostly of the same mind, and while I was drinking I heard the officers in dignified conclave talking over the same thing. It was Saturday evening, and while at home people were looking forward to a day's respite from work and care, I felt that the coming day, though never taken much notice of on board, was big with the probabilities of strife such as I at least had at present no idea of. So firmly was I possessed by the prevailing feeling.

The night was very quiet. A gentle breeze was blowing, and the sky was of the usual "Trade" character, that is, a dome of dark blue fringed at the horizon with peaceful cumulus clouds, almost motionless. I turned in at four a.m. from the middle watch and, as usual, slept like a babe. Suddenly I started wide awake, a long mournful sound sending a thrill to my very heart. As I listened breathlessly other sounds of the same character but in different tones joined in, human voices monotonously intoning in long drawn-out expirations the single word "bl-o-o-o-o-w." Then came a hurricane of noise overhead, and adjurations in no gentle language to the sleepers to "tumble up lively there, no skulking, sperm whales." At last, then, fulfilling all the presentiments of yesterday, the long dreaded moment had arrived. Happily there was no time for hesitation, in less than two minutes we were all on deck, and hurrying to our respective boats. There was no flurry or confusion, and except that orders were given more quietly than usual, with a manifest air of suppressed excitement, there was nothing to show that we were not going for an ordinary course of boat drill. The skipper was in the main crow's-nest with his binoculars. Presently he shouted, "Naow then, Mr. Count,[1] lower away soon's y'like. Small pod o'cows, an' one 'r two bulls layin' off to west'ard of 'em." Down went the boats into the water quietly enough, we all scrambled in and shoved off. A stroke or two of the oars were given to get clear of the ship, and one another, then oars were shipped and up went the sails. As I took my allotted place at the main-sheet, and the beautiful craft started off like some big bird, Mr. Count leant forward, saying

---

[1] The mate in charge of Bullen's whaling boat.

impressively to me, "Y'r a smart youngster, an' I've kinder took t'yer; but don't ye look ahead an' get gallied, 'r I'll knock ye stiff wi' th' tiller; y'hear me? N' don't ye dare to make thet sheet fast, 'r ye'll die so sudden y' won't know whar y'r hurted." I said as cheerfully as I could, "All right, sir," trying to look unconcerned, telling myself not to be a coward, and all sorts of things; but the cold truth is that I was scared almost to death because I didn't know what was coming. However, I did the best thing under the circumstances, obeyed orders and looked steadily astern, or up into the bronzed impassive face of my chief, who towered above me, scanning with eagle eyes the sea ahead. The other boats were coming flying along behind us, spreading wider apart as they came, while in the bows of each stood the harpooner with his right hand on his first iron, which lay ready, pointing over the bow in a raised fork of wood called the "crutch."

All of a sudden, at a motion of the chief's hand, the peak of our mainsail was dropped, and the boat swung up into the wind, laying "hove to," almost stationary. The centre-board was lowered to stop her drifting to leeward, although I cannot say it made much difference that ever I saw. *Now* what's the matter, I thought, when to my amazement the chief addressing me said, "Wonder why we've hauled up, don't ye?" "Yes, sir, I do," said I. "Wall," said he, "the fish hev sounded, an' 'ef we run over 'em, we've seen the last ov'em. So we wait awhile till they rise agin, 'n then we'll prob'ly git thar' 'r thareabouts before they sound agin." With this explanation I had to be content, although if it be no clearer to my readers than it then was to me, I shall have to explain myself more fully later on. Silently we lay, rocking lazily upon the gentle swell, no other word being spoken by any one. At last Louis, the harpooner, gently breathed "blo-o-o-w"; and there, sure enough, not half a mile away on the lee beam, was a little bushy cloud of steam apparently rising from the sea. At almost the same time as we kept away all the other boats did likewise, and just then, catching sight of the ship, the reason for this apparently concerted action was explained. At the main-mast head of the ship was a square blue flag, and the ensign at the peak was being dipped. These were signals well understood and promptly acted upon by those in charge of the boats, who were thus guided from a point of view at least one hundred feet above the sea.

"Stand up, Louey," the mate murmured softly. I only just stopped myself in time from turning my head to see why the order was given. Suddenly there was a bump, at the same moment the mate yelled, "Give't to him, Louey, give't to him!" and to me, "Haul that main sheet, naow haul, why don't ye?" I hauled it flat aft, and the boat shot up into the wind, rubbing sides as she did so with what to my troubled sight seemed an enormous mass of black india-rubber floating. As we *crawled* up into the wind, the whale went into convulsions befitting his size and energy. He raised a gigantic tail on high, threshing the water with deafening blows, rolling at the same time from side to side until the surrounding sea was white with froth. I felt in an agony lest we should be crushed under one of those fearful strokes, for Mr. Count appeared to be oblivious of possible danger, although we seemed to be now drifting back on to the writhing leviathan. In the agitated condition of the sea, it was a task of no ordinary difficulty to unship the tall mast, which was of course the first thing to be done. After a desperate struggle, and a narrow escape from falling overboard of one of the men, we got the long "stick," with the sail bundled around it, down and "fleeted" aft, where it was secured by the simple means of sticking the "heel" under the after thwart, two-thirds of the mast extending out over the stern. Meanwhile, we had certainly been in a position of the greatest danger, our immunity from damage being unquestionably due to anything but precaution taken to avoid it.

By the time the oars were handled, and the mate had exchanged places with the harpooner, our friend the enemy had "sounded," that is, he had gone below for a change of scene, marvelling no doubt what strange thing had befallen him. Agreeably to the accounts which I, like most boys, had read of the whale fishery, I looked for the rushing of the line round the loggerhead (a stout wooden post built into the boat aft),[2] to raise a cloud of smoke with occasional bursts of flame; so as it began

[2] The thin rope is being pulled out by the harpooned whale.

to slowly surge round the post, I timidly asked the harpooner whether I should throw any water on it. "Wot for?" growled he, as he took a couple more turns with it. Not knowing "what for," and hardly liking to quote my authorities here, I said no more, but waited events. "Hold him up, Louey, hold him up, cain't ye?" shouted the mate, and to my horror, down went the nose of the boat almost under water, while at the mate's order everybody scrambled aft into the elevated stern sheets.

The line sang quite a tune as it was grudgingly allowed to surge round the loggerhead, filling one with admiration at the strength shown by such a small rope. This sort of thing went on for about twenty minutes, in which time we quite emptied the large tub and began on the small one. As there was nothing whatever for us to do while this was going on, I had ample leisure for observing the little game that was being played about a quarter of a mile away. Mr. Cruce, the second mate, had got a whale and was doing his best to kill it; but he was severely handicapped by his crew, or rather had been, for two of them were now temporarily incapable of either good or harm. They had gone quite "batchy" with fright, requiring a not too gentle application of the tiller to their heads in order to keep them quiet. The remedy, if rough, was effectual, for "the subsequent proceedings interested them no more." Consequently his manœuvres were not so well or rapidly executed as he, doubtless, could have wished, although his energy in lancing that whale was something to admire and remember. Hatless, his shirt tail out of the waist of his trousers streaming behind him like a banner, he lunged and thrust at the whale alongside of him, as if possessed of a destroying devil, while his half articulate yells of rage and blasphemy were audible even to us.

Suddenly our boat fell backward from her "slantin-dicular" position with a jerk, and the mate immediately shouted, "Haul line, there! look lively, now! you—so on, etcetera, etcetera" (he seemed to invent new epithets on every occasion). The line came in hand over hand, and was coiled in a wide heap in the stern sheets, for silky as it was, it could not be expected in its wet state to lie very close. As it came flying in the mate kept a close gaze upon the water immediately beneath us, apparently for

the first glimpse of our antagonist. When the whale broke water, however, he was some distance off, and apparently as quiet as a lamb. Now,
had Mr. Count been a prudent or less ambitious man, our task would
doubtless have been an easy one, or comparatively so; but, being a little
over-grasping, he got us all into serious trouble. We were hauling up to
our whale in order to lance it, and the mate was standing, lance in hand,
only waiting to get near enough, when up comes a large whale right
alongside of our boat, so close, indeed, that I might have poked my finger
in his little eye, if I had chosen. The sight of that whale at liberty, and
calmly taking stock of us like that, was too much for the mate. He lifted
his lance and hurled it at the visitor, in whose broad flank it sank, like a
knife into butter, right up to the pole-hitches. The recipient disappeared
like a flash, but before one had time to think, there was an awful crash
beneath us, and the mate shot up into the air like a bomb from a mortar.
He came down in a sitting posture on the mast-thwart; but as he fell, the
whole framework of the boat collapsed like a derelict umbrella. Louis
quietly chopped the line and severed our connection with the other
whale, while in accordance with our instructions we drew each man his
oar across the boat and lashed it firmly down with a piece of line spliced
to each thwart for the purpose. This simple operation took but a minute,
but before it was completed we were all up to our necks in the sea. Still
in the boat, it is true, and therefore not in such danger of drowning as if
we were quite adrift; but, considering that the boat was reduced to a
mere bundle of loose planks, I, at any rate, was none too comfortable.
Now, had he known it, was the whale's golden opportunity; but he, poor
wretch, had had quite enough of our company, and cleared off without
any delay, wondering, no doubt, what fortunate accident had rid him of
our very unpleasant attentions.

I was assured that we were all as safe as if we were on board the ship,
to which I answered nothing; but, like Jack's parrot, I did some powerful
thinking. Every little wave that came along swept clean over our heads,
sometimes coming so suddenly as to cut a breath in half. If the wind
should increase—but no—I wouldn't face the possibility of such a dis-

agreeable thing. I was cool enough now in a double sense, for although we were in the tropics, we soon got thoroughly chilled.

By the position of the sun it must have been between ten a.m. and noon, and we, of the crew, had eaten nothing since the previous day at supper, when, as usual, the meal was very light. Therefore, I suppose we felt the chill sooner than the better-nourished mate and harpooner, who looked rather scornfully at our blue faces and chattering teeth.

In spite of all assurances to the contrary, I have not the least doubt in my own mind that a very little longer would have relieved us of *all* our burdens finally. Because the heave of the sea had so loosened the shattered planks upon which we stood that they were on the verge of falling all asunder. Had they done so we must have drowned, for we were cramped and stiff with cold and our constrained position. However, unknown to us, a bright look-out upon our movements had been kept from the crow's-nest the whole time. We should have been relieved long before, but that the whale killed by the second mate was being secured,

and another boat, the fourth mate's, being picked up, having a hole in her bilge you could put your head through. With all these hindrances, especially securing the whale, we were fortunate to be rescued as soon as we were, since it is well known that whales are of much higher commercial value than men.

However, help came at last, and we were hauled alongside. Long exposure had weakened us to such an extent that it was necessary to hoist us on board, especially the mate, whose "sudden stop," when he returned to us after his little aerial excursion, had shaken his sturdy frame considerably, a state of body which the subsequent soaking had by no means improved. In my innocence I imagined that we should be commiserated for our misfortunes by Captain Slocum, and certainly be relieved from further duties until we were a little recovered from the rough treatment we had just undergone. But I never made a greater mistake. The skipper cursed us all (except the mate, whose sole fault the accident undoubtedly was) with a fluency and vigour that was, to put it mildly, discouraging. Moreover, we were informed that he "wouldn't have no adjective skulking"; we must "turn to" and do something after wasting the ship's time and property in such a blank manner. There was a limit, however, to our obedience, so although we could not move at all for awhile, his threats were not proceeded with farther than theory.

A couple of slings were passed around the boat, by means of which she was carefully hoisted on board, a mere dilapidated bundle of sticks and raffle of gear. She was at once removed aft out of the way, the business of cutting in the whale claiming precedence over everything else just then. The preliminary proceedings consisted of rigging the "cutting stage." This was composed of two stout planks a foot wide and ten feet long, the inner ends of which were suspended by strong ropes over the ship's side about four feet from the water, while the outer extremities were upheld by tackles from the main rigging, and a small crane abreast the try-works.

These planks were about thirty feet apart, their two outer ends being connected by a massive plank which was securely bolted to them. A handrail about as high as a man's waist, supported by light iron stan-chions, ran the full length of this plank on the side nearest the ship, the whole fabric forming an admirable standing-place from whence the offi-cers might, standing in comparative comfort, cut and carve at the great mass below to their heart's content.

So far the prize had been simply held alongside by the whale-line, which at death had been "rove" through a hole cut in the solid gristle of the tail; but now it became necessary to secure the carcase to the ship in some more permanent fashion. Therefore, a massive chain like a small ship's cable was brought forward, and in a very ingenious way, by means of a tiny buoy and a hand-lead, passed round the body, one end brought through a ring in the other, and hauled upon until it fitted tight round the "small" or part of the whale next the broad spread of the tail. The free end of the fluke-chain was then passed in through a mooring-pipe for-ward, firmly secured to a massive bitt at the heel of the bowsprit (the fluke-chain-bitt), and all was ready.

. . .

The first thing to be done was to cut the whale's head off. This operation, involving the greatest amount of labour in the whole of the cutting in, was taken in hand by the first and second mates, who, armed with twelve-feet spades, took their station upon the stage, leaned over the handrail to steady themselves, and plunged their weapons vigorously down through the massive neck of the animal—if neck it could be said to have—following a well-defined crease in the blubber. At the same time the other officers passed a heavy chain sling around the long, narrow lower jaw, hooking one of the big cutting tackles into it, the "fall" of which was then taken to the windlass and hove tight, turning the whale on her back. A deep cut was then made on both sides of the rising jaw, the windlass was kept going, and gradually the whole of the throat was raised high enough for a hole to be cut through its mass, into which the strap of the second cutting tackle was inserted and secured by passing a huge toggle of oak through its eye. The second tackle was then hove taut, and the jaw, with a large piece of blubber attached, was cut off from the body with a boarding-knife, a tool not unlike a cutlass blade set into a three-foot-long wooden handle.

Upon being severed the whole piece swung easily inboard and was lowered on deck. The fast tackle was now hove upon while the third mate on the stage cut down diagonally into the blubber on the body, which the purchase ripped off in a broad strip or "blanket" about five feet wide and a foot thick. Meanwhile the other two officers carved away vigorously at the head, varying their labours by cutting a hole right through the snout. This when completed received a heavy chain for the purpose of securing the head. When the blubber had been about half stripped off the body, a halt was called in order that the work of cutting off the head might be finished, for it was a task of incredible difficulty. It was accomplished at last, and the mass floated astern by a stout rope, after which the windlass pawls clattered merrily, the "blankets" rose in quick succession, and were cut off and lowered into the square of the main hatch or "blubber-room." A short time sufficed to strip off the whole of the body-blubber, and when at last the tail was reached, the backbone was cut through, the huge mass of flesh floating away to feed the innumerable scavengers of the sea. No sooner was the last of the blubber lowered into the hold than the hatches were put on and the head hauled up alongside. Both tackles were secured to it and all hands took to the windlass levers. This was a small cow whale of about thirty barrels, that is, yielding that amount of oil, so it was just possible to lift the entire head on board; but as it weighed as much as three full-grown elephants, it was indeed a heavy lift for even our united forces, trying our tackle to the utmost. The weather was very fine, and the ship rolled but little; even then, the strain upon the mast was terrific, and right glad was I when at last the immense cube of fat, flesh, and bone was eased inboard and gently lowered on deck.

As soon as it was secured the work of dividing it began. From the snout a triangular mass was cut, which was more than half pure spermaceti. This substance was contained in spongy cells held together by layers of dense white fibre, exceedingly tough and elastic, and called by the whalers "white horse." The whole mass, or "junk" as it is called, was hauled away to the ship's side and firmly lashed to the bulwarks for the time being, so that it might not "take charge" of the deck during the rest of the operations.

The upper part of the head was now slit open lengthwise, disclosing an oblong cistern or "case" full of liquid spermaceti, clear as water. This was baled out with buckets into a tank, concreting as it cooled into a wax-like substance, bland and tasteless. There being now nothing more remaining about the skull of any value, the lashings were loosed, and the first lee-ward roll sent the great mass plunging overboard with a mighty splash. It sank like a stone, eagerly followed by a few small sharks that were hover-ing near.

As may be imagined, much oil was running about the deck, for so satu-rated was every part of the creature with it that it really gushed like water during the cutting-up process. None of it was allowed to run to waste, though, for the scupper-holes which drain the deck were all carefully plugged, and as soon as the "junk" had been dissected all the oil was carefully "squeegeed" up and poured into the try-pots.

Two men were now told off as "blubber-room men," whose duty it became to go below, and squeezing themselves in as best they could between the greasy masses of fat, cut it up into "horse-pieces" about eighteen inches long and six inches square. Doing this they became per-fectly saturated with oil, as if they had taken a bath in a tank of it; for as the vessel rolled it was impossible to maintain a footing, and every fall was upon blubber running with oil. A machine of wonderful construction had been erected on deck in a kind of shallow trough about six feet long by four feet wide and a foot deep. At some remote period of time it had no doubt been looked upon as a triumph of ingenuity, a patent mincing machine. Its action was somewhat like that of a chaff-cutter, except that the knife was not attached to the wheel, and only rose and fell, since it was not required to cut right through the "horse-pieces" with which it was fed. It will be readily understood that in order to get the oil quickly out of the blubber, it needs to be sliced as thin as possible, but for convenience in handling the refuse (which is the only fuel used) it is not chopped up in small pieces, but every "horse-piece" is very deeply scored as it were, leaving a thin strip to hold the slices together. This then was the order of work. Two harpooners attended the try-pots, replenishing them with minced blubber from the hopper at the port side, and baling out the sufficiently boiled oil into the great cooling tank on the starboard. One officer superintended the mincing, another exercised a general supervision over all. There was no man at the wheel and no look-out, for the vessel was "hove-to" under two close-reefed topsails and fore-top-mast-staysail, with the wheel lashed hard down. A look-out man was unnecessary, since we could not run anybody down, and if anybody ran us down, it would only be because all hands were asleep, for the glare of our try-works fire, to say nothing of the blazing cresset before mentioned, could have been seen for many miles. So we toiled watch and watch, six hours on and six off, the work never ceasing for an instant night or day. Though the work was hard and dirty, and the discomfort of being so continually wet through with oil great, there was only one thing dangerous about the whole business. That was the job of filling and shifting the huge casks of oil. Some of these were of enormous size, containing 350 gallons when full, and the work of moving them about the greasy deck of a rolling ship was attended with a terrible amount of risk. For only four men at most could get fair hold of a cask, and when she took it into her silly old hull to start rolling, just as we had got one half-way across the deck, with nothing to grip your feet, and the knowledge that one stumbling man would mean a sudden slide of the ton and a half weight, and a little heap of mangled corpses somewhere in the lee scuppers—well one always wanted to be very thankful when the lashings were safely passed.

The whale being a small one, as before noted, the whole business was over within three days, and the decks scrubbed and re-scrubbed until they had quite regained their normal whiteness. The oil was poured by means of a funnel and long canvas hose into the casks stowed in the ground tier at the bottom of the ship, and the gear, all carefully cleaned and neatly "stopped up," stowed snugly away below again.

ROBERT LOUIS STEVENSON

(1850–1894)

From *Travels with a Donkey in the Cévennes*

Though better known for his novels Treasure Island *and* Kidnapped, *Robert Louis Stevenson wrote two masterful travel books early in his brief career,* Travels with a Donkey *and* An Inland Voyage. *His explorer's streak was neither egocentric nor nationalistic but more akin to the romantic poets of his age—he traveled for travel's sake, and in search of inner truth. In famous lines, he declared, "The great affair is to move; to feel the needs and hitches of our life more nearly; to come off this feather-bed of civilization, and find the globe granite underfoot and strewn with cutting flints."*

Travels with a Donkey in the Cévennes is a delightfully playful, masterly written piece documenting the author's two-week journey through a low but rugged range of mountains in southwestern France in 1878. He was not alone: most of the trip was spent in a battle of wits and wills with his exasperating companion, Modestine, whom he nevertheless came to love by the end. Here he makes his donkey's acquaintance, and he and his "diminutive she-ass, not much bigger than a dog, the color of a mouse," get off to an inauspicious start. His saddlebags are packed with a Scottish romantic's essential provisions: some books, a bottle of Beaujolais, an eggbeater, and a leg of cold mutton.

In a little place called *Le Monastier,* in a pleasant highland valley fifteen miles from *Le Puy,* I spent about a month of fine days. *Monastier* is notable for the making of lace, for drunkenness, for freedom of language, and for unparalleled political dissension. There are adherents of each of the four French parties—Legitimists, Orleanists, Imperialists, and Republicans—in this little mountain-town; and they all hate, loathe, decry, and calumniate each other. Except for business purposes, or to give each other the lie in a tavern brawl, they have laid aside even the civility of speech. 'Tis a mere mountain *Poland.* In the midst of this *Babylon* I found myself a rallying-point; every one was anxious to be kind and helpful to the stranger. This was not merely from the natural hospitality of mountain people, nor even from the surprise with which I was regarded as a man living of his own free will in *Monastier,* when he might just as well have lived anywhere else in this big world; it arose a good deal from my projected excursion southward through the *Cévennes.* A traveller of my sort was a thing hitherto unheard of in that district. I was looked upon with contempt, like a man who should project a journey to the moon, but yet with a respectful interest, like one setting forth for the inclement Pole. All were ready to help in my preparations; a crowd of sympathizers supported me at the critical moment of a bargain; not a step was taken but was heralded by glasses round and celebrated by a dinner or a breakfast.

It was already hard upon *October* before I was ready to set forth, and at the high altitudes over which my road lay there was no Indian summer to be looked for. I was determined, if not to camp out, at least to have the means of camping out in my possession; for there is nothing more harassing to an easy mind than the necessity of reaching shelter by dusk, and the hospitality of a village inn is not always to be reckoned sure by those who trudge on foot. A tent, above all for a solitary traveller, is trouble-some to pitch, and troublesome to strike again; and even on the march it forms a conspicuous feature in your baggage. A sleeping-sack, on the other hand, is always ready—you have only to get into it; it serves a dou-ble purpose—a bed by night, a portmanteau by day; and it does not advertise your intention of camping out to every curious passer-by. This is a huge point. If the camp is not secret, it is but a troubled resting-place; you become a public character; the convivial rustic visits your bed-side after an early supper; and you must sleep with one eye open, and be up before the day. I decided on a sleeping-sack; and after repeated visits to *Le Puy,* and a deal of high living for myself and my advisers, a sleeping-sack was designed, constructed, and triumphally brought home.

This child of my invention was nearly six feet square, exclusive of two triangular flaps to serve as a pillow by night and as the top and bottom of the sack by day. I call it "the sack," but it was never a sack by more than courtesy: only a sort of long roll or sausage, green waterproof cart-cloth without and blue sheep's fur within. It was commodious as a valise, warm and dry for a bed. There was luxurious turning room for one; and at a pinch the thing might serve for two. I could bury myself in it up to the neck; for my head I trusted to a fur cap, with a hood to fold down over my ears and a band to pass under my nose like a respirator; and in case of heavy rain I proposed to make myself a little tent, or tentlet, with my waterproof coat, three stones, and a bent branch.

It will readily be conceived that I could not carry this huge package on my own, merely human, shoulders. It remained to choose a beast of bur-den. Now, a horse is a fine lady among animals, flighty, timid, delicate in eating, of tender health; he is too valuable and too restive to be left alone, so that you are chained to your brute as to a fellow galley-slave; a danger-ous road puts him out of his wits; in short, he's an uncertain and exacting ally, and adds thirty-fold to the troubles of the voyager. What I required was something cheap and small and hardy, and of a stolid and peaceful temper; and all these requisites pointed to a donkey.

There dwelt an old man in *Monastier,* of rather unsound intellect according to some, much followed by street-boys, and known to fame as *Father Adam*. *Father Adam* had a cart, and to draw the cart a diminutive she-ass, not much bigger than a dog, the color of a mouse, with a kindly eye and a determined under-jaw. There was something neat and high-bred, a quakerish elegance, about the rogue that hit my fancy on the spot. Our first interview was in *Monastier* market-place. To prove her good temper, one child after another was set upon her back to ride, and one after another went head over heels into the air; until a want of confidence began to reign in youthful bosoms, and the experiment was discontinued from a dearth of subjects. I was already backed by a deputation of my friends; but as if this were not enough, all the buyers and sellers came round and helped me in the bargain; and the ass and I and *Father Adam* were the centre of a hubbub for near half an hour. At length she passed into my service for the consideration of sixty-five francs and a glass of brandy. The sack had already cost eighty francs and two glasses of beer; so that *Modestine,* as I instantly baptized her, was upon all accounts the cheaper article. Indeed, that was as it should be; for she was only an appurtenance of my mattress, or self-acting bedstead on four castors.

I had a last interview with *Father Adam* in a billiard-room at the witching hour of dawn, when I administered the brandy. He professed himself greatly touched by the separation, and declared he had often bought white bread for the donkey when he had been content with black bread for himself; but this, according to the best authorities, must have been a flight of fancy. He had a name in the village for brutally misusing the ass; yet it is certain that he shed a tear, and the tear made a clean mark down one cheek.

By the advice of a fallacious local saddler, a leather pad was made for me with rings to fasten on my bundle; and I thoughtfully completed my kit and arranged my toilette. By way of armory and utensils, I took a revolver, a little spirit-lamp and pan, a lantern and some halfpenny candles, a jack-knife and a large leather flask. The main cargo consisted of two entire changes of warm clothing—besides my travelling wear of country velveteen, pilot-coat, and knitted spencer—some books, and my railway-rug, which, being also in the form of a bag, made me a double castle for cold nights. The permanent larder was represented by cakes of chocolate and tins of Bologna sausage. All this, except what I carried about my person, was easily stowed into the sheepskin bag; and by good fortune I threw in my empty knapsack, rather for convenience of carriage than from any thought that I should want it on my journey. For more immediate needs, I took a leg of cold mutton, a bottle of Beaujolais, an empty bottle to carry milk, an egg-beater, and a considerable quantity of black bread and white, like *Father Adam,* for myself and donkey, only in my scheme of things the destinations were reversed.

Monastrians, of all shades of thought in politics, had agreed in threatening me with many ludicrous misadventures, and with sudden death in many surprising forms. Cold, wolves, robbers, above all the nocturnal practical joker, were daily and eloquently forced on my attention. Yet in these vaticinations, the true, patent danger was left out. Like *Christian,* it was from my pack I suffered by the way. Before telling my own mishaps, let me, in two words, relate the lesson of my experience. If the pack is well strapped at the ends, and hung at full length—not doubled, for your life—across the pack-saddle, the traveller is safe. The saddle will certainly not fit, such is the imperfection of our transitory life; it will assuredly topple and tend to overset; but there are stones on every road-side, and a man soon learns the art of correcting any tendency to overbalance with a well-adjusted stone.

On the day of my departure I was up a little after five; by six, we began to load the donkey; and ten minutes after, my hopes were in the dust. The pad would not stay on *Modestine's* back for half a moment. I returned it to its maker, with whom I had so contumelious a passage that the street outside was crowded from wall to wall with gossips looking on and listening. The pad changed hands with much vivacity; perhaps it would be more descriptive to say that we threw it at each other's heads; and, at any rate, we were very warm and unfriendly, and spoke with a deal of freedom.

I had a common donkey pack-saddle—a *barde,* as they call it—fitted upon *Modestine;* and once more loaded her with my effects. The doubled sack, my pilot-coat (for it was warm, and I was to walk in my waistcoat), a great bar of black bread, and an open basket containing the white bread, the mutton, and the bottles, were all corded together in a very elaborate system of knots, and I looked on the result with fatuous content. In such a monstrous deck-cargo, all poised *above* the donkey's shoulders, with nothing below to balance, on a brand-new pack-saddle that had not yet been worn to fit the animal, and fastened with brand-new girths that might be expected to stretch and slacken by the way, even a very careless traveller should have seen disaster brewing. That elaborate system of knots, again, was the work of too many sympathizers to be very artfully designed. It is true they tightened the cords with a will; as many as three at a time would have a foot against *Modestine's* quarters, and be hauling with clenched teeth; but I learned afterwards that one thoughtful person, without any exercise of force, can make a more solid job than half a dozen heated and enthusiastic grooms. I was then but a novice; even after the misadventure of the pad nothing could disturb my security, and I went forth from the stable-door as an ox goeth to the slaughter.

THE BELL OF *Monastier* was just striking nine as I got quit of these preliminary troubles and descended the hill through the common. As long as I was within sight of the windows, a secret shame and the fear of some laughable defeat withheld me from tampering with *Modestine.* She tripped along upon her four small hoofs with a sober daintiness of gait; from time to time she shook her ears or her tail; and she looked so small under the bundle that my mind misgave me. We got across the ford without difficulty—there was no doubt about the matter, she was docility itself—and once on the other bank, where the road begins to mount through pine-woods, I took in my right hand the un hallowed staff, and with a quaking spirit applied it to the donkey. *Modestine* brisked up her pace for perhaps three steps, and then relapsed into her former minuet.

Another application had the same effect, and so with the third. I am worthy the name of an Englishman, and it goes against my conscience to lay my hand rudely on a female. I desisted, and looked her all over from head to foot; the poor brute's knees were trembling and her breathing was distressed; it was plain that she could go no faster on a hill. God forbid, thought I, that I should brutalize this innocent creature; let her go at her own pace, and let me patiently follow.

What that pace was, there is no word mean enough to describe; it was something as much slower than a walk as a walk is slower than a run; it kept me hanging on each foot for an incredible length of time; in five minutes it exhausted the spirit and set up a fever in all the muscles of the leg. And yet I had to keep close at hand and measure my advance exactly upon hers; for if I dropped a few yards into the rear, or went on a few yards ahead, *Modestine* came instantly to a halt and began to browse. The thought that this was to last from here to *Alais* nearly broke my heart. Of all conceivable journeys, this promised to be the most tedious. I tried to tell myself it was a lovely day; I tried to charm my foreboding spirit with tobacco; but I had a vision ever present to me of the long, long roads, up hill and down dale, and a pair of figures ever infinitesimally moving, foot by foot, a yard to the minute, and, like things enchanted in a nightmare, approaching no nearer to the goal.

In the mean time there came up behind us a tall peasant, perhaps forty years of age, of an ironical snuffy countenance, and arrayed in the green tail-coat of the country. He overtook us hand over hand, and stopped to consider our pitiful advance.

"Your donkey," says he, "is very old?"

I told him, I believed not.

Then, he supposed, we had come far.

I told him, we had but newly left *Monastier.*

"Et vous marchez comme ça!" cried he; and, throwing back his head, he laughed long and heartily. I watched him, half prepared to feel offended, until he had satisfied his mirth; and then, "You must have no pity on these animals," said he; and, plucking a switch out of a thicket, he began

to lace *Modestine* about the stern-works, uttering a cry. The rogue pricked up her ears and broke into a good round pace, which she kept up without flagging, and without exhibiting the least symptom of distress, as long as the peasant kept beside us. Her former panting and shaking had been, I regret to say, a piece of comedy.

My *deus ex machinâ,* before he left me, supplied some excellent, if inhumane, advice; presented me with the switch, which he declared she would feel more tenderly than my cane; and finally taught me the true cry or masonic word of donkey-drivers, "Proot!" All the time, he regarded me with a comical incredulous air, which was embarrassing to confront; and smiled over my donkey-driving, as I might have smiled over his orthography, or his green tail-coat. But it was not my turn for the moment.

I was proud of my new lore, and thought I had learned the art to perfection. And certainly *Modestine* did wonders for the rest of the forenoon, and I had a breathing space to look about me. It was Sabbath; the mountain-fields were all vacant in the sunshine; and as we came down through St. *Martin de Frugères,* the church was crowded to the door, there were people kneeling without upon the steps, and the sound of the priest's chanting came forth out of the dim interior. It gave me a home feeling on the spot; for I am a countryman of the Sabbath, so to speak, and all Sabbath observances, like a Scotch accent, strike in me mixed feelings, grateful and the reverse. It is only a traveller, hurrying by like a person from another planet, who can rightly enjoy the peace and beauty of the great ascetic feast. The sight of the resting country does his spirit good. There is something better than music in the wide unusual silence; and it disposes him to amiable thoughts, like the sound of a little river or the warmth of sunlight.

In this pleasant humor I came down the hill to where *Goudet* stands in a green end of a valley, with *Château Beaufort* opposite upon a rocky steep, and the stream, as clear as crystal, lying in a deep pool between them. Above and below, you may hear it wimpling over the stones, an amiable stripling of a river, which it seems absurd to call the *Loire.* On all sides, *Goudet* is shut in by mountains; rocky footpaths, practicable at best for donkeys, join it to the outer world of *France;* and the men and women drink and swear, in their green corner, or look up at the snow-clad peaks in winter from the threshold of their homes, in an isolation, you would think, like that of *Homer's* Cyclops. But it is not so; the postman reaches *Goudet* with the letter-bag; the aspiring youth of *Goudet* are within a day's walk of the railway at *Le Puy;* and here in the inn you may find an engraved portrait of the host's nephew, *Régis Senac,* "Professor of Fencing and Champion of the two *Americas,*" a distinction gained by him, along with the sum of five hundred dollars, at *Tammany Hall, New York,* on the 10th *April,* 1876.

I hurried over my midday meal, and was early forth again. But, alas, as we climbed the interminable hill upon the other side, "Proot!" seemed to have lost its virtue. I prooted like a lion, I prooted mellifluously like a sucking-dove; but *Modestine* would be neither softened nor intimidated. She held doggedly to her pace; nothing but a blow would move her, and that only for a second. I must follow at her heels, incessantly belaboring. A moment's pause in this ignoble toil, and she relapsed into her own private gait. I think I never heard of any one in as mean a situation. I must reach the lake of *Bouchet,* where I meant to camp, before sundown, and, to have even a hope of this, I must instantly maltreat this uncomplaining animal. The sound of my own blows sickened me. Once, when I looked at her, she had a faint resemblance to a lady of my acquaintance who formerly loaded me with kindness; and this increased my horror of my cruelty.

To make matters worse, we encountered another donkey, ranging at will upon the roadside; and this other donkey chanced to be a gentleman. He and *Modestine* met nickering for joy, and I had to separate the pair and beat down their young romance with a renewed and feverish bastinado. If the other donkey had had the heart of a male under his hide, he would have fallen upon me tooth and hoof; and this was a kind of consolation—he was plainly unworthy of *Modestine's* affection. But the incident saddened me, as did everything that spoke of my donkey's sex.

It was blazing hot up the valley, windless, with vehement sun upon my shoulders; and I had to labor so consistently with my stick that the sweat ran into my eyes. Every five minutes, too, the pack, the basket, and the pilot-coat would take an ugly slew to one side or the other; and I had to stop *Modestine,* just when I had got her to a tolerable pace of about two miles an hour, to tug, push, shoulder, and readjust the load. And at last, in the village of *Ussel,* saddle and all, the whole hypothec turned round and grovelled in the dust below the donkey's belly. She, none better pleased, incontinently drew up and seemed to smile; and a party of one man, two women, and two children came up, and, standing round me in a half-circle, encouraged her by their example.

I had the devil's own trouble to get the thing righted; and the instant I had done so, without hesitation, it toppled and fell down upon the other side. Judge if I was hot! And yet not a hand was offered to assist me. The man, indeed, told me I ought to have a package of a different shape. I suggested, if he knew nothing better to the point in my predicament, he might hold his tongue. And the good-natured dog agreed with me smilingly. It was the most despicable fix. I must plainly content myself with the pack for *Modestine,* and take the following items for my own share of the portage: a cane, a quart flask, a pilot-jacket heavily weighted in the pockets, two pounds of black bread, and an open basket full of meats and bottles. I believe I may say I am not devoid of greatness of soul; for I did not recoil from this infamous burden. I disposed it, Heaven knows how, so as to be mildly portable, and then proceeded to steer *Modestine* through the village. She tried, as was indeed her invariable habit, to enter every house and every courtyard in the whole length; and, encumbered as I was, without a hand to help myself, no words can render an idea of my difficulties. A priest, with six or seven others, was examining a church in process of repair, and he and his acolytes laughed loudly as they saw my plight. I remembered having laughed myself when I had seen good men struggling with adversity in the person of a jackass, and the recollection filled me with penitence. That was in my old light days, before this trouble came upon me. God knows at least that I shall never laugh again, thought I. But O, what a cruel thing is a farce to those engaged in it!

A little out of the village, *Modestine,* filled with the demon, set her heart upon a by-road, and positively refused to leave it. I dropped all my bundles, and, I am ashamed to say, struck the poor sinner twice across the face. It was pitiful to see her lift up her head with shut eyes, as if waiting for another blow. I came very near crying; but I did a wiser thing than that, and sat squarely down by the roadside to consider my situation under the cheerful influence of tobacco and a nip of brandy. *Modestine,* in the mean while, munched some black bread with a contrite hypocritical air. It was plain that I must make a sacrifice to the gods of shipwreck. I threw away the empty bottle destined to carry milk; I threw away my own white bread, and, disdaining to act by general average, kept the black bread for *Modestine;* lastly, I threw away the cold leg of mutton and the egg-whisk, although this last was dear to my heart. Thus I found room for everything in the basket, and even stowed the boating-coat on the top. By means of an end of cord I slung it under one arm; and although the cord cut my shoulder, and the jacket hung almost to the ground, it was with a heart greatly lightened that I set forth again.

I had now an arm free to thrash *Modestine,* and cruelly I chastised her. If I were to reach the lakeside before dark, she must bestir her little shanks to some tune. Already the sun had gone down into a windy-looking mist; and although there were still a few streaks of gold far off to the east on the hills and the black fir-woods, all was cold and gray about our onward path. An infinity of little country by-roads led hither and thither among the fields. It was the most pointless labyrinth. I could see my destination overhead, or rather the peak that dominates it; but choose as I pleased, the roads always ended by turning away from it, and sneaking back towards the valley, or northward along the margin of the hills. The failing light, the waning color, the naked, unhomely, stony country through which I was travelling, threw me into some despondency. I promise you, the stick was not idle; I think every decent step that *Modestine* took must have cost me at least two emphatic blows. There was not another sound in the neighborhood but that of my unwearying bastinado.

Suddenly, in the midst of my toils, the load once more bit the dust, and, as by enchantment, all the cords were simultaneously loosened, and the road scattered with my dear possessions. The packing was to begin again from the beginning; and as I had to invent a new and better system, I do not doubt but I lost half an hour. It began to be dusk in earnest as I reached a wilderness of turf and stones. It had the air of being a road which should lead everywhere at the same time; and I was falling into something not unlike despair when I saw two figures stalking towards me over the stones. They walked one behind the other like tramps, but their pace was remarkable. The son led the way, a tall, ill-made, sombre, Scotch-looking man; the mother followed, all in her Sunday's best, with an elegantly-embroidered ribbon to her cap, and a new felt hat atop, and proffering, as she strode along with kilted petticoats, a string of obscene and blasphemous oaths.

I hailed the son and asked him my direction. He pointed loosely west and north-west, muttered an inaudible comment, and, without slacking his pace for an instant, stalked on, as he was going, right athwart my path. The mother followed without so much as raising her head. I shouted and shouted after them, but they continued to scale the hillside, and turned a deaf ear to my outcries. At last, leaving *Modestine* by herself, I was constrained to run after them, hailing the while. They stopped as I drew near, the mother still cursing; and I could see she was a handsome, motherly, respectable-looking woman. The son once more answered me roughly and inaudibly, and was for setting out again. But this time I simply collared the mother, who was nearest me, and, apologizing for my violence, declared that I could not let them go until they had put me on my road. They were neither of them offended—rather mollified than otherwise; told me I had only to follow them; and then the mother asked me what I wanted by the lake at such an hour. I replied, in the Scotch manner, by inquiring if she had far to go herself. She told me, with another oath, that she had an hour and a half's road before her. And then, without salutation, the pair strode forward again up the hillside in the gathering dusk.

I returned for *Modestine,* pushed her briskly forward, and, after a sharp

ascent of twenty minutes, reached the edge of a plateau. The view, looking back on my day's journey, was both wild and sad. *Mount Mézenc* and
the peaks beyond *St. Julien* stood out in trenchant gloom against a cold
glitter in the east; and the intervening field of hills had fallen together
into one broad wash of shadow, except here and there the outline of a
wooded sugar-loaf in black, here and there a white irregular patch to represent a cultivated farm, and here and there a blot where the *Loire,* the
Gazeille, or the *Lausonne* wandered in a gorge.

Soon we were on a high-road, and surprise seized on my mind as I
beheld a village of some magnitude close at hand; for I had been told that
the neighborhood of the lake was uninhabited except by trout. The road
smoked in the twilight with children driving home cattle from the fields;
and a pair of mounted stride-legged women, hat and cap and all, dashed
past me at a hammering trot from the canton where they had been to
church and market. I asked one of the children where I was. At *Bouchet
St. Nicolas,* he told me. Thither, about a mile south of my destination,
and on the other side of a respectable summit, had these confused roads
and treacherous peasantry conducted me. My shoulder was cut, so that it
hurt sharply; my arm ached like toothache from perpetual beating; I gave
up the lake and my design to camp, and asked for the *auberge.*

MRS. ALFRED "MARY" MUMMERY

(DATES UNKNOWN)

From Alfred F. Mummery's *My Climbs in the Alps and Caucasus*

In the very center of Alfred Mummery's beloved classic hides a chapter unlike all the others, written by his fearless and high-spirited young wife. Like most of the other female mountaineers of her day, her feisty independence on the rock did not extend to her public persona as a writer, and so Mary Mummery will be forever known in print as "Mrs. Alfred." Although by the end of the 1800s several women had made headlines through their daring exploits in the Alps, the Alpine Club remained prejudiced against the "weaker sex." It would not admit them as members and would publish an article penned by a woman only if she found a man to claim it as his. Surely it was this exclusive attitude that prompted Mrs. Mummery to begin her chapter with two rousing paragraphs scolding men who think that women "should be satisfied with watching through a telescope some weedy and invertebrate masher being hauled up a steep peak by a couple of burly guides."

Luckily her husband was not one of these. Indeed, she accompanied her husband—one of the most talented climbers of his day—on many expeditions, honing her considerable athleticism and formidable wit on

vertical rock and ice. Their 1880 traverse of the highly technical
Teufelsgrat, described in the passage that follows, was one of their earli-
est adventures and is still considered one of the great husband-and-wife
accomplishments in mountaineering history. Sadly, this pair had a rela-
tively brief partnership on the rope; in 1895 Alfred Mummery disap-
peared while attempting to summit Nanga Parbat in the Himalayas.

The slopes of the Breithorn and the snows of the Weiss Thor are usually supposed to mark the limit of ascents suitable to the weaker sex—
indeed, strong prejudices are apt to be aroused the moment a woman
attempts any more formidable sort of mountaineering. It appears to me,
however, that her powers are, in actual fact, better suited to the really
difficult climbs than to the monotonous snow grinds usually considered
more fitting.

Really difficult ascents are of necessity made at a much slower pace,
halts are fairly frequent, and, with few exceptions, the alternations of
heat and cold are less extreme. Snow grinds, on the contrary, usually
involve continuous and severe exertion—halts on a wide snow field are
practically impossible—and the danger of frost-bite in the early morning
is succeeded by the certainty of sun-burning at mid-day. The masculine
mind, however, is, with rare exceptions, imbued with the idea that a
woman is not a fit comrade for steep ice or precipitous rock, and, in consequence, holds it as an article of faith that her climbing should be done
by Mark Twain's method, and that she should be satisfied with watching
through a telescope some weedy and invertebrate masher being hauled
up a steep peak by a couple of burly guides, or by listening to this same
masher when, on his return, he lisps out with a sickening drawl the many
perils he has encountered.

Alexander Burgener, however, holds many strange opinions; he
believes in ghosts, he believes also that women can climb. None the less
it was with some surprise that I heard him say, "You must go up the
Teufelsgrat." Now the Teufelsgrat, as its name implies, is a ridge of

exceptional enormity, and one, moreover, that a few days previously, while we were ascending the Matterhorn, he had pointed out to me as the very embodiment of inaccessibility. I was proud of the compliment, and we solemnly shook hands, Burgener saying the while that the nominal proprietor of the ridge and all his angels should not turn us back, once we were fairly started.

For the benefit of those who may not be well acquainted with the Alpine possessions of his Satanic Majesty, it may be pointed out that the Teufelsgrat is the south-western ridge of the Täschhorn. A short distance north of the Täsch-Alp this ridge ends in the little peak called the Strahlbelt. Our plan was to sleep at the Täsch-Alp and, crossing the Weingarten glacier, to climb up to a very obvious col immediately on the Täschhorn side of that small peak. From thence to the summit we hoped to be able to follow the ridge.

Accordingly, on July 15, 1887, we started from Zermatt to sleep in the highest châlet—in those days the Täsch Inn was still an unimagined luxury. A merry afternoon was spent on the Alp. Some friends, thinking it a good opportunity to see a sunrise, had joined our party, and, being much interested in our expedition, partook of our high spirits. We greatly astonished the various beasts of the neighbourhood by encroaching on their domain. During the afternoon an irate bull made various endeavours to slay us, and at length succeeded in driving the whole party, guides and travellers, on to the roof of the châlet. Finally, when we began to find our perch inconveniently small, a general sortie was ordered, and with wild yells and much flourishing of axes and hats, the brute was put to rout and sent bellowing down the Alp.

When the last tint of sunset had faded off the Weisshorn, we lit our candles and converted the châlet into a ball-room. It was only twelve feet square, and made perilous by low and unexpected beams. None the less, we had a brilliant dance, diversified with songs from the guides and porters. Andenmatten, our second guide, was even provided with a strange and wonderful musical instrument, from which much exhausting blowing would extract reedy dance music and other nondescript melodies. The evening's entertainment having been wound up by the usual discussion about the weather, we betook ourselves to our rugs and tried to sleep. But the boards were hard and the rugs were rough and we were all very restless, and our tempers were getting irritable, when, towards eleven o'clock, the door received a mighty bang, followed by a terrific roar. We all leapt up and seized on ice-axes and telescopes, sticks and hobnailed boots, as weapons wherewith to slay, or at any rate put to flight, the monster who had dared to attack our stronghold. The door was then thrown open and with loud shouts we sallied forth, and once more saw our old enemy the bull. Realising the vigour and fury of his assailants, he again fled, waking the echoes with his indignant snorts and grumbles.

We seized on this incident as a favourable excuse, and abandoned all further idea of sleep. Soon our preparations for the start were begun, and at 1.30 a.m. everything was ready. The two lanterns, skilfully constructed by knocking the bottoms out of empty champagne bottles, were duly lit and, saying good-bye to our friends, we plunged through the long wet grass. The track was soon hopelessly lost, so we worked our way towards the torrent and followed its left bank to the moraine.

I do not wish to make any heart ache by recalling the feelings that followed an unwholesome and indigestible supper at 8 p.m., a sleepless night, and a still less digestible breakfast at 1 a.m.; truth, however, compels me to admit that when these feelings were further accentuated by a loose and very inferior moraine lit by the flickering light of a farthing dip in a Bouvier bottle, I agreed most fully in the short and comprehensive denunciation of things in general which various masculine lips now and again expressed. As we tripped and stumbled up the endless stones we became aware that the day was breaking, and by the time we reached the snout of the Weingarten glacier, Monte Rosa was blazing in brightest sunlight. We halted a few minutes in order that Burgener might consider which of two rock couloirs immediately in front of us would offer the best route. I will confess this problem did not arouse my enthusiasm, and, turning my back to the cliffs, I watched the stately advance of the great red sun, as it drove the last lingering darkness from the lower snow fields.

Burgener's survey was soon completed, the men once more swung the knapsacks on to their shoulders, and we strode across the moraine and loose stones towards the couloir nearest the Täschhorn. The rocks proved very easy, and we made rapid progress till, at 4.45 a.m., we reached a convenient spot for breakfast. Just in front the cliff became much steeper and was intersected by more or less continuous bands of precipitous rock.

Burgener rejoiced in the approach of our first struggle, and could hardly restrain his exuberant spirits. He employed his time, when his mouth didn't happen to be more seriously occupied, by using his best English to try and shatter my nerves. He gave me various and most graphic pictures of the awful precipices which were to greet my inexperienced eyes, always ending each sentence with, "It is more beautifuls as the Matterhorn," that being the only peak we had previously ascended together.

Having exhausted the regulation time for feeding, the rope was got out and a business-like air settled on Burgener's countenance. He, of course, took the lead, I followed, then came Andenmatten, and my husband last. The rocks were fairly good for a little while, but as we got higher they became steeper and very rotten. Our leader took the greatest care not to upset any of the stones, and kept hurling frightful warnings at me to be equally careful. "You kill your man, you not like that!" I did not "kill my man," but, nevertheless, it was here that our first accident occurred.

We had reached a sort of platform cut off from the upper slopes by a precipitous wall of rock. At one point, however, where the end of an overlapping slab had weathered and decayed, it seemed just possible to surmount the barrier. Burgener was soon at work upon it, but the splinters of rock were so loose that no reliable grip could be found, and progress had to be made with foot and hand hold equally uncertain. Still he steadily advanced, and, at length, could just reach his hands over the top of the rock and clutch at a great stone which seemed firm. Firm it was to a certain extent. Firm enough not to roll over on our heads, but, alas! not firm enough to prevent a slight movement on to Burgener's hand. A stifled groan, a trickle of blood down the rocks, followed by a long and impressive sentence in patois, was all the intelligence vouchsafed us till, with a last effort, Burgener clambered on to the top of the wall. We quickly followed, and, finding a convenient ledge, proceeded to make our diagnosis. A somewhat mangled, swollen, and bleeding thumb offered an interesting problem to a student of the St. John's Ambulance Association. The bleeding was soon checked, and the offending thumb bound up in a variety of pocket-handkerchiefs, Burgener murmuring the while in most pathetic tones, "I no more strong in that hand."

We suggested an immediate retreat, but after a glance at the pinnacled ridge, now well within view, a half bottle of Bouvier (we had forgotten to bring any cognac) and a bite off the limb of a tough poulet, there issued from the invalid's lips sneering remarks at the idea of returning. "Vorwärts," he cried, and vorwärts we went, amidst a strange mixture of joyful jodels at the towering gendarmes which seemed to challenge us to wrestle from afar, and dejected looks and mournful voice repeating, "I no more strong in that hand."

About 5.30 a.m. we reached the ridge, here covered with snow. Andenmatten took the lead, and, as the snow was in excellent condition, we were able to make good pace. This was soon succeeded by queer, slabby, stratified rocks, piled at a steep angle, like rows of huge slates, one on the other. Their sharp edges, however, offered good hold for hands and feet. After a short time these broken rocks were interspersed with an occasional bold, precipitous turret, forcing our leader to show his metal. This first gendarme was, nevertheless, successfully passed, and the second stood before us—a large, piled-up mass of brownish yellow, rotten rock, blocking entirely from our view the rest of the arête.

After a short consultation between the guides the best route was singled out, and Andenmatten once more advanced to the attack. The base of the tower went well, and little by little the difficulties seemed to be yielding. Our leader's face beamed with pride and pleasure, as he stormed crag after crag, but, alas! he forgot the well-worn proverb, "Pride goeth before destruction, and a haughty spirit before a fall."

Solomon was once more to be justified, and the joyful Andenmatten was to be the victim. A last small, rocky tooth impeding his progress, and not being able to find sufficient hold, he summoned Burgener to his aid. The suggestion that he should take off the knapsack was treated as an insult, and a minute later, aided by a friendly shove, he had not merely got good hold on the top of the tooth, but was actually resting his arms on it. The tooth was to all intents and purposes climbed, when, to our horror, we saw his arms sliding off, and with a last convulsive effort to find grip for his fingers, he toppled outwards and plunged head downwards over the cliff. Long before the command "hold" could be given we saw him, heels uppermost, arms outspread, knapsack hanging by one strap, and hat rolling into space, on a sloping ice-glazed rock some fifteen feet below us. Burgener, with admirable readiness, had caught hold of the rope as Andenmatten was in the very act of falling, and his iron grip, luckily for us, had stood the strain. I was still clinging to a projecting crag, whilst our last man had thrown himself half over the opposite side of the ridge, and was ready for all emergencies. The fall being checked, all hands seized the rope, but no immediate results ensued. My husband then climbed down, and found that Andenmatten's coat had hitched on a rock. This being loosened, a few strong tugs hauled the victim on to the ridge. The deathly silence was broken only by the sobs of the nerve-shattered bundle which lay at our feet, and it was difficult to realise that this was the same active, sturdy, high-spirited man who had piped for us to dance—who had kept us merry by jodels, making the echoes resound amongst the rocks, and whose cheerfulness had made even the stony moraine and endless screes lose something of their horror. Still the silence remained unbroken save for the injured one's sobs—when, suddenly, a solemn voice remarked, "How providential both bottles of Bonvier are not broken." And, looking round, I found my husband had employed the awe-stricken moments in overhauling the contents of the knapsack. One of these same bottles was promptly opened, and a glass of the foaming fluid poured down the throat of the gasping guide.

After again displaying my great surgical skill, mainly by banging the injured one in the ribs, bending his limbs, and generally treating him in a reckless and unmerciful manner, I declared him more frightened than hurt. "Vorwärts," shouted Burgener; "Vorwärts, wir wollen nicht zurück,"[1] and once more he took the lead. I followed, then my husband and last of all Andenmatten, his face deathly pale, his limbs trembling, and his head enveloped in a voluminous red handkerchief. At every small rock that came in our way he uttered either bitter curses on the past or prayers for his future; matters, we assured him, of trivial import so long as he placed his feet firmly. A short distance further we were forced off the arête on to the Weingarten face. Every ledge and shelf was here so piled with loose, rolling *débris*, that it was impossible to move without upsetting great slabs and stones. They slid from under our feet, collecting perfect avalanches, as they bounded from ledge to ledge, before taking the last tremendous plunge to the glacier. Coming to the end of these shelves and ledges, we were pulled up by "Blatten" and forced to ascend to the ridge once more. By this time the mournful appeals of the crestfallen Andenmatten enlisted our sympathies, and we halted a few minutes to once more examine his back and apply a certain well-known remedy to his lips. At the same time a gentle hint was given that it was quite useless to develop pains of any sort, either in the back or elsewhere, until a more favourable spot should present itself for their treatment.

We then again set to work. A pyramid in front being impracticable, we were forced over on to the Kien glacier face, along a steep ice slope of most uninviting aspect. Here and there a slab of rock protruded through

---

[1] "Forward, we don't want to go back."

the ice, suggesting slight hold for the hands, but almost invariably proving to be loose and coming away at the slightest touch. The amount of step-cutting involved was extremely irksome to Burgener. His hand was by this time bleeding afresh, and a groan of pain escaped his lips as each stroke of the axe sent the brittle chips sliding and slithering down the glassy slope. In spite of the wounded hand, the step-cutting had to continue for half an hour or more—half an hour that appeared to me absolutely interminable, as I listened to the groans from in front and to the intermittent sobs and complaints from behind. Andenmatten appeared, indeed, to be in such a deplorable condition that he might faint at any moment; a contingency which suggested that, after all, the Teufelsgrat might have the best of the game.

Further progress on the ice slope was now barred by an impassable buttress of smooth, black rock, the fangs of a huge tooth which towered high above the ridge. Burgener was forced in consequence to work back to the right, and make his way to the ridge up the chimney or rock couloir by which the tooth was flanked. There was, of course, the obvious objection that this chimney would bring us to the arête on the wrong side of the great tooth, but, as our leader remarked, "Es giebt keinen andereu Weg!"[2] Some rather difficult climbing brought him into the gully. When he had found secure footing, I scrambled up and was stowed away into a small ice-filled cleft. He then kindly took my axe and perched it for me in the gully, and, with an authoritative "You stay there" to me, he proceeded on his way. Stones and chips of ice soon whizzed past, followed, a few minutes later, by a great flake which swept down, upsetting my axe, and in a moment my cherished weapon had disappeared into space.

At length the rope became taut, and in obedience to the order "come on," I climbed up the ice-glazed, snow-masked rocks to a big step cut into deeper ice near the top of the gully. Above, snow and easy rock led us to the ridge. But as we had feared, the great tower in front was impassable, and it was evident that another traverse would have to be

2 "There is no other way!"

made. On coming quite close, however, we were overjoyed to find an extraordinary cleft in the rock. The cleft was just wide enough to enable one to squeeze through, and led along the ridge, apparently turning the obstruction.

I feel sure my companions shared the thrill of delight which this awoke within me, by the inspiriting jodel which Burgener shot into the air, the merry chuckle from my husband, and the absence of sound of any sort from Andenmatten. To explore this dismal and uncanny tunnel was the next business. For this purpose one of the party unroped and dived into the semi-darkness. His grunts and groans as he squeezed himself through the narrow passage, and a final volley of those unreportable words in which the troubled masculine mind invariably seeks relief, acquainted us with the fact that the hole was a delusion, and that the mountain had been merely playing us a practical joke.

The only alternative was to get round the obstruction on the right. Burgener at once led us along a narrow ledge, which was more or less covered with the *débris* fallen from above. It was necessary to be extremely careful, as the cliff on our left was cased with a veneer of rotten stones, and it seemed as if the disturbance of any single one of them might bring the whole rickety mass down on our heads. On the right was a dizzy precipice of fifteen hundred feet or more, with the crevassed Weingarten glacier below. After a while we reached an arm of rock which blocked the ledge; climbing over, or rather round this, we found a secure nook where we sat down whilst Burgener unroped and went ahead to explore. He was soon hidden from our view by the crags, and, for a time, all the news we had of him was the ceaseless rattle of the stones he upset. At last we saw him reappear, but there was no life in his movements; his face was serious, and in response to our queries he said: "Herr Mommerie, it is quite impossible." During our enforced idleness we had bad time to thoroughly study the wall of rock cutting us off from the ridge. A very sanguine member of the party had even declared that, "If old Burgener can't get up that slope, it is a pity."

Putting on the rope once more, the great man of the party advanced to the assault. With great care he got his hands well fixed in a crevice, but above and on either side, as far as he could reach, everything he touched came away, covering me with showers of crumbling shale. I jammed my head against the cliff, but this gave scanty shelter from the sharp-edged, slate-like chips that came flying by, and by the time the order "Come on" was sounded, my fingers and arms were a good deal the worse for wear, and my eyes were full of anything and everything small enough to get into them. But the worst was now to come; how was I to get up without at least slaying those behind me, or, which seemed much more likely, upsetting the whole unstable veneer that covered the face of the cliff? Whenever one stone gave way, those above it came sweeping down in a perfect avalanche, so exciting Burgener's fears that he kept shrieking, "You kill your man if you not more careful are." My own impression was that I should not merely "kill my man," but that the whole party and most of the mountain would be hurled to the glacier beneath. It was, therefore, with a most joyful heart that I at length found myself seated securely on a rock overlooking the snow slope on the left of the arête, and could watch in comfort the miseries of my companions below.

So soon as we had thoroughly realised that no serious injury had been done either to us or the mountain, Burgener carefully examined our route. In a few moments forth came the joyful words, "Herr Monnuerie, das geht."

Once more we advanced, this time "Herr Mommerie" leading. The arête proved fairly easy, though there were short steps of precipitous rock where a shoulder from Burgener or a hoist on his axe were needed. At one place a more formidable step was encountered, and the knapsacks, coats, Andenmatten and myself were left below, while the cragsmen of the party grappled with the difficulty. Shouts at length announced their success, and with a great swish down came the rope for the various baggage. As soon as this had been hauled up, the rope came down again for me, and, with unmixed delight, I prepared to follow. My half-hour's halt had been anything but pleasant, as a bitterly cold wind had sprung up, and the sun was obscured by driving mist. A third time the rope was thrown down, and after much hauling and advice Andenmatten joined our company. We then kept along the ridge till a larger "step," precipitous and impassable, barred the way. Our leaders again consulted, and, after a short halt, led us on to the Kien glacier face, where a convenient snow slope seemed to afford an easy, though not very expeditious, method of turning the obstruction.

The snow being in good condition we got over the ground quickly, but as we advanced the axe occasionally reached the underlying ice, and at last the snow dwindled down to an inch or less in thickness, and every step had to be hacked out of hard black ice. The cautious Alexander, thinking that it was no longer a place in which an amateur should lead, unroped, and cutting a few steps below me, went to the front, and swung mighty blows against the relentless slope. It was desirable to go as fast as possible, for the rock above us was constantly sending its superfluous icicles and stones across our track, and we feared at every moment that larger missiles might follow, and sweep us with them in their mad flight of bounds and leaps to the gigantic blue crevasses far, far below. But the ice was hard, and Burgener was hampered by his wounded hand. Slowly we seemed to crawl along, and ever, when we reached rock, found nothing but smooth slabs, slippery with a glazing of ice. Wearily we plodded on. Fingers and feet had long since lost all sensation, and the only hope that buoyed our sinking spirits was the belief that, on passing a rib of rock not far in front, our difficulties would be at an end and the ascent practically accomplished. In due time we reached this rib, and beyond it the snow was certainly thicker, and, as far as we could see, there was nothing ahead that need cause us uneasiness. Judging by the time we had already spent on the mountain and the many difficulties we had surmounted, I concluded that the summit must be nearly won. The lead was again made over to my husband, and Burgener having resumed his old place on the rope, the traverse continued.

"Oh! vain hope and frivolous conclusion!" The crucial test was yet to

come. Snow, rocks and ice had astonished us in the past by their forbid-
ding nature; now, in addition to these, we were handicapped by the lateness of the hour (1.30 p.m.), a driving mist, and, worst of all, by fatigue,
cold and hunger.

The snow once more began to thin out, leaving nothing but a huge
sheet of ice. To cut across would have taken days. There was clearly
nothing for it but once more to regain the ridge. Burgener was of opinion
that we were past the more serious towers and pinnacles, and that, if we
could only reach the crest, a sure and not too lengthy road to the summit
would be ours. He therefore directed our leader to make straight up the
slope towards some great slabs of rock that projected through the ice.
These, however, soon became too precipitous and smooth, and we were
reduced, as our last chance, to cutting up a hideous ice-gully that flanked
the rocks. In places snow covered the ice, and, the gully being bent and
narrow, it afforded more or less precarious footing. Burgener's injunctions
were constant, "Keep where the snow is thickest." But the snow soon
dwindled down till it nowhere exceeded an inch or so; still, as long as the
beat of the axe could hew out a step, we advanced steadily. At length,
however, the cheery chip of the axe ceased, and in response to Burgener's
query came the reply, "Es giebt gar kein Eis."[3] To the right and to the left
the smooth slabs of the rock-gully were but thinly glazed, and above this
again was a thin coating of loose snow. The wall of rock on the right suggested, however, some possibility of continuing the ascent, and to this
our leader made his way and climbed a short distance, when it became
so ice-glazed and precipitous that he was brought to a stand. It was even
doubtful whether he could descend, and it was evident that his position
was critical in the extreme. Luckily, he had for the moment fairly reliable
footing.

Burgener's strong points now showed themselves; without a moment's
hesitation or delay he untied, and, holding the rope as a banister, rapidly
ascended by its aid. Arrived at the point where my husband had tra-

---

3 "There is no ice at all."

versed, to the right, he quitted the rope and made his way rather to the left, and succeeded in finding ice deep enough for very shallow steps. Aided here and there by a projecting stone, he worked up till the slope of the gully eased slightly, and considerable quantities of snow had accumulated. This snow was of the worst possible quality, and poured away like flour at every step; still, bad as it was it rendered progress possible, and, working upwards with indomitable courage, we saw him at last reach reliable footing. Our feelings found vent in loud shouts and jodels, but all the same it was grim work standing in a small step three-quarters of an hour, with splinters of ice and a stream of snow from above chilling fingers and toes till it seemed impossible to endure it longer. Indeed, nothing but the sure and certain knowledge that the only alternative was to move and slip, could have kept me inactive so long. Welcome were the occasional cheery assurances from above, "Hold on a bit longer and we shall get up all right." But Burgener, being unroped, could give no direct help to my husband, and it was some time before the latter could effect the traverse back into the gully and up the treacherous steps to the snow above. When the safety of the party was once more in Burgener's hands, I ascended, finding that my husband had already cut his way to the ridge. Then the order to untie reached me, and the rope was sent down for Andenmatten.

With a hasty glance at the never-to-be-forgotten gully, we bent our somewhat weary steps onward, scrambling, climbing and crawling over the various crags, pinnacles and flying buttresses which constitute the arête. Compared to our recent experiences it seemed easy, and progress was rapid. Suddenly, however, our leader came to a halt, and though Burgener urged him to proceed, he utterly refused, and after a few moments summoned Alexander to the front. I could not see his usually expressive face, but the words, "Herr Gott, unmöglich!"[4] reached my ears, and I hurried forward to see what new peril threatened us.

---

[4] "Dear God, impossible!"

To understand the position of affairs it is necessary to describe the very curious rock formation in some detail. The ridge where we stood projected in a huge rock cornice, far over the precipice. Immediately beyond, this cornice had broken away. In consequence, the ridge by which we had been ascending appeared to end abruptly, and there was no question of going forwards—immeasurable space yawned in front. Twenty feet or more to our left the true ridge, there denuded of its rock cornice, mounted rapidly in a series of precipitous steps, but from our point of view we looked, not at the ridge, but at the bare precipitous face below it. Even could we have reached that face, no climber could hope to cling to it; but we could not even reach it; between us and it was the most awful chasm it has ever been my lot to see. This formation of ridge is, so far as the experience of any member of the party extended, unique. It gave, indeed, the impression that there were two ridges, separated from each other by an impassable gulf. No wonder, then, that black horror seized us. Return was not to be thought of, and advance seemed impossible. There we four stood, absolutely powerless, our teeth chattering with the bitter cold, and the damp, cruel mist ever driving across, threatening to add obscurity to our other bewilderment.

Happily, after a few minutes we began to recover from the mental shock caused by this most dramatic break in the ridge, and proceeded to reduce its tremendous appearance to the dull and narrow limits of actual fact. So soon as we had realised that we were on a cornice overhanging the precipice, it became obvious that we must climb down the cornice to the real ridge, and from that point seek to attack the difficulties in front. This descent was not very easy, the slabby rocks shelving steeply towards the Kien glacier, and all the interstices and cracks being filled with ice. However, some slight hold was obtainable on the extreme edge, and after the ice had been dug from various irregularities and fractures my husband arrived at a point immediately above a deep cleft, which cut off the corniced section of the ridge from its uncorniced continuation. Beyond this point the comfortable assurance of the rope was gone. Any one dependent on it would necessarily swing free in mid-air, and it may well be doubted whether "all the king's horses and all the king's men" would suffice to replace that aerial dangler on the ridge. Happily, minute search revealed a small notch in the rock, and though it was evident that a rope drawn from time to time through it would be certain to slip out, it appeared likely that a fixed rope would be held in position so long as only a perfectly steady pull was applied to it. In dubious tones, therefore, came the words, "Fix the rope and I'll try." To which Burgener replied, "Herr Je, es muss gehen sonst sind wir alle caput."[5] The rope being securely lashed to a crag on the top of the cornice, the other end was passed down, and our leader squeezed it into the tiny notch. First carefully pulling it taut to prevent any "run" when his weight should come on it, we saw him swing over and disappear. An instant later we heard the welcome news, "It's all right, there is good hold all the way down."

At length he came in sight, stretching over the yawning gulf, and we saw him grip the rock beyond and climb warily along the side of a great block of uncertain stability, poised like a logan stone on the arête. An ugly ten feet or more followed, and then we heard the joyful, "Kommen sie nur, Alexander."[6] The sheet anchor of the party having got over, I had to follow, and great was my elation to find that I could accomplish without help a mauvais pas that had for a minute or two seemed impassable to the stronger and more daring members of the party.

Looking back, the crag we had just left was weird in the extreme; though at the top it was twenty feet or more in breadth, it narrowed down at the bottom of the cleft to less than two feet, and the whole mass looked as if a good blow from an ice-axe would send it bodily on to the Weingarten glacier. Indeed, as the mist whirled and eddied through the cleft, it seemed to totter as in the very act of falling. But it was already 4 p.m., and we were far from the wished for snow; so, whilst Andenmat-

[5] "Lord Jesus, it will have to work or we are all done for."
[6] "Come on along, Alexander."

ten was being coached across, my husband unroped and went to work, crawling up a steep "step" in the arête. The rope was then thrown up to him, and Alexander, scrambling up by its aid, was ready to help the rest of the party. This procedure was then repeated. Still crag followed crag, here loose rocks that rolled away at a touch, there precipitous buttresses, access to which could only be gained by using Burgener's broad shoulders as a ladder. All at once, however, difficulties seemed to cease, our leader again put on the rope, and we rattled along the arête till it broadened out into a great snow ridge.

"Der Teufelsgrat ist gemacht!" shouted Burgener, and we began to race along the snow, which rose in front and to our right into a steep crest. Up these slopes we could see the footprints left by a party which, under the leadership of Franz Burgener, had made the ordinary ascent on the previous day. "Half an hour more and it is done, and the Teufelsgrat is ours," added the excited Alexander as we hurried along, feeling that success was within our grasp. The footprints grew perceptibly larger, and on we ran till we actually placed our feet in the tracks. Here all unnecessary luggage was deposited, and Burgener, seeing I was very cold, arrayed me in his coat and gloves. We hastened up the snow, finding no difficulty other than its extreme softness. A scramble over some sharp slate-like rocks followed, then a little more snow, and at 5.30 p.m. we stood on the summit. But for one moment only. At once Burgener began with serious face to say, "I not like a thunderstorm on this ridge." There was no doubt about it, the clouds were wrapping round us, and the distant grumble rolled in our ears. "Go on, go on quicker, Herr Mommerie!" and then with a push he hustled me along the arête. "You must go on, I could a cow hold here," were the encouraging words I heard: as I went helter-skelter over anything which happened to be in the way. Soon the snow slopes were reached, and our property once more picked up. We ran our hardest through the blinding storm, almost deafened by the reverberating peals of thunder; but what mattered it? True it was late; true we were cold, hungry, and tired; true we were sinking into the snow above our knees, and the "trace" had disappeared beneath the rapidly falling snow; but "the Teufelsgrat was ours," and we cared little for these minor evils, and we laughed the tempest to scorn with jodels and triumphant shouts. A short traverse to the left and we crossed the Bergschrund; a weary drag over gentle snow slopes, a little care in winding through some open crevasses, and our dangers were ended. At 8 p.m. we reached the snout of the Kien glacier, and once more stepped on to moraine. We descended stony slopes for another hour, and then I remembered that our last meal had taken place at 10 a.m. It being obvious that we could not get to Randa that night, I suggested a halt, and the idea was received with applause. In a few minutes we were sitting on various stones munching our evening meal, the only drawback being that we were distinctly cold. My hands and feet were numb, and what remained of our clothing (we had left a good deal of it on the Teufelsgrat) was soaking wet, and, worst of all, my boots, viewed by the flickering light of a candle, seemed hardly likely to hold out till we got to Randa.

Our hunger being somewhat appeased, I noticed symptoms of sleepiness amongst the guides. In consequence, I reminded Burgener of his promise to take us, in any case, down to the trees, so that we might rejoice in a fire. We started off once more, carefully roped. The slope being steep and intersected by low cliffs, and the night being so inky black that we could see nothing, it was really necessary to take this precaution. We proceeded down the hill much as a pack of cards might be expected to do. Burgener sprawling on his back and upsetting me, and I passing the shock back to the others. This mode of advance kept up till 11 p.m., when our guides suddenly pulled up, and inquired, in an awestruck whisper, whether we could see a tiny light on the right? With great glee I said, "Yes, it must be a châlet." The suggestion was treated with silent contempt. "What can it be then?" In funereal tones Burgener said, "I do not know;" but Andenmatten timidly whispered, "Geister!"[7] From that moment I could see there was no fire for us; that we should be

[7] "Spirits!"

lucky if we could sneak under the cover of a rock to shelter us from the storm that threatened once more to burst over our heads.

A few steps further and a huge black object faced us. On examination we found it to be a suitable place for spending the next few hours. In five minutes the guides were snoring peacefully; but we, after wringing the water out of our dripping clothes, were reduced to dancing various war dances in the vain hope of keeping warm. When these exercises became unduly fatiguing, we watched the lightning play round the peaks and ridges, and finally stirred up the guides with an ice-axe and urged them to continue the descent. They did not at all approve this course of action, as they considered their quarters luxurious and most thoroughly calculated to induce refreshing sleep. The next two hours were spent in slowly slipping and tumbling down stony grass-grown slopes. We then turned to the right on to somewhat smoother ground. The men, however, refused to go further, alleging that there were fearful precipices in front, and that, in the blackness of the stormy night, it was quite impossible to do so with reasonable safety. The guides again went soundly to sleep, whilst we watched wearily for the first sign of morning. When a streak of light did at length illumine the darkness, we saw the dim outline of trees not far distant, and promptly went down to them. A fire was soon blazing, and we endeavoured to warm ourselves; but though we well nigh roasted our toes and fingers and scorched our faces, the rest of us seemed, perhaps by contrast, colder than before, and we shivered painfully before the crackling pine wood.

As soon as it was fairly light, we dragged our weary bodies through the forest and along and down the pastures, till at 5.30 a.m. we entered the little white inn at Randa. We woke the landlord, and he promptly provided us with a big fire. A hot breakfast followed, and when we had done due justice to his culinary efforts, we climbed into a shaky char-à-banc[8] and drove back to Zermatt.

Burgener was in the highest spirits; his chief source of delight

[8] Typically, an open bus for sightseers.

appeared to be a belief that our non-return the previous night would have excited alarm, and that we should probably have the proud privilege of meeting a search party, properly equipped for the transport of our shattered remains. My husband, however, did not altogether sympathise with these feelings, and seemed to have a keen appreciation of the Trinkgeld,[9] tariffs, and other pecuniary concomitants of such luxuries. Happily, we knew our friends were not very likely to think we should have come to any harm, and when two hours later we drove into Zermatt, we found they were still peacefully slumbering in their rooms.

[9] Tips.

ELIZABETH LE BLOND

(1861–1934)

From *Adventures on the Roof of the World*

The title page of this book lists the author as Mrs. Aubrey Le Blond, for like many women of her generation she wrote under her husband's name. But on my copy, in pencil below her printed name, the author has signed "Elizabeth Le Blond E.A.J. (H–W)," suggesting the many husbands and names she acquired during her long life. Her book The High Alps in Winter *is written under yet another: Mrs. Fred Burnaby.*

This energetic woman had almost as many daring first ascents to her credit as she had names, and was one of the first people to climb extensively in the Alps in winter. She was born to a well-to-do family in Ireland, was sickly as a child, and went to Switzerland in 1881 to "take the airs" and cure her health. There she discovered mountaineering and never looked back. She was deeply involved in the goings-on at London's Alpine Club, but since she couldn't officially join, she founded the Ladies Alpine Club in 1907. Although not overtly a feminist, Le Blond quietly discarded her cumbersome, wind-catching Victorian skirts while climbing (an act that was considered scandalous at the time), by taking them off once out of sight and stashing them behind a rock for the return trip. Le Blond may have done more than any other climber of her era to encourage other women to discover her beloved sport.

This short excerpt describes Le Blond's climb of the rugged Zinal Rothhorn with her two guides, Joseph and Roman Imboden. It is lifted from the only chapter of the book in which she felt bold enough to chronicle her own climbing and not the deaths, disasters, and mishaps of the men of the Alpine Club.

Ignorance of what the future has in store is often not a bad thing. Had I realised that at the hour when we ought to have been at Zinal we should be sitting—and for the second time in one day—on the top of the Rothhorn, we should hardly have set out in so light-hearted a fashion from the little inn in the Trift Valley, above Zermatt, at 4 A.M. on 14th September 1895.

The party consisted of my two guides, Joseph and Roman Imboden, father and son, and myself, and our idea was to cross the fine peak of the Rothhorn, 13,855 feet high, from Zermatt to Zinal. I had been up that mountain before, and so, on many previous occasions, had Imboden, but, oddly enough, he had never been down the other side. Roman, however, had once or twice made the traverse, and, in any case, we knew quite enough about the route from hearsay to feel sure we could hit it off even without Roman's experience.

Some fresh snow had fallen a few days previously, and the slabby part of the Rothhorn on the north side was unpleasantly white, besides which there was a strong and bitterly cold wind. We pretty well abandoned all idea of getting down on the other side when we saw how unfavourably things were turning out, and though I felt greatly disappointed I never have and never would urge a guide in whom I have confidence to undertake what he considers imprudent. We left the matter open till the last minute, however, and took both the knapsacks to the top, where we arrived at 9.15.

Warming ourselves in a sunny and sheltered corner of the by no means inhospitable summit, we had some food and a pleasant rest. I cannot say if the meal and the cheering effects of the sunshine made things look different, but it is a fact that after, perhaps, an hour's halt, Imboden shouldered his knapsack and remarked to me, "Come along, ma'am, as far as the end of the ridge; we will just have a look." Hope awakened in me, and scrambling to my feet I followed him. The wind was certainly high; I had difficulty even on those easy rocks in keeping my footing; how, I wondered, should we manage when the real climbing began? I had read of an *arête* of rock, little broader than one of the blunt knives we had used at breakfast, and the idea of passing along it with a shrieking gale trying to tear us from our perch was not alluring. Presently we reached the spot where one quits the gentle slope and comparatively broad ridge, and embarks on the profile of a slender and precipitous face of rock, with nearly vertical forehead and small and infrequent cracks for hands and feet. We were going to do more than look at it, apparently; we were about to descend it, for without any further remark Imboden began to get ready, letting Roman pass ahead. Taking hold of the rope between his son and himself he told me to stand aside while he gradually paid it out as Roman went down. The first yard or two consisted of slabs, set at a high angle. Then the ridge abruptly curved over and one saw nothing but air till the eye rested on the glacier thousands of feet below. In a few minutes Roman had disappeared, and the steady paying out of the rope alone indicated that he was climbing downwards. After a time he reached almost the end of his tether of about 30 feet—for we were on a very long rope—and his father called out, "Rope up!" "Let the lady come to the edge and give me a little more," came a voice from far down. Putting the final loop into my hand and bidding me sit down, Imboden held me hard by the cord behind until the tautness of the piece between Roman and me showed it was time to be moving. I then advanced very cautiously to what seemed like the edge of the world. Turning round with my face to the rock I had my first glance below. Far down was the top of Roman's hat, and as he saw the advancing soles of my boots he grinned with

appreciation, feeling that now we really were embarked on the enterprise. "There's a good place down here, ma'am, come along!" he called
up, with one toe on a ledge 3 inches wide, two fingers thrust into a crack,
and the rope held out of his way by being put, the remark concluded,
between his teeth. I had no doubt it was a nice place when one got there,
but meanwhile I had to make the best use I could of my eyes to find a
suitable assortment of hand- and foot-holes. Soon I, too, was clinging to
the face of the precipice, and Imboden was left above out of sight and
before long almost out of hearing. The wind here was far less trying as we
were sheltered by the topmost pinnacle of the mountain. To me the feeling of danger from a gale on a rock peak is due even more to the difficulty of hearing what one's companions are saying than to the risk of
one's balance being upset. It is extremely disconcerting, when a climber,
descending steep rocks and anxious to make a long but perhaps an easy
step downwards to good foot-hold, calls for more rope, and is promptly
swung clear out into space by an invisible guide above, who has misunderstood his orders. When a party is accustomed to work together, this
sort of thing seldom happens, still it makes all the difference in the pleasure of negotiating difficult rocks if the air is calm.

Our only trouble now was owing to the fresh snow, but this had partially consolidated, and we got down steadily and safely, gradually leaving
behind the cold wind which whistled amongst the crags above.

It was early in the day, and we went slowly, stopping once or twice to
photograph where warm and sheltered resting-places of comfortable proportions tempted us to linger. The rocky knife edge was unpleasantly
sharp for the arms bent over it, but useful ledges down the side helped to
distribute the weight and amuse and occupy the mind. When finally we
reached the end of the rocks, and had nothing but snow between us and
the Mountet Hut, we considered ourselves as good as there, and made a
long halt on the last stones.

We were wrong, however. "My boy, I will go ahead now," remarked
Imboden, stepping off into the snow. He went a few paces, and then
looked first all round him and lastly at us. *"Blue ice!"* he muttered, with

intense disgust. "Blue ice right down to the bottom!" We shrugged our shoulders; Imboden was ahead doing the work; we could afford to be philosophical. I should not like to say how many strokes of the axe each step required, but the slope was steep, a slip could not be risked, and Imboden hewed out great foot-holds in the slippery wall. After this had gone on for some time he paused. "Upon my word," remarked he, "it will take us the rest of the day to get down at this rate! I shall try another way." So we turned and remounted the slope, and sitting down once more on the stones, Imboden traced out a possible route down the face of the mountain, bearing diagonally across it. It looked dullish; besides, thought I, after all, we don't particularly want to go to Zinal. Roman put into words what, I think, sprung simultaneously into both our minds. "Let us go back to Zermatt over the top of the Rothhorn again!" "Yes, let us do that!" I exclaimed. Imboden gazed from one to the other of us in amazement. "Go back over the top of the Rothhorn?" he repeated. "Why, we should simply be out all night!" Roman didn't answer, but his eyes wandered persistently up the *arête*. His father now began to calculate, and by some strange process of arithmetic he came to the conclusion that if we hurried very much it was just possible that we might get off the difficult part of the peak before night overtook us. Still, he was far from reconciled to the idea, while every moment Roman and I liked it better. Imboden saw how keen we were, and presently exclaimed: "Well, I'll go if you both want it, but we must be quick; if we spend the night on the top of the Rothhorn and a storm comes on, we may simply lose our lives!" There was no need however, to tell Roman to be quick. He was told off to lead, and I followed, with Imboden last. The memory of that ascent has remained in my mind as a confused dream. Every scrap of my attention was given to holding on and pulling myself upwards, never pausing, except in the very worst places, to see what either of the guides was doing, and, with every foot- and hand-hold fresh in my memory, I was full of a delightful sense of security which muscles in first-class condition and complete absence of any sensation of fatigue fully justified. We rose at an incredible pace, and after an hour and twenty-five minutes of splendid exercise, we threw ourselves once more on the flat little top of the Rothhorn. We had now only the descent by the ordinary route between us and Zermatt, and this seemed a small matter compared to what we had accomplished that day.

We did not remain long on the summit, and the first part of the descent was quickly ended. We had now reached that point on the mountain where it is necessary to leave the ridge and go down for some distance on the precipitous north face. This bit of the climb, always requiring great care on account of the smoothness and steepness of the rock, was on this occasion particularly difficult because of the powdery snow which covered everything, and the bitterly cold wind to which here, and, luckily for us, here only, we were exposed. The associations of these slabs are not of a nature to reassure the timid climber. Many years ago, in fact on the very first occasion when the Rothhorn was ascended from the Zermatt side, a startling incident took place near this spot. The party consisted of Messrs Dent and Passingham, with Alexander Burgener, Ferdinand Imseng, and Franz Andermatten as guides, and they were descending the mountain when the exciting occurrence described by Mr Dent happened.[†] He has kindly allowed me to reprint his account.

Down the first portion of the steep rock slope we passed with great caution, some of the blocks of stone being treacherously loose, or only lightly frozen to the face. We had arrived at the most difficult part of the whole climb, and at a rock passage which at that time we considered was the nastiest we had ever encountered. The smooth, almost unbroken face of the slope scarcely afforded any foot-hold, and our security almost entirely depended on the rope we had laid down in our ascent. Had not the rope been in position we should have varied our route, and no doubt found a line of descent over this part much easier than the one we actually made for, even without any help from the fixed cord. Imseng was far below, working his way back to the *arête,* while the

[†] *Above the Snow Line,* by Clinton Dent.

rest of the party were holding on, moving but slowly, with their faces to the mountain. Suddenly I heard a shout from above; those below glanced up at once: a large flat slab of rock, that had afforded us good hold in ascending, but proved now to have been only frozen in to a shallow basin of ice, had been dislodged by the slightest touch from one of the party above, and was sliding down straight at us. It seemed an age, though the stone could not have had to fall more than 10 feet or so, before it reached us. Just above me it turned its course slightly; Franz, who was just below, more in its direct line of descent, attempted to stop the mass, but it ground his hands against the rock and swept by straight at Imseng. A yell from us hardly awoke him to the danger; the slab slid on faster and faster, but just as we expected to see our guide swept away, the rock gave a bound for the first time, and as, with a startled expression, he flung himself against the rock face, it leapt up, and, flying by within a few inches of his head, thundered down below. A moment or two of silence followed, and then a modified cheer from Imseng, as subdued as that of a "super" welcoming a theatrical king, announced his safety, and he looked up at us with a serious expression on his face. Franz's escape had been a remarkably lucky one, but his hands were badly cut about and bruised. In fact, it was a near thing for all of us, and the mere recollection will still call up that odd sort of thrill a man experiences on suddenly recollecting at 11 P.M. that he ought to have dined out that evening with some very particular people. Had not the rock turned its course just before it reached Franz, and bounded from the face of the mountain over Imseng's head, one or more of the party must unquestionably have been swept away. The place was rather an exceptional one, and the rock glided a remarkably long distance without a bound, but still the incident may serve to show that falling stones are not a wholly imaginary danger.

· · ·

To return to ourselves. We steadily progressed down the cold and snowy face, with rope kept taut and paid out slowly as, one by one, we moved lower. I need not follow our climb, which was without incident, and while it was still daylight, we reached the snow ridge, on the stones just below, which in ascending it is usual to pause for breakfast. We were particularly anxious to be off the stony rocks below and to gain the little glacier and pass over the moraine before dark, but this we could not manage, so in spite of our lantern we wandered about on those odious rocks for hours before we found the gully by which alone it is possible to get off them. Our various attempts entailed the descent of slippery chimneys leading to the top of black precipices, with nothing to be done but scramble up again, merely to embark in other chimneys with precisely similar consequences. I got so sick of the whole thing that I would gladly have dozed under a rock and awaited daylight. The guides, however, stuck to the business, and after a positive nightmare of gullies they at last hit off the right and only one. I have seldom felt greater satisfaction that when I stepped off those detestable rocks on to the snow, shimmering beneath our feet in the starlight. We had now only to cross the glacier and make our way down an exceedingly steep but well-defined foot-path over the sharply-crested moraine. Once we had left this behind us we had nothing more than grass-slopes between us and the Trift Inn. As soon as we reached this final stage in our day's work, we selected the most comfortable-looking hollow, and hanging the lantern to an axe stuck upright in the ground, we prepared, at a somewhat unorthodox hour and within only thirty minutes of the hotel, to enjoy a well-earned meal.

FRANCIS PARKMAN

(1823–1893)

From *The Oregon Trail*

---

*In 1846, at the age of twenty-three, Francis Parkman set out from
Saint Louis, Missouri, following the Oregon Trail west to the Rockies.
Unlike most of the travelers he met along the way, he was not an emi-
grant, fur-trader, or prospector, but a student, fresh out of college. He
wrote in the preface to his book, "My business was observation, and I
was willing to pay dearly for the opportunity of exercising it." Here he
refers to his health, which, never robust, deteriorated badly on the year-
long journey. When he returned home to Boston and started writing his
stories for publication, he had nearly lost the use of his eyes. He dic-
tated the stories to friends, and* The Oregon Trail *was published in
1849. It has since been printed in many subsequent editions.*

*Parkman became a great admirer and friend of several tribes along
the way, most notably the Sioux in and around the Black Hills of
South Dakota. He followed the trail west at a time when relations with
the Indians were still relatively untroubled by violence and deceit, and
when the land was still a place of mind-boggling abundance. The year
before his death, Parkman would write, "I remember that, as we rode*

*by the foot of Pike's Peak, when for a fortnight we met no face of man,
my companion remarked, in a tone anything but complacent, that a
time would come when those plains would be a grazing country, the
buffalo give place to tame cattle, farmhouses be scattered along the
water-courses, and wolves, bears, and Indians be numbered among the
things that were. We condoled with each other on so melancholy a
prospect, but we little thought what the future had in store. . . . The
buffalo is gone, and of all his millions nothing is left but bones. Those
discordant serenaders, the wolves that howled at evening about the
traveller's camp-fire, have succumbed to arsenic. . . . The wild Indian
is turned into an ugly caricature of his conqueror."*

In the following passage Parkman travels with the Sioux into the
Black Hills, where they set up their summer camp.

We travelled eastward for two days, and then the gloomy ridges of
the Black Hills rose up before us. The village passed along for some miles
beneath their declivities, trailing out to a great length over the arid
prairie, or winding at times among small detached hills of distorted
shapes. Turning sharply to the left, we entered a wide defile of the mountains, down the bottom of which a brook came winding, lined with tall
grass and dense copses, amid which were hidden many beaver dams and
lodges. We passed along between two lines of high precipices and rocks,
piled in utter disorder one upon another, and with scarcely a tree, a bush,
or a clump of grass to veil their nakedness. The restless Indian boys were
wandering along their edges and clambering up and down their rugged
sides, and sometimes a group of them would stand on the verge of a cliff
and look down on the array as it passed in review beneath them. As we
advanced, the passage grew more narrow; then it suddenly expanded into
a round grassy meadow, completely encompassed by mountains; and
here the families stopped as they came up in turn, and the camp rose like
magic.

The lodges were hardly erected when, with their usual precipitation, the Indians set about accomplishing the object that had brought them there; that is, the obtaining poles for supporting their new lodges. Half the population, men, women, and boys, mounted their horses and set out for the interior of the mountains. As they rode at full gallop over the shingly rocks and into the dark opening of the defile beyond, I thought I had never read or dreamed of a more strange or picturesque cavalcade. We passed between precipices more than a thousand feet high, sharp and splintering at the tops, their sides beetling over the defile or descending in abrupt declivities, bristling with black fir-trees. On our left they rose close to us like a wall, but on the right a winding brook with a narrow strip of marshy soil intervened. The stream was clogged with old beaver-dams, and spread frequently into wide pools. There were thick bushes and many dead and blasted trees along its course, though frequently nothing remained but stumps cut close to the ground by the beaver, and marked with the sharp chisel-like teeth of those indefatigable laborers. Sometimes we were diving among trees, and then emerging upon open spots, over which, Indian-like, all galloped at full speed. As Pauline[1] bounded over the rocks I felt her saddle-girth slipping, and alighted to draw it tighter; when the whole array swept past me in a moment, the women with their gaudy ornaments tinkling as they rode, the men whooping, and laughing, and lashing forward their horses. Two black-tailed deer bounded away among the rocks; Raymond[2] shot at them from horseback; the sharp report of his rifle was answered by another equally sharp from the opposing cliffs, and then the echoes, leaping in rapid succession from side to side, died away rattling far amid the mountains.

After having ridden in this manner for six or eight miles, the appearance of the scene began to change, and all the declivities around us were covered with forests of tall, slender pine-trees. The Indians began to fall

[1] Parkman's horse.

[2] Raymond, a hunter and Parkman's guide, died during John Charles Frémont's epic passage of the Rockies in the winter of 1848.

off to the right and left, and dispersed with their hatchets and knives among these woods, to cut the poles which they had come to seek. Soon I was left almost alone; but in the deep stillness of those lonely mountains, the stroke of hatchets and the sound of voices might be heard from far and near.

Reynal,[3] who imitated the Indians in their habits as well as the worst features of their character, had killed buffalo enough to make a lodge for himself and his squaw, and now he was eager to get the poles necessary to complete it. He asked me to let Raymond go with him, and assist in the work. I assented, and the two men immediately entered the thickest part of the wood. Having left my horse in Raymond's keeping, I began to climb the mountain. I was weak and weary, and made slow progress, often pausing to rest, but after an hour had elapsed, I gained a height, whence the little valley out of which I had climbed seemed like a deep, dark gulf, though the inaccessible peak of the mountain was still towering to a much greater distance above. Objects familiar from childhood surrounded me; crags and rocks, a black and sullen brook that gurgled with a hollow voice deep among the crevices, a wood of mossy distorted trees and prostrate trunks flung down by age and storms, scattered among the rocks, or damming the foaming waters of the little brook. The objects were the same, yet they were thrown into a wilder and more startling scene, for the black crags and the savage trees assumed a grim and threatening aspect, and close across the valley the opposing mountain confronted me, rising from the gulf for thousands of feet, with its bare pinnacles and its ragged covering of pines. Yet the scene was not without its milder features. As I ascended, I found frequent little grassy terraces, and there was one of these close at hand, across which the brook was stealing, beneath the shade of scattered trees that seemed artificially planted. Here I made a welcome discovery, no other than a bed of strawberries, with their white flowers and their red fruit, close nestled among

---

[3] A French frontiersman, married to a Sioux woman, who also accompanied Parkman.

the grass by the side of the brook, and I sat down by them, hailing them as old acquaintances; for among those lonely and perilous mountains, they awakened delicious associations of the gardens and peaceful homes of far-distant New-England.

Yet wild as they were, these mountains were thickly peopled. As I climbed farther, I found the broad dusty paths made by the elk, as they filed across the mountain side. The grass on all the terraces was trampled down by deer; there were numerous tracks of wolves, and in some of the rougher and more precipitous parts of the ascent, I found foot-prints different from any that I had ever seen, and which I took to be those of the Rocky Mountain sheep. I sat down upon a rock; there was a perfect stillness. No wind was stirring, and not even an insect could be heard. I recollected the danger of becoming lost in such a place, and therefore I fixed my eye upon one of the tallest pinnacles of the opposite mountain. It rose sheer upright from the woods below, and by an extraordinary freak of nature, sustained aloft on its very summit a large loose rock. Such a landmark could never be mistaken, and feeling once more secure, I began again to move forward. A white wolf jumped up from among some bushes, and leaped clumsily away; but he stopped for a moment, and turned back his keen eye and his grim bristling muzzle. I longed to take his scalp and carry it back with me, as an appropriate trophy of the Black Hills, but before I could fire, he was gone among the rocks. Soon after I heard a rustling sound, with a cracking of twigs at a little distance, and saw moving above the tall bushes the branching antlers of an elk. I was in the midst of a hunter's paradise.

Such are the Black Hills, as I found them in July; but they wear a different garb when winter sets in, when the broad boughs of the fir tree are bent to the ground by the load of snow, and the dark mountains are whitened with it. At that season the mountain-trappers, returned from their autumn expeditions, often build their rude cabins in the midst of these solitudes, and live in abundance and luxury on the game that harbors there. I have heard them relate, how with their tawny mistresses, and perhaps a few young Indian companions, they have spent months in

total seclusion. They would dig pitfalls, and set traps for the white
wolves, the sables, and the martens, and though through the whole night
the awful chorus of the wolves would resound from the frozen mountains
around them, yet within their massive walls of logs they would lie in careless ease and comfort before the blazing fire, and in the morning shoot
the elk and the deer from their very door.

THE CAMP WAS full of the newly-cut lodge-poles; some, already prepared, were stacked together, white and glistening, to dry and harden in
the sun; others were lying on the ground, and the squaws, the boys, and
even some of the warriors, were busily at work peeling off the bark and
paring them with their knives to the proper dimensions. Most of the
hides obtained at the last camp were dressed and scraped thin enough
for use, and many of the squaws were engaged in fitting them together
and sewing them with sinews, to form the coverings for the lodges. Men
were wandering among the bushes that lined the brook along the margin
of the camp, cutting sticks of red willow, or *shongsasha,* the bark of
which, mixed with tobacco, they use for smoking. Reynal's squaw was
hard at work with her awl and buffalo sinews upon her lodge, while her
proprietor, having just finished an enormous breakfast of meat, was
smoking a social pipe along with Raymond and myself. He proposed at
length that we should go out on a hunt. "Go to the Big Crow's lodge,"
said he, "and get your rifle. I'll bet the gray Wyandot pony against your
mare that we start an elk or a black-tailed deer, or likely as not, a big-
horn, before we are two miles out of camp. I'll take my squaw's old yellow
horse; you can't whip her more than four miles an hour, but she is as
good for the mountains as a mule."

I mounted the black mule which Raymond usually rode. She was a
very fine and powerful animal, gentle and manageable enough by nature;
but of late her temper had been soured by misfortune. About a week
before, I had chanced to offend some one of the Indians, who out of
revenge went secretly into the meadow and gave her a severe stab in the

haunch with his knife. The wound, though partially healed, still galled her extremely, and made her even more perverse and obstinate than the rest of her species.

The morning was a glorious one, and I was in better health than I had been at any time for the last two months. Though a strong frame and well compacted sinews had borne me through hitherto, it was long since I had been in a condition to feel the exhilaration of the fresh mountain-wind and the gay sunshine that brightened the crags and trees. We left the little valley and ascended a rocky hollow in the mountain. Very soon we were out of sight of the camp, and of every living thing, man, beast, bird, or insect. I had never before, except on foot, passed over such execrable ground, and I desire never to repeat the experiment. The black mule grew indignant, and even the redoubtable yellow horse stumbled every moment, and kept groaning to himself as he cut his feet and legs among the sharp rocks.

It was a scene of silence and desolation. Little was visible except beetling crags and the bare shingly sides of the mountains, relieved by scarcely a trace of vegetation. At length, however, we came upon a forest tract, and had no sooner done so than we heartily wished ourselves back among the rocks again; for we were on a steep descent, among trees so thick that we could see scarcely a rod in any direction.

If one is anxious to place himself in a situation where the hazardous and the ludicrous are combined in about equal proportions, let him get upon a vicious mule, with a snaffle bit, and try to drive her through the woods down a slope of forty-five degrees. Let him have a long rifle, a buckskin frock with long fringes, and a head of long hair. These latter appendages will be caught every moment and twitched away in small portions by the twigs, which will also whip him smartly across the face, while the large branches above thump him on the head. His mule, if she be a true one, will alternately stop short and dive violently forward, and his positions upon her back will be somewhat diversified and extraordinary. At one time he will clasp her affectionately, to avoid the blow of a bough overhead; at another, he will throw himself back and fling his knee forward against the side of her neck, to keep it from being crushed between the rough bark of a tree and the equally unyielding ribs of the animal herself. Reynal was cursing incessantly during the whole way down. Neither of us had the remotest idea where we were going; and though I have seen rough riding, I shall always retain an evil recollection of that five minutes' scramble.

At last we left our troubles behind us, emerging into the channel of a brook that circled along the foot of the descent; and here, turning joyfully to the left, we rode in luxury and ease over the white pebbles and the rippling water, shaded from the glaring sun by an overarching green transparency. These halcyon moments were of short duration. The friendly brook, turning sharply to one side, went brawling and foaming down the rocky hill into an abyss, which, as far as we could discern, had no bottom; so once more we betook ourselves to the detested woods. When next we came forth from their dancing shadow and sunlight, we found ourselves standing in the broad glare of day, on a high jutting point of the mountain. Before us stretched a long, wide, desert valley, winding away far amid the mountains. No civilized eye but mine had ever looked upon that virgin waste. Reynal was gazing intently; he began to speak at last:

"Many a time, when I was with the Indians, I have been hunting for gold all through the Black Hills. There's plenty of it here; you may be certain of that. I have dreamed about it fifty times, and I never dreamed yet but what it came out true. Look over yonder at those black rocks piled up against that other big rock. Don't it look as if there might be something there? It won't do for a white man to be rummaging too much about these mountains; the Indians say they are full of bad spirits; and I believe myself that it's no good luck to be hunting about here after gold. Well, for all that, I would like to have one of these fellows up here, from down below, to go about with his witch-hazel rod, and I'll guarantee that it would not be long before he would light on a gold-mine. Never mind; we'll let the gold alone for to-day. Look at those trees down below us in the hollow; we'll go down there, and I reckon we'll get a black-tailed deer."

But Reynal's predictions were not verified. We passed mountain after mountain, and valley after valley; we explored deep ravines; yet still, to my companion's vexation and evident surprise, no game could be found. So, in the absence of better, we resolved to go out on the plains and look for an antelope. With this view we began to pass down a narrow valley, the bottom of which was covered with the stiff wild-sage bushes and marked with deep paths, made by the buffalo, who, for some inexplicable reason, are accustomed to penetrate, in their long grave processions, deep among the gorges of these sterile mountains.

Reynal's eye was ranging incessantly among the rocks and along the edges of the black precipices, in hopes of discovering the mountain-sheep peering down upon us in fancied security from that giddy elevation. Nothing was visible for some time. At length we both detected something in motion near the foot of one of the mountains, and in a moment afterward a black-tailed deer, with his spreading antlers, stood gazing at us from the top of a rock, and then, slowly turning away, disappeared behind it. In an instant Reynal was out of his saddle, and running toward the spot. I, being too weak to follow, sat holding his horse and waiting the result. I lost sight of him, then heard the report of his rifle deadened among the rocks, and finally saw him reappear, with a surly look, that plainly betrayed his ill success. Again we moved forward down the long valley, when soon after we came full upon what seemed a wide and very shallow ditch, incrusted at the bottom with white clay, dried and cracked in the sun. Under this fair outside, Reynal's eye detected the signs of lurking mischief. He called me to stop, and then alighting, picked up a stone and threw it into the ditch. To my utter amazement it fell with a dull splash, breaking at once through the thin crust, and spattering round the hole a yellowish creamy fluid, into which it sank and disappeared. A stick, five or six feet long, lay on the ground, and with this we sounded the insidious abyss close to its edge. It was just possible to touch the bottom. Places like this are numerous among the Rocky Mountains. The buffalo, in his blind and heedless walk, often plunges into them unawares. Down he sinks; one snort of terror, one convulsive struggle, and the slime calmly flows above his shaggy head, the languid undulations of its sleek and placid surface alone betraying how the powerful monster writhes in his death-throes below.

We found after some trouble a point where we could pass the abyss, and now the valley began to open upon the plains which spread to the horizon before us. On one of their distant swells we discerned three or four black specks, which Reynal pronounced to be buffalo.

"Come," said he, "we must get one of them. My squaw wants more sinews to finish her lodge with, and I want some glue myself."

He immediately put the yellow horse to such a gallop as he was capable of executing, while I set spurs to the mule, who soon far outrun her plebeian rival. When we had galloped a mile or more, a large rabbit, by ill-luck, sprang up just under the feet of the mule, who bounded violently aside in full career. Weakened as I was, I was flung forcibly to the ground, and my rifle falling close to my head, went off with the shock. Its sharp, spiteful report rang for some moments in my ear. Being slightly stunned, I lay for an instant motionless, and Reynal, supposing me to be shot, rode up and began to curse the mule. Soon recovering myself, I arose, picked up the rifle and anxiously examined it. It was badly injured. The stock was cracked, and the main screw broken, so that the lock had to be tied in its place with a string; yet happily it was not rendered totally unserviceable. I wiped it out, reloaded it, and handing it to Reynal, who meanwhile had caught the mule and led her up to me, I mounted again. No sooner had I done so, than the brute began to rear and plunge with extreme violence; but being now well prepared for her, and free from incumbrance, I soon reduced her to submission. Then taking the rifle again from Reynal, we galloped forward as before.

We were now free of the mountains and riding far out on the broad prairie. The buffalo were still some two miles in advance of us. When we came near them, we stopped where a gentle swell of the plain concealed us from their view, and while I held his horse Reynal ran forward with his rifle, till I lost sight of him beyond the rising ground. A few minutes elapsed: I heard the report of his piece, and saw the buffalo running away at full speed on the right, and immediately after, the hunter himself, unsuccessful as before, came up and mounted his horse in excessive ill-humor. He cursed the Black Hills and the buffalo, swore that he was a good hunter, which indeed was true, and that he had never been out before among those mountains without killing two or three deer at least.

We now turned toward the distant encampment. As we rode along, antelope in considerable numbers were flying lightly in all directions over the plain, but not one of them would stand and be shot at. When we reached the foot of the mountain-ridge that lay between us and the village, we were too impatient to take the smooth and circuitous route; so turning short to the left, we drove our wearied animals directly upward among the rocks. Still more antelope were leaping about among these flinty hill-sides. Each of us shot at one, though from a great distance, and each missed his mark. At length we reached the summit of the last ridge. Looking down, we saw the bustling camp in the valley at our feet, and ingloriously descended to it. As we rode among the lodges, the Indians looked in vain for the fresh meat that should have hung behind our saddles, and the squaws uttered various suppressed ejaculations, to the great indignation of Reynal. Our mortification was increased when we rode up to his lodge. Here we saw his young Indian relative, the Hail-Storm, his light graceful figure reclining on the ground in an easy attitude, while with his friend the Rabbit, who sat by his side, he was making an abundant meal from a wooden bowl of *wasna,* which the squaw had placed between them. Near him lay the fresh skin of a female elk, which he had just killed among the mountains, only a mile or two from the camp. No doubt the boy's heart was elated with triumph, but he betrayed no sign of it. He even seemed totally unconscious of our approach, and his handsome face had all the tranquillity of Indian self-control; a self-control which prevents the exhibition of emotion without restraining the emotion itself. It was about two months since I had known the Hail-Storm, and within that time his character had remarkably developed. When I first saw him, he was just emerging from the habits and feelings of the boy into the ambition of the hunter and warrior. He had lately killed his first deer, and this had excited his aspirations after distinction. Since that time he had been continually in search of game, and no young hunter in the village had been so active or so fortunate as he. It will perhaps be remembered how fearlessly he attacked the buffalo-bull, as we were moving toward our camp at the Medicine Bow Mountain. All this success had produced a marked change in his character. As I first remembered him he always shunned the society of the young squaws, and was extremely bashful and sheepish in their presence; but now, in the confidence of his own reputation, he began to assume the airs and the arts of a man of gallantry. He wore his red blanket dashingly over his left shoulder, painted his cheeks every day with vermilion, and hung pendants of shells in his ears. If I observed aright, he met with very good success in his new pursuits; still the Hail-Storm had much to accomplish before he attained the full standing of a warrior. Gallantly as he began to bear himself among the women and girls, he still was timid and abashed in the presence of the chiefs and old men; for he had never yet killed a man, or stricken the dead body of an enemy in battle. I have no doubt that the handsome smooth-faced boy burned with a keen desire to flesh his maiden scalping-knife, and I would not have encamped alone with him without watching his movements with a distrustful eye.

His elder brother, the Horse, was of a different character. He was nothing but a lazy dandy. He knew very well how to hunt, but preferred to live by the hunting of others. He had no appetite for distinction, and the Hail-Storm, though a few years younger than he, already surpassed him in reputation. He had a dark and ugly face, and he passed a great part of his time in adorning it with vermilion, and contemplating it by means of a little pocket looking-glass which I gave him. As for the rest of the day, he divided it between eating and sleeping, and sitting in the sun on the outside of a lodge. Here he would remain for hour after hour, arrayed in all his finery, with an old dragoon's sword in his hand, and evidently flattering himself that he was the centre of attraction to the eyes of the surrounding squaws. Yet he sat looking straight forward with a face of the utmost gravity, as if wrapped in profound meditation, and it was only by the occasional sidelong glances which he shot at his supposed admirers that one could detect the true course of his thoughts.

Both he and his brother may represent a class in the Indian community: neither should the Hail-Storm's friend, the Rabbit, be passed by without notice. The Hail-Storm and he were inseparable: they ate, slept, and hunted together, and shared with one another almost all that they possessed. If there be any thing that deserves to be called romantic in the Indian character, it is to be sought for in friendships such as this, which are quite common among many of the prairie tribes.

Slowly, hour after hour, that weary afternoon dragged away. I lay in Reynal's lodge, overcome by the listless torpor that pervaded the whole encampment. The day's work was finished, or if it were not, the inhabitants had resolved not to finish it at all, and all were dozing quietly within the shelter of the lodges. A profound lethargy, the very spirit of indolence, seemed to have sunk upon the village. Now and then I could hear the low laughter of some girl from within a neighboring lodge, or the small shrill voices of a few restless children, who alone were moving in the deserted area. The spirit of the place infected me; I could not even think consecutively; I was fit only for musing and reverie, when at last, like the rest, I fell asleep.

When evening came, and the fires were lighted round the lodges, a select family circle convened in the neighborhood of Reynal's domicil. It was composed entirely of his squaw's relatives, a mean and ignoble clan, among whom none but the Hail-Storm held forth any promise of future distinction. Even his prospects were rendered not a little dubious by the character of the family, less however from any principle of aristocratic distinction than from the want of powerful supporters to assist him in his undertakings, and help to avenge his quarrels. Raymond and I sat down along with them. There were eight or ten men gathered around the fire, together with about as many women, old and young, some of whom were tolerably good-looking. As the pipe passed round among the men, a lively conversation went forward, more merry than delicate, and at length two or three of the elder women (for the girls were somewhat diffident and bashful) began to assail Raymond with various pungent witticisms. Some of the men took part, and an old squaw concluded by bestowing on him a ludicrous nickname, at which a general laugh followed at his expense. Raymond grinned and giggled, and made several futile attempts at repartee. Knowing the impolicy and even danger of suffering myself to be placed in a ludicrous light among the Indians, I maintained a rigid inflexible countenance, and wholly escaped their sallies.

In the morning I found, to my great disgust, that the camp was to retain its position for another day. I dreaded its languor and monotony, and to escape it, I set out to explore the surrounding mountains. I was accompanied by a faithful friend, my rifle, the only friend indeed on whose prompt assistance in time of trouble I could implicitly rely. Most of the Indians in the village, it is true, professed good will towards the whites, but the experience of others and my own observation had taught me the extreme folly of confidence, and the utter impossibility of foreseeing to what sudden acts the strange unbridled impulses of an Indian may urge him. When among this people danger is never so near as when you are unprepared for it, never so remote as when you are armed and on the alert to meet it at any moment. Nothing offers so strong a temptation to their ferocious instincts as the appearance of timidity, weakness, or security.

Many deep and gloomy gorges, choked with trees and bushes, opened from the sides of the hills, which were shaggy with forests wherever the rocks permitted vegetation to spring. A great number of Indians were stalking along the edges of the woods, and boys were whooping and laughing on the mountain-sides, practising eye and hand, and indulging their destructive propensities by following birds and small animals and killing them with their little bows and arrows. There was one glen, stretching up between steep cliffs far into the bosom of the mountain. I began to ascend along its bottom, pushing my way onward among the rocks, trees, and bushes that obstructed it. A slender thread of water trickled along its centre, which since issuing from the heart of its native rock could scarcely have been warmed or gladdened by a ray of sunshine.

After advancing for some time, I conceived myself to be entirely alone;
but coming to a part of the glen in a great measure free of trees and
undergrowth, I saw at some distance the black head and red shoulders of
an Indian among the bushes above. The reader need not prepare himself
for a startling adventure, for I have none to relate. The head and shoulders belonged to Mene-Seela, my best friend in the village. As I had
approached noiselessly with my moccasoned feet, the old man was quite
unconscious of my presence; and turning to a point where I could gain
an unobstructed view of him, I saw him seated alone, immovable as a
statue, among the rocks and trees. His face was turned upward, and his
eyes seemed riveted on a pine-tree springing from a cleft in the precipice
above. The crest of the pine was swaying to and fro in the wind, and its
long limbs waved slowly up and down, as if the tree had life. Looking for a
while at the old man, I was satisfied that he was engaged in an act of
worship, or prayer, or communion of some kind with a supernatural
being. I longed to penetrate his thoughts, but I could do nothing more
than conjecture and speculate. I knew that though the intellect of an
Indian can embrace the idea of an all-wise, all-powerful Spirit, the
supreme Ruler of the universe, yet his mind will not always ascend into
communion with a being that seems to him so vast, remote, and incom-
prehensible; and when danger threatens, when his hopes are broken,
when the black wing of sorrow overshadows him, he is prone to turn for
relief to some inferior agency, less removed from the ordinary scope of his
faculties. He has a guardian spirit, on whom he relies for succor and
guidance. To him all nature is instinct with mystic influence. Among
those mountains not a wild beast was prowling, a bird singing, or a leaf
fluttering, that might not tend to direct his destiny, or give warning of
what was in store for him; and he watches the world of nature around
him as the astrologer watches the stars. So closely is he linked with it,
that his guardian-spirit, no unsubstantial creation of the fancy, is usually
embodied in the form of some living thing; a bear, a wolf, an eagle, or a
serpent; and Mene-Seela, as he gazed intently on the old pine-tree, might
believe it to inshrine the fancied guide and protector of his life.

Whatever was passing in the mind of the old man, it was no part of sense or of delicacy to disturb him. Silently retracing my footsteps, I descended the glen until I came to a point where I could climb the steep precipices that shut it in, and gain the side of the mountain. Looking up, I saw a tall peak rising among the woods. Something impelled me to climb; I had not felt for many a day such strength and elasticity of limb. An hour and a half of slow and often intermitted labor brought me to the very summit; and emerging from the dark shadows of the rocks and pines, I stepped forth into the light, and walking along the sunny verge of a precipice, seated myself on its extreme point. Looking between the mountain-peaks to the westward, the pale blue prairie was stretching to the farthest horizon, like a serene and tranquil ocean. The surrounding mountains were in themselves sufficiently striking and impressive, but this contrast gave redoubled effect to their stern features.

MARK TWAIN (SAMUEL L. CLEMENS)

(1835–1910)

From *Roughing It*

In 1872, Mark Twain published his second major travel book, Roughing It, *which he described as "a record of several years of variegated
vagabondizing" in the American West. Those several years included a
disastrous stint as a silver prospector in Nevada in 1860, before he
found his career in journalism. With trademark Twain humor, he takes
the occasion to mock himself—and therefore everyone else who ever
tried a get-rich-quick scheme in the West—turning the book into an
irreverent anti-adventure story and good-natured social critique.*

*Twain embraced the notion of the open road and its promise of free-
dom and experience wholeheartedly, and yet in reality he was a reluc-
tant and often uncomfortable traveler.* Roughing It *begins with the
flush of youthful enthusiasm: "I never had been away from home, and
that word 'travel' had a seductive charm for me." But as he goes by
coach and rail from the Missouri River to Nevada, then by horseback
through deserts and mountains, he can not help tempering his excitement and reverence for the scenery around him with some irony. By the
time he heads for Lake Tahoe with his friend Johnny K, he is in full-*

blown comic mode, where romantic expectations have been offset by mishap, and gallantry has given way to laziness. In the following passage, the adventurer, setting claim to a piece of the frontier, has become the klutz, setting fire to a forest while trying to fry up some bacon.

It was the end of August, and the skies were cloudless and the weather superb. In two or three weeks I had grown wonderfully fascinated with the curious new country, and concluded to put off my return to "the States" awhile. I had grown well accustomed to wearing a damaged slouch hat, blue woolen shirt, and pants crammed into boot-tops, and gloried in the absence of coat, vest and braces. I felt rowdy-ish and "bully," (as the historian Josephus phrases it, in his fine chapter upon the destruction of the Temple). It seemed to me that nothing could be so fine and so romantic. I had become an officer of the government, but that was for mere sublimity. The office was an unique sinecure. I had nothing to do and no salary. I was private Secretary to his majesty the Secretary[1] and there was not yet writing enough for two of us. So Johnny K———and I devoted our time to amusement. He was the young son of an Ohio nabob and was out there for recreation. He got it. We had heard a world of talk about the marvellous beauty of Lake Tahoe, and finally curiosity drove us thither to see it. Three or four members of the Brigade had been there and located some timber lands on its shores and stored up a quantity of provisions in their camp. We strapped a couple of blankets on our shoulders and took an axe apiece and started—for we intended to take up a wood ranch or so ourselves and become wealthy. We were on foot. The reader will find it advantageous to go horseback. We were told that the distance was eleven miles. We tramped a long time on level ground, and then toiled laboriously up a mountain about a thousand miles high and looked over. No lake there. We descended on the

---

[1] "His Majesty" is Twain's brother, appointed secretary of the Nevada Territory. Twain's excuse for the journey was that his brother needed an undersecretary.

other side, crossed the valley and toiled up another mountain three or four thousand miles high, apparently, and looked over again. No lake yet. We sat down tired and perspiring, and hired a couple of Chinamen to curse those people who had beguiled us. Thus refreshed, we presently resumed the march with renewed vigor and determination. We plodded on, two or three hours longer, and at last the Lake burst upon us—a noble sheet of blue water lifted six thousand three hundred feet above the level of the sea, and walled in by a rim of snow-clad mountain peaks that towered aloft full three thousand feet higher still! It was a vast oval, and one would have to use up eighty or a hundred good miles in traveling around it. As it lay there with the shadows of the mountains brilliantly photographed upon its still surface I thought it must surely be the fairest picture the whole earth affords.

We found the small skiff belonging to the Brigade boys, and without loss of time set out across a deep bend of the lake toward the landmarks that signified the locality of the camp. I got Johnny to row—not because I mind exertion myself, but because it makes me sick to ride backwards when I am at work. But I steered. A three-mile pull brought us to the camp just as the night fell, and we stepped ashore very tired and wolfishly hungry. In a "cache" among the rocks we found the provisions and the cooking utensils, and then, all fatigued as I was, I sat down on a boulder and superintended while Johnny gathered wood and cooked supper. Many a man who had gone through what I had, would have wanted to rest.

It was a delicious supper—hot bread, fried bacon, and black coffee. It was a delicious solitude we were in, too. Three miles away was a saw-mill and some workmen, but there were not fifteen other human beings throughout the wide circumference of the lake. As the darkness closed down and the stars came out and spangled the great mirror with jewels, we smoked meditatively in the solemn hush and forgot our troubles and our pains. In due time we spread our blankets in the warm sand between two large boulders and soon feel asleep, careless of the procession of ants that passed in through rents in our clothing and explored our persons. Nothing could disturb the sleep that fettered us, for it had been fairly earned, and if our consciences had any sins on them they had to adjourn court for that night, any way. The wind rose just as we were losing consciousness, and we were lulled to sleep by the beating of the surf upon the shore.

It is always very cold on that lake shore in the night, but we had plenty of blankets and were warm enough. We never moved a muscle all night, but waked at early dawn in the original positions, and got up at once, thoroughly refreshed, free from soreness, and brim full of friskiness. There is no end of wholesome medicine in such an experience. That morning we could have whipped ten such people as we were the day before—sick ones at any rate. But the world is slow, and people will go to "water cures" and "movement cures" and to foreign lands for health. Three months of camp life on Lake Tahoe would restore an Egyptian mummy to his pristine vigor, and give him an appetite like an alligator. I do not mean the oldest and driest mummies, of course, but the fresher ones. The air up there in the clouds is very pure and fine, bracing and delicious. And why shouldn't it be?—it is the same the angels breathe. I think that hardly any amount of fatigue can be gathered together that a man cannot sleep off in one night on the sand by its side. Not under a roof, but under the sky; it seldom or never rains there in the summer time. I know a man who went there to die. But he made a failure of it. He was a skeleton when he came, and could barely stand. He had no appetite, and did nothing but read tracts and reflect on the future. Three months later he was sleeping out of doors regularly, eating all he could hold, three times a day, and chasing game over mountains three thousand feet high for recreation. And he was a skeleton no longer, but weighed part of a ton. This is no fancy sketch, but the truth. His disease was consumption. I confidently commend his experience to other skeletons.

I superintended again, and as soon as we had eaten breakfast we got in the boat and skirted along the lake shore about three miles and disembarked. We liked the appearance of the place, and so we claimed some three hundred acres of it and stuck our "notices" on a tree. It was yellow pine timber land—a dense forest of trees a hundred feet high and from one to five feet through at the butt. It was necessary to fence our property or we could not hold it. That is to say, it was necessary to cut down trees here and there and make them fall in such a way as to form a sort of enclosure (with pretty wide gaps in it). We cut down three trees apiece, and found it such heart-breaking work that we decided to "rest our case" on those; if they held the property, well and good; if they didn't, let the property spill out through the gaps and go; it was no use to work ourselves to death merely to save a few acres of land. Next day we came back to build a house—for a house was also necessary, in order to hold the property. We decided to build a substantial log-house and excite the envy of the Brigade boys; but by the time we had cut and trimmed the first log it seemed unnecessary to be so elaborate, and so we concluded to build it of saplings. However, two saplings, duly cut and trimmed, compelled recognition of the fact that a still modester architecture would satisfy the law, and so we concluded to build a "brush" house. We devoted the next day to this work, but we did so much "sitting around" and discussing, that by the middle of the afternoon we had achieved only a half-way sort of affair which one of us had to watch while the other cut brush, lest if both turned our backs we might not be able to find it again, it had such a strong family resemblance to the surrounding vegetation. But we were satisfied with it.

We were land owners now, duly seized and possessed, and within the protection of the law. Therefore we decided to take up our residence on our own domain and enjoy that large sense of independence which only such an experience can bring. Late the next afternoon, after a good long rest, we sailed away from the Brigade camp with all the provisions and cooking utensils we could carry off—borrow is the more accurate word— and just as the night was falling we beached the boat at our own landing.

IF THERE IS any life that is happier than the life we led on our timber ranch for the next two or three weeks, it must be a sort of life which I have not read of in books or experienced in person. We did not see a human being but ourselves during the time, or hear any sounds but those that were made by the wind and the waves, the sighing of the pines, and now and then the far-off thunder of an avalanche. The forest about us was dense and cool, the sky above us was cloudless and brilliant with sunshine, the broad lake before us was glassy and clear, or rippled and breezy, or black and storm-tossed, according to Nature's mood; and its circling border of mountain domes, clothed with forests, scarred with land-slides, cloven by cañons and valleys, and helmeted with glittering snow, fitly framed and finished the noble picture. The view was always fascinating, bewitching, entrancing. The eye was never tired of gazing, night or day, in calm or storm; it suffered but one grief, and that was that it could not look always, but must close sometimes in sleep.

We slept in the sand close to the water's edge, between two protecting boulders, which took care of the stormy night-winds for us. We never took any paregoric to make us sleep. At the first break of dawn we were always up and running foot-races to tone down excess of physical vigor and exuberance of spirits. That is, Johnny was—but I held his hat. While smoking the pipe of peace after breakfast we watched the sentinel peaks put on the glory of the sun, and followed the conquering light as it swept down among the shadows, and set the captive crags and forests free. We watched the tinted pictures grow and brighten upon the water till every little detail of forest, precipice and pinnacle was wrought in and finished, and the miracle of the enchanter complete. Then to "business."

That is, drifting around in the boat. We were on the north shore. There, the rocks on the bottom are sometimes gray, sometimes white. This gives the marvelous transparency of the water a fuller advantage than it has elsewhere on the lake. We usually pushed out a hundred yards or so from shore, and then lay down on the thwarts, in the sun, and let the boat drift by the hour whither it would. We seldom talked. It interrupted the Sabbath stillness, and marred the dreams the luxurious rest and indolence brought. The shore all along was indented with deep, curved bays and coves, bordered by narrow sand-beaches; and where the sand ended, the steep mountain-sides rose right up aloft into space—

rose up like a vast wall a little out of the perpendicular, and thickly wooded with tall pines.

So singularly clear was the water, that where it was only twenty or thirty feet deep the bottom was so perfectly distinct that the boat seemed floating in the air! Yes, where it was even *eighty* feet deep. Every little pebble was distinct, every speckled trout, every hand's-breadth of sand. Often, as we lay on our faces, a granite boulder, as large as a village church, would start out of the bottom apparently, and seem climbing up rapidly to the surface, till presently it threatened to touch our faces, and we could not resist the impulse to seize an oar and avert the danger. But the boat would float on, and the boulder descend again, and then we could see that when we had been exactly above it, it must still have been twenty or thirty feet below the surface. Down through the transparency of these great depths, the water was not *merely* transparent, but dazzlingly, brilliantly so. All objects seen through it had a bright, strong vividness, not only of outline, but of every minute detail, which they would not have had when seen simply through the same depth of atmosphere. So empty and airy did all spaces seem below us, and so strong was the sense of floating high aloft in mid-nothingness, that we called these boat-excursions "balloon-voyages."

We fished a good deal, but we did not average one fish a week. We could see trout by the thousand winging about in the emptiness under us, or sleeping in shoals on the bottom, but they would not bite—they could see the line too plainly, perhaps. We frequently selected the trout we wanted, and rested the bait patiently and persistently on the end of his nose at a depth of eighty feet, but he would only shake it off with an annoyed manner, and shift his position.

We bathed occasionally, but the water was rather chilly, for all it looked so sunny. Sometimes we rowed out to the "blue water," a mile or two from shore. It was as dead blue as indigo there, because of the immense depth. By official measurement the lake in its centre is one thousand five hundred and twenty-five feet deep!

Sometimes, on lazy afternoons, we lolled on the sand in camp, and smoked pipes and read some old well-worn novels. At night, by the camp-fire, we played euchre and seven-up to strengthen the mind—and played them with cards so greasy and defaced that only a whole summer's acquaintance with them could enable the student to tell the ace of clubs from the jack of diamonds.

We never slept in our "house." It never recurred to us, for one thing; and besides, it was built to hold the ground, and that was enough. We did not wish to strain it.

By and by our provisions began to run short, and we went back to the old camp and laid in a new supply. We were gone all day, and reached home again about night-fall, pretty tired and hungry. While Johnny was carrying the main bulk of the provisions up to our "house" for future use, I took the loaf of bread, some slices of bacon, and the coffee-pot, ashore, set them down by a tree, lit a fire, and went back to the boat to get the frying-pan. While I was at this, I heard a shout from Johnny, and looking up I saw that my fire was galloping all over the premises!

Johnny was on the other side of it. He had to run through the flames to get to the lake shore, and then we stood helpless and watched the devastation.

The ground was deeply carpeted with dry pine-needles, and the fire touched them off as if they were gunpowder. It was wonderful to see with what fierce speed the tall sheet of flame traveled! My coffee-pot was gone, and everything with it. In a minute and a half the fire seized upon a dense growth of dry manzanita chapparal six or eight feet high, and then the roaring and popping and crackling was something terrific. We were driven to the boat by the intense heat, and there we remained, spell-bound.

Within half an hour all before us was a tossing, blinding tempest of flame! It went surging up adjacent ridges—surmounted them and disappeared in the cañons beyond—burst into view upon higher and farther ridges, presently—shed a grander illumination abroad, and dove again—flamed out again, directly, higher and still higher up the mountain-side—threw out skirmishing parties of fire here and there, and sent them trailing their crimson spirals away among remote ramparts and ribs and

gorges, till as far as the eye could reach the lofty mountain-fronts were webbed as it were with a tangled network of red lava streams. Away across the water the crags and domes were lit with a ruddy glare, and the firmament above was a reflected hell!

Every feature of the spectacle was repeated in the glowing mirror of the lake! Both pictures were sublime, both were beautiful; but that in the lake had a bewildering richness about it that enchanted the eye and held it with the stronger fascination.

We sat absorbed and motionless through four long hours. We never thought of supper, and never felt fatigue. But at eleven o'clock the conflagration had traveled beyond our range of vision, and then darkness stole down upon the landscape again.

Hunger asserted itself now, but there was nothing to eat. The provisions were all cooked, no doubt, but we did not go to see. We were homeless wanderers again, without any property. Our fence was gone, our house burned down; no insurance. Our pine forest was well scorched, the dead trees all burned up, and our broad acres of manzanita swept away. Our blankets were on our usual sand-bed, however, and so we lay down and went to sleep. The next morning we started back to the old camp, but while out a long way from shore, so great a storm came up that we dared not try to land. So I baled out the seas we shipped, and Johnny pulled heavily through the billows till we had reached a point three or four miles beyond the camp. The storm was increasing, and it became evident that it was better to take the hazard of beaching the boat than go down in a hundred fathoms of water; so we ran in, with tall white-caps following, and I sat down in the stern-sheets and pointed her head-on to the shore. The instant the bow struck, a wave came over the stern that washed crew and cargo ashore, and saved a deal of trouble. We shivered in the lee of a boulder all the rest of the day, and froze all the night through. In the morning the tempest had gone down, and we paddled down to the camp without any unnecessary delay. We were so starved that we ate up the rest of the Brigade's provisions, and then set out to Carson to tell them about it and ask their forgiveness. It was accorded, upon payment of damages.

We made many trips to the lake after that, and had many a hairbreadth escape and blood-curdling adventure which will never be recorded in any history.

DILLON WALLACE

(1863–1939)

From *The Lure of the Labrador Wild*

Young, idealistic, and bored with bourgeois life in New York, journalist Leonidas Hubbard, Jr., had by the late 1800s become obsessed with the "uncharted" interior of Labrador. When he came into some money, he convinced his friend Dillon Wallace and a Cree guide by the name of George to join him on a daring adventure that he could later write up for his publisher. He found adventure of the most desperate kind. He didn't live to write it up for anyone. Wallace published his heart-wrenching, suspenseful account of the journey as a memorial to his friend.

A ship dropped the three men on the eastern coast of Labrador, and with little more than a canoe, compass, some pea flour, bacon, and a couple of rifles, they set out in the direction of Lake Michikamau, famous as a mecca for caribou each fall. In a fateful moment of care-lessness, the men take the wrong river out of Grand Lake and are soon lost in a maze of lakes. On portage after portage, they find little game and slowly weaken from starvation. Still pressing on, and still lost, they reach the point of no return, where they know that, in their debilitated state, their chances of getting to a settlement before winter sets in and the rivers freeze are next to none. Hubbard dies on the way back, and only by the slimmest of margins do the other two survive.

Hubbard's disastrous trip to the Far North spawned two other books by followers. In 1905, Mina Hubbard paddled her husband's intended route across Labrador with Indian guides and wrote A Woman's Way Across Unknown Labrador. *And more recently, two journalists retraced Hubbard's original, ill-fated route and wrote the classic adventure tale,* Great Heart. *Wallace's account stands out for its unflinching honesty and dignity in the face of extreme hardship, and its vivid portrayal of the psychological as well as physical deterioration he and the others experience. Here we join them in the days before and after their crucial decision to turn back.*

From the northwesterly end of Lake Disappointment[1] we portaged on Friday (August 28) across a neck of land to two small, shallow lakes that lay to the northward, and in the teeth of a gale paddled to the northern shore of the farther lake. There we went into camp for the day in order that Hubbard might rest, as he was still weak from the effects of his recent illness. We took advantage of the opportunity to patch up our moccasins and clothing as best we could, and held a long consultation, the outcome of which was, that it was decided that for the present, at least, we should leave behind us our canoe and the bulk of our camp equipment, including the tent, and push on with light packs, consisting of one blanket for each man, an axe, the two pistols, one rifle, and our stock of food.

Before us there apparently stretched miles of rough, rocky country. Our equipment and stock of food at this time made up into four packs of about 100 pounds each. The canoe, water-soaked and its crevices filled

---

[1] So named because they hoped this lake would be a key waterway connecting them to Lake Michikamau, but it was landlocked.

with sand, must now have weighed nearly a hundred pounds. It was a most awkward thing to carry over one's head when the wind blew, and where there were rocks there was danger of the carrier falling and breaking, not only the canoe, but his own bones. This meant that if our entire outfit were taken along, practically every bit of land we travelled would have to be covered twice. In leaving the canoe behind, we, of course, should have to take chances on meeting intervening lakes; but, once in the region of northern Michikamau, there seemed a fair chance of our falling in with Indians that would take us down the George River,[2] and the advantages of light travel were obvious with winter fast approaching.

The stock of food we had to carry would not weigh us down. The dried venison had been reduced to a few pounds, so that we had to eat of it sparingly and make our principal diet on boiled fish and the water in which it was cooked. We had just a bit of flour, enough to serve bread at rare intervals as a great dainty. Nothing remained of our caribou tallow and marrow grease. It is true we held in reserve the "emergency ration"; but this consisted only of eighteen pounds of pea meal, a pint of rice, and a small piece of bacon. This ration we had pledged ourselves to use only in case of the direst necessity, should we be compelled to make a forced retreat, and we felt we must not think of it at this time as food on hand.

In camp on Friday night I could see that Hubbard was worrying considerably. Nervously active by habit, he found delay doubly hard. The days we had spent on Lake Disappointment in a vain search for a river had been particularly trying on his nerves, and had left him a prey to many fears. The spectre of an early winter in this sub-Arctic land began to haunt him constantly. The days were slipping away and were becoming visibly shorter with each sunset. If we could get to the Indians on the George, we should be safe; for they would give us warm skins for clothing and replenish our stock of food. But should we meet with more

---

[2] Their plans depended on reaching Michikamau before the caribou hunt was over. There they hoped to find Indians to help them back to coastal settlements via the George River.

delays, and arrive on the George too late for the caribou migration, and fail to find the Indians, what then? Well, then, our fate would be sealed. Hubbard was the leader of the expedition, and he felt himself responsible, not only for his own life, but, to a large extent, for ours. It is little wonder, therefore, that he brooded over the possibilities of calamity, but with youth, ambition, and the ardent spirit that never will say die, he invariably fought off his fears, and bent himself more determinedly than ever to achieve the purpose for which he had set out. Frequently he confided his fears to me, but was careful to conceal all traces of them from George.

In light marching order we went out on Saturday morning (August 29), making rapid progress to the northward, through a thick growth of small spruce timber and over a low ridge; but scarcely had we gone a mile when we were compelled to halt. There in front of us was a small lake extending east and west. It was not more than an eighth of a mile across it, but a long distance around it. Back we went for the canoe, and at the same time brought forward the whole camp outfit. Again we tried light marching order, and again a lake compelled us to go back for the canoe and outfit. And thus it was all day: a stretch of a mile or so; then a long, narrow lake to cross, until finally we were forced to admit that our plan of proceeding with light packs and without the canoe was impracticable.

Hubbard was feeling stronger on Saturday evening, and we had a pleasant camp. George made a big fire of tamarack, and we lay before it on a couch of spruce boughs and ate tough boiled venison and drank the broth; and, feeling we had made some progress, we were happy, despite the fact that we were in the midst of a trackless wilderness with our way to Michikamau and the Indians as uncertain as ever.

Sunday morning (August 30) broke superbly beautiful, and the day continued clear and mild. We made an early start; for every hour had become precious. While we were doing this cross-country work without any streams to guide us, it was George's custom to go ahead all the way from half a mile to two miles and blaze a trail, so that when we were travelling back and forth bringing up the packs and the canoe we might not go astray. In the course of the morning we came to two small lakes, which we paddled over.

We had believed that our goose chases were over; for these birds now having grown their feathers, could fly, and were generally beyond the reach of our pistols and the uncertain aim of a rifle at anything on the wing. For two days we had heard them flying, and now and then would see them high in the air. But while we were crossing one of the small lakes this Sunday, five geese walked gravely down the bank and into the water ahead of the canoe. One of them we got with a pistol shot; the others flew away. In another lake we reached late in the day we came upon five or six ducks. They were not far away, but dived so frequently we were unable to shoot them with pistol or rifle. A shotgun might have enabled us to get nearly all the geese as well as the ducks and other game we saw on the wing and in the water on other occasions. We often expressed the regret that we had no shotgun with us. At one time Hubbard had intended that one should be taken, but later decided that the ammunition would be too bulky.

A low, semi-barren ridge running east and west lay just beyond the small blue-green lake in which we saw the ducks towards evening. About seven miles beyond the ridge to the north was a short range of high, barren mountains that were perhaps a trifle lower than the Kipling Mountains. Upon ascending the ridge we heard the rushing of water on the other side, which sound proved to come from a small fall on a stream expanding and stretching out to the eastward in long, narrow lakes. Apparently these lakes were the headquarters of a small river flowing to the southeast, and in all probability here was the source of the Red River, which, as I have described, flows into the Nascaupee some fifteen or eighteen miles above Grand Lake.[3]

The whole character of the country had now changed. It was very

[3] Having taken the wrong river out of Grand Lake, but not knowing where they went wrong, the men have only a hazy understanding of the watersheds they are traversings, and no map.

rocky and steadily growing more barren. Ridges and hills extended to the mountains on the north. Great boulders were piled in confusion behind us and in front of us. Portaging over them had been most difficult and dangerous. A misstep might have meant a broken leg, and as it was, the skin had been pretty nearly all knocked off of our shins from the instep to the knee.

Below the fall we had discovered was a deep pool in which Hubbard caught, with his emergency kit and a tamarack pole, twenty trout averaging twelve inches in length. We camped near this pool. The hard work of the day had brought on Hubbard another attack of his old illness; apparently it was only by a great exertion of will-power that he kept moving at all during the afternoon, and at night he was very weak. Before supper he drank a cup of strong tea as a stimulant, and was taken immediately with severe vomiting.

Watching his suffering, the thought came to me whether, disregarding all other considerations, I should not at this point strongly insist on the party turning back. I was aware, however, of the grim determination of the man to get his work done, and was convinced of the uselessness of any attempt to sway him from his purpose. Moreover, I myself was hopeful of our ability to reach the caribou grounds; I felt sure that Hubbard's grit would carry him through. Looking back now, I can see I should have at least attempted to turn him back, but I am still convinced it would have been useless. I thoroughly believe only one thing would have turned the boy back at that time—force.

. . .

In the afternoon I took my rod and went about three miles to the westward, where I came upon an isolated pond with no apparent outlet. Everywhere I could see the trout jumping, and by sundown had as long a string of them as I could conveniently carry. It was an hour after dark when I reached camp. George had returned, and they were beginning to fear that I was lost.

George had climbed the mountains, and he reported a fair line of travel to the northwest, with a "long lake that looked like a river," and, some distance northwest of that, "big water" and a tolerably good route for portages. What he told us led Hubbard to decide to continue on with the canoe and our entire outfit. George brought back with him two grouse he had shot.

The next morning (Tuesday, September 1) Hubbard was much better, and we began September with a renewed effort. It was rough and painful portaging over rocks and knolls. Every forty or fifty rods we came upon deep ponds with water so clear we could see the pebbles on the bottom. Between these ponds boulders were piled indiscriminately. In directing our course to the northwest we avoided the mountains that had lain just ahead. For two days we pushed on among the boulders, then over a wide marsh and through a heavy spruce growth, which brought us, on September 3d, to George's "lake that looked like a river." Let us call it Mary Lake.

Along Lake Mary we paddled, in the pouring rain that began that day, some five miles to its western end; and there, near a creek that flowed into it, we found the remains of an old Indian camp. George looked the camp over critically and remarked:

"The beggars killed two caribou, and they broke every bone up and boiled out the last drop of grease."

"What was it—a summer or a winter camp?" asked Hubbard.

"A summer," said George. "And they'd been fishing, too. There's a good fishing place—just try it."

We did try it, and we had a fairly good catch of large trout. For supper we had a few of the trout boiled, together with the water, with one spoonful of flour for each man stirred in. We ate the fish entire, entrails, head, and all, and from that time on we let no part of the fish we caught be thrown away. Everything now in the way of food George divided carefully into three equal parts, even the fish broth. By this time we had not enough flour on hand to make more than half a dozen cakes of bread, and we continued to use only a spoonful or two a day for each man, mixing it with game or fish broth; in this way we hoped it would satisfy to some extent our craving for grain, and last longer.

As evening approached the sky cleared, and a big full moon tipped the fir trees with silver and set Lake Mary to gleaming. The air was filled with the perfume of the balsam and spruce, and it acted as a tonic on our spirits and drove away the depression of the day's work in the rain. Hubbard seemed to be as full of vim as ever, and all of us were quite contented.

Sitting on the couch of boughs, George looked up at the sky and said:

"There's a fine Indian story about that moon."

Of course Hubbard and I begged that he tell it to us.

"Well," said George, "it's a long story about a boy and girl that lived together in a wigwam by a great water. Their father and mother were dead, and the boy had learned to be a great hunter, because he had to hunt for them both, though he was young. One day he found a tree that was very high, and he climbed it, and told his sister to climb it with him; and they climbed higher and higher, and as they climbed, the tree grew taller and taller; and after a while they reached the moon. And then the boy laid down to sleep, and after a while he woke up with a bright light shinin' in his face—it was the sun passin' 'long that way. The boy said he would set a snare for the sun and catch it, and the next night he had his snare set when the sun came 'long, and he caught the sun, and then it was always bright on the moon.

"There's a lot more to that story," added George, after a pause, "and I'll tell it to you some time; but it's too long and too late to tell it to-night."

Unfortunately we never heard the continuation of the tale. George often hinted at interesting folklore stories about the milky way and different stars, and various other things in nature; but this was the nearest approach to a story we ever wrung from him.

From our last camp on Lake Disappointment to our camp at the western end of Lake Mary we had travelled about twenty-five miles. In leaving the latter camp on September 4th we inclined our course directly west, to reach the "big water" George had seen from his mountain. During the next four days we encountered bad weather. As evening came on the sky would clear and remain clear until morning, when the clouds and rain would reappear. On the 4th there was sleet with the rain, and on the 6th we had our first snow, which soon was washed away, however, by rain.

Our progress on the 4th was along the edge of a marsh between two low, wooded ridges, and then over the marsh and through several ponds, upon the shore of one of which we camped early in order that George might climb a hill, view the country and decide upon the shortest and best route to the "big water." He reported it about three miles ahead.

It had been our rule to defer our bathing until the evening's chill had quieted the flies, but now there was no need of that, as the colder weather had practically killed them for the season. About this time I noticed that Hubbard did not take his usual bath, and I remarked:

"The weather is getting pretty cold for bathing in the open, isn't it?"

"Yes," said Hubbard; "but I wouldn't let that stop me if I weren't ashamed of my bones. To tell you the truth, Wallace, I'm like a walking skeleton."

It was true. We were all very thin, but our lack of food told upon Hubbard's appearance the most, as he was naturally slender.

The "big water" George thought was only three miles away proved to be like the wisp of hay that is held before the donkey's nose to lead him on. Day after day we floundered through swamps and marshes, over rocky, barren hills, and through thick growths of willows and alders, and at the end of the day's journey it would apparently be as far off as ever. The explanation was that in the rarefied atmosphere of interior Labrador distances are very deceptive; when George reported that the "big water" was three miles ahead it must have been fully fifteen.

On the 5th, while crossing the barrens we came upon some blueberries and after eating our fill we were able to gather enough to supply each man with a big dish of them for supper. We were working our way over some bluffs on the afternoon of the 6th, when George, who was carrying the canoe, became separated from Hubbard and me. The wind was blowing hard, and he had difficulty in keeping the boat above his head. Suddenly I heard a call, and, looking back, saw George running after me, empty-handed. Hubbard did not hear the call, and went on. I dropped my pack, and waited for George to come up.

"You fellus better wait for me," he panted. "I can't manage the canoe alone in the wind, and if we get separated, I might strike the lake one place and you somewhere else. And," added George, sententiously, "you fellus have got the grub."

We shouted to Hubbard to wait, and when he answered, George and I returned for the canoe. Hubbard, however, kept on, and George and I carried the canoe ahead until we reached the thick woods into which he had disappeared; then George went back for my pack. Presently we heard Hubbard call from the depths of the woods, and a little later the sound of an axe.

As we learned later, he had dropped his pack, and was blazing a trail towards us in order that he might find it again. He was as nervous as George had been over his narrow escape from being permanently separated from the rest of the party, and at a time when such a happening would have had serious consequences for us all. Under the best of circumstances, the prospect of being left alone in the midst of that inhospitable wilderness was enough to appal.

On the 7th we reached a creek, and launched the canoe. Hubbard went ahead to fish below the rapids in the creek while George and I brought down the canoe and outfit, making several short portages. That night we camped two miles down the stream. Hubbard had caught, by hard work, thirty small trout, half of which we ate for supper.

We were still ravenously hungry after we finished the trout, but the bag contained only one more meal of venison and we did not dare draw on it. This, together with the difficulty we were having in reaching the "big water," set Hubbard to worrying again. He was especially anxious about the sufficiency of the material he had gathered for a story, fearing that if he failed to reach the caribou grounds there would not be enough to satisfy his publishers. I told him I thought he already had enough for a "bang-up" story.

"Anyway," I said, "we'll reach the caribou grounds, and see the Indians yet. George and I will go with you to the last ditch; you can count on us to the finish."

"All right," said Hubbard, evidently relieved. "If you boys aren't sick of it, it's on to the caribou grounds, late or no late. But I feel I've got you fellows in a tight place."

"We came with our eyes open," I replied, "and it's not your fault."

On the morning of September 8th, following our stream out to a shoal, rocky bay, we reached the "big water" at last. It was the great body of water that I have mapped out as Windbound Lake. Forty miles we had portaged from Lake Disappointment. We were practically out of food of any kind. Looking over the great expanse of water stretching miles away to the westward, we wondered what our new lake had in store for us of hope and success, of failure and despair. Would it lead us to Michikamau? If not, what were we to do?

On its farther shore, about twenty miles to the northwest, rose in solemn majesty a great, grey mountain, holding its head high above all the surrounding world. It shall be known as Mount Hubbard. To this mountain we decided to paddle and view the country. Instinctively we felt that Michikamau lay on the other side. We launched our canoe after a light luncheon of trout and a small ptarmigan George had shot. Once in the course of the afternoon we stopped paddling to climb a low ridge near the shore and eat cranberries, which we found in abundance on its barren top. From the ridge we could see water among the hills in every direction. In the large lake at our feet were numerous wooded islands.

We camped at dusk on one of these islands, and on Wednesday, September 9th, launched our canoe at day-break, to resume our journey to Mount Hubbard. We reached its base before ten o'clock. Blueberries grew in abundance on the side of the mountain, which, together with the country near it, had been burned. One of us, it was decided, should remain behind to pick berries, while the others climbed to the summit. I volunteered for the berrypicking, but I shall always regret it was not possible for me to go along.

Before Hubbard and George returned, I had our mixing basin filled with berries, and the kettle half full. The day was clear, crisp and delight-ful—one of those perfect days when the atmosphere is so pure and trans-parent that minute objects can be distinguished for miles. On the earth and on the water, not a thing of life was to be seen. The lake, relieved here and there with green island-spots; the cold rocks of distant moun-tains to the northeast; the low, semi-barren ridges and hills that we had travelled over bounding the lake to the eastward, and a ridge of green hills west of the lake that extended southward from behind Mount Hub-bard as far as the eye could reach—all combined to complete a scene of vast and solemn beauty; and I, alone on the mountain side picking blue-berries, felt an inexpressible sense of loneliness—felt myself the only thing of life in all that boundless wilderness-world.

From the moment Hubbard and George had left me, I had not seen or heard them. But up the mountain they went through the burnt spruce forest, up for four miles over rocks, up and up to the top; and then to the westernmost side of the peak they went and looked—looked to the west; and there, only a few miles away, lay Michikamau with its ninety-mile expanse of water—the lake we so long had sought for and fought so des-perately to reach. It was there, just beyond the ridge I had seen extending to the southward.

· · ·

Towards evening we took a northwesterly course in the canoe in search of the lake's outlet to Michikamau. While paddling we got a seven-pound namaycush, which enabled us to eat that night. Our camp was on a rock-bound island, partially covered with stunted gnarled spruce and fir trees. The weather had cleared and the heavens were bright with stars when we drew our canoe high upon the boulder-strewn shore, clear of the break-ing waves. The few small trout we had caught we stowed away in the bow of the canoe, as they were to be reserved for breakfast.

Early in the morning (September 12th) we were awakened by a north-east gale that threatened every moment to carry our tent from its fasten-ings, and as we peered out through the flaps, rain and snow dashed in our faces. The wind also was playing high jinks with the lake; it was white with foam, and the waves, dashing against the rocks on the shore, threw the spray high in the air. Evidently, there was no hope of launching the canoe that day, and assuming indifference of the driving storm that threatened to uncover us, we settled down for a much-needed morning sleep. At ten o'clock George crawled out to build a fire in the lee of some bushes and boil trout for a light breakfast. Soon he stuck his head in the tent, and his face told us something had happened even before he said:

"Well, that's too bad."

"What's too bad?" asked Hubbard anxiously.

"Somebody's stole the trout we left in the canoe."

"Who?" asked Hubbard and I together.

"Otter or somebody—maybe a marten." (George always referred to animals as persons.)

We all went again to look and make sure the fish were not there somewhere; but they were really gone, and we looked at one another and laughed, and continued to make light of it as we ate a breakfast of soup made of three little slices of bacon, with two or three spoonfuls of flour and rice.

. . .

Perhaps I should say here that these were the hungriest days of our journey. What we suffered later on, the good Lord only knows; but we never felt the food-craving, the hunger-pangs as now. In our enforced idleness it was impossible for us to prevent our thoughts from dwelling on things to eat, and this naturally accentuated our craving. Then, again, as everyone that has had such an experience knows, the pangs of hunger are mitigated after a certain period has been passed.

In the afternoon George and I took the pistols and ascended a low ridge in the rear of the camp to look for ptarmigans. Soon George exclaimed under his breath:

"There's two! Get down low and don't let 'em see you; the wind blows so they'll be mighty wild. I'll belly round to that bush over there and take a shot."

He crawled or wriggled along to the bush, which was the nearest cover and about forty yards from the birds. With a dinner in prospect, I watched him with keen anxiety. I could see him lying low and carefully aiming his pistol. Suddenly, bang!—and one of the birds fluttered straight up high in the air, trying desperately to sustain itself; then fell into the brush on the hillside below. At that George raised his head and gave a peculiar laugh—a laugh of wild exultation—an Indian laugh. He was the Indian hunter then. I never heard him laugh so again, nor saw him look quite as he did at that moment. As the other bird flew away, he rose to his feet and shouted:

"I hit 'im!—did you see how he went? Now we'll find 'im."

But we didn't. We beat the bushes high and low for an hour, and finally in disappointment and disgust gave up the search. The bird lay there dead somewhere, but we never found it, and we returned to camp empty-handed and perhaps, through anticipation, hungrier than ever.

On Tuesday (September 15th) the high west wind had not abated, and the occasional sleet-squalls continued. We were dreary and disconsolate when we came out of the tent and huddled close to the fire. For the first time Hubbard heard George tell his stories of Indians that starved. And there we were still windbound and helpless, with stomachs crying continually for food. And the caribou migration was soon to begin, if it had not already begun, and there seemed no prospect of the weather clearing.

We made an inventory of the food we were hoarding for an emergency, and found that in addition to about two pounds of flour, we had eighteen pounds of pea meal, a little less than a pint of rice, and a half a pound of bacon. George then told another story of Indians that starved. At length he stopped talking, and we sat silent for a long while, staring blankly at the blazing logs.

Slowly the minutes crawled. In great gusts the wind swept down, howling dismally among the trees and driving the sleet into our faces. Still we sat cowering in silence when Hubbard arose, pushed the loose ends of the partially burned sticks into the fire and stood with his back to the blaze, apparently deep in thought. Presently, turning slowly towards the lake, he walked down through the intervening brush and stood alone on the sandy shore contemplating the scene before him—the dull, lowering skies, the ridges in the distance, the lake in its angry mood protesting against his further advance, the low, wooded land that hid the gate to Michikamau.

Weather-beaten, haggard, gaunt and ragged, he stood there watching; then seemed to be lost completely in thought, forgetful of the wind and weather and dashing spray. Finally he turned about briskly, and, with quick, nervous steps, pushed through the brush to the fire, where George and I were still sitting in silence. Suddenly, and without a word of introduction, he said:

"Boys, what do you say to turning back?"

FOR A MOMENT I was dazed at the thought—the thought of turning back without ever seeing the Indians or caribou hunt, and I could not speak. George, however, soon found his tongue. He was still willing to go on, if need be, and risk his life with us.

"I came to go with you fellus," he said, "and I want to do what you fellus do."

"But," I said to Hubbard, "don't you think it will be easier to reach the Indians on the George, or even the George River Post, than Northwest River Post? We must surely be near the Indians; we shall probably see the smoke of their wigwams when we reach Michikamau. It is likely we shall find them camping on the big lake—either Mountaineers or Nascaupee—and if we get to them they'll surely help us."

"Yes," answered Hubbard, "if we get to them they'll help us; but these miserable westerly and northwesterly gales may keep us on these waters indefinitely, or even on the shore of Michikamau at a spot where we may not be able to launch our canoe or reach the Indians for days, and that would be fatal. The caribou migration is surely begun, and perhaps is over already, and there's no use in going ahead."

I saw his point and acquiesced. "I suppose it's best to turn back as soon as the wind will let us," I said; "for it's likely to subside only for a few hours at a time at this season, and perhaps if we don't get out when we can, we may never get out at all. But what does George say?" I asked, turning to our plucky companion.

"Oh," said he, "I'd like to turn back, and I think it's safest; but I'm goin' to stick to you fellus, and I'm goin' where you go."

"Well," said Hubbard, "what's the vote?—shall we turn back or go on?"

"Turn back," said I.

"Very well, then," he replied quietly; "that's settled."

. . .

To our ever-increasing dismay, the northwest gale continued to blow almost unceasingly during the next few days. Sometimes towards evening the wind would moderate sufficiently to permit us to troll with difficulty along the lee shore of an island, but seldom were we rewarded with more than a single namaycush, and so far from our getting enough fish to carry us over our long portage to Lake Disappointment, we did not catch enough for our daily needs, and were compelled to draw on our little store of emergency provisions. On Wednesday (September 16th) we ate the last bit of bacon and the last handful of rice we had so carefully hoarded. We succeeded that day in reaching the rapid where we caught the few trout that some animal stole from us, and there we camped. From this point we believed we could more readily gain the bay where we had entered the lake, and begin our retreat when the wind subsided.

. . .

Despite the steady gnaw, gnaw at the pit of our stomachs, we had cut down our meals to the minimum amount of food that would keep us alive; we were so weak we no longer were sure where our feet were going to when we put them down. But all the fish we had to smoke was two or three. And on Friday night we ate the last bit of our flour; it was used to thicken the water in which we boiled for supper some entrails, a namaycush head and the two little trout we had caught during the day.

All that night the northwest gale was accompanied by gusts of rain and snow. On Saturday (September 19th) the mercury dropped to 32 degrees, and the air was raw. Not a single fish were we able to catch.

George and I smoked a pipe for breakfast, while Hubbard imbibed the atmosphere. A bit of the smoked fish we had hoped to keep, boiled with a dash of pea meal in the water, did us for luncheon and supper.

Heretofore we had slept each rolled in his own blanket, but it was so cold in the tent that night we had to make a common bed by spreading one blanket beneath us on a tarpaulin and lying spoon-fashion with the other two blankets drawn over us. The blankets were decidedly narrow for three men to get under, and it was necessary for us to lie very close together indeed; but our new method enabled us to keep fairly warm and we continued its use.

On Sunday (September 20th) the temperature dropped to 29 and the squalls continued. In desperation we broke camp in the morning and tried to cross the lake with our outfit, but the wind soon drove us back to shelter. While we were out on the lake we caught a namaycush on the troll, and this fish we had for luncheon, together with some cranberries we found on a ridge near where we had taken refuge on the shore. A little later I was attacked with vomiting and faintness. When I tried to swing an axe, I reeled and all but lost consciousness.

Late in the afternoon the squalls subsided, and we made another attempt to escape from the prison in which we were slowly starving. Fortunately the wind continued fair and there were no cross-seas; and on and on we paddled in the direction of—home! Oh, the great relief of it! For nearly two weeks we had been held on that dreadful lake. Day after day the relentless storm had raged, while hunger leered at us and tormented us with its insistent clamour as we, with soaked rags and shivering bodies, strove vainly to prevent the little stock of food from diminishing that we felt was our only hold on life. And now we were going home!

Darkness had long since fallen when we reached an island near the point where we had entered the lake. In a driving rain we pitched our camp. For supper we had the last of the little stock of fish that we had been able to dry. This meant that, in addition to our stock of tea, the only food we had left on hand was sixteen pounds of pea meal. But we did not worry. We were going home. And on Monday morning, September 21st, though the wind was again blowing a gale, and the passage among the spray-covered rocks was filled with risk, we paddled over to the mainland, ready to begin our race for life down the trail we had fought so hard to ascend.

UPON REACHING THE mainland we stopped to assort and dry our baggage. All of us felt we had entered upon a race against starvation, and everything that was not strictly necessary to aid our progress to Northwest River Post we threw away. In addition to many odds and ends of clothing we abandoned about three pounds of tea. Tea was the one thing of which we had carried an abundance, and though we had used it freely, we had more than we deemed necessary to carry us through.

While we were nearing the shore, we sighted three little ducklings bobbing up and down in the tumbling waves and repeatedly diving. They were too far off to reach with a pistol, and Hubbard took his rifle. It seemed almost like attacking a fly with a cannon, but with our thoughts on grub, none of us was impressed with its incongruity then. After Hubbard had fired two or three shots, one of the ducklings suddenly turned over. We paddled to it with feverish haste, and found that it had been stunned by a ball that had barely grazed its bill. It was a lucky shot; for if the bullet had gone through the duckling's body there would have been little left of it to eat.

While George and I were drying the camp equipment, Hubbard caught five small trout in the stream that emptied into the lake at this point—the stream we had followed down. These fish we ate for luncheon. Once more ready to start, we pushed up the stream to the place where we had last camped before reaching the lake, and there we again pitched our tent. For supper we made soup of the duckling. It was almost like coming home to reach this old camping ground, and it cheered us considerably. The first day of the forty-mile portage we had to make before reaching fairly continuous water had been, as a whole, depressing.

Rain, accompanied by a cold wind, began to fall early in the afternoon. The weather was so cold, in fact, that the trout would not rise after we caught the five near the lake, and this made us uneasy as to how the fishing would prove farther down the trail. The day's journey, moreover, had made it clear, in spite of our efforts to hide the fact from one another, that we were much weaker than when we last had made portages. We had reached the stage where none of us could carry the canoe alone. Decidedly we were not the same men that had set out so blithely from the post eight weeks before. As for myself, I had shortened my belt thirteen inches since July 15th.

It became the custom now for George and me to go ahead with the canoe for a mile or so while Hubbard brought forward in turn each of the three packs for about an eight of a mile. Then George and I would return to him, and, each taking a pack, we would advance to the place where the canoe had been left. Sometimes, however, this routine was varied, Hubbard now and then helping George with the canoe while I juggled with the packs until they returned to me. Despite the fact that we had fewer as well as lighter packs to carry than on the up trail, our progress was slower because of our increasing weakness. Whereas it had taken us three days on the up trail to portage the fifteen miles between Lake Mary and Windbound Lake, it now took us five days to cover the same ground.

On Tuesday, the 22d, the second day of our portage, it rained all the time, and for the greater part of the day we floundered through marshes and swamps. We caught no fish and killed no game. Hubbard tried to stalk a goose in a swamp, wading above his knees in mud and water to get a shot; but he finally had to fire at such long range that he missed, and the bird flew away, to our great disappointment. Our day's food consisted of half a pound of pea meal for each man. During the day Hubbard had an attack of vomiting, and at night, when we reached our second camping ground above the lake, we were all miserable and thoroughly soaked, though still buoyed up by the knowledge that we were going home.

The cold rain continued on the 23d until late in the day, when the sky cleared and evening set in cold and crisp. That day I was attacked with vomiting. Our food was the same as on the day previous, with the addition of some mossberries and cranberries we found on the barren ridge over which we crossed. It was another day of hard portaging on stomachs crying for food, and when we pitched our camp we were so exhausted that we staggered like drunken men. Silent and depressed, we took our places on the seat of boughs that George had prepared by the roaring fire; but after we had eaten our meagre supper and drunk our tea, and our clothes had begun to dry in the genial glow, we found our tongues again; and, half forgetting that, starving and desperate, we were still in the midst of the wilderness, far from human help, we once more talked of the homes that were calling to us over the dreary wastes; talked of the dear people that would welcome us back and of the good things they would give us to eat; talked until far into the night, dreading to go to the cold tent and the wet blankets.

FILIPPO DE FILIPPI

(1869–1938)

From *The Ascent of Mount St. Elias*

When we think of travel a century ago, we often picture half-starved men stranded on icebergs or missionaries dying of fever in the jungle. And those images are real—the privations and isolation possible in those days can hardly be imagined. But at the same time that these explorers lacked the huge advantages of modern equipment and communication devices, well-heeled travelers of the time packed along provisions that would seem absurdly extravagant to us today. Any account of the Italian Duke of Abruzzi (whose full name is Prince Luigi Amedeo Giuseppe Di Savoia and who is referred to in the book simply as H.R.H.) is an example of blue-blooded travel at its finest.

On his Alaskan journey, the Duke took along enough gear to fill four 750-pound sleds, including ten iron bedsteads that the men dragged all the way to 10,000 feet (the outfit didn't include dogs). And though the Duke was not one to invite privations, he was one of the finest and boldest mountaineers of the century. He made first ascents of major summits in the Alps, Caucasus, Ruwenzori, and Alaska, and made the first attempt on K2 in 1909. His ascent of Mount St. Elias set a new *standard for endurance and effort in alpinism. Accompanying the Duke to most of these ranges was his friend Vittorio Sella, whose riveting photographs are among the finest ever made. The author of this book, Filippo de Filippi, was the Duke's surgeon and narrator on many of his journeys.*

Mount St. Elias was "discovered" and named by Danish explorer Vitus Bering in 1741. It was long thought to be North America's highest mountain because of its awesome vertical relief and overbearing profile in the range. The Malaspina Glacier covering the summit is the largest ice sheet on the continent. It was attempted seven times before the Duke of Abruzzi and his party successfully summitted the peak in 1897. The mountain was considered a notable conquest not because of its altitude (18,008 feet) and technical difficulty but its inaccessibility; the climb required traversing over 100 miles of glacial ice from the coast and climbing 14,000 feet above snowline. The weather during their five-week expedition was wet and stormy and avalanches a consistent threat.

The following passage describes that strangely anticlimactic moment that climbers know so well, when the men's euphoria at reaching the summit is dampened by exhaustion, the effects of altitude, and the view of a long descent.

C alled up at 1 o'clock a.m. (July 30th), we set about preparing for the penultimate stage of the ascent. The *col* between Mount Newton and St. Elias was to be climbed that day. Thence we hoped, by the long north-east ridge, to win the great peak on the following morning. So confident were we now of success that hope amounted almost to certainty. The supplies to be taken with us had been most carefully chosen, and comprised the following articles:—

Two Whymper[1] tents, ten sleeping bags, rations for two and a half

---

[1] Popular canvas tents of the time, designed by Edward Whymper.

days, one petroleum cooking stove, one spirit lamp ditto, meteorological instruments, the smaller of Sella's photographic machines, Gonella's small camera, and a few extra flannels.

We started at 4 o'clock, divided into three parties, along the route marked out by the guides, who had prepared a track right up to the *col* on the previous day. It was a bright, cold morning, with a perfectly clear sky. The snow was firm enough in the beaten track, but loose everywhere else, and covered with a thin crust of ice that gave under our feet. The strip of plateau, extending for about two miles and a half ahead to the flank of the *col,* lies at the very foot of the north-east face of St. Elias. This face is rocky at the steeper parts, but showed almost everywhere a coating of ice overlapping its precipices that threatened us with formidable avalanches. The condition of the snow warned us of this danger, seeing that for a stretch of over one mile it was no longer loose, but hardened avalanche snow, which crackled under the nails of our shoes, and was thickly sprinkled with *sérac* fragments fallen from a height of over 3,000 feet. Fortunately for us, most of the accumulated fresh snow had already come down during the past three days of fine weather, and the rest of it had had time to harden a little; but what chiefly served to keep the ice safely bound to the precipitous rocks was the intense cold of early morning.

After about an hour's march, the slope of the glacier gradually began to increase, and we soon reached the foot of the cliff where the real ascent begins. The wall rises in a series of somewhat steep slopes, separated by great transversal *crevasses,* and varying from 400 to 600 feet in height. We zig-zagged obliquely up these snow-slopes, the surface of which was pretty good for long stretches, where the guides had found it necessary to cut steps on the previous day. The first *crevasse* immediately beneath the isolated rock that projects from the middle of the wall cost us some trouble, and nearly half an hour's labour. The first two caravans crossed it easily enough by a snow-bridge, but this broke down when attempted by Sella, the leader of the third rope. After searching vainly for some solid foothold on the snow-vault, the third party finally managed to reach the other side by leaping boldly across the gap in the bridge. But the last guide unluckily dropped his jacket as he jumped, and had to be let down to a good depth in the fissure to recover it.

Keeping to the left of the rocks, we then mounted to the second *crevasse*, which cuts straight across the steep incline in such a way that its upper edge overlaps the lower one like a roof, leaving an interval of about seven feet. At a short distance, however, along the lower side, we discovered a point where the edges drew a little closer together. By mounting on a guide's shoulders, we managed to get safely across, and our loads were hauled up after us. Another snow-slope, a last and easily negotiated *crevasse*, and then, at about 10 o'clock a.m., we landed on the top of the *col*.

Our tents were pitched a little beneath the crest, on the east side, facing the Newton Glacier, 12,297 feet above the sea, and 3,636 feet higher than our previous camp. H.R.H. named the *col* after I. C. Russell, who was the first to conquer it, in 1891.

As soon as we reached the *col*, we turned eager glances to the new region revealed to us towards the north-west. At our feet we beheld a very extensive level glacier, covered with snow, and with no signs of *crevasses;* but its eastern and western boundaries were hidden from us by the mountains at either side. Beyond the portion fronting us lay an interminable stretch of snow and ice, an infinite series of low mountain chains bristling with numberless jagged, sharp-pointed and precipitous peaks, where rocks and ice-fields were closely intermingled. Towards the horizon we had a confused view of some very high ranges. We realized that from the summit we should see the whole of this region more distinctly mapped out.

The view to the north was blocked by Mount Newton, which now took the shape of a sharp-pointed snow-cone. Just to its left, and farther back, we discerned the pinnacled rock forming the western extremity of the Logan chain. From Mount Newton an irregular ridge runs down to the *col*, edged, to the north, by a bulky snow-cornice, and cut by deep indentations forming the heads of the gullies of stones and ice which score the mountain side towards Newton Glacier. The great ridge of Mount St.

Elias is of wholly dissimilar structure, for being so wide it resembles a *slope*, and cannot be easily identified with the even, straight crest seen from below. Viewed from the *col*, it appears to be broken by projections of varying steepness, amongst which three distinct clusters of rocks rise above the snow; while the wide, rounded summit seems to soar upwards at a short distance from the last group of crags, and apparently very little higher; whereas, from the valley below, these rocks seemed to stand about midway between the *col* and the summit of the mountain.

Beneath the Newton and St. Elias ridges the mountain sides become precipitous. Masses of snow, ice, and rock, set loose by the first rays of the morning sun, thunder and hurtle down into the valley with a roar which reaches us distinctly, raising clouds of pulverized ice in their descent.

More than 3,000 feet below us the spacious Newton valley descends to the east. At this distance the ice-cascades, with their piled *séracs*, seem mere tracts of rugged, wrinkled glacier between the smooth, level plateaux. We identify all the peaks around us, and in the depth beneath, the white, flat stretch of the Malaspina Glacier, bounded by its black lines of forest and marginal moraine. Beyond, and more than 62 miles off, lies the blue expanse of Yakutat Bay.

The afternoon hours pass rapidly and almost unheeded, and the pure cold evening is an omen of splendid weather for the morrow. Northwards all is cold shade under a steel blue sky, but the rest of the horizon is orange red. Little by little Mount Augusta crimsons like a fiery volcano. The thermometer is at 18° Fahr., and a chill north-west wind drives us to our tents. Lying down closely packed in these narrow shelters, we try to get some rest to fit us for the last and most serious effort; but most of us are too excited by the thought of the morrow's task to be able to sleep.

At midnight we all turn out, and swallow a bowl of hot coffee before packing the loads. These consist of one day's rations, a small spirit stove, a mercurial barometer, two aneroids, a hygrometer, spirit and mercurial thermometer, and photographic apparatus. The night is perfectly clear and still; Venus shines serenely over the summit of Mount Newton. The temperature stands at 18° Fahr. We are roped in three separate parties. H.R.H., Lieutenant Cagni, the two guides Petigax and Maquignaz are on the first rope; Gonella with Croux and Botta on the second; Sella and myself with Pellissier on the third. We are too excited to talk. We feel that we are on the very point of realizing the hope which has sustained us through prolonged days of toil and through the painful anxiety which, during the last stages, kept us questioning the barometer or the direction of the wind every few minutes.

The crest of the ridge where it reaches the *col* forms an ice cliff, which we skirt on the right. The powdery surface snow is very unequally distrib-uted, here and there leaving uncovered the harder layer beneath, in which steps have to be cut by the first guide. Petigax and Maquignaz go on in front, each taking the lead for half an hour in turn, and we all mount rapidly at a steady pace.

On reaching the top of the cliff, we cross to the east flank of the ridge running down to Newton Valley, where the snow is firmer, being more exposed to the sun. The surface is uneven and ribbed, reminding us of winter snow-slopes in the Alps.

After about an hour's climb, we come to the first rocks, which are formed of black splinters of *diorite,* round which we soon make our way through the snow. A little higher up, while skirting a fissured hump of ice, blasts of frozen north wind drive the powdery snow against our faces. Far above us, the summit is gilded by the first rays of the sun, and gradu-ally the great golden disk rises to the right of Mount Newton. As we climb higher, this summit rapidly sinks, and before long we see its peak beneath us, while behind it, and more than twenty miles off, rises the south flank of the Logan chain. Towards 5 o'clock a.m. we reached the last crags, and speedily surmounted them.[†]

[†] These crags (about 14,500 feet above the sea) form the highest point attained by Russell in 1891. In making the ascent, one does not approach the intermediate rock-group seen from below, but passes it at some distance to the left.

Our ascent was favoured by completely calm weather, and an ideal temperature, unusual in the high mountains, neither inconveniently cold nor oppressively hot. At 6.30, H.R.H. called a short halt; we breakfasted and were off again in half an hour. Soon the aneroids proved that we had reached the altitude of Mont Blanc (about 15,700 feet), and some of our party began to feel the diminished pressure in the shape of palpitation and difficult breathing, which although too slight to impede progress, yet sufficed to suggest that some of us might be prevented from reaching the summit.

At 8 o'clock Cagni arranged his instruments and took meteorological observations. We were now at an altitude of over 16,500 feet; and the temperature was 16° to 17° Fahr. There was an extraordinarily fine view to the east. The peak of Mount Augusta, although now beneath our level, preserved its daring grandeur of outline. But the Logan chain to the north was the most majestic of all. On our right, stretched the vast, precipitous north crest of St. Elias, all rocky save the upper portion, which was covered with snow. About midway it is broken by a towering crag, at whose feet a small glacier descends from the ridge. Around us there was nothing but dazzling snow, its whiteness just softened by faint opalescent tinges of colour.

The observations being duly registered, we resume our way up the tiring, monotonous slope. Less than 1,600 feet now separate us from the summit, but they will cost us more labour than the 4,200 already won. Almost all of us are suffering more or less from the rarefaction of the air, some being attacked by headache, others by serious difficulty of breathing and general exhaustion. H.R.H. slackens the pace of his caravan, and sometimes calls a halt, to wait for those who have fallen in the rear. He is determined to keep us all together, knowing the sense of discouragement felt by any one left behind by the rest of the party. The ascent is very monotonous on the whole and perfectly easy, leading either over the great rounded hump of the crest, or along its eastern flank. Luckily there is only a thin stratum of loose snow, so that one barely sinks into it ankle-deep; while now and again we strike a belt of hard snow in which the leading guide has to cut steps with a few strokes of his axe.

Before long we all experience those alternations of hope and disappointment which are typical symptoms of over-fatigue. Every slope ahead seems as though it must be the last; every ice pinnacle is mistaken for the great *gendarme* near the top of the crest which we had discerned from below. Even the guides make strange blunders regarding the extent of slope still to be won.

Our rate of progress is now of the slowest. We climb for ten minutes, and then rest for five or six. One or two of us lie down panting on the snow; some sit or crouch, while others take their rest standing, and lean on their ice-axes. H.R.H., Sella, and two of the guides are the only persons showing no signs of distress. Gonella suffers from headache; Cagni, myself, and Botta have to fight against the drowsiness which comes over us at every halt. The two remaining guides have slight symptoms of mountain sickness.

Our legs seem heavy as lead. Every step requires a distinct effort of the will, and we get on by dint of certain devices familiar to all who have made ascents when tired out—leaning both hands on the knees, or planting the axe in the snow ahead and dragging the body up by it, while at every step we pause for breath. Still, we manage to climb somehow; we are spurred on by excitement, and our nerves are strung to the highest pitch.

At last, after untold disappointments, a little after 11 o'clock, a sharp ice-pinnacle soared above us, and to the right of it and somewhat higher, the ample curve of a snow-dome. For some minutes past no one had spoken a word. Suddenly we all exclaimed: "The summit!" Only an ice-slope about 150 feet high had still to be surmounted. It was steep, and in our exhausted condition we had to attack it in a slanting direction, resting for breath every few steps. On reaching the top of this incline, we again came to a halt. Before us rose gently towards the west a slope which, in the dazzling light, appeared to be of vast extent. We had actually passed from the crest to the eastern limit of the terminal dome, and scarcely realized that we were so near to the summit.

The leading caravan started ahead, the two others lagged about 150 feet behind. Suddenly we saw the leading guides, Petigax and Maquignaz, move aside to make way for the Prince. They were within a few paces of the top. H.R.H. stepped forward, and was the first to plant his foot on the summit. We hastened breathlessly to join in his triumphant hurrah!

Every trace of fatigue disappeared in the joy of success. This moment was the reward of our thirty-eight days of labour and hardship.

It was the 31st of July, a quarter to 12 a.m. A few minutes later, H.R.H. hoisted our little tricolour flag on an ice-axe, and we nine gathered round him to join in his hearty shout for Italy and the king. Then all pressed the hand of the Prince, who had so skillfully led the expedition, and had maintained our courage and strength to the last by the force of his inspiring example.

Our excitement was of short duration. Once our object attained, we experienced the inevitable reaction after so many months devoted to the pursuit of one idea. Nevertheless, it was needful to pull ourselves together, and set to work taking observations. It was the most favourable hour for them. At mid-day, Mr. Hendriksen, at Yakutat, always registered the indications given by the meteorological instruments we had left in his charge. Therefore it was most important that simultaneous observations should be noted on the summit of St. Elias. The Fortin barometer marked a pressure of 15 inches 2 lines. With the due corrections and rectifications, it indicated an altitude of 18,090 feet, which very nearly agreed with the angular calculation made by Mr. Russell in 1891, fixing the height at 18,100 feet. All preceding calculations had proved discordant and untrustworthy. Only one gave an approximately correct result;

† In chap. iv. I have already given the principal observations on the altitude of Mount St. Elias, taken by explorers of that region. I now add the most recent, made in 1892–93, by J. E. MacGrath, of the "U.S. Coast Survey," kindly communicated to us by Prof. J. C. Russell. This fixes the height of Mount St. Elias at 18,024 feet.

namely, that made by the Italian navigator Malaspina in 1792, fixing the altitude of Mount St. Elias at 17,847 feet.†

We had risen 5,793 feet from the *col* to the summit. The ascent had occupied ten hours and a half; but we must deduct from this the thirty minutes spent over lunch, and another half-hour devoted to meteorological observations. During the first five hours we had climbed 3,400 feet, at an average rate of 680 feet per hour; and 2,400 feet in the last four hours and a half, at an average rate of about 600 feet an hour.

The summit of Mount St. Elias consists of a spacious plateau stretching, with a slight inclination, from south-east to north-west. The highest point stands north, and forms a raised platform about 40 square yards in extent. The temperature in the sun stood at 10° Fahr.; there was no wind, but a light breeze sufficed to chill us. We found some shelter a few yards from the top, and without leaving the terminal dome. Here we sat down to take some refreshment, trying to overcome the repugnance to food induced by fatigue and mountain sickness.

Beneath us, on every side, lay an indescribable panorama, glittering in the intense mid-day light. Only the Malaspina Glacier and the sea were covered by a low-hanging curtain of fog; in every other direction the horizon was perfectly clear. The enormous extent of snow-fields, glaciers, and mountains revealed to our sight, surpassed all imagination.

Those majestic peaks which two days before towered above us, while we were painfully struggling through the snows of Newton Glacier, now lay at our feet. We traced along the valleys the long course we had followed, while memory recalled difficulties and obstacles now lost in the distance. Often had we turned longing glances from the depths towards this small ledge outlined against the sky, as if imploring encouragement from the lofty summit!

The peak of Mount Augusta, still imposing, although nearly 4,000 feet below us, now assumed the form of a huge pyramid, turning a rocky face southwards, but covered, on the north side, with ice that spreads up to the terminal cupola. Beyond the Seward Glacier soars Mount Cook; and to the left of this another and more remote snow-summit, that must be either Mount Hubbard or Mount Irving, but which of the two it is hard to decide. From the sea of mist shrouding the Malaspina Glacier, the higher peaks of the Samovar and Hitchcock chains thrust up like isolated rocks. Lastly, in the far distance, to the south-east, we distinguish the summit of Mount Fairweather.

About twenty miles away to the north, and running parallel with the Newton-Augusta range, we see the vast chain of Mount Logan, the sole competitor disputing the supremacy of Mount St. Elias.[†] The lengthy crest constituting its summit rises gradually from west to east, in an almost uninterrupted *arête,* without depressions or deep *cols,* broken only by a few rocky pinnacles and ice-domes, and reaching its greatest height in a snow-peak at the eastern extremity.

. . .

The whole north-west region to the left of Mount Logan is an unexplored waste of glaciers and mountains, a vast zone bristling with sharp peaks and crags, rugged and precipitous to the south, snow-covered to the north, and surrounded by vast snow-fields free from *crevasses,* and connected with each other by the snowy *cols* of the mountain chains. The medium altitude of the snow-fields is about 7,000 feet, that of the mountains from 9,000 to 10,000 feet. No words can express the desolation of this immeasurable waste of ice, which Russell has compared with the ice-sheet that covers Greenland. No smallest trace of vegetation can be discerned on it, no running water, no lake. It might be a tract of primitive

[†] Mr. Russell, who first discovered and gave a name to this mountain in 1890, assigned it a height of 19,500 feet. J. E. MacGrath gave it that of 19,539 feet. As far back as 1838, Topham had already judged that the highest point of the mountain system would be found north of St. Elias, having observed that the chief bulk of the Guyot and Malaspina Glaciers came down from the region situated north and northeast of that peak. From the summit of St. Elias, we failed to prove the superior height of Mount Logan; at so great a distance, observation with the prismatic compass gave only negative results. Later on, however, during the return voyage off the Fairweather coast, we noticed that the Logan peak disappeared from the horizon, while the whole terminal cone of St. Elias was still clearly visible. Russell had already made the same observation in 1891.

chaos untouched by the harmonizing forces of nature. Surveying this strange scene, we realized for the first time that we were close to the limits of the mysterious Polar world. Such is the region forming the northwest boundary of the Columbus Glacier. Numerous tributaries pour into the latter from the lower hills; and the most considerable of these affluents, running into the Columbus on the immediate left of Mount Logan, was named by H.R.H. after Quintino Sella, the illustrious pioneer of Italian Alpinism.

On the far horizon, somewhere between fifty and one hundred miles off, a broad summit towered up behind the western corner of Mount Logan, which was ascertained by the compass to be at 328°. H.R.H. named this peak "Lucania," in remembrance of the ship that had brought us to America. West of this new peak, at about the same distance and due north of St. Elias, we descried another great mountain at 326°, which we believed to be identical with the peak christened Mount Bear by Russell in 1891. Finally, to the north-west, some 200 miles off, a conical peak soared up at 311°, apparently of even greater height than the other two. This was christened the "Bona," after a racing yacht then belonging to H.R.H. These three peaks really seem to rival Mount St. Elias in height, and must approach 18,000 feet in height. None of them showed any sign of volcanic activity.

While we scanned the wide prospect, endeavouring to fix in our memory each detail of the wondrous scene, multitudinous thoughts and feelings crowded upon us. The labyrinth of dark lines, the pure white plains, the chaos of rock and ice, blended in our minds with familiar scenes of marvellous beauty in our own Alpine world.

But sheer physical weariness soon unfits the mind for contemplation of so much supernatural grandeur. We feel vaguely crushed by the immensity; a desolating sense of isolation comes to us from those infinite wastes of ice, and from the solemn, oppressive silence of nature. Once the first excitement worn off, we are dazed by the radiance of the sunlight striking through the cold air; we suffer from distress caused by the altitude, and before long our only desire is to hasten down the peak as fast as we can.

By 1 o'clock p.m. we had gathered up our few possessions, arranged the different caravans, and begun the descent in the same order observed during the climb. We had spent an hour and a half on the summit.

Long glissades bore us quickly down the slopes we had so laboriously toiled up, and the few *crevasses,* being mostly filled with snow, were easily crossed. A little wind blowing in sudden gusts swept the face of the mountain, and assailed us with volleys of icy dust. As we drew near to the *col* the snow was in worse condition, and we had to plough through it knee-deep for long intervals. Nevertheless, we got on fast, slipping, falling, regaining our feet, plastered with snow from head to foot, but eager to reach camp, to escape from all that blinding, white glare, into the comforting shade of our tents. Between 4 and 5 o'clock p.m. we overtook on the *col* H.R.H.'s caravan, which had descended the great snowslope in two hours and a half.

We had only a little broken sleep that night, and awoke early on the 1st of August in a very battered, aching, and stiffened condition. The same evening we camped again on the upper Newton plateau.

CAPTAIN JOHN CLAUS VOSS

(1858–1922)

From *The Venturesome Voyages of Captain Voss*

In 1901, Canadian sea captain John Voss bought an old dugout canoe from a Native American on Vancouver Island. Responding to the challenge by a journalist who asked him if he thought he could sail around the world in a vessel smaller than Joshua Slocum's beloved thirty-five-foot Spray, Voss outfitted the canoe with three masts, a keel, deck, and rudimentary cabin. That summer, the eccentric loner set out to take his "canoe," the Tilikum, 40,000 miles around the globe. He sailed from Canada south to Australia, then around the Cape of Good Hope and north to England, ending the voyage in the fall of 1904. Although he wasn't always alone and didn't circumnavigate the globe, the journey established him, with Slocum, as one of the most accomplished small-boat sea captains in the world. Voss's Venturesome Voyages, published in 1913, became a minor classic in sailing literature. The Tilikum, which was toured and celebrated in England for a while, then sold and abandoned, has now been restored and is on display in the Maritime Museum in Victoria, British Columbia.

Voss's voyage was not without controversy. The journalist George Lux-

ton went with him for part of the journey, promising to finance Voss if he made it across two oceans, and to write a book about their adventures. The two men fell out, Luxton deserted the expedition in Fiji, and a young sailor named Louis Begent took his place. In the following passage, Begent is lost overboard when the boat is nearly capsized by a freak wave more than 1200 miles from Australia. Having lost his compass as well as his mate, Voss must navigate by dead reckoning, that is, by watching his course in relation to the direction of the ocean swell.

On October 20th Mr. Luxton came to me and said, "Look here, John, I have got a good seaman to take my place for the run with you to Sydney, and if you are willing to take him along I propose to take passage on a steamship, and on your arrival there I will join you again and complete the voyage, as I am satisfied now that the *Tilikum* is quite able to make it."

I accepted his proposal, and the next morning my new mate came on board. By the looks of him he appeared to be what he later on proved himself, a first-class seaman. His name was Louis Begent, aged thirty-one, a native of Louchester, Tasmania. I told Begent to go to work and get the boat ready for sea, saying that we were going to sail during the afternoon. However, having made quite a few friends in Fiji, we did not get away till the following afternoon at three o'clock. Captain Clark was good enough to give us a tow out as far as the lighthouse. An hour later he turned back with his launch, and we, with a moderate south-easterly breeze, shaped our course for Sydney, a distance of about eighteen hundred miles. Just about sunset, about seven miles outside the bay, we got into a channel between two islands, and as this looked very dangerous for navigation, I ran close to a beach in smooth water and anchored.

The following morning, at daybreak, when we were in the act of getting under sail again, we found that our anchor was foul of the bottom, and were therefore unable to get it up. My mate offered to dive down to clear it, but as the water was full of sharks I cut the anchor rope instead, and with a fresh easterly breeze we steered again on our westerly course. The wind kept fresh and the weather clear until the morning of the 27th, when the sky became cloudy, and during the day the wind freshened up to a strong breeze. At ten o'clock that night, I took in the foresail and spanker, and under the mainsail and staysail, with a strong easterly wind, and steering south-west, the *Tilikum* went along quite comfortably, now and then taking over a little water, but nothing to speak of.

It was my watch on deck from eight till twelve, and about half an hour before midnight the compass light went out. As the night was quite clear, with a good many stars shining brightly in the south-west, I picked out one of the stars nearly ahead of the boat and steered by it till my watch came to an end, when I called my mate, who got up and took my place at the rudder. I told him to keep the boat going by the star ahead till the light was fixed up. I then took the box, which contained the compass and light, down to the cabin. My mate was well able to keep the canoe on her course by the stars, so there was no particular hurry about the compass, and instead of getting the lamp lit at once, I lit a cigar for myself, another for my mate, and passed it out to him. I then set to work on the compass light. While I was thus employed my mate was telling me how he enjoyed the sailing in the *Tilikum* and how he would like to make the trip to London in her.

"If we keep this wind," he said, "we will be in Sydney in time for the Melbourne Cup Race. I expect my brother-in-law to be in Melbourne by that time, perhaps you know him? His name is Castella, and he is in command of the American ship *Hawaian Island*."

"I am well acquainted with Captain Castella and his wife," I answered. (The ship in question was at that time the largest and finest steel ship under the American flag.) After that I became very much interested in my mate, and for a minute forgot all about the compass, till he said, "It is getting cloudy ahead of us, so will you pass the compass out?"

While we were chatting away the *Tilikum* went along at her best, answering her helm beautifully. I had lit the lamp and handed the binnacle out to my mate, who, for a second, let go the tiller in order to place it in front of him on the seat of the cockpit, and just as he put the binnacle back in its place, I saw a large breaking sea coming up near the stern of the boat. Knowing by the appearance of the sea that it was a bad one, I shouted loudly, "Hold on"; but before I had the words out of my mouth the breaker had struck us.

I had braced myself in the cabin door to keep the water out, but when the sea struck it knocked me down. However, I was up in a second to see if any damage had been done on deck. I could not see my mate, and the boat was just about half-way round coming up to the wind. I peered forward, thinking that my mate was getting the sea anchor out or doing some other kind of work, but he was not to be seen. I shouted, but got no answer. I knew then that he was overboard, and of course that he must be to windward, as the boat had been going very fast, and therefore must have left him some distance astern ere she came to the wind. To try and beat back to where he had gone overboard was an impossible task owing to the strong wind and large seas. Therefore I put the helm hard down, lowered the sails, and put the sea anchor out to prevent the boat drifting too much. Thinking that he might be able to swim to the boat, and that this was the only way his life could be saved, I continued calling him by name, but got no reply. All my shouting and calling, which I kept up for a long time, was in vain. Nothing but the sound of the wind, and now and then a breaking sea, was to be heard. Ten minutes passed; twenty minutes; thirty minutes; an hour; and still no sign of my unfortunate companion. Then I knew that he was dead.

The loss of my mate was partly due to negligence, as I always had a life-line, one end of which was fastened to the boat; the other end to be put round the helmsman's body. I told him, when he first came on board, never to neglect to put that life-line around himself whenever he took the rudder, as I always did, and if he had followed my advice he may have gone overboard from the effects of the sea, but would never have got away from the boat.

The sea that took my mate overboard was by no means very dangerous. Of course there was water enough in it to carry a man away if he was not holding on to anything. However, later on during the cruise the boat shipped larger seas than this one, but I never again had a deplorable accident of this kind.

After I had given up all hope of ever seeing my mate again I went down to the cabin, and there found everything afloat. The bedding was soaked and everything else in the cabin was very wet. I then baled the *Tilikum* out, after which I went on deck again, and sat down in the cockpit thinking over the loss I had sustained. I was approaching the southern limit of the south-east trade wind, but instead of a trade wind it developed into a howling gale during the morning hours. I was just going to have a look at the compass to see if the wind was still in the same direction when I discovered to my dismay that the compass and binnacle had gone too!

When daylight came, and the sun made its appearance on the eastern horizon, I got on top of the cabin deck and took a good look round for my missing mate. But there was nothing to be seen but the large seas with their breaking summits, and the passing clouds in the sky above, while the *Tilikum* under her sea anchor and a storm sail over the stern, rose bravely to every sea as it came along.

At eight o'clock I hoisted my little Canadian flag half-mast, and then proceeded to search for a small pocket compass, which I knew my former companion had, when we were hunting in the forest of Vancouver Island. Being unable to find it, it struck me that Mr. Luxton kept the same in one of his valises, and doubtless without thinking of it took the compass with him when he left me in Suva. Consequently, I was alone at sea without a compass.

My position was then about six hundred miles south-west from Suva, and about twelve hundred from Sydney, isolated, no compass to steer by, everything soaking wet, and the boat hove to in a gale. For some time I was completely taken aback, and did not know what to do or what would become of me. The first thought that occurred to me was that I might wait there for a passing vessel. Then again, it struck me that I was out of the track of vessels and might lay there for months and not see one.

During the forenoon the wind abated somewhat. At midday the sun was shining brightly. I took my quadrant, and getting on top of the cabin deck, with one arm round the mast to prevent myself from falling overboard, tried to get the noon altitude. While standing there watching the sun slowly rising to the meridian to the north of me, I said to myself, "Well, there is north." By facing north the wind was about ten points to my right and the sea running from the same quarter, which of course made the direction of the wind and sea from the E.S.E. The latter observation almost satisfied me that I could make a fairly good course by steering in clear weather by the sun, moon or stars, and in thick weather do the best I could, steering by the ocean swell.

A little after noon the wind had moderated considerably and the seas had lost their breaking tops. I hauled in my sea anchor, and under the forestaysail swung the *Tilikum* on her course to the south-westward, steering by the ocean swell which was running from the E.S.E. By steering the boat so that the E.S.E. swell would strike her two points abaft the port beam, was to give her a S.W. course.

The guides I had to steer by were the sun, moon, stars, and the ocean swell, but I soon discovered that the ocean swell was by far the best to keep the boat making a good course. Then, again, I was obliged to use the heavenly bodies to get the set of the swell. The only trouble I had in finding the course was when after I got up from a sleep and found the weather thick and overcast. Still worse, when there was a cross swell I was helpless, and obliged to heave to until the weather cleared up.

For two days after the accident it kept blowing from the E.S.E., and as I was unable to sleep I kept her going night and day until the third day, when the wind died out and I lay becalmed.

From the time of the accident till the calm was two and a half days, during which time I had no sleep, and very little to eat, and that cold; I may say that I was just about played out. I therefore went to work and made myself some warm food, and after a fairly good meal, laid down to have a sleep. I laid in my little bunk for quite a while, turning from side to side and thinking over the past few days. However, I eventually dozed off only to dream about all kinds of things. I thought I saw my lost companion look in at the cabin door, and it gave me an awful start. On looking up the time I found to my surprise that I had only been asleep about ten minutes. I tried again and again to sleep, but in vain. However, I laid down for a few hours; then I fancied I felt a breeze come in through the cabin door, and sure enough when I got on deck there was a moderate breeze from the south. The great trouble was that whenever I retired to my bunk to sleep I could not do so, and when sailing, especially in light winds, I could not keep awake. Still, I set sail and did the best I could to keep the *Tilikum* going towards Sydney.

The wind and weather kept about the same till the following day. It was in the afternoon, while I was nearly asleep, when a heavy southerly squall struck the *Tilikum* under all sails, and over she went on her beam ends. So did I; it was only through a piece of luck that I did not go overboard, for the boat was on the port tack, with the sheets hauled by the wind. I was sitting on the port side dozing when she went over on her beam ends. Landing against the lee washboards, which kept me from going overboard, I nearly broke my neck. As luck happened the foremast snapped, and the boat righted at once.

From the fall I got a kink in the neck, and laid for a little while in the cockpit before I was able to realise what had happened. When I came to my proper senses, I looked round and saw the foresail, part of the foremast, forestaysail and all the head gear hanging overboard. The mainsail and mizzen were still set, and these, with the aid of the fore gear hanging overboard, kept the vessel nicely head to wind. After stripping her of the mainsail, and hauling in the mizzen sheet, the *Tilikum* laid as well as if she was riding to her sea anchor.

For the next few hours, while I was thinking of my miserable plight and what would next happen to the *Tilikum* and myself, I let her drift as she was. By and by I came to the conclusion that while there is life there is hope, and where there is a will there is a way; and being still in the possession of both, I went to work and picked up all the head gear and sails that were hanging overboard, secured it on deck, and as it kept blowing hard for two days I let the boat drift under her sea anchor and storm sail. All that time I was, of course, unable to do anything toward repairing the damage, but by keeping a riding light on deck during the night I got all the sleep I possibly could.

During the second night the wind gradually died out, and at daybreak the weather was calm and clear. After the large seas had gone down I went to work to splice the foremast and put everything back in its place, and in the afternoon I was ready for another breeze. I did not have to wait long for it, a moderate breeze coming up the same night. From then I experienced light winds and weather until October 14th, and when my position was about a hundred and fifty miles north-east from Sydney a strong breeze came in from the rear. I kept running before it as long as I thought it safe to do so, but when the wind increased to a howling gale and the seas commenced to break I hove to in the usual way. I put a light on deck, and then turned in "all standing" (with all my clothes on). Now and then I would get up and see if the light on deck was burning.

About midnight I got up to see if the light was all right, but to my surprise it was extinguished, and, to make matters worse, a green, red and bright light appeared ahead. Of course, I knew at once that these were a steamer's lights, and that the vessel was coming straight towards me. There was no time to lose. I had to let the lookout on the steamer know that I was ahead of her or in another five minutes she would have run me down. I knew that I had no time to fix my light, so pulled off one of my socks, soaked it with kerosene, and set it ablaze. I felt a good deal better when I saw the green light disappearing from my sight. They had seen my signal, and in less than five minutes a large steamer passed by.

The gale kept up its fury for three days and nights, after which the wind moderated, but as I had seen neither sun, moon nor stars, and had completely lost my position, I kept the boat under her sea anchor till noon, when I got the position, which put me about a hundred miles south-east of Sydney. By that time the wind had died down and the sea became quite calm. Two hours later the sky was as clear as crystal, with the exception of a very heavy cloud rising from the south-west. I watched this as it grew larger and larger. In a little while, when it rose to about forty-five degrees above the horizon, it looked like a huge arch supported on the bosom of the ocean, one abutment in the south-west and the other in the south-east, and it certainly appeared as if I was getting into another heavy gale. I therefore secured all my sails and prepared for the storm; but the cloud rose no higher, and while I was looking at it I saw what appeared to be a long, sharp point forming underneath the centre of the span, which was gradually approached by a similar point rising out of the ocean, and as soon as the two points met they formed a large water-spout. I at once made a dive down into my cabin to get my rifle on deck, which did not take longer than half a minute, and by the time I was on deck again there were two. Then, one after the other they formed until, in a very short time, there were six, the nearest at the very most, one mile from me; but there they stopped, and owing to the perfect calm I could hear the water rushing up in the cloud, which sounded something like a distant waterfall. Shortly afterwards one of the spouts broke; then another; then another would rise; and so they kept on rising and falling, one after the other, for about three hours. The cloud got larger and larger till six o'clock, when the last spout dropped.

I may mention here that I had sailed across the South Pacific several times, and on different occasions I have seen water-spouts, but never, before or since, have I witnessed spouts of the same nature. All other water-spouts I have seen moved more or less in a slanting position, while those in question were all perfectly vertical.

During the afternoon, from about three till six o'clock, there must have been at least thirty spouts that I saw from my boat, and the nearest at any time I should judge was about a mile distant. I fired several shots at the spouts, and one of them broke shortly after I fired, but whether it broke from the effects of the vibration of the shot or from natural conse-quences I cannot say. I have been told by ship-masters who have had experience with water-spouts that they will break every time from the vibration of a gun-shot, if it is discharged within two hundred yards. I, however, was well pleased that they kept where they were, as, had they come near my vessel, and had I been unable to break them with my gun, the *Tilikum* and I might still be sailing in the sky.

At six o'clock the bank that had up to then formed a large arch, and by the looks of it had imbibed from the ocean thousands upon thousands of tons of water, broke up and covered the sky in a few minutes with dark and threatening clouds. At the same time the weather still kept calm, but I heard light thunder; then a flash of lightning was followed by a loud peal of thunder, and I then experienced a very severe thunderstorm. There was no wind with it, but occasionally very heavy rain squalls. The lightning was apparently very near my boat, for it would make the dark and cloudy night as bright as day. I knew I was absolutely unable to prevent the lightning from striking my boat, so went below and laid down in my bunk to await further developments.

The thunderbolts seemed to be very close to the *Tilikum,* and I was apprehensive that the next flash of lightning would strike the canoe and put the two of us out of existence. However, nothing happened to me or my boat, and later the thunder diminished, until at midnight it stopped altogether. I got up, opened the cabin door, and took a look round. There was then no cloud to be seen anywhere, and the sky was dotted with stars. There was also a light breeze from the south-east, and as I had all the stars I wanted to guide me on my way, I at once got sails on the *Tilikum* and directed my course for Sydney.

The south-easterly breeze kept light during the night, but freshened in the morning. At noon I had as much wind as she could stand under all sails, and this condition continued until dark, when the breeze gradually moderated, and at nine o'clock I said to myself, "If my reckoning is right I should see the Sydney light before long."

From that time I kept looking for the light, and in fifteen minutes sighted it.

THOMAS GASKELL ALLEN, JR., AND WILLIAM LEWIS SACHTLEBEN

(DATES UNKNOWN)

From *Across Asia on a Bicycle*

Like many modern-day college students, the two American protagonists of this remarkable story decided to set off on a low-budget adventure the day after graduation. But they did something unheard of in 1890: they set off clear around the world, and—even more original—by bicycle, a contraption that had been invented not long before. Although they went without fanfare, with no desire to make any "firsts," in the end they pedaled 15,044 miles, at the time the longest continuous land journey ever made.

The most dangerous part of their ride was the desolate steppe of western China. Before the last decade of the nineteenth century, no European since Marco Polo had successfully crossed the Gobi desert and the length of the Chinese empire. Given the fierce resistance of the Chinese to intruders and the unforgiving nature of the vast unpopulated terrain, few were foolish enough to try. Knowing what they set out to do—and accomplished in a little over two years—it is astonishing that more of the authors' hardships do not come through in these pages. The brief mention of illness in the following passage, where they cross the Gobi and reach the Great Wall, is a rare glimpse into their physical lives. Like so many travelogues of the age, this one focuses on the cultural aspects of the journey and is full of comments on the customs, dress, and character of the Turks and Chinese.

It is amusing to read this book and understand that the Chinese love affair with the bicycle had its origin with these two unsuspecting American youths. In every chapter is a highly amusing passage about the unanimously open-mouthed reaction the cyclists got to the "iron horses" they rode. No one in Asia Minor had seen anything like the bicycle before; the riders were mobbed in every village and town, from Constantinople to Peking. In China the reception was particularly hysterical: "In one out-of-the-way village of northwestern China, we were evidently taken for some species of Centaurs," they wrote. Before they left, the Chinese government ordered a blacksmith to draw up a pattern from one of their battered steeds, and the rest is history.

In a glowing sunset, at the end of a hot day's climb, we looked for the last time over the Ili valley, and at dusk, an hour later, rolled into one of the Kirghiz aouls that are here scattered among the rich pasturage of the plateau.

Even here we found that our reputation had extended from Kuldja. The chief advanced with *amans* of welcome, and the heavy-matted curtains in the kibitka doorway were raised, as we passed, in token of honor. When the refreshing kumiss was served around the evening campfire, the dangers of the journey through China were discussed among our hosts with frequent looks of misgiving. Thus, from first to last, every judgment was against us, and every prediction was of failure, if not of something worse; and now, as we stole out from the tent by the light of the rising moon, even the specter-like mountain-peaks around us, like symbols of coming events, were casting their shadows before. There was something so illusive in the scene as to make it very impressive. In the morning, early, a score of horsemen were ready to escort us on the road.

At parting they all dismounted and uttered a prayer to Allah for our safety; and then as we rode away, drew their fingers across their throats in silence, and waved a solemn good-by. Such was the almost superstitious fear of these western nomads for the land which once sent forth a Yengiz Khan along this very highway.

Down the narrow valley of the Kuitun, which flows into the Ebi-nor, startling the mountain deer from the brink of the tree-arched rivulet, we reached a spot which once was the haunt of a band of those border-robbers about whom we had heard so much from our apprehensive friends. At the base of a volcano-shaped mountain lay the ruins of their former dens, from which only a year ago they were wont to sally forth on the passing caravans. When they were exterminated by the government, the head of their chief, with its dangling quene, was mounted on a pole near-by, and preserved in a cage from birds of prey, as a warning to all others who might aspire to the same notoriety. In this lonely spot we were forced to spend the night, as here occurred, through the careless-ness of the Kuldja Russian blacksmith, a very serious break in one of our gear wheels. It was too late in the day to walk back the sixteen miles to

the Kirghiz encampment, and there obtain horses for the remaining fifty-
eight miles to Kuldja, for nowhere else, we concluded, could such a
break be mended. Our sleeping-bags were now put to a severe test
between the damp ground and the heavy mountain dew. The penetrating
cold, and the occasional panther-like cry of some prowling animal, kept
us awake the greater part of the night, awaiting with revolvers in hand
some expected attack.

Five days later we had repassed this spot and were toiling over the
sand and saline-covered depression of the great "Han-Hai," or Dried-up
Sea. The mountain freshets, dissolving the salt from their sandy channels, carry it down in solution and deposit it with evaporation in massive
layers, forming a comparatively hard roadway in the midst of the shifting
sand-dunes. Over these latter our progress was extremely slow. One
stretch of fifteen miles, which it took us six hours to cover, was as formidable as any part of the Turkoman desert along the Transcaspian railway.
At an altitude of only six hundred feet above the sea, according to our
aneroid barometer, and beneath the rays of a July sun against which even
our felt caps were not much protection, we were half-dragging, half-
pushing, our wheels through a foot of sand, and slapping at the mosquitos swarming upon our necks and faces. These pests, which throughout
this low country are the largest and most numerous we have ever met,
are bred in the intermediate swamps, which exist only through the negligence of the neighboring villagers. At night smoldering fires, which half
suffocate the human inmates, are built before the doors and windows to
keep out the intruding insects. All travelers wear gloves, and a huge hood
covering the head and face up to the eyes, and in their hands carry a
horse-tail switch to lash back and forth over their shoulders. Being without such protection we suffered both day and night.

The mountain freshets all along the road to Urumtsi were more frequent and dangerous than any we had yet encountered. Toward evening
the melting snows, and the condensing currents from the plain heated
during the day, fill and overflow the channels that in the morning are
almost dry. One stream, with its ten branches, swept the stones and

boulders over a shifting channel one mile in width. It was when wading through such streams as this, where every effort was required to balance ourselves and our luggage, that the mosquitos would make up for lost time with impunity.

. . .

With constant wading and tramping, our Russian shoes and stockings, one of which was almost torn off by the sly grab of a Chinese spaniel, were no longer fit for use. In their place we were now obliged to purchase the short, white cloth Chinese socks and string sandals, which for mere cycling purposes and wading streams proved an excellent substitute, being light and soft on the feet and very quickly dried. The calves of our legs, however, being left bare, we were obliged, for state occasions at least, to retain and utilize the upper portion of our old stockings. It was owing to this scantiness of wardrobe that we were obliged when taking a bath by the roadside streams to make a quick wash of our linen, and put it on wet to dry, or allow it to flutter from the handle-bars as we rode along. It was astonishing even to ourselves how little a man required when once beyond the pale of Western conventionalities.

From Manas to Urumtsi we began to strike more tillage and fertility. Maize, wheat, and rice were growing, but rather low and thin. The last is by no means the staple food of China, as is commonly supposed, except in the southern portion. In the northern, and especially the outlying, provinces it is considered more a luxury for the wealthy. Millet and coarse flour, from which the *mien* or dough-strings are made, is the foundation, at least, for more than half the subsistence of the common classes. Nor is there much truth, we think, in the assertion that Chinamen eat rats, although we sometimes regretted that they did not. After a month or more without meat a dish of rats would have been relished, had we been able to get it.

. . .

On entering a Chinese city we always made it a rule to run rapidly through until we came to an inn, and then lock up our wheels before the crowd could collect. Urumtsi, however, was too large and intricate for such a manœuver. We were obliged to dismount in the principal through-fare. The excited throng pressed in upon us. Among them was a China-man who could talk a little Russian, and who undertook to direct us to a comfortable inn at the far end of the city. This street parade gathered to the inn yard an overwhelming mob, and announced to the whole com-munity that "the foreign horses" had come. It had been posted, we were told, a month before, that "two people of the new world" were coming through on "strange iron horses," and every one was requested not to molest them. By this, public curiosity was raised to the highest pitch. When we returned from supper at a neighboring restaurant, we were treated to a novel scene. The doors and windows of our apartments had been blocked with boxes, bales of cotton, and huge cart-wheels to keep out the irrepressible throng. Our host was agitated to tears; he came out wringing his hands, and urging upon us that any attempt on our part to enter would cause a rush that would break his house down. We listened to his entreaties on the condition that we should be allowed to mount to the roof with a ladder, to get away from the annoying curiosity of the crowd. There we sat through the evening twilight, while the crowd below, somewhat balked, but not discouraged, stood taking in every move. Nightfall and a drizzling rain came at last to our relief.

The next morning a squad of soldiers was despatched to raise the siege, and at the same time presents began to arrive from the various offi-cials, from the Tsongtu, or viceroy, down to the superintendent of the local prisons. The matter of how much to accept of a Chinese present, and how much to pay for it, in the way of a tip to the bearer, is one of the finest points of that finest of fine arts, Chinese etiquette; and yet in the midst of such an abundance and variety we were hopelessly at sea. Fruits and teas were brought, together with meats and chickens, and even a live sheep. Our Chinese visiting-cards—with the Chinese the great insignia of rank—were now returned for those sent with the presents, and the hour appointed for the exhibition of our bicycles as requested.

Long before the time, the streets and housetops leading from the inn to the viceroy's palace at the far end of the city began to fill with people, and soldiers were detailed at our request to make an opening for us to ride through abreast. This, however, did not prevent the crowd from pushing us against each other, or sticking sticks in the wheels, or throwing their hats and shoes in front of us, as we rode by. When in sight of the viceroy's palace, they closed in on us entirely. It was the worst jam we had ever been in. By no possibility could we mount our machines, although the mob was growing more and more impatient. They kept shouting for us to ride, but would give us no room. Those on the outside pushed the inner ones against us. With the greatest difficulty could we preserve our equilibrium, and prevent the wheels from being crushed, as we surged along toward the palace gate; while all the time our Russian interpreter, Mafoo, on horseback in front, continued to shout and gesticulate in the wildest manner above their heads. Twenty soldiers had been stationed at the palace gate to keep back the mob with cudgels. When we reached them, they pulled us and our wheels quickly through into the inclosure, and then tried to stem the tide by belaboring the heads and shoulders in reach, including those of our unfortunate interpreter, Mafoo. But it was no use. Everything was swept away before this surging wave of humanity. The viceroy himself, who now came out to receive us, was powerless. All he could do was to request them to make room around the palace courtyard for the coming exhibition. Thousands of thumbs were uplifted that afternoon, in praise of the wonderful *twee-tah-cheh,* or two-wheeled carts, as they witnessed our modest attempt at trick riding and special manœuvering. After refreshments in the palace, to which we were invited by the viceroy, we were counseled to leave by a rear door, and return by a round-about way to the inn, leaving the mob to wait till dark for our exit from the front.

. . .

It was already dusk on the evening of August 10 when we drew up to the hamlet of Shang-loo-shwee at the end of the Hami oasis. The Great Gobi, in its awful loneliness, stretched out before us, like a vast ocean of endless space. The growing darkness threw its mantle on the scene, and left imagination to picture for us the nightmare of our boyhood days. We seemed, as it were, to be standing at the end of the world, looking out into the realm of nowhere. Foreboding thoughts disturbed our repose, as we contemplated the four hundred miles of this barren stretch to the Great Wall of China. With an early morning start, however, we struck out at once over the eighty-five miles of the Takla Makan sands. This was the worst we could have, for beyond the caravan station of Kooshee we would strike the projecting limits of Mongolian Kan-su. This narrow tract, now lying to our left between Hami and the Nan Shan mountains, is characterized by considerable diversity in its surface, soil, and climate. Traversed by several copious streams from the Nan Shan mountains, and the moisture-laden currents from the Bay of Bengal and the Brahmaputra valley, its "desert" stretches are not the dismal solitudes of the Tarim basin or the "Black" and "Red" sands of central Asia. Water is found almost everywhere near the surface, and springs bubble up in the hollows, often encircled by exterior oases. Everywhere the ground is traversable by horses and carts. This comparatively fertile tract, cutting the Gobi into two great sections, has been, ever since its conquest two thousand years ago, of vast importance to China, being the only feasible avenue of communication with the western provinces, and the more important link in the only great highway across the empire. A regular line of caravan stations is maintained by the constant traffic both in winter and summer. But we were now on a bit of the genuine Gobi—that is, "Sandy Desert"—of the Mongolian, or "Shamo" of the Chinese. Everywhere was the same interminable picture of vast undulating plains of shifting reddish sands, interspersed with quartz pebbles, agates, and carnelians, and relieved here and there by patches of wiry shrubs, used as fuel at the desert stations, or lines of hillocks succeeding each other like waves on the surface of the shoreless deep. The wind, even more than the natural barrenness of the soil, prevents the growth of any vegetation except low, pliant herbage. Withered plants are uprooted and scattered by the gale like patches of foam on the stormy sea. These terrible winds, which of course were against us, with the frequently heavy cart-tracks, would make it quite impossible to ride. The monotony of many weary hours of plodding was relieved only by the bones of some abandoned beast of burden, or the occasional train of Chinese carts, or rather two-wheeled vans, loaded with merchandise, and drawn by five to six horses or mules. For miles away they would see us coming, and crane their necks in wondering gaze as we approached. The mulish leaders, with distended ears, would view our strange-looking vehicles with suspicion, and then lurch far out in their twenty-foot traces, pulling the heavily loaded vehicles from the deep-rutted track. But the drivers were too busy with their eyes to notice any little divergence of this kind. Dumb with astonishment they continued to watch us till we disappeared again toward the opposite horizon. Farther on we would meet a party of Chinese emigrants or exiles, on their way to the fertile regions that skirt the northern and southern slopes of the Tian Shan mountains. By these people even the distant valley of the Ili is being largely populated. Being on foot, with their extraordinary loads balanced on flexible shoulder-poles, these poor fellows could make only one station, or from twelve to twenty miles a day. In the presence of their patience and endurance, we were ashamed to think of such a thing as hardship.

The station-houses on the desert were nothing more than a collection of mud huts near a surface well of strongly brackish water. Here, most of the caravans would put up during the day, and travel at night. There was no such thing as a restaurant; each one by turn must do his own cooking in the inn kitchen, open to all. We, of course, were expected to carry our own provisions and do our own culinary work like any other respectable travelers. This we had frequently done before where restaurants were not to be found. Many a time we would enter an inn with our arms filled with provisions, purchased at the neighboring bazaars, take possession of the oven and cooking utensils, and proceed to get up an American meal, while all the time a hundred eyes or more would be staring at us in blank amazement. But here on the desert we could buy nothing but very coarse flour. When asked if they had an egg or a piece of vegetable, they would shout *"Ma-you"* ("There is none") in a tone of rebuke, as much as to say: "My conscience! man, what do you expect on the Gobi!" We would have to be content with our own tea made in the iron pot, fitting in the top of the mud oven, and a kind of sweetened bread made up with our supply of sugar brought from Hami. This we nicknamed our "Gobi cake," although it did taste rather strongly of brackish water and the garlic of previous contents of the one common cooking-pot. We would usually take a large supply for road use on the following day, or, as sometimes proved, for the midnight meal of the half-starved inn-dog. The interim between the evening meal and bedtime was always employed in writing notes by the feeble, flickering light of a primitive taper-lamp, which was the best we had throughout the Chinese journey.

A description of traveling in China would by no means be complete without some mention of the vermin which infest, not only inns and houses, but the persons of nearly all the lower classes. Lice and fleas seem to be the *sine qua non* of Chinese life, and in fact the itching with some seems to furnish the only occasion for exercise. We have seen even shopkeepers before their doors on a sunny afternoon, amusing them-selves by picking these insidious creatures from their inner garments. They are one of the necessary evils it seems, and no secret is made of it. The sleeping *kangs* of the Chinese inns, which are made of beaten earth and heated in winter like an oven, harbor these pests the year round, not to mention the filthy coverlets and greasy pillows that were sometimes offered us. Had we not had our own sleeping-bags, and used the camera, provision-bag, and coats for pillows, our life would have been intolerable. As it was there was but little rest for the weary.

The longest station on the desert was thirty-one miles. This was the only time that we suffered at all with thirst. In addition to the high mean elevation of the Gobi, about four thousand feet, we had cloudy weather for a considerable portion of the journey, and, in the Kan-su district, even a heavy thunder-shower. These occasional summer rains form, here and there, temporary meres and lakes, which are soon evaporated, leaving nothing behind except a saline efflorescence. Elsewhere the ground is furrowed by sudden torrents tearing down the slopes of the occasional hills or mountains. These dried up river-beds furnished the only continuously hard surfaces we found on the Gobi; although even here we were sometimes brought up with a round turn in a chuck hole, with the sand flying above our heads.

Our aneroid barometer registered approximately six thousand five hundred feet, when we reached at dusk the summit of the highest range of hills we encountered on the desert journey. But instead of the station-hut we expected to find, we were confronted by an old Mongolian monastery. These institutions, we had found, were generally situated as this one, at the top of some difficult mountain-pass or at the mouth of some cavernous gorge, where the pious intercessors might, to the best advantage, strive to appease the wrathful forces of nature. In this line of duty the lama was no doubt engaged when we walked into his feebly-lighted room, but, like all Orientals, he would let nothing interfere with the performance of his religious duties. With his gaze centered upon one spot, his fingers flew over the string of beads in his lap, and his tongue over the stereotyped prayers, with a rapidity that made our head swim. We stood unnoticed till the end, when we were at once invited to a cup of tea, and directed to our destination, five *li* beyond. Toward this we plodded through the growing darkness and rapidly cooling atmosphere; for in its extremes of temperature the Gobi is at once both Siberian and Indian, and that, too, within the short period of a few hours. Some of the mornings of what proved to be very hot days were cold enough to make our extremities fairly tingle.

A constant diet of bread and tea, together with the hard physical exercise and mental anxiety, caused our strength at length to fail.

The constant drinking of brackish water made one of us so ill that he could retain no food. A high fever set in on the evening of August 15, and as we pulled into the station of Bay-doon-sah, he was forced to go to bed at once. The other, with the aid of our small medicine supply, endeavored to ward off the ominous symptoms. In his anxiety, however, to do all that was possible he made a serious blunder. Instead of antipyrin he administered the poison, sulphate of zinc, which we carried to relieve our eyes when inflamed by the alkali dust. This was swallowed before the truth was discovered. It was an anxious moment for us both when we picked up the paper from the floor and read the inscription. We could do nothing but look at each other in silence. Happily it was an overdose, and the vomiting which immediately followed relieved both the patient and the anxious doctor. What to do we did not know. The patient now suggested that his companion should go on without him, and, if possible, send back medical aid or proper food; but not to remain and get worse himself. He, on the other hand, refused to leave without the other. Then too, the outlying town of Ngan-si-chou, the first where proper food and water could be obtained, was only one day's journey away. Another effort was decided upon. But when morning came, a violent hurricane from the southeast swept the sand in our faces, and fairly blew the sick man over on his wheel. Famishing with thirst, tired beyond expression, and burning with fever as well as the withering heat, we reached at last the bank of the Su-la-ho. Eagerly we plunged into its sluggish waters, and waded through under the walls of Ngan-si-chou.

Ngan-si-chou was almost completely destroyed during the late Dungan rebellion. Little is now to be seen except heaps of rubbish, ruined temples, and the scattered fragments of idols. The neglected gardens no longer check the advancing sands, which in some places were drifting over the ramparts. Through its abandoned gateway we almost staggered with weakness, and directed our course to the miserable bazaar. The only meat we could find was pork, that shibboleth between Mohammedanism and Confucianism. The Dungan restaurant-keeper would not cook it, and only after much persuasion consented to have it prepared outside and brought back to be eaten beneath his roof. With better water and more substantial food we began, from this time on, to recuperate. But before us still a strong head wind was sweeping over the many desert stretches that lay between the oases along the Su-la-ho, and with the constant walking our sandals and socks were almost worn away. For this reason we were delayed one evening in reaching the town of Dyou-min-shan. In the lonely stillness of its twilight a horseman was approaching across the barren plain, bearing a huge Chinese lantern in his hand, and

singing aloud, as is a Chinaman's custom, to drive off the evil spirits of the night. He started back, as we suddenly appeared, and then dismounted, hurriedly, to throw his lantern's glare upon us. "Are you the two Americans?" he asked in an agitated manner. His question was surprising. Out in this desert country we were not aware that our identity was known, or our visit expected. He then explained that he had been instructed by the magistrate of Dyou-min-shan to go out and look for us, and escort us into the town. He also mentioned in this connection the name of Ling Darin—a name that we had heard spoken of almost with veneration ever since leaving Urumtsi. Who this personage was we were unable to find out beyond that he was an influential mandarin in the city of Su-chou, now only a day's journey away.

Near that same fortieth parallel of latitude on which our Asiatic journey was begun and ended, we now struck, at its extreme western limit, the Great Wall of China. The Kiayu-kuan, or "Jade Gate," by which it is here intersected, was originally so called from the fact that it led into the Khotan country, whence the Chinese traders brought back the precious

mineral. This, with the Shanghai-kuan near the sea, and the Yuamin-
kuan, on the Nankow pass, are the principal gateways in this "wall of ten
thousand *li*," which, until forced by Yengiz Khan, protected the empire
from the Mongolian nomads for a period of fourteen hundred years. In
its present condition the Great Wall belongs to various epochs. With the
sudden and violent transitions of temperature in the severe Mongolian
climate, it may be doubted whether any portion of Shi Hoangti's original
work still survives. Nearly all the eastern section, from Ordos to the Yellow Sea, was rebuilt in the fifth century, and the double rampart along
the northwest frontier of the plains of Peking was twice restored in the
fifteenth and sixteenth. North of Peking, where this prodigious structure
has a mean height of about twenty-six feet, and width of twenty feet, it is
still in a state of perfect repair, whereas in many western districts along
the Gobi frontier, as here before us, it is little more than an earthen rampart about fifteen feet in height, while for considerable distances, as
along the road from Su-chou to Kan-chou, it has entirely disappeared for
miles at a stretch. Both the gate and the wall at this point had been
recently repaired. We could now see it rising and falling in picturesque
undulations as far as the Tibetan ranges. There it stops altogether, after a
westward course of over fifteen hundred miles. In view of what was
before us, we could not but smile as we thought of that French abbé who
undertook, in an elaborate volume, to prove that the "Great Wall of
China" was nothing more than a myth.

PART III

Lifelong Quests

I could not comprehend in the least what lay before us. . . . Yet it is our destiny to move on, whatever direction it may be that that narrow winding path, running among tall grasses and down into gullies and across small streams, takes us, until we penetrate that cold, dark, still horizon before us. . . .

—HENRY MORTON STANLEY

I think I cannot preserve my health and spirits, unless I spend four hours a day at least,—and it is commonly more than that,—sauntering through the woods and over the hills and fields, absolutely free from all wordly engagements . . .

—HENRY DAVID THOREAU

FRANCIS EDWARD YOUNGHUSBAND

(1863–1942)

From *Among the Celestials*

---

*The early exploration of the Himalayas is a difficult story to make
coherent. Unlike most parts of the world being swarmed over by Europeans in the nineteenth century, the Himalayas were not thought to
have value for imperial or intrinsic reasons, but merely as a geopolitical
boundary, shielding British India from the north. Its people were misunderstood and its geography gravely underestimated. What's more,
those few explorers who described the region were mostly surveyors or
military men with the driest of writing styles. Younghusband was a rare
exception.*

*One of the great figures of the age and known for his courage and
charisma, Younghusband was a captain in the British exploring outfit
grandly named the King's Dragoon Guards. Although the Alps were
where most British climbers cut their teeth, Younghusband fell in love
with the mountains in the unparalleled vertical world of the
Himalayas. Before joining the foreign army as a young man he had
never climbed, and yet he would go on to be one of the very first to
attempt Mount Everest.*

In 1887, then twenty-four years old, Younghusband set out on an intelligence mission with a group of horsemen, porters, and guides across the Gobi desert and back to India through the Karakoram Range. Perhaps the most significant aspect of his journey was his successful crossing of the steep and crevasse-ridden 19,000-foot Mustagh Pass, described in the following passage. For this 180-mile trek through the snow, the men wore thin leather moccasins, and none had a tent, sleeping bag, or coat warmer than a sheepskin. Taking great risks, they broke the trail for an important new route through the heart of the Himalayas. He came to call this particular climb his "baptism of fear," and exploring the high passes became his all-consuming passion and lifelong spiritual quest from that point onward.

The Mustagh Pass, which we were now approaching, is on the main watershed, which both divides the rivers of India from the rivers of Turkestan, and also the British from the Chinese dominions. Peaks along the watershed, in the vicinity of the pass, had been fixed by trigonometrical observations from the Indian side at 24,000, 26,000, and as we have seen in one case at over 28,000 feet in height, so I could scarcely doubt that the pass across the range must be lofty and difficult. It was, therefore, all the more worth conquering, and as it would be the final and greatest obstacle on my long journey from Peking, I set out to tackle it with the determination to overcome it at almost any cost. Every other difficulty had been successfully negotiated, and this last remaining obstacle, though the most severe of all, was not to be permitted at the climax of my journey to keep me from my goal.

These were my feelings as I advanced up the valley, at the head of which lay the Mustagh Pass. But I had little idea of the magnitude of the difficulties which in reality lay before me and these were soon to commence.

Scarcely a mile from our bivouac of the previous night we came to a point where the valley was blocked by what appeared to be enormous heaps of broken stones and fragments of rock. These heaps were between two and three hundred feet in height, and stretched completely across the valley. I had gone on ahead by myself, and when I saw these mounds of *débris*, I thought we might have trouble in taking ponies over such rough obstacles; but I was altogether taken aback when, on coming up to the heaps, I found that they were masses of solid ice, merely covered over on the surface with a thin layer of this rocky *débris*, which served to conceal the surface of the ice immediately beneath. And my dismay can be imagined when, on ascending one of the highest of the mounds, I found that they were but the end of a series which extended without interruption for many miles up the valley to the snows at the foot of the pass. We were, in fact, at the extremity of an immense glacier. This was the first time I had actually stood on a glacier, and I had never realised till now how huge and continuous a mass of ice it is. Here and there, breaking through the mounds of stone, I had seen cliffs of what I thought was black rock, but on coming close up to these found them to be nothing but solid dark green ice. I discovered caverns, too, with transparent walls of clear, clean ice, and long, tapering icicles hanging in delicate fringes from the roof. It was an astonishing and wonderful sight; but I was destined to see yet more marvellous scenes than this in the icy region upon which I was now entering.

To take a caravan of ponies up a glacier like this seemed to me an utter impossibility. The guides thought so too, and I decided upon sending the ponies round by the Karakoram Pass, 180 miles to the eastward, to Leh, and going on myself over the Mustagh Pass with a couple of men. This would have been a risky proceeding, for if we did not find our way over the pass we should have scarcely enough provisions with us to last us till we could return to an inhabited place again. Supplies altogether were running short, and the longer we took in reaching the pass, the harder we should fare if we did not succeed in getting over. But while I was deciding upon sending the ponies back, the caravan men were making a gallant attempt to lead them up the glacier. I rejoined them, and we all helped the ponies along as well as we could; hauling at them in front, pushing at them behind, and sometimes unloading and ourselves carrying the loads up the stone-covered mounds of ice. But it was terribly hard and trying work for the animals. They could get no proper foothold, and as they kept climbing up the sides of a mound they would scratch away the thin layer of stones on the surface, and then, coming on to the pure ice immediately below, would slip and fall and cut their knees and hocks about in a way which went directly to my heart. I did not see how this sort of thing could last. We had only advanced a few hundred yards, and there were still from fifteen to twenty miles of glacier ahead. I therefore halted the ponies for the day, and went on with a couple of men to reconnoitre. We fortunately found, in between the glacier and the mountainside, a narrow stretch of less impracticable ground, along which it would be possible to take the ponies. This we marked out, and returned to our bivouac after dark.

That night we passed, as usual, in the open, thoroughly exhausted after the hard day's work, for at the high altitudes we had now reached the rarefaction of the air makes one tired very quickly, and the constant tumbling about on the slippery glacier in helping the ponies over it added to one's troubles. My boots were cut through, my hands cut all over, and my elbows a mass of bruises.

At daybreak on the following morning we started again, leading the ponies up the route we had marked out; but a mile from the point where our previous exploration had ended we were confronted by another great glacier flowing down from the left. We now had a glacier on one side of us, mountains on the other, and a second glacier right across our front. At this time my last remaining pair of boots were completely worn out, and my feet so sore from the bruises they received on the glacier I could scarcely bear to put them to the ground. So I stayed behind with the ponies, while two men went on to find a way through the obstacles before us. The men returned after a time, and said they could find no possible way for the ponies; but they begged me to have a look myself, saying that perhaps by my good fortune I might be able to find one.

I accordingly, with a couple of men, retraced my steps down the edge of the main glacier for some little distance, till we came to a point where it was possible to get ponies on to the glacier itself and take them right out into the middle. We then ascended a prominent spot on the glacier, from which we could obtain a good view all round. We were in a sea of ice. There was now little of the rocky moraine stuff with which the ice of the glacier had been covered in its lower part, and we looked out on a vast river of pure white ice, broken up into myriads of sharp needle-like points. Snowy mountains rose above us on either hand, and down their sides rolled the lesser glaciers, like clotted cream pouring over the lip of a cream-jug; and rising forbiddingly before us was the cold icy range we should have to cross.

This, marvellous as it was to look upon, was scarcely the country through which to take a caravan of ponies, but I made out a line of moraine extending right up the main glacier. We got on to this, and, following it up for some distance, found, to our great relief, that it would be quite possible to bring ponies up it on to the smooth snow of the *névé* at the head of the glacier. Having ascertained this beyond a doubt, we returned late in the afternoon towards the spot where we had left our ponies. Darkness, however, overtook us before we reached it. We wandered about on the glacier for some time, and nearly lost our way; but at last, quite worn out, reached our little caravan once more.

That night we held a council of war as to which of the two Mustagh Passes we should attack. There are two passes, known as the Mustagh, which cross the range. One, to the east, that is to our left as we were ascending the glacier, is known as the Old Mustagh Pass, and was in use in former days, till the advance of ice upon it made it so difficult that a new one was sought for, and what is known as the New Mustagh Pass, some ten miles farther west along the range, had been discovered. It was over this latter pass that the guides hoped to conduct our party. They said that even ponies had in former times been taken across it by means of ropes and by making rough bridges across the crevasses. No European had crossed either of them, but Colonel Godwin-Austen, in 1862, reached the southern foot of the new pass in the course of his survey of

Baltistan. This New Mustagh Pass seemed the more promising of the two, and I therefore decided upon sending two men on the following morning to reconnoitre it and report upon its practicability.

At the first streak of daylight the reconnoiterers set out, and the remainder of us afterwards followed with the ponies along the route which we had explored on the previous day. We took the ponies up the glacier without any serious difficulty, and in the evening halted close up to the head of the glacier where snowy mountains of stupendous height shut us in on every hand. At dusk the two men who had been sent out to reconnoitre the new pass returned, to say that the ice had so accumulated on it that it would be now quite impossible to take ponies over, and that it would be difficult even for men to cross it. The plan which they therefore suggested was to leave the ponies behind, and cross the range by the Old Mustagh Pass, push on to Askoli, the first village on the south side of the range, and from there send back men with supplies for the ponies and the men with them sufficient to enable the caravan to reach Shahidula, on the usual trade route beteen Yarkand and Kashmir. This was evidently all we could do. We could not take the ponies any farther, and we could not send them back as they were, for we had nearly run out of supplies, and Shahidula the nearest point at which fresh supplies could be obtained, was one hundred and eighty miles distant. All now depended upon our being able to cross the pass. If we were not able to, we should have to march this one hundred and eighty miles back through the mountains with only three or four days' supplies to support us. We might certainly have eaten the ponies, so would not actually have starved; but we should have had a hard struggle for it, and there would still have been the range to cross at another point.

Matters were therefore approaching a critical stage, and that was an anxious night for me. I often recall it, and think of our little bivouac in the snow at the foot of the range we had to overcome. The sun sank behind the icy mountains, the bright glow gently disappeared, and they became steely hard while the grey cold of night settled shimmering down upon them. All around was pure white snow and ice, breathing out cold upon us. The little pools and streamlets of water which the heat of the sun had poured off the glacier during the day were now gripped by the frost, which seemed to creep around ourselves too, and huddle us up together. We had no tent to shelter us from the biting streams of air flowing down from the mountain summits, and we had not sufficient fuel to light a fire round which we might lie. We had, indeed, barely enough brushwood to keep up a fire for cooking; but my Chinese servant cooked a simple meal of rice and mutton for us all. We gathered round the fire to eat it hot out of the bowl, and then rolled ourselves up in our sheepskins and went to sleep, with the stars twinkling brightly above, and the frost gripping closer and closer upon us.

Next morning, while it was yet dark, Wali, the guide, awoke us. We each had a drink of tea and some bread, and then we started off to attack the pass. The ponies, with nearly all the baggage, were left behind under the charge of Liu-san, the Chinaman, and some of the older men. All we took with us was a roll of bedding for myself, a sheepskin coat for each man, some native biscuits, tea and a large tea-kettle, and a bottle of brandy. The ascent to the pass was easy but trying, for we were now not far from nineteen thousand feet above sea-level, and at that height, walking uphill through deep snow, we quickly became exhausted. We could only take a dozen or twenty steps at a time, and we would then bend over on our sticks and pant as if we had been running hard uphill. We were tantalised, too, by the apparent nearness of the pass. Everything here was on a gigantic scale, and what seemed to be not more than an hour's walk from the bivouac was in fact a six hours' climb.

It was nearly midday when we reached the top of the pass, and what we saw there makes me shudder even now to think upon. There was nothing but a sheer precipice before us, and those first few moments on the summit of the Mustagh Pass were full of intensest anxiety to me. If we could but get over, the crowning success of my expedition would be gained. But the thing seemed to me simply an impossibility. I had had no experience of Alpine climbing, and I had no ice-axes or other mountaineering appliances with me. I had not even proper boots. All I had for

foot-gear were some native boots of soft leather, without nails and without heels—mere leather stockings, in fact—which gave no sort of grip
upon an icy surface. How, then, I should ever be able to get down the icy
slopes and rocky precipices I now saw before me I could not by any possibility imagine; and if it had rested with me alone, the probability is we
never should have got over the pass at all.

What, however, saved our party was my holding my tongue. I kept
quite silent as I looked over the pass, and waited to hear what the men
had to say about it. They meanwhile were looking at me, and, imagining
that an Englishman never went back from an enterprise he had once
started on, took it as a matter of course that, as I gave no order to go
back, I necessarily meant to go on. So they set about their preparations
for the descent. We had brought an ordinary pickaxe with us, and Wali[1]
went on ahead with this, while the rest of us followed one by one behind
him, each hanging on to a rope tied round Wali's waist to support him in
case he slipped while hewing steps across an ice-slope leading to a rocky
precipice which seemed to afford the only possible means of descending
the pass. This slope was of hard ice, very steep, and, thirty yards or so
below the line we took, ended in an ice-fall, which again terminated
many hundreds of feet beneath in the head of a glacier at the foot of the
pass. Wali with his pickaxe hewed a way step by step across the ice-
slope, so as to reach the rocky cliff by which we should have to descend
on to the glacier below.

We slowly edged across the slope after him, but it was hard to keep
cool and steady. From where we stood we could see nothing over the end
of the slope but the glacier hundreds of feet below us. Some of the men
were so little nervous that they kicked the fragments of ice hewed out by
Wali down the slope, and laughed as they saw them hop down it and
with one last bound disappear altogether. But an almost sickening feeling
came on me as I watched this, for we were standing on a slope as steep
as the roof of a house. We had no ice-axes with which to anchor our-

---

[1] One of Younghusband's Ladakhi guides.

selves or give us support; and though I tied handkerchiefs, and the men bits of leather and cloth, round the insteps of our smooth native boots, to give us a little grip on the slippery ice, I could not help feeling that if any one of us had lost his foothold the rest would never have been able to hold him up with the rope, and that in all likelihood the whole party would have been carried away and plunged into the abyss below.

Outwardly I kept as cool and cheerful as I could, but inwardly I shuddered at each fresh step I took. The sun was now pouring down and just melted the surface of the steps after they were hewn, so that by the time those of us who were a few paces behind Wali reached a step the ice was just covered over with water and this made it still more slippery for our soft leather boots, which had now become almost slimy on the surface. It was under these circumstances that my Ladaki servant Drogpa gave in. He was shaking all over in an exaggerated shiver, and so unsteady, I thought he would slip at any moment and perhaps carry us all with him. We were but at the beginning of our trials. We had not even begun the actual descent yet, but were merely crossing to a point from which we should make it. And to have such a man with us might have endangered the safety of the whole party; so I told him he might return to the ponies and go round with them. It rather upset me to see a born hillman so affected, but I pretended not to care a bit and laughed it off, *pour encourager les autres,* as the thing had to be done.

At last we reached the far side of the slope, and found ourselves on a projecting piece of rock protruding through the ice. Here we could rest, but only with the prospect of still further difficulties before us. We were at the head of the rocky precipice, the face of which we should have to descend to reach the ice-slopes which extended to the glacier at the foot of the pass. At such heights as those which we had now reached, where the snow and ice lie sometimes hundreds of feet thick, it is only where it is very steep that the bare rock shows through. The cliff we had now to descend was an almost sheer precipice; its only saving feature was that it was rough and rugged, and so afforded some little hold for our hands and feet. Yet even then we seldom got a hold for the whole hand or whole foot. All we generally found was a little ledge, upon which we could grip with the tips of the fingers or side of the foot. The men were most good to me, whenever possible guiding my foot into some secure hold, and often supporting it there with their hands; but at times it was all I could do to summon sufficient courage to let myself down on to the veriest little crevices which had to support me. There was a constant dread, too, that fragments of these ledges might give way with the weight upon them; for the rock was very crumbly, as it generally is when exposed to severe frosts, and once I heard a shout from above, as a huge piece of rock which had been detached came crashing past me, and as nearly as possible hit two of the men who had already got half-way down.

We reached the bottom of the cliff without accident, and then found ourselves at the head of a long ice-slope extending down to the glacier below. Protruding through the ice were three pieces of rock, which would serve us as successive halting-places, and we determined upon taking a line which led by them. We had brought with us every scrap of rope that could be spared from the ponies' gear, and we tied these and all the men's turbans and waist-clothes together into one long rope, by which we let a man down the ice-slope on to the first projecting rock. As he went down he cut steps, and when he had reached the rock we tied the upper end of the rope firmly on to a rock above, and then one by one we came down the slope, hanging on to the rope and making use of the steps which had been cut. This was, therefore, a comparatively easy part of the descent; but one man was as nearly as possible lost. He slipped, fell over on his back, and came sliding down the slope at a frightful pace. Luckily, however, he still managed to keep hold of the rope with one hand, and so kept himself from dashing over the ice-fall at the side of the slope; but when he reached the rock his hand was almost bared of skin, and he was shivering with fright. Wali, however, gave him a sound rating for being so careless, and on the next stage made him do all the hardest part of the work.

The other men got down the slope without mishap, and then came the last man. He, of course, could not have the benefit of a rope to hang on by, for he would have to untie it from the rock and bring it with him. Wali had selected for this, the most dangerous piece of work in the whole descent, the man who had especially troubled me by knocking pieces of ice over the precipice when we were on the ice-slope at the head of the pass. He was one of the slaves I had released at Yarkand[2] an incessant grumbler, and very rough, but, next to Wali, the best man I had for any really hard work. He tied the end of the rope round his waist, and then slowly and carefully came down the steps which had been hewn in the slope. We at the end of the rope pulled it in at every step he took, so that if he slipped, though he might fall past us, we should be able to haul in the rope fast, and so perhaps save him from the ice-fall. He reached our rock of refuge in safety, and we then in the same manner descended two more stages of the ice-slope, and finally reached a part where the slope was less steep, and we could proceed without cutting steps the whole way.

At last, just as the sun set, we reached the glacier at the foot of the pass. We were in safety once more. The tension of six crucial hours was over, and the last and greatest obstacle in my journey had been success-fully surmounted. Those moments when I stood at the foot of the pass are long to be remembered by me—moments of intense relief, of glowing pride and of deep gratitude for the success that had been granted. But such feelings as mine were now cannot be described in words; they are known only to those who have had their heart set on one great object and have accomplished it.

I took a last look at the pass, never before nor since seen by a European, and which, viewed from below, looked utterly impracticable to any human being. Then we started away down the glacier to find some bare spot on which to lay our rugs and rest.

The sun had now set, but, fortunately for us, there was an abundance of light, and the night was marvelously beautiful, so that, tired as I was, I could not but be impressed by it. The moon was nearly full, the sky with-

2 North of the Karakorams, near Kashmir.

out a cloud, and in the amphitheatre of snowy mountains and among the icy seracs of the glacier, not one speck of anything but the purest white was visible. The air at these altitudes, away from dust and with no misty vapour in it, was absolutely clear, and the soft silvery rays of the moon struck down upon the glistening mountains in unsullied radiance. The whole effect was of some enchanting fairy scene; and the sternness of the mountains was slowly softened down till lost, and their beauty in its purest form alone remained.

With our senses enervated by such a scene as this, and overcome with delight as we were at having successfully crossed the pass, we pushed on down the glacier in a dreamy, careless way, perfectly regardless of the dangers which lay hidden around us. Under ordinary circumstances we should have proceeded cautiously down a glacier which, beautiful though it was, had its full share of crevasses; and it was only when I turned round and found one man missing, that I realised how negligent we had been. We retraced our steps, and found the poor fellow had dropped down a crevasse, the mouth of which had been covered with a thin coating of ice and snow, which had given way under his weight, so that he had dropped through. Very fortunately the crevasse was not wide, and after falling about fifteen feet he had been wedged in between the two sides by the load of my bedding which he was carrying; so by letting a rope down we were able to extricate him in safety. This taught us a lesson, and for the rest of the way we went along roped together, as we ought to have been from the first, and tested each step as we advanced.

I now kept in the rear, and the man with my bedding was in front of me. As we were closed up during a temporary halt, I detected a strong smell of brandy coming from the bundle of bedding. A distracting thought occurred to me. I tore open the bundle, and there was my last bottle of brandy—broken! Lady Walsham, on my leaving Peking, had insisted upon giving me at least two bottles of brandy for the journey. I had drunk one in the Gobi Desert, and I had made up my mind to keep the other till the day I had crossed the Mustagh Pass, but there it was broken, and the brandy wasted, just when both the men and myself were really needing something to pull us together. The bundle of bedding had been thrown over the pass to save carrying it down, and though the bottle had been wrapped up in my sheepskin sleeping-bag, it had been smashed to pieces.

About eleven o'clock we at last reached a piece of ground on the mountain-side free from snow, and here we halted for the night. There was no wood, and only a few roots of weeds about with which to light a fire, so we had to break up a couple of our alpenstocks to make a small fire, by which we managed to boil sufficient water to make a few cups of tea. We had some buscuit with that, and then I got into my sheepskin bag, and the men wrapped themselves up in their sheepskin coats, and we lay down and slept as if nothing could ever wake us again. The work and anxiety on the last few days had been great, and on this day we had been on the move for eighteen hours continuously. Now the worst was over, and I slept with my mind at ease and happy.

But at daybreak the next morning we were on our legs again. We had still a long way to go before we could reach Askoli, the nearest village, and our men remaining behind on the pass were waiting for supplies. Yet freezing as it was we had to start without anything to warm us, for we could find no materials for a fire; but at about ten o'clock, at a point near where our glacier joined the great Baltoro glacier, we found an old hut, built at the time when this route was in use, and from the fragments of wood about we made up the first good fire we had had for a week past, and had a fairly substantial meal. But we could not indulge ourselves at all freely, for we were very short of provisions. We had left with the men on the pass all but just sufficient to carry us through to Askoli; and a few mouthfuls of meat, with some biscuit and some tea, were all we could allow ourselves. Having eaten this and rested for an hour, we again pushed on, and struck the Baltoro glacier nearly opposite the great Masher Brum peak, which stands up over twenty-five thousand feet high just across the glacier. Then, turning to our left in the opposite direction to Askoli, we could see far away up this, the largest mountain glacier in the world, other peaks of even greater height, rising like snowy spires in the distance. Four peaks over twenty-six thousand feet, stand out at the head of the Baltoro glacier, and away to our left, though hidden from us, was the peak K.2, which I had seen from the northern side of the Mustagh Pass. Five years afterwards, Sir William Conway's party explored the entire length of the glacier, and ascended a peak twenty-three thousand feet in height at its head; but, fascinating though it would have been to have wandered among these mountain giants, in a region unsurpassed for sublimity and grandeur by any in the world, I could only now think of reaching an inhabited spot again as rapidly as possible.

We turned to the right, then down the glacier, keeping along the moraine close to the mountain-side. This and the two following were days of agony to me, for my native boots were now in places worn through till the bare skin of my foot was exposed, and I had to hobble along on my toes or my heels to keep the worn-out part by the balls of my feet from the sharp stones and rocky *débris* of the glacier. On account of this tenderness of my feet, I was always slipping, too, falling and bruising my elbows, or cutting my hands on the rough stones in trying to save myself.

All that day we plodded wearily along down the glacier, till at sunset we came upon a little clump of fir trees on the mountain-side. Here we were able to make up as big a fire as we wished, and if we could only have had more to eat, would have been perfectly happy; but there was now no meat left, and tea and biscuit was all we had. Next day we reached the end of the glacier, and sleeping that night in a cave, on the following day made our last march into Askoli. Never did I think we were going to reach that spot! By midday we saw its green trees and fields in the distance; but I could only drag myself slowly along, as the way was rough and stony, and I was footsore and exhausted. At last, however, at four o'clock, we really entered the village. We sent for the headman, and told him to bring us some food. A bed was brought me to lie on, and then, with a stewed fowl and some rice to eat, fresh life and energy came into me, and I could realise the satisfaction of having reached the first inhabited spot in Indian territory.

A. HENRY SAVAGE LANDOR

(1867–1924)

From *In the Forbidden Land*

Landor may have suffered the same flaw of character as the American John Ledyard, who in 1786 set out to cross Siberia, the Bering Sea, and all of North America on foot (he made it to Siberia, where he was promptly arrested by Catherine the Great). Of Ledyard, Thomas Jefferson wrote: "He is a person of ingenuity and information. Unfortunately, he has too much imagination."

In some Victorian minds, Landor gave exploring a bad name. These were the days of stiff upper lips and proper manners, when arrogance and posturing were in healthy supply but exhibited only on natives and arch rivals, rarely on one's reading public. Landor, who traveled extensively in Japan, Tibet, Africa, and South America, apparently endured starvation, kidnappings, torture, and other extravagant hardships. Still, vainglorious sensationalist or not, if even half of what Landor wrote is true, he gets high marks for his brazen courage and extraordinary lust for adventure.

The highly entertaining In the Forbidden Land describes Landor's journey across the Himalayas and into the closed kingdom of Tibet, *where only a handful of Westerners had gained entry by 1897. There he was captured by Tibetan guards and allegedly tortured by various means, including being run on horseback while bound to a saddle of spikes. Finally he was freed and forced out, all but naked, via the snowbound Lumpia Pass. This excerpt has him crossing the mountains on his way to Tibet, ditching all common sense and risking his life on an impulsive and harrowing ascent of a 21,000-foot summit along the route.*

From Kuti I had despatched a sturdy Shoka, named Nattoo, to ascertain whether it was possible to cross the chain over the high Mangshan Pass, as in this case I should be enabled to get many marches into Tibet by the jungle without fear of being detected. I should thus get behind the force of soldiers which I was informed the Jong Pen of Taklakot had concentrated at the Lippu Pass to prevent my entering the country, and before they could have time to discover my whereabouts I should be too far ahead for them to find me. Nattoo arrived in camp almost simultaneously with ourselves and had a long tale of woe to relate. He had been half way up the mountain. The snow was deep and there were huge and treacherous cracks in the ice. As he was on his way up, an avalanche had fallen, and it was merely by the skin of his teeth that he had escaped with his life. This was to him an evil omen, and he had turned back without reaching the summit of the pass. He seemed scared and worn out, and declared that it was impossible for us to proceed that way. Unfortunately the thrilling account of the Kutial's[1] misfortunes had a depressing effect on my men. What with the intense cold, the fatigue of carrying heavy loads at high elevations over such rough country, and the fearful rivers which they dreaded, and so many of which we had crossed, my carriers became absolutely demoralised at the thought of new hardships ahead,

[1] Nattoo's.

all the more when I assured them that I did not believe Nattoo, and that I should go and see for myself.

It was 4:30 in the afternoon, and therefore some time before sunset. There would be moonlight. I had on that day marched eight miles,[†] and though the soles of my feet were cut and sore I was not really tired. Our camp was at an elevation of 16,150 feet, a pretty respectable altitude considering that the highest mountain in Europe is only 15,781 feet. Dr. Wilson insisted on accompanying me to the top, and Kachi Ram and a Rongba coolie volunteered to come as well. Bijesing, the Johari, got on his feet after some persuasion, and that completed our little exploration party. Chanden Sing,[2] who was really the only man I could trust, was left in charge of the camp, with strict orders to punish severely any one who might attempt to turn back during my absence.

We set out almost immediately after reaching camp, following up stream the course of the Mangshan River, which is boxed in between high cliffs. . . . There was no track, and the walking was extremely difficult and troublesome, over large slippery stones, between which one's feet constantly slipped and got jammed, straining and injuring one's ankles. Little trusting my followers, who seemed on the verge of mutiny, I did not care to leave behind in camp the heavy load of silver rupees (R. 800) sewn in my coat, which, by the way, I always carried on my person, as well as my rifle, two compasses (prismatic and luminous), two aneroids, one half-chronometer, and another watch and some thirty cartridges. The combined weight of these articles was considerable, and I felt it especially during the first days of my march. On this particular afternoon it was almost too much for my strength. However, one gets accustomed to most things, and after a while I felt comparatively little discomfort in marching under it. I persisted in thus weighting myself

[†] It must be remembered that at high elevations the exertion of walking eight miles would be equivalent to that of marching about twice the distance at much lower altitudes.

---

[2] Landor's hired servant.

simply to be on the safe side, so as to be always prepared in case my men revolted or abandoned me.

We proceeded up and down the series of hillocks and in and out of the innumerable channels that the melting snow and ice had, with the aid of centuries, cut deep into the mass of rolling stones. At the point where the two ranges met there stood before us the magnificent pale green ice-terraces of the Mangshan glacier, surmounted by extensive snowfields winding their way to the summit of the mountain range. Clouds enveloped the higher peaks. The clear Alpine ice showed vertical streaks, especially in the lower part of the glacier, where it was granulated to a certain extent. The base, the sides and top being covered with a thick coat of fresh snow, and my time being very limited, I was unable to make careful investigations to ascertain the recent movement and oscillations of this glacier.

. . .

The Mangshan River rises from this glacier, but we left the glacier (17,800 feet) to the right, and, turning sharply northwards, began our ascent towards the pass. To gaze upon the incline before us was alone sufficient to deter one from attempting to climb it, had one a choice; in addition to this, the snow we struggled over was so soft and deep that we sank into it up to our waists. Occasionally the snow alternated with patches of loose *débris* and rotten rock, on which we were no better off; in fact, the fatigue of progressing over them was simply overpowering. Having climbed up half-a-dozen steps among the loose cutting stones, we felt ourselves sliding back to almost our original point of departure, followed by a small avalanche of shifting material that only stopped when it got to the foot of the mountain.

At 19,000 feet we were for a considerable distance on soft snow, covering an ice-field with deep crevasses and cracks in it. We had to feel our way with great caution, particularly as there was only the light of the moon to depend upon.

Fortunately, as we rose higher, there were no more crevasses, but I began to feel a curious exhaustion that I had never experienced before.

At sunset the thermometer which Kachi carried for me had descended forty degrees within a few minutes, and the sudden change in the temperature seemed to affect us all more or less; but we went on, with the exception of Bijesing, who was seized with mountain sickness so violently that he was unable to proceed. The doctor, too, a man of powerful build, was suffering considerably. His legs, he said, had become like lead, and each seemed to weigh a ton. The effort of lifting, or even moving, them required all his energy. Although he was terribly blown and gasping for breath, yet he would not give in, and he struggled on bravely until we reached an altitude of 20,500 feet. Here he was seized with such exhaustion and pain that he was unable to proceed. Kachi Ram, the Rongba and I went ahead, but we also were suffering, Kachi complaining of violent beating in his temples and loud buzzing in his ears. He also gasped and staggered dangerously, threatening to collapse at any moment. At 21,000 feet he fell flat on the snow. He was instantly asleep, breathing heavily and snoring raspingly. His hands and feet were icy cold, and I rubbed them. But what caused me more anxiety than anything was the irregular beating and throbbing of his heart. I wrapped him up in his blanket and my waterproof, and, having seen to his general comfort, I shouted to the doctor, telling him what had happened, and that I was going to push on as much higher as I could stand, the Rongba being now the only one of the party who was able to keep up.

A thick mist came on and enveloped us, which considerably added to our trials. Our efforts to get on after we left Kachi at 21,000 feet were desperate, our lungs in convulsion as if about to burst, our pulses hastened, our hearts throbbing (mine being ordinarily very regular) as if they would beat themselves out of our bodies. Exhausted and seized by irresistible drowsiness, the Rongba and I nevertheless at last reached the top. It was a satisfaction to have got there, to have reached such an altitude, although I had long realised the impossibility of getting my men over by this way. It served me also to ascertain the amount of snow on the other side of the range, which, when the fog lifted somewhat, I found to be greater on the northern slope than on the southern. Although almost fainting with fatigue, I registered my observations. The altitude was 22,000 feet, the hour 11 P.M., and there was a strong, cutting North-East wind. I had stupidly forgotten to take my thermometer out of Kachi's pocket when I left him, and was unable to register the temperature, but the cold was intense. The stars were extraordinarily brilliant and the moon shone bright for a while over the panorama around me, and though it was a view of utter desolation, it had nevertheless a curious indescribable fascination. Below me, to the south, were mountainous masses buried in snow, and to the South-West and North-East were peaks even higher than the one on which I stood. To the north stretched the immense, dreary Tibetan plateau with undulations and intricate hill ranges, beyond which a high mountain range with snow peaks could just be perceived in the distance. I could see very little snow near by, except on the northern slope of the range I was standing on, and on the hill-tops which dotted the plateau.

I had barely taken it in, barely realised the wonder of nature asleep when the mist again rose before me and I saw a gigantic phantom rising out of it. It stood in the centre of a luminous circle, a tall, dark figure in the folds of an enormous veil of mist. The effect was overwhelming, and it was only after some moments that I realised that the spectre wore my features, was a liquid presentation of my own proportions colossally enlarged; that I stood in the centre of a lunar rainbow, and that I was gazing on the reflection of myself in the mist. As I moved my arms, my body, or my head, the ghost-like figure moved, and I felt myself irresistibly changing my postures—oddly and nervously at first—then, with an awakening sense of the ridiculous in my actions—so as to make my image change and do as I did. I felt like a child placed for the first time in front of a mirror.

· · ·

The Rongba had fallen exhausted, and I felt so faint with the awful pressure on my lungs, that, despite all my efforts to resist it, I collapsed on the snow. The coolie and I, shivering pitifully, shared the same blanket for additional warmth. Both of us were seized with irresistible drowsiness, as if we had taken a strong narcotic. I fought hard against it, for I well knew that if my eyelids once closed they would almost certainly remain so for ever. I called to the Rongba. He was fast asleep. I summoned up my last atom of vitality to keep my eyes open. The wind blew hard and biting, with a hissing noise. How that hiss still sounds in my ears! It seemed like the whisper of death. The Rongba, crouched with teeth chattering, was moaning, and his sudden shudders bespoke great pain. It seemed only common charity to let him have the blanket, which was in any case too small for both, so I wrapped it tightly round his head and body. He was doubled up with his chin on his knees. This small exertion was quite sufficient to make me lose the tug-of-war in which I was pulling against nature. Just like the subject who, under hypnotic influence, feels his own will and power suddenly going from him, so I felt the entire hopelessness of further struggle against the supernatural forces I was contending with. Falling backwards on the snow, I made a last desperate effort to gaze at the glittering stars . . . my sight became dim and obscured. . . .

For how long this semi-consciousness lasted, I do not know. "God! how ghastly! Doctor! Kachi!" I tried to articulate. My voice seemed choked in my throat. Was what I saw before me real? The two men, as if frozen to death by the side of each other, seemed lying on that vast white sheet of snow, motionless as statues of ice. In my dream I attempted to raise them. They were quite rigid. I knelt beside them, calling them and frantically striving to bring them back to consciousness and life. Bewildered, I turned round to look for Bijesing, and, as I did so, all sense of vitality seemed to freeze within me. I saw myself enclosed in a quickly contracting tomb of transparent ice. It was easy to realise that I too would shortly be nothing but a solid block of ice, like my companions. My legs, my arms were already congealed. Horror-stricken as I was at the approach of such a hopeless, ghastly death, my sensations were accompanied by a languor and lassitude indescribable but far from unpleasant. To some extent thought or wonderment was still alive. Should I dwindle painlessly away, preferring rest and peace to effort, or should I make a last struggle to save myself? The ice seemed to close in more and more every moment. I was choking.

I tried to scream! to force myself through the suffocating weight on me! I gave a violent plunge, and then everything had vanished. The frozen Kachi, the doctor, the transparent tomb! Nothingness!

At last I was able to open my eyes, which ached as if needles had been stuck into them. It was snowing hard. I had temporarily lost the use of my legs and fingers. They were frozen. So violent was the shock of realising how very near death I had really been, that in waking up from the ghastly nightmare I became acutely alive to the full importance of instantly making my way down to a lower level. I was already covered with a layer of snow, and I suppose it was the frigid pressure on my forehead that caused the dream. It is, however, probable that, had it not been for the hideous vision that shook my nerves free of paralysing torpor, I should never have awakened from that spell-bound silence.

I sat up with difficulty, and by rubbing and beating them, slowly regained the use of my lower limbs. I roused the Rongba, rubbed him, and shook him till he was able to move. We began our descent.

No doubt the satisfaction of going up high mountains is very great; but can it be compared to that of coming down?

Descending was dangerous but not wearisome. The incline being extremely steep, we took gigantic strides on the snow, and when we came to patches of *débris,* we slid ten or fifteen feet each step amidst a deafening roar from the huge mass of loose stones set in motion by our descent.

"Hark!" I said to the Rongba, "what is that?"

We waited till all was silence, and with hands up to our ears listened attentively. It was still snowing.

"*Ao, ao, ao! Faldi ao! Tumka hatte?* Come, come, come quickly! Where are you?" cried a faint distressed voice from far down below.

We quickened our pace; having hardly any control over our legs, our descent was precipitous. The snow-fall ceased and we became enveloped in a thick mist which pierced into our very bones.

Guided by the anxious cries of the doctor, whose voice we recognised, we continued our breakneck journey downward. The cries got more and more distinct, and at last, to my great joy, we came face to face with Wilson, who, thank Heaven, was alive but almost helpless, as he said his legs were still like lead, and it was all he could do to move them.

Owing to his anxiety about us, he had been shouting for a long time, and getting no answer, he became very uneasy, all the more so as he found he could in no way come to our help. He had quite given us up for lost.

We looked for and found Kachi. He had slept like a top, curled up in his warm blanket and my overcoat, and was now quite refreshed, so all united again, we continued our race downwards, exchanging our experiences and sensations. We had no very serious mishaps, and life and strength gradually came back to us again when we descended to lower elevations. The ascent from the glacier at the bottom of the mountain to the summit occupied four and a half hours; the precipitous descent, without counting stoppages, only the ninth part of that time.

Over the same trying stony valley we reached camp during the early hours of the morning. The distance from camp to the altitude reached and back was over ten miles; therefore, during the twenty-four hours I had altogether gone eighteen miles (quite a record at such great altitudes). I may here also remark that, since breakfast at six o'clock the previous morning, I had taken no food of any kind, thus making an interval of twenty-three hours between one meal and the next. The anxiety of my men in camp was intense. They had lost all hope of seeing us again, and they were quite reassured when I told them that we would proceed later in the morning by the Lumpiya Pass, which was believed to be far easier.

In no time they had lighted a fire of dung, and after having had (at five o'clock in the morning) a handsome feed of rice, *chapatis,* extract of meat, and strengthening emergency food, we felt we were entitled to a well-deserved rest.

EDWARD WHYMPER

(1840–1911)

From *The Ascent of the Matterhorn*

The Alps were where mountaineering began, and where the sport was pursued with a frenzy that has never been equalled. Even so, by the middle of the nineteenth century the range's crown jewel, the Matterhorn, remained aloof and mysterious, a giant pointed face of crumbling rock that most believed was impenetrable. Two men, Edward Whymper—an implacable and solitary wood engraver—and John Tyndall, a brilliant Irish scientist with a hot temper—were equally determined to be the first to stand atop mountaineering's ultimate challenge. Their race and rivalry gripped the climbing world for three years.

In 1865, after seven previous attempts, Whymper made the first ascent of the Matterhorn, a major accomplishment that ended in infamy. On the descent, four men fell to their deaths when high on a difficult ridge one slipped and the rope snapped. The accident captivated the imaginations of an entire public, its details debated for years to come. Whymper's life became defined by the tragedy; shortly thereafter, this mountaineer whose ambition for conquering peaks in the Alps had known no bounds, stopped climbing altogether.

Whymper's account of the famous fall would be an obvious choice
for this anthology, but a rather more engaging and full-blown tale is
that of Whymper's adventure alone on the Matterhorn in 1862. It says
a lot about his character that what befell him on the mountain that
day left him not only unphased but also all the more determined to
return to the object of his obsession and summit on another try. It was
only later in life, after his success was marred by the terrible fate of his
four friends, that Whymper became reflective about the dangers of his
sport. In now famous lines he wrote: "Climb if you will, but remember
that courage and strength are nought without prudence. . . . Do noth-
ing in haste; look well to each step, and from the beginning think what
may be the end."

I t is unnecessary to enter into a minute description of the Matterhorn,
after all that has been written about that famous mountain. Those by
whom this book is likely to be read will know that that peak is nearly
15,000 feet high, and that it rises abruptly, by a series of cliffs which may
properly be termed precipices, a clear 5000 feet above the glaciers which
surround its base. They will know too that it was the last great Alpine
peak which remained unscaled,—less on account of the difficulty of
doing so, than from the terror inspired by its invincible appearance.
There seemed to be a *cordon* drawn around it, up to which one might go,
but no farther.

· · ·

The Matterhorn looks equally imposing from whatever side it is seen; it
never seems commonplace; and in this respect, and in regard to the
impression it makes upon spectators, it stands almost alone amongst
mountains. It has no rivals in the Alps, and but few in the world.

· · ·

Three times I had essayed the ascent of this mountain, and on each
occasion had failed ignominiously. I had not advanced a yard beyond my
predecessors. Up to the height of nearly 13,000 feet there were no

extraordinary difficulties; the way so far might even become "a matter of amusement." Only 1800 feet remained; but they were as yet untrodden, and might present the most formidable obstacles. No man could expect to climb them by himself. A morsel of rock only seven feet high might at any time defeat him, if it were perpendicular. Such a place might be possible to two, or a bagatelle to three men. It was evident that a party should consist of three men at least. But where could the other two men be obtained? Carrel[1] was the only man who exhibited any enthusiasm in the matter; and he, in 1861, had absolutely refused to go unless the party consisted of at least *four* persons. Want of men made the difficulty, not the mountain.

The weather became bad again, so I went to Zermatt on the chance of picking up a man, and remained there during a week of storms.[†] Not one of the better men, however, could be induced to come, and I returned to Breil on the 17th, hoping to combine the skill of Carrel with the willingness of Meynet[2] on a new attempt, by the same route as before; for the Hörnli ridge, which I had examined in the meantime, seemed to be entirely impracticable. Both men were inclined to go, but their ordinary occupations prevented them from starting at once.[††]

My tent had been left rolled up at the second platform, and whilst waiting for the men it occurred to me that it might have been blown away during the late stormy weather; so I started off on the 18th to see if this were so or not. The way was by this time familiar, and I mounted rapidly, astonishing the friendly herdsmen—who nodded recognition as I flitted past them and the cows—for I was alone, because no man was available. But more deliberation was necessary when the pastures were passed, and climbing began, for it was needful to mark each step, in case of mist, or

[†] During this time making the ascent of Monte Rosa.
[††] They were not guides by profession.

---

[1] In 1862, Jean-Antoine Carrel probably had more experience on the Matterhorn than anyone else, including Tyndall and Whymper.
[2] Luc Meynet, a porter.

surprise by night. It is one of the few things which can be said in favour of mountaineering alone (a practice which has little besides to commend it), that it awakens a man's faculties, and makes him observe. When one has no arms to help, and no head to guide him except his own, he must needs take note even of small things, for he cannot afford to throw away a chance; and so it came to pass, upon my solitary scramble, when above the snow-line, and beyond the ordinary limits of flowering plants, when peering about, noting angles and landmarks, that my eyes fell upon the tiny straggling plants—oftentimes a single flower on a single stalk—pioneers of vegetation, atoms of life in a world of desolation, which had found their way up—who can tell how?—from far below, and were obtaining bare sustenance from the scanty soil in protected nooks; and it gave a new interest to the well-known rocks to see what a gallant fight the survivors made (for many must have perished in the attempt) to ascend the great mountain. The Gentian, as one might have expected, was there; but it was run close by Saxifrages, and by *Linaria alpina,* and was beaten by *Thlaspi rotundifolium,* which latter plant was the highest I was able to secure, although it too was overtopped by a little white flower which I knew not, and was unable to reach.

The tent was safe, although snowed up; and I turned to contemplate the view, which, when seen alone and undisturbed, had all the strength and charm of complete novelty. The highest peaks of the Pennine chain were in front—the Breithorn (13,685 feet), the Lyskamm (14,889), and Monte Rosa (15,217); then, turning to the right, the entire block of mountains which separated the Val Tournanche from the Val d'Ayas was seen at a glance, with its dominating summit the Grand Tournalin (11,155). Behind were the ranges dividing the Val d'Ayas from the Valley of Gressoney, backed by higher summits. . . . Such a view is hardly to be excelled in the Alps, and *this* view is very rarely seen, as I saw it, perfectly unclouded.

Time sped away unregarded, and the little birds which had built their nests on the neighbouring cliffs had begun to chirp their evening hymn before I thought of returning. Half mechanically I turned to the tent,

unrolled it, and set it up; it contained food enough for several days, and I resolved to stay over the night. I had started from Breil without provisions, or telling Favre—the innkeeper, who was accustomed to my erratic ways—where I was going. I returned to the view. The sun was setting, and its rosy rays, blending with the snowy blue, had thrown a pale, pure violet far as the eye could see; the valleys were drowned in purple gloom, whilst the summits shone with unnatural brightness: and as I sat in the door of the tent, and watched the twilight change to darkness, the earth seemed to become less earthy and almost sublime; the world seemed dead, and I, its sole inhabitant. By and by, the moon as it rose brought the hills again into sight, and by a judicious repression of detail rendered the view yet more magnificent. Something in the south hung like a great glow-worm in the air; it was too large for a star, and too steady for a meteor; and it was long before I could realise the incredible fact that it was the moonlight glittering on the great snow-slope on the north side of Monte Viso, at a distance, as the crow flies, of 98 miles. Shivering, at last I entered the tent and made my coffee. The night was passed comfortably, and the next morning, tempted by the brilliancy of the weather, I proceeded yet higher in search of another place for a platform.

Solitary scrambling over a pretty wide area had shown me that a single individual is subjected to many difficulties which do not trouble a party of two or three men, and that the disadvantages of being alone are more felt while descending than during the ascent. In order to neutralise these inconveniences, I devised two little appliances, which were now brought into use for the first time. One was a claw—a kind of grapnel—about five inches long, made of shear steel, one-fifth of an inch thick. This was of use in difficult places, where there was no hold within arm's length, but where there were cracks or ledges some distance higher. The claw could be stuck on the end of the alpenstock and dropped into such places, or, on extreme occasions, flung up until it attached itself to something. The edges that laid hold of the rocks were serrated, which tended to make them catch more readily: the other end had a ring to which a rope was fastened. It must not be understood that this was employed for hauling one's-self up for any great distance, but that it was used in ascending, at the most, for only a few yards at a time. In descending, however, it could be prudently used for a greater distance at a time, as the claws could be planted firmly; but it was necessary to keep the rope taut, and the pull constantly in the direction of the length of the implement, otherwise it had a tendency to slip away. The second device was merely a modification of a dodge practised by all climbers. It is frequently necessary for a single man (or for the last man of a party) during a descent, to make a loop in the end of his rope, to pass it over some rocks, and to come down holding the free end. The loop is then jerked off, and the process may be repeated. But as it sometimes happens that there are no rocks at hand which will allow a loose loop to be used, a slip-knot has to be resorted to, and the rope is drawn in tightly. Consequently it will occur that it is not possible to jerk the loop off, and the rope has to be cut and left behind. To prevent this, I had a wrought-iron ring (two and a quarter inches in diameter and three-eights of an inch thick) attached to one end of my rope. A loop could be made in a moment by passing the other end of the rope through this ring, which of course slipped up and held tightly as I descended holding the free end. A strong piece of cord was also attached to the ring, and, on arriving at the bottom, this was pulled; the ring slid back again, and the loop was whipped off readily. By means of these two simple appliances I was able to ascend and descend rocks, which otherwise would have been completely impassable for a single person. The combined weight of these two things amounted to less than half-a-pound.[3]

It has been mentioned . . . that the rocks of the south-west ridge are by no means difficult for some distance above the Col du Lion. This is true of the rocks up to the level of the Chimney, but they steepen when that is passed, and remaining smooth and with but few fractures, and still continuing to dip outwards, present some steps of a very uncertain kind, particularly when they are glazed with ice. At this point (just above the Chimney) the climber is obliged to follow the southern (or Breil) side of the ridge, but, in a few feet more, one must turn over to the northern (or Z'Mutt) side, where, in most years, nature kindly provides a snow-slope. When this is surmounted, one can again return to the crest of the ridge, and follow it, by easy rocks, to the foot of the Great Tower. This was the highest point attained by Mr. Hawkins in 1860, and it was also our highest on the 9th of July.

This Great Tower is one of the most striking features of the ridge. It stands out like a turret at the angle of a castle. Behind it a battlemented wall leads upwards to the citadel. Seen from the Théodule pass, it looks only an insignificant pinnacle, but as one approaches it (on the ridge) so

---

[3] Whymper invented a number of climbing safety aids, versions of which are still used today.

it seems to rise, and, when one is at its base, it completely conceals the upper parts of the mountain. I found here a suitable place for the tent; which, although not so well protected as the second platform, possessed the advantage of being 300 feet higher up; and fascinated by the wildness of the cliffs, and enticed by the perfection of the weather, I went on to see what was behind.

The first step was a difficult one. The ridge became diminished to the least possible width—it was hard to keep one's balance—and just where it was narrowest, a more than perpendicular mass barred the way. Nothing fairly within arm's reach could be laid hold of; it was necessary to spring up, and then to haul one's-self over the sharp edge by sheer strength. Progression directly upwards was then impossible. Enormous and appalling precipices plunged down to the Tiefenmatten glacier on the left, but round the right-hand side it was just possible to go. One hindrance then succeeded another, and much time was consumed in seeking the way. I have a vivid recollection of a gully of more than usual perplexity at the side of the Great Tower, with minute ledges and steep walls; of the ledges dwindling down and at last ceasing; and of finding myself, with arms and legs divergent, fixed as if crucified, pressing against the rock, and feeling each rise and fall of my chest as I breathed; of screwing my head round to look for hold, and not seeing any, and of jumping sideways on to the other side. 'Tis vain to attempt to describe such places. Whether they are sketched with a light hand, or wrought out in laborious detail, one stands an equal chance of being misunderstood. Their enchantment to the climber arises from their calls on his faculties, in their demands on his strength, and on overcoming the impediments which they oppose to his skill. The non-mountaineering reader cannot feel this, and his interest in descriptions of such places is usually small, unless he supposes that the situations are perilous. They are not necessarily perilous, but I think that it is impossible to avoid giving such an impression if the difficulties are particularly insisted upon.

About this part there was a change in the quality of the rock, and there was a change in the general appearance of the ridge. The rocks (talcose gneiss) below this spot were singularly firm; it was rarely necessary to test one's hold; the way led over the living rock, and not up rent-off fragments. But here, all was decay and ruin. The crest of the ridge was shattered and cleft, and the feet sank in the chips which had drifted down; while above, huge blocks, hacked and carved by the hand of time, nodded to the sky, looking like the grave-stones of giants. Out of curiosity I wandered to a notch in the ridge, between two tottering piles of immense masses, which seemed to need but a few pounds on one or the other side to make them fall; so nicely poised that they would literally have rocked in the wind, for they were put in motion by a touch; and based on support so frail that I wondered they did not collapse before my eyes. In the whole range of my Alpine experience I have seen nothing more striking than this desolate, ruined, and shattered ridge at the back of the Great Tower. I have seen stranger shapes,—rocks which mimic the human form, with monstrous leering faces—and isolated pinnacles, sharper and greater than any here; but I have never seen exhibited so impressively the tremendous effects which may be produced by frost, and by the long-continued action of forces whose individual effects are barely perceptible.

It is needless to say that it is impossible to climb by the crest of the ridge at this part; still one is compelled to keep near to it, for there is no other way. Generally speaking, the angles on the Matterhorn are too steep to allow the formation of considerable beds of snow, but here there is a corner which permits it to accumulate, and it is turned to gratefully, for, by its assistance, one can ascend four times as rapidly as upon the rocks.

The Tower was now almost out of sight, and I looked over the central Pennine Alps to the Grand Combin, and to the chain of Mont Blanc. My neighbour, the Dent d'Hérens, still rose above me, although but slightly, and the height which had been attained could be measured by its help. So far, I had no doubts about my capacity to descend that which had been ascended; but, in a short time, on looking ahead, I saw that the cliffs steepened, and I turned back (without pushing on to them, and getting into inextricable difficulties), exulting in the thought that they would be passed when we returned together, and that I had, without assistance, got nearly to the height of the Dent d'Hérens, and considerably higher than any one had been before.[†] My exultation was a little premature.

About 5 P.M. I left the tent again, and thought myself as good as at Breil. The friendly rope and claw had done good service, and had smoothened all the difficulties. I lowered myself through the Chimney, however, by making a fixture of the rope, which I then cut off, and left behind, as there was enough and to spare. My axe had proved a great nuisance in coming down, and I left it in the tent. It was not attached to the bâton, but was a separate affair,—an old navy boarding-axe. While cutting up the different snow-beds on the ascent, the bâton trailed behind fastened to the rope; and, when climbing, the axe was carried behind, run through the rope tied round my waist, and was sufficiently out of the way. But in descending, when coming down face outwards (as is always best where it is possible), the head or the handle of the weapon caught frequently against the rocks, and several times nearly upset me. So, out of laziness if you will, it was left in the tent. I paid dearly for the imprudence.

The Col du Lion was passed, and fifty yards more would have placed me on the "Great Staircase," down which one can run. But on arriving at an angle of the cliffs of the Tête du Lion, while skirting the upper edge of the snow which abuts against them, I found that the heat of the two past days had nearly obliterated the steps which had been cut when coming up. The rocks happened to be impracticable just at this corner, so nothing could be done except make the steps afresh. The snow was too hard to beat or tread down, and at the angle it was all but ice. Half-a-dozen steps only were required, and then the ledges could be followed again. So

---

[†] A remarkable streak of snow (marked "cravate" in the outline of the Matterhorn, as seen from the Théodule) runs across the cliff at this part of the mountain. My highest point was somewhat higher than the lowest part of this snow, and was consequently about 13,400 feet above the sea.

I held to the rock with my right hand, and prodded at the snow with the point of my stick until a good step was made, and then, leaning round the angle, did the same for the other side. So far well, but in attempting to pass the corner (to the present moment I cannot tell how it happened) I slipped and fell.

The slope was steep on which this took place, and was at the top of a gully that led down through two subordinate buttresses towards the Glacier du Lion—which was just seen, a thousand feet below. The gully narrowed and narrowed, until there was a mere thread of snow lying between two walls of rock, which came to an abrupt termination at the top of a precipice that intervened between it and the glacier. Imagine a funnel cut in half through its length, placed at an angle of 45 degrees, with its point below and its concave side uppermost, and you will have a fair idea of the place.

The knapsack brought my head down first, and I pitched into some rocks about a dozen feet below; they caught something and tumbled me off the edge, head over heels, into the gully; the bâton was dashed from my hands, and I whirled downwards in a series of bounds, each longer than the last; now over ice, now into rocks; striking my head four or five times, each time with increased force. The last bound sent me spinning through the air, in a leap of fifty or sixty feet, from one side of the gully to the other, and I struck the rocks, luckily, with the whole of my left side. They caught my clothes for a moment, and I fell back on to the snow with motion arrested. My head fortunately came the right side up, and a few frantic catches brought me to a halt, in the neck of the gully, and on the verge of the precipice. Bâton, hat, and veil skimmed by and disappeared, and the crash of the rocks—which I had started—as they fell on to the glacier, told how narrow had been the escape from utter destruction. As it was, I feel nearly 200 feet in seven or eight bounds. Ten feet more would have taken me in one gigantic leap of 800 feet on to the glacier below.

The situation was sufficiently serious. The rocks could not be left go for a moment, and the blood was spirting out of more than twenty cuts.

The most serious ones were in the head, and I vainly tried to close them with one hand, whilst holding on with the other. It was useless; the blood jerked out in blinding jets at each pulsation. At last, in a moment of inspiration, I kicked out a big lump of snow, and stuck it as a plaster on my head. The idea was a happy one, and the flow of blood diminished.

Then, scrambling up, I got, not a moment too soon, to a place of safety, and fainted away. The sun was setting when consciousness returned, and it was pitch dark before the Great Staircase was descended; but, by a combination of luck and care, the whole 4800 feet of descent to Breil was accomplished without a slip, or once missing the way. I slunk past the cabin of the cowherds, who were talking and laughing inside, utterly ashamed of the state to which I had been brought by my imbecility, and entered the inn stealthily, wishing to escape to my room unnoticed. But Favre met me in the passage, demanded "Who is it?" screamed with fright when he got a light, and aroused the household. Two dozen heads then held solemn council over mine, with more talk than action. The natives were unanimous in recommending that hot wine (syn. vinegar), mixed with salt, should be rubbed into the cuts. I protested, but they insisted. It was all the doctoring they received. Whether their rapid healing was to be attributed to that simple remedy, or to a good state of health, is a question; they closed up remarkably quickly, and in a few days I was able to move again.

JOHN MUIR

(1838–1914)

From *Travels in Alaska*

Although he will forever be associated with Yosemite and the High Sierra, John Muir, a self-styled "poetico-trampo-geologist-botanist and ornith-naturalist, etc." explored up and down the Americas. As a young man he walked over 1,000 miles from the upper Midwest where he grew up to the Gulf coast, and his restlessness never left him. Later in life, he discovered Alaska, traveling as far north as Point Barrow and the northeastern coast of Siberia. He first journeyed to Alaska in 1879, drawn by his study of glaciers, a lifelong fascination that began with his wanderings in the High Sierra.

Muir returned to southeastern Alaska in 1880 and 1890. Travels in Alaska, which was unfinished when he died in 1914, combines his essays and journals from the three journeys. After his journeys but before his death, one of the most prominent glaciers and a peak in the Glacier Bay area were named after him, and he refers to them by name here.

Travels in Alaska reflects a more mature, self-restrained Muir than his classic and wildly ecstatic early work, My First Summer in the

Sierra. *But he can't help including rhapsodic passages about the scenery around him and the occasional diatribe about groups of tourists "who look only at what they are directed to look at." By midlife Muir may have slowed down some, but as he once wrote, "I am hopelessly and forever a mountaineer. . . . Civilization and fever, and all the morbidness that has been hooted at me, have not dimmed my glacial eyes, and I care to live only to entice people to look at Nature's loveliness."*

In the following passage we see evidence of many of the traits that made Muir legendary even in his time: his tireless fascination with the natural world, his great physical endurance and delight in physical hardship, and his commitment to a simple, ascetic existence close to the wild.

I never saw Alaska looking better than it did when we bade farewell to Sum Dum[1] on August 22 and pushed on northward up the coast toward Taku. The morning was clear, calm, bright—not a cloud in all the purple sky, nor wind, however gentle, to shake the slender spires of the spruces or dew-laden grass around the shores. Over the mountains and over the broad white bosoms of the glaciers the sunbeams poured, rosy as ever fell on fields of ripening wheat, drenching the forests and kindling the glassy waters and icebergs into a perfect blaze of colored light. Every living thing seemed joyful, and nature's work was going on in glowing enthusiasm, not less appreciable in the deep repose that brooded over every feature of the landscape, suggesting the coming fruitfulness of the icy land and showing the advance that has already been made from glacial winter to summer. The care-laden commercial lives we lead close our eyes to the operations of God as a workman, though openly carried on that all who will look may see. The scarred rocks here and the moraines make a vivid showing of the old winter-time of the glacial period, and mark the bounds of the *mer-de-glace* that once filled the bay and covered the sur-

[1] Sum Dum Bay.

rounding mountains. Already that sea of ice is replaced by water, in which multitudes of fishes are fed, while the hundred glaciers lingering about the bay and the streams that pour from them are busy night and day bringing in sand and mud and stones, at the rate of tons every minute, to fill it up. Then, as the seasons grow warmer, there will be fields here for the plough.

Our Indians,[2] exhilarated by the sunshine, were garrulous as the gulls and plovers, and pulled heartily at their oars, evidently glad to get out of the ice with a whole boat.

"Now for Taku," they said, as we glided over the shining water. "Good-bye, Ice-Mountains; good-bye, Sum Dum." Soon a light breeze came, and they unfurled the sail and laid away their oars and began, as usual in such free times, to put their goods in order, unpacking and sunning provisions, guns, ropes, clothing, etc. Joe has an old flintlock musket suggestive of Hudson's Bay times, which he wished to discharge and reload. So, stepping in front of the sail, he fired at a gull that was flying past before I could prevent him, and it fell slowly with outspread wings alongside the canoe, with blood dripping from its bill. I asked him why he had killed the bird, and followed the question by a severe reprimand for his stupid cruelty, to which he could offer no other excuse than that he had learned from the whites to be careless about taking life. Captain Tyeen denounced the deed as likely to bring bad luck.

· · ·

Toward evening at the head of a picturesque bay we came to a village belonging to the Taku tribe. We found it silent and deserted. Not a single shaman or policeman had been left to keep it. These people are so happily rich as to have but little of a perishable kind to keep, nothing worth fretting about. They were away catching salmon, our Indians said. All the Indian villages hereabout are thus abandoned at regular periods every year, just as a tent is left for a day, while they repair to fishing, berrying,

---

[2] Muir is traveling with a missionary named Mr. Young and three Indians—Captain Tyeen, Hunter Joe, and Smart Billy.

and hunting stations, occupying each in succession for a week or two at a time, coming and going from the main, substantially built villages. Then, after their summer's work is done, the winter supply of salmon dried and packed, fish-oil and seal-oil stored in boxes, berries and spruce bark pressed into cakes, their trading-trips completed, and the year's stock of quarrels with the neighboring tribe patched up in some way, they devote themselves to feasting, dancing, and hootchenoo drinking. The Takus, once a powerful and warlike tribe, were at this time, like most of the neighboring tribes, whiskied nearly out of existence. They had a larger village on the Taku River, but, according to the census taken that year by the missionaries, they numbered only 269 in all,—109 men, 79 women, and 81 children, figures that show the vanishing condition of the tribe at a glance.

Our Indians wanted to camp for the night in one of the deserted houses, but I urged them on into the clean wilderness until dark, when we landed on a rocky beach fringed with devil's-clubs, greatly to the disgust of our crew. We had to make the best of it, however, as it was too dark to seek farther. After supper was accomplished among the boulders, they retired to the canoe, which they anchored a little way out, beyond low tide, while Mr. Young and I at the expense of a good deal of scrambling and panax stinging, discovered a spot on which we managed to sleep.

The next morning, about two hours after leaving our thorny camp, we rounded a great mountain rock nearly a mile in height and entered the Taku fiord. It is about eighteen miles long and from three to five miles wide, and extends directly back into the heart of the mountains, draining hundreds of glaciers and streams.

. . .

While I sat sketching [the glaciers] from a point among the drifting icebergs where I could see far back into the heart of their distant fountains, two Taku seal-hunters, father and son, came gliding toward us in an extremely small canoe. Coming alongside with a goodnatured "Sagh-a-ya," they inquired who we were, our objects, etc., and gave us information about the river, their village, and two other large glaciers that descend nearly to the sea-level a few miles up the river cañon. Crouching in their little shell of a boat among the great bergs, with paddle and barbed spear, they formed a picture as arctic and remote from anything to be found in civilization as ever was sketched for us by the explorers of the Far North.

Making our way through the crowded bergs to the extreme head of the fiord, we entered the mouth of the river, but were soon compelled to turn back on account of the strength of the current. The Taku River is a large stream, nearly a mile wide at the mouth, and, like the Stickeen, Chilcat, and Chilcoot, draws its sources from far inland, crossing the mountain-chain from the interior through a majestic cañon, and draining a multitude of glaciers on its way.

The Taku Indians, like the Chilcats, with a keen appreciation of the advantages of their position for trade, hold possession of the river and compel the Indians of the interior to accept their services as middle-men, instead of allowing them to trade directly with the whites.

When we were baffled in our attempt to ascend the river, the day was nearly done, and we began to seek a camp-ground. After sailing two or three miles along the left side of the fiord, we were so fortunate as to find a small nook described by the two Indians, where firewood was abundant, and where we could drag our canoe up the bank beyond reach of the berg-waves. Here we were safe, with a fine outlook across the fiord to the great glaciers and near enough to see the birth of the icebergs and the wonderful commotion they make, and hear their wild, roaring rejoicing. The sunset sky seemed to have been painted for this one mountain mansion, fitting it like a ceiling. After the fiord was in shadow the level sunbeams continued to pour through the miles of bergs with ravishing beauty, reflecting and refracting the purple light like cut crystal. Then all save the tips of the highest became dead white. These, too, were speedily quenched, the glowing points vanishing like stars sinking beneath the horizon. And after the shadows had crept higher, submerging the glaciers and the ridges between them, the divine alpenglow still lingered on their highest fountain peaks as they stood transfigured in glorious array. Now the last of the twilight purple has vanished, the stars begin to shine, and all trace of the day is gone. Looking across the fiord the water seems perfectly black, and the two great glaciers are seen stretching dim and ghostly into the shadowy mountains now darkly massed against the starry sky.

Next morning it was raining hard, everything looked dismal, and on the way down the fiord a growling head wind battered the rain in our faces, but we held doggedly on and by 10 A.M. got out of the fiord into Stephens Passage. A breeze sprung up in our favor that swept us bravely on across the passage and around the end of Admiralty Island by dark. We camped in a boggy hollow on a bluff among scraggy, usnea-bearded spruces. The rain, bitterly cold and driven by a stormy wind, thrashed us well while we floundered in the stumpy bog trying to make a fire and supper.

When daylight came we found our camp-ground a very savage place. How we reached it and established ourselves in the thick darkness it would be difficult to tell.

. . .

I set off early the morning of August 30 before any one else in camp had stirred, not waiting for breakfast, but only eating a piece of bread. I had intended getting a cup of coffee, but a wild storm was blowing and calling, and I could not wait. Running out against the rain-laden gale and turning to catch my breath, I saw that the minister's little dog had left his bed in the tent and was coming boring through the storm, evidently determined to follow me. I told him to go back, that such a day as this had nothing for him.

"Go back," I shouted, "and get your breakfast." But he simply stood with his head down, and when I began to urge my way again, looking around, I saw he was still following me. So I at last told him to come on if he must and gave him a piece of the bread I had in my pocket.

Instead of falling, the rain, mixed with misty shreds of clouds, was flying in level sheets, and the wind was roaring as I had never heard wind roar before. Over the icy levels and over the woods, on the mountains, over the jagged rocks and spires and chasms of the glacier it boomed and moaned and roared, filling the fiord in even, gray, structureless gloom, inspiring and awful. I first struggled up in the face of the blast to the east end of the ice-wall, where a patch of forest had been carried away by the glacier when it was advancing. I noticed a few stumps well out on the moraine flat, showing that its present bare, raw condition was not the condition of fifty or a hundred years ago. In front of this part of the glacier there is a small moraine lake about half a mile in length, around the margin of which are a considerable number of trees standing knee-deep, and of course dead. This also is a result of the recent advance of the ice.

Pushing up through the ragged edge of the woods on the left margin of the glacier, the storm seemed to increase in violence, so that it was difficult to draw breath in facing it; therefore I took shelter back of a tree to enjoy it and wait, hoping that it would at last somewhat abate. Here the glacier, descending over an abrupt rock, falls forward in grand cascades, while a stream swollen by the rain was now a torrent,—wind, rain, ice-torrent, and water-torrent in one grand symphony.

At length the storm seemed to abate somewhat, and I took off my heavy rubber boots, with which I had waded the glacial streams on the flat, and laid them with my overcoat on a log, where I might find them on my way back, knowing I would be drenched anyhow, and firmly tied my mountain shoes, tightened my belt, shouldered my ice-axe, and, thus free and ready for rough work, pushed on, regardless as possible of mere rain. Making my way up a steep granite slope, its projecting polished bosses encumbered here and there by boulders and the ground and bruised ruins of the ragged edge of the forest that had been uprooted by the glacier during its recent advance, I traced the side of the glacier for two or three miles, finding everywhere evidence of its having encroached on the woods, which here run back along its edge for fifteen or twenty miles. Under the projecting edge of this vast ice-river I could see down beneath it to a depth of fifty feet or so in some places, where logs and branches were being crushed to pulp, some of it almost fine enough for paper, though most of it stringy and coarse.

After thus tracing the margin of the glacier for three or four miles, I chopped steps and climbed to the top, and as far as the eye could reach, the nearly level glacier stretched indefinitely away in the gray cloudy sky, a prairie of ice. The wind was now almost moderate, though rain continued to fall, which I did not mind, but a tendency to mist in the drooping draggled clouds made me hesitate about attempting to cross to the opposite shore. Although the distance was only six or seven miles, no traces at this time could be seen of the mountains on the other side, and in case the sky should grow darker, as it seemed inclined to do, I feared that when I got out of sight of land and perhaps into a maze of crevasses I might find difficulty in winning a way back.

Lingering a while and sauntering about in sight of the shore, I found this eastern side of the glacier remarkably free from large crevasses. Nearly all I met were so narrow I could step across them almost anywhere, while the few wide ones were easily avoided by going up or down along their sides to where they narrowed. The dismal cloud ceiling showed rifts here and there, and, thus encouraged, I struck out for the west shore, aiming to strike it five or six miles above the front wall, cautiously taking compass bearings at short intervals to enable me to find my way back should the weather darken again with mist or rain or snow. The structure lines of the glacier itself were, however, my main guide. All went well. I came to a deeply furrowed section about two miles in width where I had to zigzag in long, tedious tacks and make narrow doublings, tracing the edges of wide longitudinal furrows and chasms until I could find a bridge connecting their sides, oftentimes making the direct distance ten times over. The walking was good of its kind, however, and by dint of patient doubling and axe-work on dangerous places, I gained the opposite shore in about three hours, the width of the glacier at this point being about seven miles. Occasionally, while making my way, the clouds lifted a little, revealing a few bald, rough mountains sunk to the throat in the broad, icy sea which encompassed them on all sides, sweeping on forever and forever as we count time, wearing them away, giving them the shape they are destined to take when in the fullness of time they shall be parts of new landscapes.

Ere I lost sight of the east-side mountains, those on the west came in sight, so that holding my course was easy, and, though making haste, I halted for a moment to gaze down into the beautiful pure blue crevasses and to drink at the lovely blue wells, the most beautiful of all Nature's water-basins, or at the rills and streams outspread over the ice-land prairie, never ceasing to admire their lovely color and music as they glided and swirled in their blue crystal channels and potholes, and the rumbling of the moulins, or mills, where streams poured into blue-walled pits of unknown depth, some of them as regularly circular as if bored with augers. Interesting, too, were the cascades over blue cliffs, where streams fell into crevasses or slid almost noiselessly down slopes so smooth and frictionless their motion was concealed. The round or oval wells, however, from one to ten feet wide, and from one to twenty or thirty feet deep, were perhaps the most beautiful of all, the water so pure as to be almost invisible. My widest views did not probably exceed fifteen miles, the rain and mist making distances seem greater.

On reaching the farther shore and tracing it a few miles to northward, I found a large portion of the glacier-current sweeping out westward in a bold and beautiful curve around the shoulder of a mountain as if going direct to the open sea. Leaving the main trunk, it breaks into a magnificent uproar of pinnacles and spires and up-heaving, splashing wave-shaped masses, a crystal cataract incomparably greater and wilder than a score of Niagaras.

Tracing its channel three or four miles, I found that it fell into a lake, which it fills with bergs. The front of this branch of the glacier is about three miles wide. I first took the lake to be the head of an arm of the sea, but, going down to its shore and tasting it, I found it fresh, and by my aneroid perhaps less than a hundred feet above sea-level. It is probably separated from the sea only by a moraine dam. I had not time to go around its shores, as it was now near five o'clock and I was about fifteen miles from camp, and I had to make haste to recross the glacier before dark, which would come on about eight o'clock. I therefore made haste up to the main glacier, and, shaping my course by compass and the struc ture lines of the ice, set off from the land out on to the grand crystal prairie again. All was so silent and so concentred, owing to the low dragging mist, the beauty close about me was all the more keenly felt, though tinged with a dim sense of danger, as if coming events were casting shadows. I was soon out of sight of land, and the evening dusk that on cloudy days precedes the real night gloom came stealing on and only ice was in sight, and the only sounds, save the low rumbling of the mills and the rattle of falling stones at long intervals, were the low, terribly earnest moanings of the wind or distant waterfalls coming through the thickening gloom. After two hours of hard work I came to a maze of crevasses of appalling depth and width which could not be passed apparently either up or down. I traced them with firm nerve developed by the danger, making wide jumps, poising cautiously on dizzy edges after cutting footholds, taking wide crevasses at a grand leap at once frightful and inspiring. Many a mile was thus traveled, mostly up and down the glacier, making but little real headway, running much of the time as the danger of having to pass the night on the ice became more and more imminent. This I could do, though with the weather and my rain-soaked condition it would be trying at best. In treading the mazes of this crevassed section I had frequently to cross bridges that were only knife-edges for twenty or thirty feet, cutting off the sharp tops and leaving them flat so that little Stickeen[3] could follow me. These I had to straddle, cutting off the top as I progressed and hitching gradually ahead like a boy riding a rail fence. All this time the little dog followed me bravely, never hesitating on the brink of any crevasse that I had jumped, but now that it was becoming dark and the crevasses became more troublesome, he followed close at my heels instead of scampering far and wide, where the ice was at all smooth, as he had in the forenoon. No land was now in sight. The mist fell lower and darker and snow began to fly. I could not see far enough up and down the glacier to judge how best to work out of the bewildering labyrinth, and how hard I tried while there was yet hope of reaching

[3] Mr. Young's dog.

camp that night! a hope which was fast growing dim like the sky. After dark, on such ground, to keep from freezing, I could only jump up and down until morning on a piece of flat ice between the crevasses, dance to the boding music of the winds and waters, and as I was already tired and hungry I would be in bad condition for such ice work. Many times I was put to my mettle, but with a firm-braced nerve, all the more unflinching as the dangers thickened, I worked out of that terrible ice-web, and with blood fairly up Stickeen and I ran over common danger without fatigue. Our very hardest trial was in getting across the very last of the sliver bridges. After examining the first of the two widest crevasses, I followed its edge half a mile or so up and down and discovered that its narrowest spot was about eight feet wide, which was the limit of what I was able to jump. Moreover, the side I was on—that is, the west side—was about a foot higher than the other, and I feared that in case I should be stopped by a still wider impassable crevasse ahead that I would hardly be able to take back that jump from its lower side. The ice beyond, however, as far as I could see it, looked temptingly smooth. Therefore, after carefully making a socket for my foot on the rounded brink, I jumped, but found that I had nothing to spare and more than ever dreaded having to retrace my way. Little Stickeen jumped this, however, without apparently taking a second look at it, and we ran ahead joyfully over smooth, level ice, hoping we were now leaving all danger behind us. But hardly had we gone a hundred or two yards when to our dismay we found ourselves on the very widest of all the longitudinal crevasses we had yet encountered. It was about forty feet wide. I ran anxiously up the side of it to northward, eagerly hoping that I could get around its head, but my worst fears were realized when at a distance of about a mile or less it ran into the crevasse that I had just jumped. I then ran down the edge for a mile or more below the point where I had first met it, and found that its lower end also united with the crevasse I had jumped, showing dismally that we were on an island two or three hundred yards wide and about two miles long and the only way of escape from this island was by turning back and jumping again that crevasse which I dreaded, or venturing ahead across the giant crevasse by the very worst of the sliver bridges I had ever seen. It was so badly weathered and melted down that it formed a knife-edge, and extended across from side to side in a low, drooping curve like that made by a loose rope attached at each end at the same height. But the worst difficulty was that the ends of the down-curving sliver were attached to the sides at a depth of about eight or ten feet below the surface of the glacier. Getting down to the end of the bridge, and then after crossing it getting up the other side, seemed hardly possible. However, I decided to dare the dangers of the fearful sliver rather than to attempt to retrace my steps. Accordingly I dug a low groove in the rounded edge for my knees to rest in and, leaning over, began to cut a narrow foothold on the steep, smooth side. When I was doing this, Stickeen came up behind me, pushed his head over my shoulder, looked into the crevasses and along the narrow knife-edge, then turned and looked in my face, muttering and whining as if trying to say, "Surely you are not going down there." I said, "Yes, Stickeen, this is the only way." He then began to cry and ran wildly along the rim of the crevasse, searching for a better way, then, returning baffled, of course, he came behind me and lay down and cried louder and louder.

After getting down one step I cautiously stooped and cut another and another in succession until I reached the point where the sliver was attached to the wall. There, cautiously balancing, I chipped down the upcurved end of the bridge until I had formed a small level platform about a foot wide, then, bending forward, got astride of the end of the sliver, steadied myself with my knees, then cut off the top of the sliver, hitching myself forward an inch or two at a time, leaving it about four inches wide for Stickeen. Arrived at the farther end of the sliver, which was about seventy-five feet long, I chipped another little platform on its upcurved end, cautiously rose to my feet, and with infinite pains cut narrow notch steps and finger-holds in the wall and finally got safely across. All this dreadful time poor little Stickeen was crying as if his heart was broken, and when I called to him in as reassuring a voice as I could muster, he only cried the louder, as if trying to say that he never, never

could get down there—the only time that the brave little fellow appeared
to know what danger was. After going away as if I was leaving him, he
still howled and cried without venturing to try to follow me. Returning to
the edge of the crevasse, I told him that I must go, that he could come if
he only tried, and finally in despair he hushed his cries, slid his little feet
slowly down into my footsteps out on the big sliver, walked slowly and
cautiously along the sliver as if holding his breath, while the snow was
falling and the wind was moaning and threatening to blow him off. When
he arrived at the foot of the slope below me, I was kneeling on the brink
ready to assist him in case he should be unable to reach the top. He
looked up along the row of notched steps I had made, as if fixing them in
his mind, then with a nervous spring he whizzed up and passed me out
on to the level ice, and ran and cried and barked and rolled about fairly
hysterical in the sudden revulsion from the depth of despair to triumphant joy. I tried to catch him and pet him and tell him how good and
brave he was, but he would not be caught. He ran round and round,
swirling like autumn leaves in an eddy, lay down and rolled head over
heels. I told him we still had far to go and that we must now stop all non-
sense and get off the ice before dark. I knew by the ice-lines that every
step was now taking me nearer the shore and soon it came in sight. The
headland four or five miles back from the front, covered with spruce
trees, loomed faintly but surely through the mist and light fall of snow
not more than two miles away. The ice now proved good all the way
across, and we reached the lateral moraine just at dusk, then with trembling limbs, now that the danger was over, we staggered and stumbled
down the bouldery edge of the glacier and got over the dangerous rocks
by the cascades while yet a faint light lingered. We were safe, and then,
too, came limp weariness such as no ordinary work ever produces, however hard it may be. Wearily we stumbled down through the woods, over
logs and brush and roots, devil's-clubs pricking us at every faint blunder-
ing tumble. At last we got out on the smooth mud slope with only a mile
of slow but sure dragging of weary limbs to camp. The Indians had been
firing guns to guide me and had a fine supper and fire ready, though fear-

ing they would be compelled to seek us in the morning, a care not often applied to me. Stickeen and I were too tired to eat much, and, strange to say, too tired to sleep. Both of us, springing up in the night again and again, fancied we were still on that dreadful ice bridge in the shadow of death.

Nevertheless, we arose next morning in newness of life. Never before had rocks and ice and trees seemed so beautiful and wonderful, even the cold, biting rainstorm that was blowing seemed full of loving-kindness, wonderful compensation for all that we had endured, and we sailed down the bay through the gray, driving rain rejoicing.

HENRY DAVID THOREAU

(1817–1862)

From *The Maine Woods*

---

*Exploration, Henry David Thoreau reminded us, often has more to do
with depth than distance. "Two or three hours' walking will carry me to
as strange a country as I expect ever to see," he wrote about his "saun-
terings" around his home in Concord, Massachusetts. This was not a
jaded statement, but quite the opposite. Thoreau walked "in search of
the springs of life" and to be "free from all worldly engagements," and
in that sense he was one of the most original travelers and observers, as
well as influential writer-philosophers of our time.*

*Once in a great while Thoreau ventured farther afield, beyond the
agricultural landscapes of Massachusetts to something wilder. His
three walking and canoeing journeys to Maine, made in 1846, 1853,
and 1857, made a great impression on him. His essays and journal
entries were collected posthumously in the 1864 book, The Maine
Woods. Nature appeared more menacing and unpredictable in the
deep, "untamable" wild, and Thoreau's sense of belonging—even of the
meaning of human existence—was shaken. "Nature here was some-*

*thing savage and awful, though beautiful," he wrote in an essay about
his climb of Mount Katahdin.*

*In the essay that follows, Thoreau paddles Lake Chesuncook with a
friend and an Indian guide named Joe. Thoreau is more interested in
botanizing, but he gets pulled into a moose hunt. His vivid descriptions
of the woods and the animals and his changing emotions as the events
of the hunt unfold transform a commonplace adventure into a story of
elemental drama.*

At mid-afternoon we embarked on the Penobscot. Our birch was
nineteen and a half feet long by two and a half at the widest part, and
fourteen inches deep within, both ends alike, and painted green, which
Joe thought affected the pitch and made it leak. This, I think, was a mid-
dling-sized one. That of the explorers was much larger, though probably
not much longer. This carried us three with our baggage, weighing in all
between five hundred and fifty and six hundred pounds. We had two
heavy, though slender, rock-maple paddles, one of them of bird's-eye
maple. Joe placed birch-bark on the bottom for us to sit on, and slanted
cedar splints against the cross-bars to protect our backs, while he himself
sat upon a cross-bar in the stern. The baggage occupied the middle or
widest part of the canoe. We also paddled by turns in the bows, now sitting with our legs extended, now sitting upon our legs, and now rising
upon our knees; but I found none of these positions endurable, and was
reminded of the complaints of the old Jesuit missionaries of the torture
they endured from long confinement in constrained positions in canoes,
in their long voyages from Quebec to the Huron country; but afterwards I
sat on the cross-bars, or stood up, and experienced no inconvenience.

It was deadwater for a couple of miles. The river had been raised about
two feet by the rain, and lumberers were hoping for a flood sufficient to
bring down the logs that were left in the spring. Its banks were seven or
eight feet high, and densely covered with white and black spruce,—
which, I think, must be the commonest trees thereabouts,—fir, arbor-

vitæ, canoe, yellow and black birch, rock, mountain, and a few red maples, beech, black and mountain ash, the large-toothed aspen, many civil-looking elms, now imbrowned, along the stream, and at first a few hemlocks also. We had not gone far before I was startled by seeing what I thought was an Indian encampment, covered with a red flag, on the bank, and exclaimed, "Camp!" to my comrades. I was slow to discover that it was a red maple changed by the frost. The immediate shores were also densely covered with the speckled alder, red osier, shrubby willows or sallows, and the like. There were a few yellow lily pads still left, half-drowned, along the sides, and sometimes a white one. Many fresh tracks of moose were visible where the water was shallow, and on the shore, the lily stems were freshly bitten off by them.

After paddling about two miles, we parted company with the explorers, and turned up Lobster Stream, which comes in on the right, from the southeast. This was six or eight rods wide, and appeared to run nearly parallel with the Penobscot. Joe said that it was so called from small fresh-water lobsters found in it. It is the Matahumkeag of the maps. My companion wished to look for moose signs, and intended, if it proved worth the while, to camp up that way, since the Indian advised it. On account of the rise of the Penobscot, the water ran up this stream to the pond of the same name, one or two miles. The Spencer Mountains, east of the north end of Moosehead Lake, were now in plain sight in front of us. The kingfisher flew before us, the pigeon woodpecker was seen and heard, and nuthatches and chickadees close at hand. Joe said that they called the chickadee *kecunnilessu* in his language. I will not vouch for the spelling of what possibly was never spelt before, but I pronounced after him till he said it would do. We passed close to a woodcock, which stood perfectly still on the shore, with feathers puffed up, as if sick. This Joe said they called *nipsquecohossus*. The kingfisher was *skuscumonsuck;* bear was *wassus;* Indian devil, *lunxus;* the mountain-ash, *upahsis*. This was very abundant and beautiful. Moose tracks were not so fresh along this stream, except in a small creek about a mile up it, where a large log had lodged in the spring, marked "W-cross-girdle-crow-foot." We saw a pair of moose-horns on the shore, and I asked Joe if a moose had shed them; but he said there was a head attached to them, and I knew that they did not shed their heads more than once in their lives.

After ascending about a mile and a half, to within a short distance of Lobster Lake, we returned to the Penobscot. Just below the mouth of the Lobster we found quick water, and the river expanded to twenty or thirty rods in width. The moose-tracks were quite numerous and fresh here. We noticed in a great many places narrow and well-trodden paths by which they had come down to the river, and where they had slid on the steep and clayey bank. Their tracks were either close to the edge of the stream, those of the calves distinguishable from the others, or in shallow water; the holes made by their feet in the soft bottom being visible for a long time. They were particularly numerous where there was a small bay, or pokelogan, as it is called, bordered by a strip of meadow, or separated from the river by a low peninsula covered with coarse grass, wool-grass, etc., wherein they had waded back and forth and eaten the pads. We detected the remains of one in such a spot. At one place, where we landed to pick up a summer duck, which my companion had shot, Joe peeled a canoe birch for bark for his hunting-horn. He then asked if we were not going to get the other duck, for his sharp eyes had seen another fall in the bushes a little farther along, and my companion obtained it. I now began to notice the bright red berries of the tree-cranberry, which grows eight or ten feet high, mingled with the alders and cornel along the shore. There was less hard wood than at first.

After proceeding a mile and three quarters below the mouth of the Lobster, we reached, about sundown, a small island at the head of what Joe called the Moosehorn Deadwater (the Moosehorn, in which he was going to hunt that night, coming in about three miles below), and on the upper end of this we decided to camp. On a point at the lower end lay the carcass of a moose killed a month or more before. We concluded merely to prepare our camp, and leave our baggage here, that all might be ready when we returned from moose-hunting. Though I had not come a-hunting, and felt some compunctions about accompanying the hunters, I wished to see a moose near at hand, and was not sorry to learn how the Indian managed to kill one. I went as reporter or chaplain to the hunters,—and the chaplain has been known to carry a gun himself. After clearing a small space amid the dense spruce and fir trees, we covered the damp ground with a shingling of fir twigs, and, while Joe was preparing his birch horn and pitching his canoe,—for this had to be done whenever we stopped long enough to build a fire, and was the principal labor which he took upon himself at such times,—we collected fuel for the night, large, wet, and rotting logs, which had lodged at the head of the island, for our hatchet was too small for effective chopping; but we did not kindle a fire, lest the moose should smell it. Joe set up a couple of forked stakes, and prepared half a dozen poles, ready to cast one of our blankets over in case it rained in the night, which precaution, however, was omitted the next night. We also plucked the ducks which had been killed for breakfast.

While we were thus engaged in the twilight, we heard faintly, from far down the stream, what sounded like two strokes of a woodchopper's axe, echoing dully through the grim solitude. We are wont to liken many sounds, heard at a distance in the forest, to the stroke of an axe, because they resemble each other under those circumstances, and that is the one we commonly hear there. When we told Joe of this, he exclaimed, "By George, I'll bet that was a moose! They make a noise like that." These sounds affected us strangely, and by their very resemblance to a familiar one, where they probably had so different an origin, enhanced the impression of solitude and wildness.

At starlight we dropped down the stream, which was a deadwater for three miles, or as far as the Moosehorn; Joe telling us that we must be very silent, and he himself making no noise with his paddle, while he urged the canoe along with effective impulses. It was a still night, and suitable for this purpose,—for if there, is wind, the moose will smell you,—and Joe was very confident that he should get some. The Harvest

Moon had just risen, and its level rays began to light up the forest on our right, while we glided downward in the shade on the same side, against the little breeze that was stirring. The lofty, spiring tops of the spruce and fir were very black against the sky, and more distinct than by day, close bordering this broad avenue on each side; and the beauty of the scene, as the moon rose above the forest, it would not be easy to describe. A bat flew over our heads, and we heard a few faint notes of birds from time to time, perhaps the myrtle-bird for one, or the sudden plunge of a musquash, or saw one crossing the stream before us, or heard the sound of a rill emptying in, swollen by the recent rain. About a mile below the island, when the solitude seemed to be growing more complete every moment, we suddenly saw the light and heard the crackling of a fire on the bank, and discovered the camp of the two explorers; they standing before it in their red shirts, and talking aloud of the adventures and profits of the day. They were just then speaking of a bargain, in which, as I understood, somebody had cleared twenty-five dollars. We glided by without speaking, close under the bank, within a couple of rods of them; and Joe, taking his horn, imitated the call of the moose, till we suggested that they might fire on us. This was the last we saw of them, and we never knew whether they detected or suspected us.

I have often wished since that I was with them. They search for timber over a given section, climbing hills and often high trees to look off; explore the streams by which it is to be driven, and the like; spend five or six weeks in the woods, they two alone, a hundred miles or more from any town, roaming about, and sleeping on the ground where night over-takes them, depending chiefly on the provisions they carry with them, though they do not decline what game they come across; and then in the fall they return and make report to their employers, determining the number of teams that will be required the following winter. Experienced men get three or four dollars a day for this work. It is a solitary and adventurous life, and comes nearest to that of the trapper of the West, perhaps. They work ever with a gun as well as an axe, let their beards grow, and live without neighbors, not on an open plain, but far within a wilderness.

This discovery accounted for the sounds which we had heard, and destroyed the prospect of seeing moose yet awhile. At length, when we had left the explorers far behind, Joe laid down his paddle, drew forth his birch horn,—a straight one, about fifteen inches long and three or four wide at the mouth, tied round with strips of the same bark,—and, standing up, imitated the call of the moose,—*ugh-ugh-ugh,* or *oo-oo-oo-oo,* and then a prolonged *oo-o-o-o-o-o-o-o,* and listened attentively for several minutes. We asked him what kind of noise he expected to hear. He said that if a moose heard it, he guessed we should find out; we should hear him coming half a mile off; he would come close to, perhaps into, the water, and my companion must wait till he got fair sight, and then aim just behind the shoulder.

The moose venture out to the riverside to feed and drink at night. Earlier in the season the hunters do not use a horn to call them out, but steal upon them as they are feeding along the sides of the stream, and often the first notice they have of one is the sound of the water dropping from its muzzle. An Indian whom I heard imitate the voice of the moose, and also that of the caribou and the deer, using a much longer horn than Joe's, told me that the first could be heard eight or ten miles, sometimes; it was a loud sort of bellowing sound, clearer and more sonorous than the lowing of cattle, the caribou's a sort of snort, and the small deer's like that of a lamb.

At length we turned up the Moosehorn, where the Indians at the carry had told us that they killed a moose the night before. This is a very meandering stream, only a rod or two in width, but comparatively deep, coming in on the right, fitly enough named Moosehorn, whether from its windings or its inhabitants. It was bordered here and there by narrow meadows between the stream and the endless forest, affording favorable places for the moose to feed, and to call them out on. We proceeded half a mile up this as through a narrow, winding canal, where the tall, dark spruce and firs and arbor-vitæ towered on both sides in the moonlight, forming a perpendicular forest-edge of great height, like the spires of a Venice in the forest. In two places stood a small stack of hay on the bank, ready for the lumberer's use in the winter, looking strange enough there. We thought of the day when this might be a brook winding through smooth-shaven meadows on some gentleman's grounds; and seen by moonlight then, excepting the forest that now hems it in, how little changed it would appear!

Again and again Joe called the moose, placing the canoe close by some favorable point of meadow for them to come out on, but listened in vain to hear one come rushing through the woods, and concluded that they had been hunted too much thereabouts. We saw, many times, what to our imaginations looked like a gigantic moose, with his horns peering from out the forest edge; but we saw the forest only, and not its inhabitants, that night. So at last we turned about. There was now a little fog on the water, though it was a fine, clear night above. There were very few sounds to break the stillness of the forest. Several times we heard the hooting of a great horned owl, as at home, and told Joe that he would call out the moose for him, for he made a sound considerably like the horn; but Joe answered, that the moose had heard that sound a thousand times, and knew better; and oftener still we were startled by the plunge of a musquash. Once, when Joe had called again, and we were listening for moose, we heard, come faintly echoing, or creeping from far through the moss-clad aisles, a dull, dry, rushing sound with a solid core to it, yet as if half smothered under the grasp of the luxuriant and fungus-like forest, like the shutting of a door in some distant entry of the damp and shaggy wilderness. If we had not been there, no mortal had heard it. When we asked Joe in a whisper what it was, he answered, "Tree fall." There is something singularly grand and impressive in the sound of a tree falling in a perfectly calm night like this, as if the agencies which overthrow it did not need to be excited, but worked with a subtle, deliberate, and conscious force, like a boa-constrictor, and more effectively then than even in a windy day. If there is any such difference, perhaps it is because trees with the dews of the night on them are heavier than by day.

Having reached the camp, about ten o'clock, we kindled our fire and went to bed. Each of us had a blanket, in which he lay on the fir twigs, with his extremities toward the fire, but nothing over his head. It was worth the while to lie down in a country where you could afford such great fires; that was one whole side, and the bright side, of our world. We had first rolled up a large log some eighteen inches through and ten feet long, for a backlog, to last all night, and then piled on the trees to the height of three or four feet, no matter how green or damp. In fact, we burned as much wood that night as would, with economy and an air-tight stove, last a poor family in one of our cities all winter. It was very agreeable, as well as independent, thus lying in the open air, and the fire kept our uncovered extremities warm enough. The Jesuit missionaries used to say, that, in their journeys with the Indians in Canada, they lay on a bed which had never been shaken up since the creation, unless by earthquakes. It is surprising with what impunity and comfort one who has always lain in a warm bed in a close apartment, and studiously avoided drafts of air, can lie down on the ground without a shelter, roll himself in a blanket, and sleep before a fire, in a frosty autumn night, just after a long rain-storm, and even come soon to enjoy and value the fresh air.

I lay awake awhile, watching the ascent of the sparks through the firs, and sometimes their descent in half-extinguished cinders on my blanket. They were as interesting as fireworks, going up in endless, successive crowds, each after an explosion, in an eager, serpentine course, some to five or six rods above the tree-tops before they went out. We do not suspect how much our chimneys have concealed; and now air-tight stoves have come to conceal all the rest. In the course of the night, I got up once or twice and put fresh logs on the fire, making my companions curl up their legs.

When we awoke in the morning (Saturday, September 17), there was considerable frost whitening the leaves. We heard the sound of the chickadee, and a few faintly lisping birds, and also of ducks in the water about the island. I took a botanical account of stock of our domains before the dew was off, and found that the ground-hemlock, or American yew, was the prevailing undershrub. We breakfasted on tea, hard-bread, and ducks.

Before the fog had fairly cleared away we paddled down the stream again, and were soon past the mouth of the Moosehorn. These twenty miles of the Penobscot, between Moosehead and Chesuncook lakes, are comparatively smooth, and a great part deadwater; but from time to time it is shallow and rapid, with rocks or gravel beds, where you can wade across. There is no expanse of water, and no break in the forest, and the meadow is a mere edging here and there. There are no hills near the river nor within sight, except one or two distant mountains seen in a few places. The banks are from six to ten feet high, but once or twice rise gently to higher ground. In many places the forest on the bank was but a thin strip, letting the light through from some alder swamp or meadow behind. The conspicuous berry-bearing bushes and trees along the shore were the red osier, with its whitish fruit, hobble-bush, mountain-ash, tree-cranberry, choke-cherry, now ripe, alternate cornel, and naked viburnum. Following Joe's example, I ate the fruit of the last, and also of the hobble-bush, but found them rather insipid and seedy. I looked very narrowly at the vegetation, as we glided along close to the shore, and frequently made Joe turn aside for me to pluck a plant, that I might see by comparison what was primitive about my native river. Horehound, horse-mint, and the sensitive fern grew close to the edge, under the willows and alders, and wool-grass on the islands, as along the Assabet River in Concord. It was too late for flowers, except a few asters, goldenrods, etc. In several places we noticed the slight frame of a camp, such as we had prepared to set up, amid the forest by the riverside, where some lumberers or hunters had passed a night, and sometimes steps cut in the muddy or clayey bank in front of it.

We stopped to fish for trout at the mouth of a small stream called Rag-muff, which came in from the west, about two miles below the Moosehorn. Here were the ruins of an old lumbering-camp, and a small space, which had formerly been cleared and burned over, was now densely overgrown with the red cherry and raspberries. While we were trying for trout, Joe, Indian-like, wandered off up the Ragmuff on his own errands, and when we were ready to start was far beyond call. So we were compelled to make a fire and get our dinner here, not to lose time. Some dark reddish birds, with grayer females (perhaps purple finches), and myrtle-birds in their summer dress, hopped within six or eight feet of us and our smoke. Perhaps they smelled the frying pork. The latter bird, or both, made the lisping notes which I had heard in the forest. They suggested that the few small birds found in the wilderness are on more familiar terms with the lumberman and hunter than those of the orchard and clearing with the farmer. I have since found the Canada jay, and partridges, both the black and the common, equally tame there, as if they had not yet learned to mistrust man entirely. The chickadee, which is at home alike in the primitive woods and in our wood-lots, still retains its confidence in the towns to a remarkable degree.

Joe at length returned, after an hour and a half, and said that he had been two miles up the stream exploring, and had seen a moose, but, not having the gun, he did not get him. We made no complaint, but concluded to look out for Joe the next time. However, this may have been a mere mistake, for we had no reason to complain of him afterwards. As we continued down the stream, I was surprised to hear him whistling, "O Susanna" and several other airs, while his paddle urged us along. Once he said, "Yes, sir-ee." His common word was "Sartain." He paddled, as usual, on one side only, giving the birch an impulse by using the side as a fulcrum. I asked him how the ribs were fastened to the side rails. He answered, "I don't know, I never noticed." Talking with him about subsisting wholly on what the woods yielded,—game, fish, berries, etc.,—I suggested that his ancestors did so; but he answered that he had been brought up in such a way that he could not do it. "Yes," said he, "that's the way they got a living, like wild fellows, wild as bears. By George! I shan't go into the woods without provision,—hard-bread, pork, etc." He had brought on a barrel of hard-bread and stored it at the carry for his hunting. However, though he was a Governor's son, he had not learned to read.

. . .

After passing through some long rips, and by a large island, we reached an interesting part of the river called the Pine Stream Deadwater, about six miles below Ragmuff, where the river expanded to thirty rods in width and had many islands in it, with elms and canoe-birches, now yellowing, along the shore, and we got our first sight of Ktaadn.[1]

Here, about two o'clock, we turned up a small branch three or four rods wide, which comes in on the right from the south, called Pine Stream, to look for moose signs. We had gone but a few rods before we saw very recent signs along the water's edge, the mud lifted up by their feet being quite fresh, and Joe declared that they had gone along there but a short time before. We soon reached a small meadow on the east side, at an angle in the stream, which was, for the most part, densely covered with alders. As we were advancing along the edge of this, rather more quietly than usual, perhaps, on account of the freshness of the signs,—the design being to camp up this stream, if it promised well,—I heard a slight crackling of twigs deep in the alders, and turned Joe's attention to it; whereupon he began to push the canoe back rapidly; and we had receded thus half a dozen rods, when we suddenly spied two moose standing just on the edge of the open part of the meadow which we had passed, not more than six or seven rods distant, looking round the alders at us. They made me think of great frightened rabbits, with their long ears and half-inquisitive, half-frightened looks; the true denizens of the forest (I saw at once), filling a vacuum which now first I discovered had not been filled for me,—*moose*-men, *wood-eaters*, the word is said to mean,—clad in a sort of Vermont gray, or homespun. Our Nimrod, owing to the retrograde movement, was now the farthest from the game; but being warned of its neighborhood, he hastily stood up, and, while we

[1] Mount Katahdin, the highest peak in Maine.

ducked, fired over our heads one barrel at the foremost, which alone he saw, though he did not know what kind of creature it was; whereupon this one dashed across the meadow and up a high bank on the northeast, so rapidly as to leave but an indistinct impression of its outlines on my mind. At the same instant, the other, a young one, but as tall as a horse, leaped out into the stream, in full sight, and there stood cowering for a moment, or rather its disproportionate lowness behind gave it that appearance, and uttering two or three trumpeting squeaks. I have an indistinct recollection of seeing the old one pause an instant on the top of the bank in the woods, look toward its shivering young, and then dash away again. The second barrel was leveled at the calf, and when we expected to see it drop in the water, after a little hesitation, it, too, got out of the water, and dashed up the hill, though in a somewhat different direction. All this was the work of a few seconds, and our hunter, having never seen a moose before, did not know but they were deer, for they stood partly in the water, nor whether he had fired at the same one twice or not. From the style in which they went off, and the fact that he was not used to standing up and firing from a canoe, I judged that we should not see anything more of them. The Indian said that they were a cow and her calf,—a yearling, or perhaps two years old, for they accompany their dams so long; but, for my part, I had not noticed much difference in their size. It was but two or three rods across the meadow to the foot of the bank, which, like all the world thereabouts, was densely wooded; but I was surprised to notice, that, as soon as the moose had passed behind the veil of the woods, there was no sound of footsteps to be heard from the soft, damp moss which carpets that forest, and long before we landed, perfect silence reigned. Joe said, "If you wound 'em moose, me sure get 'em."

We all landed at once. My companion reloaded; the Indian fastened his birch, threw off his hat, adjusted his waistband, seized the hatchet, and set out. He told me afterward, casually, that before we landed he had seen a drop of blood on the bank, when it was two or three rods off. He proceeded rapidly up the bank and through the woods, with a peculiar, elastic, noiseless, and stealthy tread, looking to right and left on the ground, and stepping in the faint tracks of the wounded moose, now and then pointing in silence to a single drop of blood on the handsome, shining leaves of the *Clintonia borealis,* which, on every side, covered the ground, or to a dry fern stem freshly broken, all the while chewing some leaf or else the spruce gum. I followed, watching his motions more than the trail of the moose. After following the trail about forty rods in a pretty direct course, stepping over fallen trees and winding between standing ones, he at length lost it, for there were many other moose-tracks there, and, returning once more to the last blood-stain, traced it a little way and lost it again, and, too soon, I thought, for a good hunter, gave it up entirely. He traced a few steps, also, the tracks of the calf; but, seeing no blood, soon relinquished the search.

I observed, while he was tracking the moose, a certain reticence or moderation in him. He did not communicate several observations of interest which he made, as a white man would have done, though they may have leaked out afterward. At another time, when we heard a slight crackling of twigs and he landed to reconnoitre, he stepped lightly and gracefully, stealing through the bushes with the least possible noise, in a way in which no white man does,—as it were, finding a place for his foot each time.

About half an hour after seeing the moose, we pursued our voyage up Pine Stream, and soon, coming to a part which was very shoal and also rapid, we took out the baggage, and proceeded to carry it round, while Joe got up with the canoe alone. We were just completing our portage and I was absorbed in the plants, admiring the leaves of the *Aster macrophyllus,* ten inches wide, and plucking the seeds of the great round-leaved orchis, when Joe exclaimed from the stream that he had killed a moose. He had found the cow moose lying dead, but quite warm, in the middle of the stream, which was so shallow that it rested on the bottom, with hardly a third of its body above water. It was about an hour after it was shot, and it was swollen with water. It had run about a hundred rods and sought the stream again, cutting off a slight bend. No doubt a better hunter would have tracked it to this spot at once. I was surprised at its great size, horselike, but Joe said it was not a large cow moose. My companion went in search of the calf again. I took hold of the ears of the moose, while Joe pushed his canoe downstream toward a favorable shore, and so we made out, though with some difficulty, its long nose frequently sticking in the bottom, to drag it into still shallower water. It was a brownish-black, or perhaps a dark iron-gray, on the back and sides, but lighter beneath and in front. I took the cord which served for the canoe's painter, and with Joe's assistance measured it carefully, the greatest distances first, making a knot each time. The painter being wanted, I reduced these measures that night with equal care to lengths and fractions of my umbrella, beginning with the smallest measures, and untying the knots as I proceeded; and when we arrived at Chesuncook the next day, finding a two-foot rule there, I reduced the last to feet and inches; and, moreover, I made myself a two-foot rule of a thin and narrow strip of black ash, which would fold up conveniently to six inches. All this pains I took because I did not wish to be obliged to say merely that the moose was very large. Of the various dimensions which I obtained I will mention only two. The distance from the tips of the hoofs of the fore feet, stretched out, to the top of the back between the shoulders, was seven feet and five inches. I can hardly believe my own measure, for this is about two feet greater than the height of a tall horse. (Indeed, I am now satisfied that this measurement was incorrect, but the other measures given here I can warrant to be correct, having proved them in a more recent visit to those woods.) The extreme length was eight feet and two inches. Another cow moose, which I have since measured in those woods with a tape, was just six feet from the tip of the hoof to the shoulders, and eight feet long as she lay.

When afterward I asked an Indian at the carry how much taller the male was, he answered, "Eighteen inches," and made me observe the height of a cross-stake over the fire, more than four feet from the ground, to give me some idea of the depth of his chest. Another Indian, at Oldtown, told me that they were nine feet high to the top of the back, and that one which he tried weighed eight hundred pounds. The length of the spinal projections between the shoulders is very great. A white hunter, who was the best authority among hunters that I could have, told me that the male was *not* eighteen inches taller than the female; yet he agreed that he was sometimes nine feet high to the top of the back, and weighed a thousand pounds. Only the male has horns, and they rise two feet or more above the shoulders,—spreading three or four, and sometimes six feet,—which would make him in all, sometimes, eleven feet high! According to this calculation, the moose is as tall, though it may not be as large, as the great Irish elk, *Megaceros Hibernicus*, of a former period, of which Mantell says that it "very far exceeded in magnitude any living species, the skeleton" being "upward of ten feet high from the ground to the highest point of the antlers." Joe said, that, though the moose shed the whole horn annually, each new horn has an additional prong; but I have noticed that they sometimes have more prongs on one side than on the other. I was struck with the delicacy and tenderness of the hoofs, which divide very far up, and the one half could be pressed very much behind the other, thus probably making the animal surer-footed on the uneven ground and slippery moss-covered logs of the primitive forest. They were very unlike the stiff and battered feet of our horses and oxen. The bare, horny part of the fore foot was just six inches long, and the two portions could be separated four inches at the extremities.

The moose is singularly grotesque and awkward to look at. Why should it stand so high at the shoulders? Why have so long a head? Why have no tail to speak of? for in my examination I overlooked it entirely. Naturalists say it is an inch and a half long. It reminded me at once of the camelopard,[2] high before and low behind,—and no wonder, for, like it, it is fitted to browse on trees. The upper lip projected two inches beyond the lower for this purpose. This was the kind of man that was at home there; for, as near as I can learn, that has never been the residence, but rather the hunting-ground of the Indian. The moose will, perhaps, one

[2] Giraffe.

day become extinct; but how naturally then, when it exists only as a fossil relic, and unseen as that, may the poet or sculptor invent a fabulous animal with similar branching and leafy horns,—a sort of fucus or lichen in bone,—to be the inhabitant of such a forest as this!

Here, just at the head of the murmuring rapids, Joe now proceeded to skin the moose with a pocket-knife, while I looked on; and a tragical business it was,—to see that still warm and palpitating body pierced with a knife, to see the warm milk stream from the rent udder, and the ghastly naked red carcass appearing from within its seemly robe, which was made to hide it. The ball had passed through the shoulder-blade diagonally and lodged under the skin on the opposite side, and was partially flattened. My companion keeps it to show to his grandchildren. He has the shanks of another moose which he has since shot, skinned and stuffed, ready to be made into boots by putting in a thick leather sole. Joe said, if a moose stood fronting you, you must not fire, but advance toward him, for he will turn slowly and give you a fair shot. In the bed of this narrow, wild, and rocky stream, between two lofty walls of spruce and firs, a mere cleft in the forest which the stream had made, this work went on. At length Joe had stripped off the hide and dragged it trailing to the shore, declaring that it weighed a hundred pounds, though probably fifty would have been nearer the truth. He cut off a large mass of the meat to carry along, and another, together with the tongue and nose, he put with the hide on the shore to lie there all night, or till we returned. I was surprised that he thought of leaving this meat thus exposed by the side of the carcass, as the simplest course, not fearing that any creature would touch it; but nothing did. This could hardly have happened on the bank of one of our rivers in the eastern part of Massachusetts; but I suspect that fewer small wild animals are prowling there than with us. Twice, however, in this excursion, I had a glimpse of a species of large mouse.

This stream was so withdrawn, and the moose-tracks were so fresh, that my companions, still bent on hunting, concluded to go farther up it and camp, and then hunt up or down at night. Half a mile above this, at a place where I saw the *Aster puniceus* and the beaked hazel, as we pad-

dled along, Joe, hearing a slight rustling amid the alders, and seeing
something black about two rods off, jumped up and whispered, "Bear!"
but before the hunter had discharged his piece, he corrected himself to
"Beaver!"—"Hedgehog!" The bullet killed a large hedgehog more than
two feet and eight inches long. The quills were rayed out and flattened
on the hinder part of its back, even as if it had lain on that part, but were
erect and long between this and the tail. Their points, closely examined,
were seen to be finely bearded or barbed, and shaped like an awl, that is,
a little concave, to give the barbs effect. After about a mile of still water,
we prepared our camp on the right side, just at the foot of a considerable
fall. Little chopping was done that night, for fear of scaring the moose.
We had moose meat fried for supper. It tasted like tender beef, with perhaps more flavor,—sometimes like veal.

After supper, the moon having risen, we proceeded to hunt a mile up
this stream, first "carrying" about the falls. We made a picturesque sight,
wending single file along the shore, climbing over rocks and logs, Joe,
who brought up the rear, twirling his canoe in his hands as if it were a
feather, in places where it was difficult to get along without a burden. We
launched the canoe again from the ledge over which the stream fell, but
after half a mile of still water, suitable for hunting, it became rapid again,
and we were compelled to make our way along the shore, while Joe
endeavored to get up in the birch alone, though it was still very difficult
for him to pick his way amid the rocks in the night. We on the shore
found the worst of walking, a perfect chaos, of fallen and drifted trees,
and of bushes projecting far over the water, and now and then we made
our way across the mouth of a small tributary on a kind of network of
alders. So we went tumbling on in the dark, being on the shady side,
effectually scaring all the moose and bears that might be thereabouts. At
length we came to a standstill, and Joe went forward to reconnoitre; but
he reported that it was still a continuous rapid as far as he went, or half a
mile, with no prospect of improvement, as if it were coming down from a
mountain. So we turned about, hunting back to the camp through the
still water. It was a splendid moonlight night, and I, getting sleepy as it

grew late,—for I had nothing to do,—found it difficult to realize where I was. This stream was much more unfrequented than the main one, lumbering operations being no longer carried on in this quarter. It was only three or four rods wide, but the firs and spruce through which it trickled seemed yet taller by contrast. Being in this dreamy state, which the moonlight enhanced, I did not clearly discern the shore, but seemed, most of the time, to be floating through ornamental grounds,—for I associated the fir-tops with such scenes;—very high up some Broadway, and beneath or between their tops, I thought I saw an endless succession of porticoes and columns, cornices and façades, verandas and churches. I did not merely fancy this, but in my drowsy state such was the illusion. I fairly lost myself in sleep several times, still dreaming of that architecture and the nobility that dwelt behind and might issue from it: but all at once I would be aroused and brought back to a sense of my actual position by the sound of Joe's birch horn in the midst of all this silence calling the moose, *ugh, uhg, oo-oo-oo-oo-oo-oo*, and I prepared to hear a furious moose come rushing and crashing through the forest, and see him burst out on to the little strip of meadow by our side.

But, on more accounts than one, I had had enough of moose-hunting. I had not come to the woods for this purpose, nor had I foreseen it, though I had been willing to learn how the Indian manœuvred; but one moose killed was as good, if not as bad, as a dozen. The afternoon's tragedy, and my share in it, as it affected the innocence, destroyed the pleasure of my adventure. It is true, I came as near as is possible to come to being a hunter and miss it, myself; and as it is, I think that I could spend a year in the woods, fishing and hunting just enough to sustain myself, with satisfaction. This would be next to living like a philosopher on the fruits of the earth which you had raised, which also attracts me. But this hunting of the moose merely for the satisfaction of killing him,—not even for the sake of his hide,—without making any extraordinary exertion or running any risk yourself, is too much like going out by night to some wood-side pasture and shooting your neighbor's horses. These are God's own horses, poor, timid creatures, that will run fast enough as soon as they smell you, though they *are* nine feet high. Joe told us of some hunters who a year or two before had shot down several oxen by night, somewhere in the Maine woods, mistaking them for moose. And so might any of the hunters; and what is the difference in the sport, but the name? In the former case, having killed one of God's and *your own* oxen, you strip off its hide,—because that is the common trophy, and, moreover, you have heard that it may be sold for moccasins,—cut a steak from its haunches, and leave the huge carcass to smell to heaven for you. It is no better, at least, than to assist at a slaughter-house.

This afternoon's experience suggested to me how base or coarse are the motives which commonly carry men into the wilderness. The explorers and lumberers generally are all hirelings, paid so much a day for their labor, and as such they have no more love for wild nature than wood-sawyers have for forests. Other white men and Indians who come here are for the most part hunters, whose object is to slay as many moose and other wild animals as possible. But, pray, could not one spend some weeks or years in the solitude of this vast wilderness with other employments than these,—employments perfectly sweet and innocent and ennobling? For one that comes with a pencil to sketch or sing, a thousand come with an axe or rifle. What a coarse and imperfect use Indians and hunters make of nature! No wonder that their race is so soon exterminated. I already, and for weeks afterward, felt my nature the coarser for this part of my woodland experience, and was reminded that our life should be lived as tenderly and daintily as one would pluck a flower.

With these thoughts, when we reached our camping-ground, I decided to leave my companions to continue moose-hunting down the stream, while I prepared the camp, though they requested me not to chop much nor make a large fire, for fear I should scare their game. In the midst of the damp fir wood, high on the mossy bank, about nine o'clock of this bright moonlight night, I kindled a fire, when they were gone, and, sitting on the fir twigs, within sound of the falls, examined by its light the botanical specimens which I had collected that afternoon, and wrote down some of the reflections which I have here expanded; or I walked along the shore and gazed up the stream, where the whole space above the falls was filled with mellow light. As I sat before the fire on my fir-twig seat, without walls above or around me, I remembered how far on every hand that wilderness stretched, before you came to cleared or cultivated fields, and wondered if any bear or moose was watching the light of my fire; for Nature looked sternly upon me on account of the murder of the moose.

ISABELLA BIRD

(1831–1904)

From *A Lady's Life in the Rocky Mountains*

Isabella Bird was a sickly young woman with no experience of the world beyond chilly Victorian drawing rooms when in 1854 she was sent from England on a long sea voyage to find her health. And find it she did, marvelously, while tapping into an innate lust for adventure and instinct for survival that would remain with her for the rest of her long life. On that first voyage to America, she collected the sketches and stories she would later publish anonymously as An Englishwoman in America. *With that first tentative literary foray, she also found her high-spirited voice.*

Bird's later books about her peripatetic life, Six Months in the Sandwich Isles, Unbeaten Tracks in Japan, Journeys in Persia and Kurdistan, Among the Tibetans, *and several others, found an adoring audience. A series of letters sent home to her sister during her second sojourn in America in 1879 resulted in* A Lady's Life in the Rocky Mountains, *an instant success in her day and still in print. Remarkable for its honesty and spontaneity, the book reveals the American West—and the author, despite her occasional Old World pretentions— in all its innocence, spunk, and rough-hewn youth.*

Here, Bird, an intrepid horsewoman, joins a cattle drive, then sets out to explore remote regions of the Rockies on her beloved mare, Birdie, just as winter arrives with full force.

We were to have had a grand cattle-hunt yesterday, beginning at 6.30, but the horses were all lost. Often out of fifty horses all that are worth anything are marauding, and a day is lost in hunting for them in the canyons. However, before daylight this morning Evans[1] called through my door, "Miss Bird, I say, we've got to drive cattle fifteen miles, I wish you'd lend a hand; there's not enough of us; I'll give you a good horse."

The scene of the drive is at a height of 7500 feet, watered by two rapid rivers. On all sides mountains rise to an altitude of from 11,000 to 15,000 feet, their skirts shaggy with pitch-pine forests, and scarred by deep canyons, wooded and boulder-strewn, opening upon the mountain pasture previously mentioned. Two thousand head of half-wild Texan cattle are scattered in herds throughout the canyons, living on more or less suspicious terms with grizzly and brown bears, mountain lions, elk, mountain sheep, spotted deer, wolves, lynxes, wild cats, beavers, minks, skunks, chipmonks, eagles, rattlesnakes, and all the other two-legged, four-legged, vertebrate and invertebrate inhabitants of this lonely and romantic region. On the whole, they show a tendency rather to the habits of wild than of domestic cattle. They march to water in Indian file, with the bulls leading, and when threatened, take strategic advantage of ridgy ground, slinking warily along in the hollows, the bulls acting as sentinels, and bringing up the rear in case of an attack from dogs. Cows have to be regularly broken in for milking, being as wild as buffaloes in their unbroken state; but, owing to the comparative dryness of the grasses, and the system of allowing the calf to have the milk during the daytime, a dairy of 200 cows does not produce as much butter as a Devonshire dairy of fifty. Some "necessary" cruelty is involved in the stockman's business, however humane he may be. The system is one of terrorism, and from the time

[1] Evans is the rancher Bird stays with for a short time.

that the calf is bullied into the branding-pen, and the hot iron burns into his shrinking flesh, to the day when the fatted ox is driven down from his boundless pastures to be slaughtered in Chicago, "the fear and dread of man" are upon him.

The herds are apt to penetrate the savage canyons which come down from the Snowy Range, when they incur a risk of being snowed up and starved, and it is necessary now and then to hunt them out and drive them down to the "park." On this occasion, the whole were driven down for a muster, and for the purpose of branding the calves.

After a 6.30 breakfast this morning, we started, the party being composed of my host, a hunter from the Snowy Range, two stockmen from the Plains, one of whom rode a violent buck-jumper, and was said by his comrade to be the "best rider in North Americay," and myself. We were all mounted on Mexican saddles, rode, as the custom is, with light snaffle bridles, leather guards over our feet, and broad wooden stirrups, and each carried his lunch in a pouch slung on the lassoing horn of his saddle. Four big, badly-trained dogs accompanied us. It was a ride of nearly thirty miles, and of many hours, one of the most splendid I ever took. We never got off our horses except to tighten the girths, we ate our lunch with our bridles knotted over our saddle-horns, started over the level at full gallop, leapt over trunks of trees, dashed madly down hillsides rugged with rocks or strewn with great stones, forded deep, rapid streams, saw lovely lakes and views of surpassing magnificence, startled a herd of elk with uncouth heads and monstrous antlers, and in the chase, which for some time was unsuccessful, rode to the very base of Long's Peak, over 14,000 feet high, where the bright waters of one of the affluents of the Platte burst from the eternal snows through a canyon of indescribable majesty. The sun was hot, but at a height of over 8000 feet the air was crisp and frosty, and the enjoyment of riding a good horse under such exhilarating circumstances was extreme. In one wild part of the ride we had to come down a steep hill, thickly wooded with pitch-pines, to leap over the fallen timber, and steer between the dead and living trees to avoid being "snagged," or bringing down a heavy dead branch by an unwary touch.

Emerging from this, we caught sight of a thousand Texan cattle feeding in a valley below. The leaders scented us, and, taking fright, began to move off in the direction of the open "park," while we were about a mile from and above them. "Head them off, boys!" our leader shouted; "all aboard; hark away!" and with something of the "High, tally-ho in the morning!" away we all went at a hand-gallop down-hill. I could not hold my excited animal; down-hill, up-hill, leaping over rocks and timber, faster every moment the pace grew, and still the leader shouted, "Go it, boys!" and the horses dashed on at racing speed, passing and repassing each other, till my small but beautiful bay was keeping pace with the immense strides of the great buck-jumper ridden by "the finest rider in North Americay," and I was dizzied and breathless by the pace at which we were going. A shorter time than it takes to tell it brought us close to and abreast of the surge of cattle. The bovine waves were a grand sight: huge bulls, shaped like buffaloes, bellowed and roared, and with great oxen and cows with yearling calves, galloped like racers, and we galloped alongside of them, and shortly headed them, and in no time were placed as sentinels across the mouth of the valley. It seemed like infantry awaiting the shock of cavalry as we stood as still as our excited horses would allow. I almost quailed as the surge came on, but when it got close to us my comrades hooted fearfully, and we dashed forward with the dogs, and, with bellowing, roaring, and thunder of hoofs, the wave receded as it came. I rode up to our leader, who received me with much laughter. He said I was "a good cattleman," and that he had forgotten that a lady was of the party till he saw me "come leaping over the timber, and driving with the others."

It was not for two hours after this that the real business of driving began, and I was obliged to change my thoroughbred for a well-trained cattle-horse—a *broncho,* which could double like a hare, and go over any ground. I had not expected to work like a *vachero,* but so it was, and my Hawaiian[2] experience was very useful. We hunted the various canyons

[2] Bird rode horses while in the Sandwich Islands (now Hawaii), before going to America.

and known "camps," driving the herds out of them; and, until we had secured 850 head in the *corral* some hours afterwards, we scarcely saw each other to speak to. Our first difficulty was with a herd which got into some swampy ground, when a cow, which afterwards gave me an infinity of trouble, remained at bay for nearly an hour, tossing the dog three times, and resisting all efforts to dislodge her. She had a large yearling calf with her, and Evans told me that the attachment of a cow to her first calf is sometimes so great that she will kill her second that the first may have the milk. I got a herd of over a hundred out of a canyon by myself, and drove them down to the river with the aid of one badly-broken dog, which gave me more trouble than the cattle. The getting over was most troublesome; a few took to the water readily and went across, but others smelt it, and then, doubling back, ran in various directions; while some attacked the dog as he was swimming, and others, after crossing, headed back in search of some favourite companions which had been left behind, and one specially vicious cow attacked my horse over and over again. It took an hour and a half of time and much patience to gather them all on the other side.

It was getting late in the day, and a snowstorm was impending, before I was joined by the other drivers and herds, and as the former had diminished to three, with only three dogs, it was very difficult to keep the cattle together. You drive them as gently as possible, so as not to frighten or excite them,† riding first on one side, then on the other, to guide them; and if they deliberately go in a wrong direction, you gallop in front and

---

† In several visits to America I have observed that the Americans are far in advance of us and our colonial kinsmen in their treatment of horses and other animals. This was very apparent with regard to this Texan herd. There were no stock-whips, no needless worrying of the animals in the excitement of sport. Any dog seizing a bullock by his tail or heels would have been called off and punished, and quietness and gentleness were the rule. The horses were ridden without whips, and with spurs so blunt that they could not hurt even a human skin, and were ruled by the voice and a slight pressure on the light snaffle bridle. This is the usual plan, even where, as in Colorado, the horses are *bronchos,* and inherit ineradicable vice. I never yet saw a horse *bullied* into submission in the United States.

head them off. The great excitement is when one breaks away from the herd and gallops madly up and down hill, and you gallop after him anywhere, over and among rocks and trees, doubling when he doubles, and heading him till you get him back again. The bulls were quite easily managed, but the cows with calves, old or young, were most troublesome. By accident I rode between one cow and her calf in a narrow place, and the cow rushed at me and was just getting her big horns under the horse, when he reared, and spun dexterously aside. This kind of thing happened continually. There was one very handsome red cow which became quite mad. She had a calf with her nearly her own size, and thought every one its enemy, and though its horns were well developed, and it was quite able to take care of itself, she insisted on protecting it from all fancied dangers. One of the dogs, a young, foolish thing, seeing that the cow was excited, took a foolish pleasure in barking at her, and she was eventually quite infuriated. She turned to bay forty times at least; tore up the ground with her horns, tossed the great hunting dogs, tossed and killed the calves of two other cows, and finally became so dangerous to the rest of the herd that, just as the drive was ending, Evans drew his revolver and shot her, and the calf for which she had fought so blindly lamented her piteously. She rushed at me several times mad with rage, but these trained cattle-horses keep perfectly cool, and, nearly without will on my part, mine jumped aside at the right moment, and foiled the assailant. Just at dusk we reached the corral—an acre of grass enclosed by stout post-and-rail fences seven feet high, and by much patience and some subtlety lodged the whole herd within its shelter, without a blow, a shout, or even a crack of a whip, wild as the cattle were. It was fearfully cold. We galloped the last mile and a half in four and a half minutes, reached the cabin just as snow began to fall, and found strong, hot tea ready.

October 18.

Snow-bound for three days! I could not write yesterday, it was so awful. People gave up all occupation, and talked of nothing but the storm. The hunters all kept by the great fire in the living-room, only going out to bring in logs and clear the snow from the door and windows. I never spent a more fearful night than two nights ago, alone in my cabin in the storm, with the roof lifting, the mud cracking and coming off, and the fine snow hissing through the chinks between the logs, while splittings and breaking of dead branches, wind-wrung and snow-laden, went on incessantly, with screechings, howlings, thunder and lightning, and many unfamiliar sounds besides. After snowing fiercely all day, another foot of it fell in the early night, and, after drifting against my door, blocked me effectually in. About midnight the mercury fell to zero, and soon after a gale rose, which lasted for ten hours. My window frame is swelled, and shuts, apparently, hermetically; and my bed is six feet from it. I had gone to sleep with six blankets on, and a heavy sheet over my face. Between two and three I was awoke by the cabin being shifted from underneath by the wind, and the sheet was frozen to my lips. I put out my hands, and the bed was thickly covered with fine snow. Getting up to investigate matters, I found the floor some inches deep in parts in fine snow, and a gust of fine, needle-like snow stung my face. The bucket of water was solid ice. I lay in bed freezing till sunrise, when some of the men came to see if I "was alive," and to dig me out. They brought a can of hot water, which turned to ice before I could use it. I dressed standing in snow, and my brushes, boots, and etceteras were covered with snow. When I ran to the house, not a mountain or anything else could be seen, and the snow on one side was drifted higher than the roof. The air, as high as one could see, was one white, stinging smoke of now-drift—a terrific sight. In the living-room, the snow was driving through the chinks, and Mrs. Dewy was shovelling it from the floor. Mr. D.'s beard was hoary with frost in a room with a fire all night. Evans was lying ill, with his bed covered with snow. Returning from my cabin after breakfast, loaded with occupations for the day, I was lifted off my feet, and deposited in a drift, and all my things, writing-book and letter included, were carried in different directions. Some, including a valuable photograph, are irrecoverable. The writing-book was found, some hours afterwards, under three feet of snow.

There are tracks of bears and deer close to the house, but no one can hunt in this gale, and the drift is blinding. We have been slightly over-crowded in our one room. Chess, music, and whist have been resorted to. One hunter, for very *ennui*, has devoted himself to keeping my ink from freezing. We all sat in great cloaks and coats, and kept up an enormous fire, with the pitch running out of the logs. The isolation is extreme, for we are literally snowed-up, and the other settler in the Park and "Mountain Jim"[3] are both at Denver. Late in the evening the storm ceased. In some places the ground is bare of snow, while in others all irregularities are levelled, and the drifts are forty feet deep. Nature is grand under this new aspect. The cold is awful; the high wind with the mercury at zero would skin any part exposed to it.

. . .

Halls Gulch, November 6.

I have ridden 150 miles since I wrote last. On leaving Twin Rock on Saturday I had a short day's ride to Colonel Kittridge's[4] cabin at Oil Creek, where I spent a quiet Sunday with agreeable people. The ride was all through parks and gorges, and among pine-clothed hills, about 9000 feet high, with Pike's Peak always in sight. I have developed much sagacity in finding a trail, or I should not be able to make use of such directions as these: "Keep along a gulch four or five miles till you get Pike's Peak on your left, then follow some wheel-marks till you get to some timber, and keep to the north till you come to a creek, where you'll find a great many elk tracks; then go to your right and cross the creek three times, then you'll see a red rock to your left," etc. etc. The K.'s cabin was very small and lonely, and the life seemed a hard grind for an educated and refined woman. There were snow flurries after I arrived, but the first Sunday of November was as bright and warm as June, and the atmosphere had resumed its exquisite purity. Three peaks of Pike's Peak are seen from Oil

[3] A mountainman Bird becomes friendly, perhaps even romantically involved with.
[4] Another settler.

Creek, above the nearer hills, and by them they tell the time. We had been in the evening shadows for half an hour before those peaks ceased to be transparent gold. On leaving Colonel Kittridge's hospitable cabin I dismounted, as I had often done before, to lower a bar, and, on looking round, Birdie[5] was gone! I spent an hour in trying to catch her, but she had taken an "ugly fit," and would not let me go near her; and I was getting tired and vexed, when two passing trappers, on mules, circumvented and caught her. I rode the twelve miles back to Twin Rock, and then went on, a kindly teamster, who was going in the same direction, taking my pack. I must explain that every mile I have travelled since leaving Colorado Springs has taken me farther and higher into the mountains. That afternoon I rode through lawn-like upland parks, with the great snow mass of Pike's Peak behind, and in front mountains bathed in rich atmospheric colouring of blue and violet, all very fine, but threatening to become monotonous, when the waggon road turned abruptly to the left, and crossed a broad, swift, mountain river, the head-waters of the Platte. There I found the ranch to which I had been recommended, the quarters of a great hunter named Link, which much resembled a good country inn. There was a pleasant, friendly woman, but the men were all away, a thing I always regret, as it gives me half an hour's work at the horse before I can write to you. I had hardly come in when a very pleasant German lady, whom I met at Manitou, with three gentlemen, arrived, and we were as sociable as people could be. We had a splendid though rude supper. While Mrs. Link was serving us, and urging her good things upon us, she was orating on the greediness of English people, saying that "you would think they travelled through the country only to gratify their palates;" and addressed me, asking me if I had not observed it! I am nearly always taken for a Dane or a Swede, never for an Englishwoman, so I often hear a good deal of outspoken criticism. In the evening Mr. Link returned, and there was a most vehement discussion between him, an old hunter, a miner, and the teamster who brought my pack, as to the

5 Bird's horse.

route by which I should ride through the mountains for the next three or four days—because at that point I was to leave the waggon road—and it was renewed with increased violence the next morning, so that if my nerves had not been of steel I should have been appalled. The old hunter acrimoniously said he "must speak the truth," the miner was directing me over a track where for twenty-five miles there was not a house, and where, if snow came on, I should never be heard of again. The miner said he "must speak the truth," the hunter was directing me over a pass where there were five feet of snow, and no trail. The teamster said that the only road possible for a horse was so-and-so, and advised me to take the waggon road into South Park, which I was determined not to do. Mr. Link said he was the oldest hunter and settler in the district, and he could not cross any of the trails in snow. And so they went on. At last they partially agreed on a route—"the worst road in the Rocky Mountains," the old hunter said, with two feet of snow upon it, but a hunter said, with two feet of snow upon it, but a hunter had hauled an elk over part of it, at any rate. The upshot of the whole you shall have in my next letter.

Hall's Gulch, Colorado, November 6.

IT was another cloudless morning, one of the many here on which one awakes early, refreshed, and ready to enjoy the fatigues of another day. In our sunless, misty climate you do not know the influence which persistent fine weather exercises on the spirits. I have been ten months in almost perpetual sunshine, and now a single cloudy day makes me feel quite depressed. I did not leave till 9.30, because of the slipperiness, and shortly after starting turned off into the wilderness on a very dim trail. Soon seeing a man riding a mile ahead, I rode on and overtook him, and we rode eight miles together, which was convenient to me, as without him I should several times have lost the trail altogether. Then his fine American horse, on which he had only ridden two days, broke down, while my "mad, bad broncho," on which I had been travelling for a fortnight, cantered lightly over the snow. He was the only traveller I saw in a day of nearly twelve hours. I thoroughly enjoyed every minute of that ride. It concentrated all my faculties of admiration and of locality, for truly the track was a difficult one. I sometimes thought it deserved the bad name given to it at Link's. For the most part it keeps in sight of Tarryall Creek, one of the large affluents of the Platte, and is walled in on both sides by mountains, which are sometimes so close together as to leave only the narrowest canyon between them, at others breaking wide apart, till, after winding and climbing up and down for twenty-five miles, it lands one on a barren rock-girdled park, watered by a rapid fordable stream as broad as the Ouse at Huntingdon,[6] snow-fed and ice-fringed, the park bordered by fantastic rocky hills, snow-covered and brightened only by a dwarf growth of the beautiful silver spruce. I have not seen anything hitherto so thoroughly wild and unlike the rest of these parts.

I rode up one great ascent where hills were tumbled about confusedly; and suddenly across the broad ravine, rising above the sunny grass and the deep-green pines, rose in glowing and shaded red against the glittering blue heaven a magnificent and unearthly range of mountains, as shapely as could be seen, rising into colossal points, cleft by deep blue ravines, broken up into sharks' teeth, with gigantic knobs and pinnacles rising from their inaccessible sides, very fair to look upon—a glowing, heavenly, unforgettable sight, and only four miles off. Mountains they looked not of this earth, but such as one sees in dreams alone, the blessed ranges of "the land which is very far off." They were more brilliant than those incredible colours in which painters array the fiery hills of Moab and the Desert, and one could not believe them for ever uninhabited, for on them rose, as in the East, the similitude of stately fortresses, not the gray castellated towers of feudal Europe, but gay, massive, Saracenic architecture, the outgrowth of the solid rock. They were vast ranges, apparently of enormous height, their colour indescribable, deepest and reddest near the pine-draped bases, then gradually softening into wonderful tenderness, till the highest summits rose all flushed, and with an illusion of transparency, so that one might believe that they were

---

[6] A river in England with which Bird's sister would be familiar.

taking on the hue of sunset. Below them lay broken ravines of fantastic rocks, cleft and canyoned by the river, with a tender unearthly light over all, the apparent warmth of a glowing clime, while I on the north side was in the shadow among the pure unsullied snow.

. . .

I rode up and down hills laboriously in snow-drifts, getting off often to ease my faithful Birdie by walking down ice-clad slopes, stopping constantly to feast my eyes upon that changeless glory, always seeing some new ravine, with its depths of colour or miraculous brilliancy of red, or phantasy of form. Then below, where the trail was locked into a deep canyon where there was scarcely room for it and the river, there was a beauty of another kind in solemn gloom. There the stream curved and twisted marvellously, widening into shallows, narrowing into deep boiling eddies, with pyramidal firs and the beautiful silver spruce fringing its banks, and often falling across it in artistic grace, the gloom chill and deep, with only now and then a light trickling through the pines upon the cold snow, when suddenly turning round I saw behind, as if in the glory of an eternal sunset, those flaming and fantastic peaks. The effect of the combination of winter and summer was singular. The trail ran on the north side the whole time, and the snow lay deep and pure white, while not a wreath of it lay on the south side, where abundant lawns basked in the warm sun.

The pitch pine, with its monotonous and somewhat rigid form, had disappeared; the white pine became scarce, both being displaced by the slim spires and silvery green of the miniature silver spruce. Valley and canyon were passed, the flaming ranges were left behind, the upper altitudes became grim and mysterious. I crossed a lake on the ice, and then came on a park surrounded by barren contorted hills, overtopped by snow mountains. There, in some brushwood, we crossed a deepish stream on the ice, which gave way, and the fearful cold of the water stiffened my limbs for the rest of the ride. All these streams become bigger as you draw nearer to their source, and shortly the trail disappeared in a broad rapid river, which we forded twice. The trail was very difficult to recover. It ascended ever in frost and snow, amidst scanty timber dwarfed by cold and twisted by storms, amidst solitudes such as one reads of in the High Alps; there were no sounds to be heard but the crackle of ice and snow, the pitiful howling of wolves, and the hoot of owls. The sun to me had long set; the peaks which had blushed were pale and sad; the twilight deepened into green; but still "Excelsior!" There were no happy homes with light of household fires; above, the spectral mountains lifted their cold summits. As darkness came on I began to fear that I had confused the cabin to which I had been directed with the rocks. To confess the truth, I was cold, for my boots and stockings had frozen on my feet, and I was hungry too, having eaten nothing but raisins for fourteen hours. After riding 30 miles I saw a light a little way from the track, and found it to be the cabin of the daughter of the pleasant people with whom I had spent the previous night. Her husband had gone to the plains, yet she, with two infant children, was living there in perfect security. Two pedlars, who were peddling their way down from the mines, came in for a night's shelter soon after I arrived—ill-looking fellows enough. They admired Birdie in a suspicious fashion, and offered to "swop" their pack-horse for her. I went out the last thing at night and the first thing in the morning to see that "the powny" was safe, for they were very importunate on the subject of the "swop." I had before been offered 150 dollars for her. I was obliged to sleep with the mother and children, and the pedlars occupied a room within ours. It was hot and airless. The cabin was papered with the *Phrenological Journal,* and in the morning I opened my eyes on the very best portrait of Dr. Candlish I ever saw, and grieved truly that I should never see that massive brow and fantastic face again.

Mrs. Link was an educated and very intelligent young woman. The pedlars were Irish Yankees, and the way in which they "traded" was as amusing as "Sam Slick." They not only wanted to "swop" my pony, but to "trade" my watch. They trade their souls, I know. They displayed their wares for an hour with much dexterous flattery and persuasiveness, but Mrs. Link was untemptable, and I was only tempted into buying a handkerchief to keep the sun off. There was another dispute about my route. It was the most critical day of my journey. If a snowstorm came on, I might be detained in the mountains for many weeks; but if I got through the snow and reached the Denver waggon-road, no detention would signify much. The pedlars insisted that I could not get through, for the road was not broken. Mrs. L. thought I could, and advised me to try, so I saddled Birdie and rode away.

More than half of the day was far from enjoyable. The morning was magnificent, but the light too dazzling, the sun too fierce. As soon as I got out I felt as if I should drop off the horse. My large handkerchief kept the sun from my neck, but the fierce heat caused soul and sense, brain and eye, to reel. I never saw or felt the like of it. I was at a height of 12,000 feet, where, of course, the air was highly rarefied, and the snow was so pure and dazzling that I was obliged to keep my eyes shut as much as possible to avoid snow blindness. The sky was a different and terribly fierce colour; and when I caught a glimpse of the sun, he was white and unwinking like a lime-ball light, yet threw off wicked scintillations. I suffered so from nausea, exhaustion, and pains from head to foot, that I felt as if I must lie down in the snow. It may have been partly the early stage of *soroche,* or mountain sickness. We plodded on for four hours, snow all round, and nothing else to be seen but an ocean of glistening peaks against that sky of infuriated blue. How I found my way I shall never know, for the only marks on the snow were occasional footprints of a man, and I had no means of knowing whether they led in the direction I ought to take. Earlier, before the snow became so deep, I passed the last great haunt of the magnificent mountain bison, but, unfortunately, saw nothing but horns and bones. Two months ago Mr. Link succeeded in separating a calf from the herd, and has partially domesticated it. It is a very ugly thing at seven months old, with a thick beard, and a short, thick, dark mane on its heavy shoulders. It makes a loud grunt like a pig. It can outrun their fastest horse, and it sometimes leaps over the high fence of the corral, and takes all the milk of five cows.

The snow grew seriously deep. Birdie fell thirty times, I am sure. She seemed unable to keep up at all, so I was obliged to get off and stumble along in her footmarks. By that time my spirit for overcoming difficulties had somewhat returned, for I saw a lie of country which I knew must contain South Park, and we had got under cover of a hill which kept off the sun. The trail had ceased; it was only one of those hunter's tracks which continually mislead one. The getting through the snow was awful work. I think we accomplished a mile in something over two hours. The snow was two feet eight inches deep, and once we went down in a drift the surface of which was rippled like sea sand, Birdie up to her back, and I up to my shoulders! At last we got through, and I beheld, with some sadness, the goal of my journey, "The Great Divide," the snowy range, and between me and it South Park, a rolling prairie seventy-five miles long and over 10,000 feet high, treeless, bounded by mountains, and so rich in sun-cured hay that one might fancy that all the herds of Colorado could find pasture there. Its chief centre is the rough mining town of Fairplay, but there are rumours of great mineral wealth in various quarters. The region has been "rushed," and mining camps have risen at Alma and elsewhere, so lawless and brutal that vigilance committees are forming as a matter of necessity. South Park is closed, or nearly so, by snow during an ordinary winter; and just now the great freight waggons are carrying up the last supplies of the season, and taking down women and other temporary inhabitants. . . . But I came down upon it from regions of ice and snow; and as the snow which had fallen on it had all disappeared by evaporation and drifting, it looked to me quite lowland and livable, though lonely and indescribably mournful, "a silent sea," suggestive of "the muffled oar." I cantered across the narrow end of it, delighted to have got through the snow; and when I struck the "Denver stage-road" I supposed that all the difficulties of mountain travel were at an end, but this has not turned out to be exactly the case.

A horseman shortly joined me and rode with me, got me a fresh horse, and accompanied me for ten miles. He was a picturesque figure and rode a very good horse. He wore a big slouch hat, from under which a number of fair curls hung nearly to his waist. His beard was fair, his eyes blue, and his complexion ruddy. There was nothing sinister in his expression, and his manner was respectful and frank. He was dressed in a hunter's buckskin suit ornamented with beads, and wore a pair of exceptionally big brass spurs. His saddle was very highly ornamented. What was unusual was the number of weapons he carried. Besides a rifle laid across his saddle and a pair of pistols in the holsters, he carried two revolvers and a knife in his belt, and a carbine slung behind him. I found him what is termed "good company." He told me a great deal about the country and its wild animals, with some hunting adventures, and a great deal about Indians and their cruelty and treachery. All this time, having crossed South Park, we were ascending the Continental Divide by what I think is termed the Breckenridge Pass, on a fairly good waggon-road. We stopped at a cabin, where the woman seemed to know my companion, and, in addition to bread and milk, produced some venison steaks. We rode on again, and reached the crest of the Divide, and saw snow-born streams starting within a quarter of a mile from each other, one for the Colorado and the Pacific, the other for the Platte and the Atlantic. Here I wished the hunter good-bye, and reluctantly turned north-east. It was not wise to go up the Divide at all, and it was necessary to do it in haste. On my way down I spoke to the woman at whose cabin I had dined, and she said, "I am sure you found Comanche Bill a real gentleman;" and I then knew that, if she gave me correct information, my intelligent, courteous companion was one of the most notorious desperadoes of the Rocky Mountains, and the greatest Indian exterminator on the frontier—a man whose father and family fell in a massacre at Spirit Lake by the hands of Indians, who carried away his sister, then a child of eleven. His life has since been mainly devoted to a search for this child, and to killing Indians wherever he can find them.

After riding twenty miles, which made the distance for that day fifty, I remounted Birdie to ride six miles farther, to a house which had been mentioned to me as a stopping-place. The road ascended to a height of 11,000 feet, and from thence I looked my last at the lonely, uplifted prairie sea. "Denver stage-road!" The worst, rudest, dismallest, darkest road I have yet travelled on, nothing but a winding ravine, the Platte canyon, pine-crowded and pine-darkened, walled in on both sides for six miles by pine-skirted mountains 12,000 feet high! Along this abyss for forty miles there are said to be only five houses, and were it not for miners going down, and freight-waggons going up, the solitude would be awful. As it was, I did not see a creature. It was four when I left South Park, and between those mountain walls and under the pines it soon became quite dark, a darkness which could be felt. The snow which had melted in the sun had refrozen, and was one sheet of smooth ice. Birdie slipped so alarmingly that I got off and walked, but then neither of us could keep our feet, and in the darkness she seemed so likely to fall upon me, that I took out of my pack the man's socks which had been given me at Perry's Park, and drew them on over her fore feet—an expedient which for a time succeeded admirably, and which I commend to all travellers similarly circumstanced. It was unutterably dark, and all these operations had to be performed by the sense of touch only. I remounted, allowed her to take her own way, as I could not see even her ears, and though her hind legs slipped badly, we contrived to get along through the narrowest part of the canyon, with a tumbling river close to the road. The pines were very dense, and sighed and creaked mournfully in the severe frost, and there were other *eerie* noises not easy to explain. At last, when the socks were nearly worn out, I saw the blaze of a camp fire, with two hunters sitting by it, on the hill-side, and at the mouth of a gulch something which looked like buildings. We got across the river partly on ice and partly by fording, and I found that this was the place where, in spite of its somewhat dubious reputation, I had been told that I could put up. A man came out in the sapient and good-natured stage of intoxication, and, the door being opened, I was confronted by a rough bar and a smoking, blazing kerosene lamp without a chimney. This is the worst place I have put up at as to food, lodging, and general character; an old and very dirty log-cabin, not chinked, with one dingy room used for cooking and feeding, in which a miner was lying very ill of fever; then a large roofless shed with a canvas side, which is to be an addition, and then the bar.

They accounted for the disorder by the building operations. They asked me if I were the English lady written of in the *Denver News*, and for once I was glad that my fame had preceded me, as it seemed to secure me against being quietly "put out of the way." A horrible meal was served— dirty, greasy, disgusting. A celebrated hunter, Bob Craik, came in to supper with a young man in tow, whom, in spite of his rough hunter's or miner's dress, I at once recognised as an English gentleman. It was their camp-fire which I had seen on the hill-side. This gentleman was lording it in true caricature fashion, with a Lord Dundreary drawl and a general execration of everything; while I sat in the chimney corner, speculating on the reason why many of the upper class of my countrymen—"High Toners," as they are called out here—make themselves so ludicrously absurd. They neither know how to hold their tongues or to carry their personal pretensions. An American is nationally assumptive, an Englishman personally so. He took no notice of me till something passed which showed him I was English, when his manner at once changed into courtesy, and his drawl was shortened by a half. He took pains to let me know that he was an officer in the Guards, of good family, on four months' leave, which he was spending in slaying buffalo and elk, and also that he had a profound contempt for everything American. I cannot think why Englishmen put on these broad, mouthing tones, and give so many personal details. They retired to their camp, and the landlord having passed into the sodden, sleepy stage of drunkenness, his wife asked if I should be afraid to sleep in the large canvas-sided, unceiled doorless shed, as they could not move the sick miner. So I slept there on a shake-down, with the stars winking overhead through the roof, and the mercury showing 30(of frost. I never told you that I once gave an unwary promise that I would not travel alone in Colorado unarmed, and that in consequence I left Estes Park with a Sharp's revolver loaded with ball-cartridge in my pocket, which has been the plague of my life. Its bright ominous barrel peeped out in quiet Denver shops, children pulled it out to play with, or when my riding-dress hung up with it in the pocket, pulled the whole from the peg to the floor; and I cannot conceive of any circumstances in which I could feel it right to make any use of it, or in which it could do me any possible good. Last night, however, I took it out, cleaned and oiled it, and laid it under my pillow, resolving to keep awake all night. I slept as soon as I lay down, and never woke till the bright morning sun shone through the roof, making me ridicule my own fears and abjure pistols for ever!

MARY KINGSLEY

(1862–1900)

From *Travels in West Africa*

Mary Kingsley belongs to that selective group of Englishwomen who
had good breeding, poor health, unconventional intellects, and a lust
for the exotic. Like Gertrude Bell, Isabella Bird, and a handful of others, Mary Kingsley came into her own when she cut loose from the con-
straints of Victorian society and began a life of traveling abroad. Her
ultima thule was West Africa, a place she'd heard about from her
explorer-physician father, Charles Kingsley. Her parents died when she
was thirty, leaving her free from domestic responsibilities for the first
time in her life. She was interested in collecting natural history specimens for the British Museum, and she wanted to continue her father's
study of religious fetishes. Fish and fetishes were her purpose she said
(and she did return with "one absolutely new fish," which was named
after her), but she soon found that everything about Africa captured
her imagination.

   She made two journeys to West Africa, in 1893 and again in
1894–95. She published Travels with great success in 1897. When
the Boer War broke out a few years later, she returned to nurse prison-

ers of war in Cape Town. But within a few months she caught enteric fever and died at the age of thirty-eight.

Kingsley traveled alone, with so little money that she bartered for food and often slept under the sky. The fact that she never came down with a tropical illness, or came to grief while whacking her way through the jungle or running the rapids on the Ogowé (as in the following passage), is nothing short of a miracle. But in fact, there never was a more lighthearted and stalwart traveler, and she approached every danger with a peculiar combination of understatement and wonder. Entirely undisciplined and unrefined, her writing sings with a rare wit, clarity, and her disarming force of personality.

M me Forget received me most kindly and hospitably, she, with her husband and her infant daughter, and M. and Mme Gacon represent the Mission Évangélique and the white race at Talagouga. Mme Forget is a perfectly lovely French girl, with a pale transparent skin and the most perfect great dark eyes, with indescribable charm, grace of manner, and vivacity in conversation. It grieves me to think of her, wasted on this savage wilderness surrounded by its deadly fever air. Oranie Forget, otherwise the baby, although I am not a general admirer of babies of her age—a mere matter of months—is also charming; I am not saying this because she flattered me by taking to me—all babies and children do that—but she has great style, and I have no doubt she will grow up to be a beauty too, but she would have made a dead certainty of it, if she had taken after her mother.

The mission station at Talagouga is hitched on to the rocky hillside, which rises so abruptly from the river that there is hardly room for the narrow footpath which runs along the river frontage of it. And when you are on the Forgets' verandah it seems as if you could easily roll right off it into the dark, deep, hurrying Ogowé. I suggest this to Mme Forget as an awful future for Oranie, but she has thought of it and wired the verandah up. You go up a steep flight of steps into the house, which is raised on poles some fifteen feet above the ground in front, and you walk through it against the hillside, made up mostly of enormous boulders of quartz, for Talagouga mountains are the western termination of the side of the Sierra del Cristal range. When you get through the house you come to more stairs, cut out now in the hillside rock and leading to the kitchen to the right, and to the store buildings; to the left they continue up to the church, which is still higher up the hill-face. That church is the prettiest I have seen in Africa. I do not say I should like to sit in it, because there seems to me no proper precautions taken to exclude snakes, lizards, or insects, and there would be great difficulty in concentrating one's mind on the higher life in the presence of these fearfully prevalent lower forms.

Across the other side of the ravine and high up, is perched the house which Dr Nassau built, when he first established mission work on the Upper Ogowé. The house is now in ruins; but in front of it, as an illustration of the transitory nature of European life in West Africa, is the grave of Mrs Nassau, among the great white blocks of quartz rock, its plain stone looking the one firm, permanent, human-made-thing about the place.

Talagouga is grand, but its scenery is undoubtedly grim, and its name, signifying the gateway of misery, seems applicable. It must be a melancholy place to live in, the very air lies heavy and silent. I never saw the trees stirred by a breeze the whole time I was there, even the broad plantain leaves seemed to stand sleeping day out and day in, motionless. The only sign of motion you get is in the Ogowé; if you look at it you see, in spite of its dark quiet face, that it is sweeping past at a terrific pace. One great gray rock sticks up through it just below the mission beach, and from that lies ever a silver streak from the hindrance it gives the current. Every now and again you will notice a canoe full of wild, naked, or nearly naked savages, silent because they are Fans, and don't sing like Igalwas or M'pongwe when in canoes. They are either paddling very hard and creeping very slowly upwards, against one of the banks, or just keeping her head straight and going rapidly down. Now and again you will hear the laboured

beat of the engines of either the *Mové* or *Éclaireur,* before you see the vessel and hear the warning shriek of their whistles; and you can watch her
as she comes up fighting her way to Njole, or see her as she comes down,
slipping past like a dream in a few seconds, and that is all.

I spent the succeeding days in buying fish from the natives, who
brought it in quantities, mostly of two sorts, and of course wanted enormous prices for it; but I confess I rather enjoy the give-and-take fun of
bartering against their extortion, and my trading with them introduced us
to each other so that when we met in the course of the long climbing
walks I used to take beetle-hunting in the bush behind the mission station, we knew about each other, and did not get much shocked or frightened.

That forest round Talagouga was one of the most difficult bits of country to get about in I ever came across, for it was dense and there were no
bush paths. No Fan village wants to walk to another Fan village for social
civilities, and all their trade goes up and down the river in canoes. No
doubt some miles inland there are bush paths, but I never struck one, so
they must be pretty far away. Neither did I come across any villages in
the forest, they seem all to be on the river bank round here.

Now and again, on exposed parts of the hillside, one comes across great
falls of timber which have been thrown down by tornadoes either flat on
to the ground—in which case under and among them are snakes and
scorpions, and getting over them is slippery work; or thrown sideways and
hanging against their fellows, all covered with gorgeous drapery of climbing, flowering plants—in which case they present to the human atom a
wall made up of strong tendrils and climbing grasses, through which the
said atom has to cut its way with a matchette and push into the crack so
made, getting, the while covered with red driver-ants, and such like, and
having sensational meetings with blue-green snakes, dirty green snakes
with triangular horned heads, black cobras, and boa constrictors. I never
came back to the station without having been frightened half out of my
wits, and with one or two of my small terrifiers in cleft sticks to bottle.

When you get into the way, catching a snake in a cleft stick is perfectly
simple. Only mind you have the proper kind of stick, split far enough up,

and keep your attention on the snake's head, that's his business end, and the tail which is whisking and winding round your wrist does not matter: there was one snake, by the way, of which it was impossible to tell, in the forest, which was his head. The natives swear he has one at each end; so you had better "Lef 'em", even though you know the British Museum would love to have him, for he is very venomous, and one of the few cases of death from snake-bite I have seen, was from this species.

Several times, when further in the forest, I came across a trail of flattened undergrowth, for fifty or sixty yards, with a horrid musky smell that demonstrated it had been the path of a boa constrictor, and nothing more.

It gave me more trouble and terror to get to the top of those Talagouga hillsides than it gave me to go twenty miles in the forests of Old Calabar, and that is saying a good deal, but when you got to the summit there was the glorious view of the rest of the mountains, stretching away, interrupted only by Mount Talagouga to the S.E. by E. and the great, grim, dark forest, under the lowering gray sky common during the dry season on the Equator. No glimpse or hint did one have of the Ogowé up here, so deep down in its ravine does it flow. A person coming to the hill tops close to Talagouga from the N. or N.N.W. and turning back in his track from here might be utterly unconscious that one of the great rivers of the world was flowing, full and strong, within some 800 feet of him. There is a strange sense of secretiveness about all these West African forests; but I never saw it so marked as in these that shroud the Sierra del Cristal. I very rarely met any natives in this part; those that I did were hunters, big, lithe men with all their toilet attention concentrated on their hair. On two occasions I ran some risk from having been stalked in mistake for game by these hunters. I escaped, however, because these men get as close as they can to their prey before firing; and when they found out their mistake they were not such cockney sportsmen as to kill me because I was something queer, and we stood and stared at each other, said a few words in our respective languages, and parted. One thing that struck me very much in these forests was the absence of signs of fetish worship which are so much in evidence in Calabar, where you constantly come across trees worshipped as the residences of spirits, and little huts put up over offerings to bush souls.

All the balance of the time I was at Talagouga I spent in trying to find means to get up into the rapids above Njole, for my heart got more and more set on them now that I saw the strange forms of the Talagouga fishes, and the differences between them and the fishes at Lambaréné. For some time no one whom I could get hold of regarded it as a feasible scheme, but, at last, M. Gacon thought it might be managed; I said I would give a reward of 100 francs to any one who would lend me a canoe and a crew, and I would pay the working expenses, food, wages, &c. M. Gacon had a good canoe and could spare me two English-speaking Igal-was, one of whom had been part of the way with MM. Allégret and Teis-serès, when they made their journey up to Franceville and then across to Brazzaville and down the Congo two years ago. He also thought we could get six Fans to complete the crew.

I was delighted, packed my small portmanteau with a few things, got some trade goods, wound up my watch, ascertained the date of the day of the month, and borrowed three hairpins from Mme Forget, then down came disappointment. On my return from the bush that evening, Mme Forget said M. Gacon said "it was impossible," the Fans round Talagouga wouldn't go at any price above Njole, because they were certain they would be killed and eaten by the up-river Fans. Internally consigning the entire tribe to regions where they will get a rise in temperature, even in this climate, I went with Mme Forget to M. Gacon, and we talked it over; finally, M. Gacon thought he could let me have two more Igalwas from Hatton and Cookson's beach across the river. Sending across there we found this could be done, so I now felt I was in for it, and screwed my courage to the sticking point—no easy matter after all the information I had got into my mind regarding the rapids of the River Ogowé.

I ESTABLISH MYSELF on my portmanteau comfortably in the canoe, my back is against the trade box, and behind that is the usual mound of pillows, sleeping mats, and mosquito-bars of the Igalwa crew; the whole surmounted by the French flag flying from an indifferent stick.

M. and Mme Forget provide me with everything I can possibly require, and say, that the blood of half my crew is half alcohol; on the whole it is patent they don't expect to see me again, and I forgive them, because they don't seem cheerful over it; but still it is not reassuring—nothing is about this affair, and it's going to rain. It does, as we go up the river to Njole, where there is another risk of the affair collapsing, by the French authorities declining to allow me to proceed. On we paddled, M'bo the head man standing in the bows of the canoe in front of me, to steer, then I, then the baggage, then the able-bodied seamen, including the cook also standing and paddling; and at the other extremity of the canoe—it grieves me to speak of it in this unseamanlike way, but in these canoes both ends are alike, and chance alone ordains which is bow and which is stern—stands Pierre, the first officer, also steering; the paddles used are all of the long-handled, leaf-shaped Igalwa type.

. . .

Two hours after leaving Njole we are facing our first rapid. Great gray-black masses of smoothed rock rise up out of the whirling water in all directions. These rocks have a peculiar appearance which puzzle me at the time, but in subsequently getting used to it I accepted it quietly and admired. When the sun shines on them they have a soft light blue haze round them, like a halo. The effect produced by this, with the forested hillsides and the little beaches of glistening white sand was one of the most perfect things I have ever seen.

We kept along close to the right-hand bank, dodging out of the way of the swiftest current as much as possible. Ever and again we were unable to force our way round projecting parts of the bank, so we then got up just as far as we could to the point in question, yelling and shouting at the tops of our voices. M'bo said "Jump for bank, sar," and I "up and jumped," followed by half the crew. Such banks! sheets, and walls, and rubbish heaps of rock, mixed up with trees fallen and standing. One appalling corner I shall not forget, for I had to jump at a rock wall, and hang on to it in a manner more befitting an insect than an insect-hunter, and then scramble up it into a close-set forest, heavily burdened with boulders of all sizes.

I wonder whether the rocks or the trees were there first? There is evidence both ways, for in one place you will see a rock on the top of a tree, the tree creeping out from underneath it, and in another place you will see a tree on the top of a rock, clasping it with a network of roots and getting its nourishment, goodness knows how, for these are by no means tender, digestible sand-stones, but uncommon hard gneiss and quartz which has no idea of breaking up into friable small stuff, and which only takes on a high polish when it is vigorously sanded and canvassed by the Ogowé. While I was engaged in climbing across these promontories, the crew would be busy shouting and hauling the canoe round the point by means of the strong chain provided for such emergencies fixed on to the bow. When this was done, in we got again and paddled away until we met our next affliction.

M'bo had advised that we should spend our first night at the same village that M. Allégret did: but when we reached it, a large village on the north bank, we seemed to have a lot of daylight still in hand, and thought it would be better to stay at one a little higher up, so as to make a shorter day's work for tomorrow, when we wanted to reach Kondo Kondo; so we went against the bank just to ask about the situation and character of the up-river villages. The row of low, bark huts was long, and extended its main frontage close to the edge of the river bank. The inhabitants had been watching us as we came, and when they saw we intended calling that afternoon, they charged down to the river-edge hopeful of excitement.

They had a great deal to say, and so had we. To M'bo's questions they gave a dramatic entertainment as answer, after the manner of these brisk, excitable Fans. One chief, however, soon settled down to definite details, prefacing his remarks with the silence-commanding "Azuna! Azuna!" and his companions grunted approbation of his observations. He took a piece of plantain leaf and tore it up into five different-sized bits. These he laid along the edge of our canoe at different intervals of space, while he told M'bo things, mainly scandalous, about the characters of the villages these bits of leaf represented, save of course about bit A, which represented his own. The interval between the bits was proportional to the interval between the villages, and the size of the bits was proportional to the size of the village. Village number four was the only one he should recommend our going to.

When all was said, I gave our kindly informants some heads of tobacco and many thanks. Then M'bo sang them a hymn, with the assistance of Pierre, half a line behind him in a different key, but every bit as flat. The Fans seemed impressed, but any crowd would be by the hymn-singing of my crew, unless they were inmates of deaf and dumb asylums. Then we took our farewell, and thanked the village elaborately for its kind invitation to spend the night there on our way home, shoved off and paddled away in great style just to show those Fans what Igalwas could do.

We hadn't gone 200 yards before we met a current coming round the end of a rock reef that was too strong for us to hold our own in, let alone progress. On to the bank I was ordered and went; it was a low slip of rugged confused boulders and fragments of rocks, carelessly arranged, and evidently under water in the wet season. I scrambled along, the men yelled and shouted and hauled the canoe, and the inhabitants of the village, seeing we were becoming amusing again, came, legging it like lamplighters, after us, young and old, male and female, to say nothing of the dogs. Some good souls helped the men haul, while I did my best to amuse the others by diving headlong from a large rock on to which I had elaborately climbed, into a thick clump of willow-leaved shrubs. They applauded my performance vociferously, and then assisted my efforts to extricate myself, and during the rest of my scramble they kept close to me, with keen competition for the front row, in hopes that I would do something like it again. But I refused the *encore*, because, bashful as I am, I could not but feel that my last performance was carried out with all the superb reckless *abandon* of a Sarah Bernhardt, and a display of art of this order should satisfy any African village for a year at least. At last I got across the rocks on to a lovely little beach of white sand, and stood there talking, surrounded by my audience, until the canoe got over its difficulties and arrived almost as scratched as I; and then we again said farewell and paddled away, to the great grief of the natives, for they don't get a circus up above Njole every week, poor dears.

. . .

About 8 P.M. we came to a corner, a bad one; but we were unable to leap on to the bank and haul round, not being able to see either the details or the exact position of the said bank, and we felt, I think naturally, disinclined to spring in the direction of such bits of country as we had had experience of during the afternoon. We fought our way round that corner, yelling defiance at the water, and dealt with succeeding corners on the *vi et armis* plan, breaking, ever and anon, a pole.

About 9.30 we got into a savage rapid. We fought it inch by inch. The canoe jammed herself on some barely sunken rocks in it. We shoved her off over them. She tilted over and chucked us out. The rocks round being just a wash, we survived and got her straight again, and got into her and drove her unmercifully; she struck again and bucked like a broncho, and we fell in heaps upon each other, but stayed inside that time—the men by the aid of their intelligent feet, I by clinching my hands into the bush rope lacing which ran round the rim of the canoe and the meaning of which I did not understand when I left Talagouga.

We sorted ourselves out hastily and sent her at it again. Smash went a sorely tried pole and a paddle. Round and round we spun in an exultant whirlpool, which, in a light-hearted, maliciously joking way, hurled us tail first out of it into the current. Now the grand point in these canoes of having both ends alike declared itself; for at this juncture all we had to do was to revolve on our own axis and commence life anew with what had been the bow for the stern. Of course we were defeated, we could not go up any further without the aid of our lost poles and paddles, so we had to go down for shelter somewhere, anywhere, and down at a terrific pace in the white water we went.

M'bo and Pierre, provided with our surviving poles, stood in the bows to fend us off rocks, as we shot towards them; while we midship paddles sat, helping to steer, and when occasion arose, which occasion did with lightning rapidity, to whack the whirlpools with the flat of our paddles, to break their force. Cook crouched in the stern concentrating his mind on steering only. We dashed full tilt towards high rocks, things twenty to fifty feet above water. Midship backed and flapped like fury; M'bo and Pierre received the shock on their poles; sometimes we glanced success-fully aside and flew on; sometimes we didn't. The shock being too much for M'bo and Pierre they were driven back on me, who got flattened on to the cargo of bundles which, being now firmly tied in, couldn't spread the confusion further aft; but the shock of the canoe's nose against the rock did so in style, and the rest of the crew fell forward on to the bundles, me, and themselves. So shaken up together were we several times that night, that it's a wonder to me, considering the hurry, that we sorted our-selves out correctly with our own particular legs and arms. And although we in the middle of the canoe did some very spirited flapping, our whirlpool-breaking was no more successful than M'bo and Pierre's fend-ing off, and many a wild waltz we danced that night with the waters of the River Ogowé.

Unpleasant as going through the rapids was, when circumstances took us into the black current we fared no better. For good all-round incon-venience, give me going full tilt in the dark into the branches of a fallen tree at the pace we were going then—and crash, swish, crackle and there you are, hung up, with a bough pressing against your chest, and your hair being torn out and your clothes ribboned by others, while the wicked river is trying to drag away the canoe from under you. After a good hour and more of these experiences, we went hard on to a large black reef of rocks. So firm was the canoe wedged that we in our rather worn-out state couldn't move her so we wisely decided to "lef'em" and see what could be done towards getting food and a fire for the remainder of the night. Our eyes, now trained to the darkness, observed pretty close to us a big lump of land, looming up out of the river. This we subsequently found out was Kembe Island. The rocks and foam on either side stretched away into the darkness, and high above us against the star-lit sky stood out clearly the summits of the mountains of the Sierra del Cristal.

The most interesting question to us now was whether this rock reef communicated sufficiently with the island for us to get to it. Abandoning conjecture; tying very firmly our canoe up to the rocks, a thing that seemed, considering she was jammed hard and immovable, a little unnecessary—but you can never be sufficiently careful in this matter with any kind of boat—off we started among the rock boulders. I would climb up on to a rock table, fall off it on the other side on to rocks again, with more or less water on them—then get a patch of singing sand under my feet, then with varying suddenness get into more water, deep or shallow, broad or narrow pools among the rocks; out of that over more rocks, &c., &c., &c.: my companions, from their noises, evidently were going in for the same kind of thing, but we were quite cheerful, because the probability of reaching the land seemed increasing. Most of us arrived into deep channels of water which here and there cut in between this rock reef and the bank.

M'bo was the first to find the way into certainty; he was, and I hope still is, a perfect wonder at this sort of work. I kept close to M'bo, and when we got to the shore, the rest of the wanderers being collected, we said "chances are there's a village round here"; and started to find it. After a gay time in a rock-encumbered forest, growing in a tangled, matted way on a rough hill-side, at an angle of 45 degrees, M'bo sighted the gleam of fires through the tree stems away to the left, and we bore down on it, listening to its drum. Viewed through the bars of the tree stems the scene was very picturesque. The village was just a collection of palm mat-built huts, very low and squalid. In its tiny street, an affair of some sixty feet long and twenty wide, were a succession of small fires. The villagers themselves, however, were the striking features in the picture. They were painted vermilion all over their nearly naked bodies, and were dancing enthusiastically to the good old rump-a-tump-tump-tump tune, played energetically by an old gentleman on a long, high-standing, white-and-black painted drum. They said that as they had been dancing when we arrived they had failed to hear us.

M'bo secured a—well, I don't exactly know what to call it—for my use. It was, I fancy, the remains of the village club-house. It had a certain amount of palm-thatch roof and some of its left-hand side left, the rest of the structure was bare old poles with filaments of palm mat hanging from them here and there; and really if it hadn't been for the roof one wouldn't have known whether one was inside or outside it. The floor was trodden earth and in the middle of it a heap of white ash and the usual two bush lights, laid down with their burning ends propped up off the ground with stones, and emitting, as is their wont, a rather mawkish, but not altogether unpleasant smell, and volumes of smoke which finds its way out through the thatch, leaving on the inside of it a rich oily varnish of a bright warm brown colour. They give a very good light, provided someone keeps an eye on them and knocks the ash off the end as it burns gray; the bush lights' idea of being snuffed. Against one of the open-work sides hung a drum covered with raw hide, and a long hollow bit of tree trunk, which served as a cupboard for a few small articles.

I gathered in all these details as I sat on one of the hard wood benches, waiting for my dinner, which Isaac was preparing outside in the street. The atmosphere of the hut, in spite of its remarkable advantages in the way of ventilation, was oppressive, for the smell of the bush lights, my wet clothes, and the natives who crowded into the hut to look at me, made anything but a pleasant combination. The people were evidently exceedingly poor; clothes they had very little of. The two head men had on old French military coats in rags; but they were quite satisfied with their appearance, and evidently felt through them in touch with European culture, for they lectured to the others on the habits and customs of the white man with great self-confidence and superiority.

The majority of the village had a slight acquaintance already with this interesting animal, being, I found, Adoomas. They had made a settlement on Kembe Island some two years or so ago. Then the Fans came and attacked them, and killed and ate several. The Adoomas left and fled to the French authority at Njole and remained under its guarding shadow until the French came up and chastised the Fans and burnt their village; and the Adoomas—when things had quieted down again and the Fans had gone off to build themselves a new village for their burnt one—came back to Kembe Island and their plantain patch. They had only done this a few months before my arrival and had not had time to rebuild, hence the dilapidated state of the village. As soon as my dinner arrived they politely cleared out, and I heard the devout M'bo holding a service for them, with hymns, in the street, and this being over they returned to their drum and dance, keeping things up distinctly late, for it was 11.10 P.M., when we first entered the village.

While the men were getting their food I mounted guard over our little possessions, and when they turned up to make things tidy in my hut, I walked off down to the shore by a path, which we had elaborately avoided when coming to the village, a very vertically inclined, slippery little path, but still the one whereby the natives went up and down to their canoes, which were kept tied up amongst the rocks. The moon was rising, illumining the sky, but not yet sending down her light on the foaming, flying Ogowé in its deep ravine. The scene was divinely lovely; on every side out of the formless gloom rose the peaks of the Sierra del Cristal. Tomanjawki, on the further side of the river surrounded by his companion peaks, looked his grandest, silhouetted hard against the sky. In the higher valleys where the dim light shone faintly, one could see wreaths and clouds of silver-gray mist lying, basking lazily or rolling to and fro. Olangi seemed to stretch right across the river, blocking with his great blunt mass all passage; while away to the N.E. a cone-shaped peak showed conspicuous, which I afterwards knew as Kangwe.

In the darkness round me flitted thousands of fire-flies and out beyond this pool of utter night flew by unceasingly the white foam of the rapids; sound there was none save their thunder. The majesty and beauty of the scene fascinated me, and I stood leaning with my back against a' rock pinnacle watching it. Do not imagine it gave rise, in what I am pleased to call my mind, to those complicated, poetical reflections natural beauty seems to bring out in other people's minds. It never works that way with me; I just lose all sense of human individuality, all memory of human life, with its grief and worry and doubt, and become part of the atmosphere. If I have a heaven, that will be mine, and I verily believe that if I were left alone long enough with such a scene as this, or on the deck of an African liner in the Bights, watching her funnel and masts swinging to and fro in the great long leisurely roll against the sky, I should be found soulless and dead; but I never have a chance of that.

This night my absent Kras, as my Fanti friends would call them, were sent hurrying home badly scared to their attributive body by a fearful shriek tearing through the voice of the Ogowé up into the silence of the hills. I woke with a shudder and found myself sore and stiff, but made hastily in the direction of the shriek, fancying some of our hosts had been spearing one of the crew—a vain and foolish fancy I apologise for. What had happened was that my men, thinking it wiser to keep an eye on our canoe, had come down and built a fire close to her and put up their mos-quito-bars as tents. One of the men, tired out by his day's work, had sat down on one of the three logs, whose ends, pointed to a common centre where the fire is, constitute the universal stove of this region. He was taking a last pipe before turning in, but sleep had taken him, and the wretch of a fire had sneaked along in the log under him and burnt him suddenly. The shriek was his way of mentioning the fact. Having got up these facts I left the victim seated in a remedial cool pool of water and climbed back to the village, whose inhabitants, tired at last, were going to sleep. M'bo, I found, had hung up my mosquito-bar over one of the hard wood benches, and going cautiously under it I lit a night-light and read myself asleep with my damp dilapidated old Horace.

Woke at 4 A.M. lying on the ground among the plantain stems, having by a reckless movement fallen out of the house. Thanks be there are no mosquitoes. I don't know how I escaped the rats which swarm here, run-ning about among the huts and the inhabitants in the evening, with a tameness shocking to see. I turned in again until six o'clock, when we started getting things ready to go up river again, carefully providing ourselves with a new stock of poles, and subsidising a native to come with us and help us to fight the rapids.

We left the landing place rocks of Kembe Island about 8, and no sooner had we got afloat, than, in the twinkling of an eye, we were swept, broadside on, right across the river to the north bank, and then engaged in a heavy fight with a severe rapid. After passing this, the river is fairly uninterrupted by rock for a while, and is silent and swift. When you are ascending such a piece the effect is strange; you see the water flying by the side of your canoe, as you vigorously drive your paddle into it with short rapid strokes, and you forthwith fancy you are travelling at the rate of a North-Western express; but you just raise your eyes, my friend, and look at that bank, which is standing very nearly still, and you will realise that you and your canoe are standing very nearly still too; and that all your exertions are only enabling you to creep on at the pace of a crushed snail, and that it's the water that is going the pace. It's a most quaint and unpleasant disillusionment.

A bad rapid, called by our ally from Kembe Island "Unfanga," being surmounted, we seem to be in a mountain-walled lake, and keeping along the left bank of this, we get on famously for twenty whole restful minutes, which lulls us all into a false sense of security, and my crew sing M'pongwe songs, descriptive of how they go to their homes to see their wives, and families, and friends, giving chaffing descriptions of their friends' characteristics and of their failings, which cause bursts of laughter from those among us who recognise the allusions, and how they go to their boxes, and take out their clothes, and put them on—a long bragging inventory of these things is given by each man as a solo, and then the chorus, taken heartily up by his companions, signifies their admiration and astonishment at his wealth and importance—and then they sing how, being dissatisfied with that last dollar's worth of goods they got from `Holty's', they have decided to take their next trade to Hatton and Cookson, or *vice versa;* and then comes the chorus, applauding the wisdom of such a decision, and extolling the excellence of Hatton and Cookson's goods or Holty's.

These M'pongwe and Igalwa boat songs are all very pretty, and have very elaborate tunes in a minor key. I do not believe there are any old words to them; I have tried hard to find out about them, but I believe the tunes, which are of a limited number and quite distinct from each other, are very old. The words are put in by the singer on the spur of the moment, and only restricted in this sense, that there would always be the domestic catalogue—whatever its component details might be—sung to the one fixed tune, the trade information sung to another, and so on. A good singer, in these parts, means the man who can make up the best song—the most impressive, or the most amusing; I have elsewhere mentioned pretty much the same state of things among the Ga's and Krumen and Bubi, and in all cases the tunes are only voice tunes, not for instrumental performance. The instrumental music consists of that marvellously developed series of drum tunes—the attempt to understand which has taken up much of my time, and led me into queer company—and the many tunes played on the 'mrimba and the orchid-root-stringed harp: they are, I believe, entirely distinct from the song tunes.

On we go singing elaborately, thinking no evil of nature, when a current, a quiet devil of a thing, comes round from behind a point of the bank and catches the nose of our canoe; wringing it well, it sends us scuttling right across the river in spite of our ferocious swoops at the water, upsetting us among a lot of rocks with the water boiling over them; this lot of rocks being however of the table-top kind, and not those precious, close-set pinnacles rising up sheer out of profound depths, between which you are so likely to get your canoe wedged in and split. We, up to our knees in water that nearly tears our legs off, push and shove the canoe free, and re-embarking return singing across the river, to have it out with that current. We do; and at its head find a rapid, and notice on the mountain-side a village clearing, the first sign of human habitation we have seen to-day.

Above this rapid we get a treat of still water, the main current of the Ogowé flying along by the south bank. On our side there are sandbanks with their graceful sloping backs and sudden ends, and there is a very strange and beautiful effect produced by the flakes and balls of foam thrown off the rushing main current into the quiet water. These whirl among the eddies and rush backwards and forwards as though they were still mad with wild haste, until, finding no current to take them down, they drift away into the land-locked bays, where they come to a standstill as if they were bewildered and lost and were trying to remember where they were going to and whence they had come; the foam of which they are composed is yellowish-white, with a spongy sort of solidity about it.

In a little bay we pass we see eight native women, Fans clearly, by their bright brown faces, and their loads of brass bracelets and armlets, intent on breaking up a stockaded fish-trap. We pause and chat, and watch them collecting the fish in baskets, and I acquire some specimens; and then, shouting farewells when we are well away, in the proper civil way, resume our course.

The middle of the Ogowé here is simply forested with high rocks, looking, as they stand with their grim forms above the foam, like a regiment of strange strong creatures breasting it, with their straight faces up river, and their more flowing curves down, as though they had on black mantles which were swept backwards. Our channel was free until we had to fight round the upper end of our bay into a long rush of strong current with bad whirlpools curving its face; then the river widens out and quiets down and then suddenly contracts—a rocky forested promontory running out from each bank. There is a little village on the north bank's promontory, and, at the end of each, huge monoliths rise from the water, making what looks like a gateway which had once been barred and through which the Ogowé had burst.

For the first time on this trip I felt discouraged; it seemed so impossible that we, with our small canoe and scanty crew, could force our way up through that gateway, when the whole Ogowé was rushing down through it. But we clung to the bank and rocks with hands, poles, and paddle, and did it; really the worst part was not in the gateway but just before it, for here there is a great whirlpool, its centre hollowed some two or three feet below its rim. It is caused, my Kembe islander says, by a great cave opening beneath the water. Above the gate the river broadens out again and we see the arched opening to a large cave in the south bank; the mountain-side is one mass of rock covered with the unbroken forest; and the entrance to this cave is just on the upper wall of the south bank's promontory; so, being sheltered from the current here, we rest and examine it leisurely. The river runs into it, and you can easily pass in at this season, but in the height of the wet season, when the river level would be some twenty feet or more above its present one, I doubt if you could. They told me this place is called Boko Boko, and that the cave is a very long one, extending on a level some way into the hill, and then ascending and coming out near a mass of white rock that showed as a speck high up on the mountain.

If you paddle into it you go "far far," and then "no more water live," and you get out and go up the tunnel, which is sometimes broad, sometimes narrow, sometimes high, sometimes so low that you have to crawl, and so get out at the other end.

One French gentleman has gone through this performance, and I am told found "plenty plenty" bats, and hedgehogs, and snakes. They could not tell me his name, which I much regretted. As we had no store of bush lights we went no further than the portals; indeed, strictly between ourselves, if I had had every bush light in Congo Français I personally should not have relished going further. I am terrified of caves; it sends a creaming down my back to think of them.

SIR RICHARD FRANCIS BURTON

(1821–1890)

From *Personal Narrative of a Pilgrimage to Al-Madinah and Meccah*

Burton is famous for his intense rivalry with John Hanning Speke and their bitter dispute over the source of the White Nile. But before he became wrapped up in that most elusive of geographical quests, Burton had stirred up a good deal of drama elsewhere. One of the most widely traveled of nineteenth-century explorers, Burton was also a brilliant, opinionated, enigmatic, and prolific writer. About his travels in India, Arabia, Africa, South America, Iceland, and America he wrote some seventy volumes. One of his earliest and most fascinating describes his sensational undercover journey to Al-Madinah and Mecca.

In 1852, feeling his usual restlessness for a new quest, Burton presented himself to the Royal Geographic Society and offered to remove "the huge white blot which in our maps still notes the Eastern and Central regions of Arabia." His geographical motive was an excuse for his true obsession—to set foot in a dangerous and mysterious land where Europeans had for the most part never entered or never returned. He desired to enter Meccah itself in order to study Islam's inner realm. A number of European adventurers tried to steal through the forbidden gates of Middle Eastern and Asian cities during the eighteenth century, but none was so successful or such a master of disguise as Sir Richard Burton. There is considerable evidence that he even went so far as to get circumcised, so as to appear a more likely Arab if his "external evidence" was examined. His phenomenal aptitude for languages and for cultural assimilation was unsurpassed, as was his boldness and curiosity. He went to Meccah disguised as a Persian wanderer, merchant, philosopher, and mystic—a character that suited him to perfection. Here he joins a mass of other pilgrims on his way to the Holy City and finds himself in the midst of a violent raid by a score of highway bandits.

We started at ten A.M. (Monday, 5th September) in a South-Easterly direction, and travelled over a flat, thinly dotted with Desert vegetation. At one P.M. we passed a basaltic ridge; and then, entering a long depressed line of country, a kind of valley, paced down it five tedious hours. The Samum[1] as usual was blowing hard, and it seemed to affect the travellers' tempers. In one place I saw a Turk, who could not speak a word of Arabic, violently disputing with an Arab who could not understand a word of Turkish. The pilgrim insisted upon adding to the camel's load a few dry sticks, such as are picked up for cooking. The camel-man as perseveringly threw off the extra burthen. They screamed with rage, hustled each other, and at last the Turk dealt the Arab a heavy blow. I afterwards heard that the pilgrim was mortally wounded that night, his stomach being ripped open with a dagger. On enquiring what had become of him, I was assured that he had been comfortably wrapped up in his shroud, and placed in a half-dug grave. This is the general practice in the case of the poor and solitary, whom illness or accident incapaci-

[1] Desert wind.

tates from proceeding. It is impossible to contemplate such a fate without horror: the torturing thirst of a wound,[†] the burning sun heating the brain to madness, and—worst of all, for they do not wait till death—the attacks of the jackal, the vulture, and the raven of the wild.

At six P.M., before the light of day had faded, we traversed a rough and troublesome ridge. Descending it our course lay in a southerly direction along a road flanked on the left by low hills of red sandstone and bright porphyry.[2] About an hour afterwards we came to a basalt field, through whose blocks we threaded our way painfully and slowly, for it was then dark. At eight P.M. the camels began to stumble over the dwarf dykes of the wheat and barley fields, and presently we arrived at our halting-place, a large village called Al-Sufayna. The plain was already dotted with tents and lights. We found the Baghdad Caravan, whose route here falls into the Darb al-Sharki. It consists of a few Persians and Kurds, and collects the people of North-Eastern Arabia, Wahhabis and others. They are escorted by the Agayl tribe and by the fierce mountaineers of Jabal Shammar. Scarcely was our tent pitched, when the distant pattering of musketry and an ominous tapping of the kettle-drum sent all my companions in different directions to enquire what was the cause of quarrel. The Baghdad Cafilah, though not more than 2000 in number, men, women and children, had been proving to the Damascus Caravan, that, being perfectly ready to fight, they were not going to yield any point of precedence. From that time the two bodies encamped in different places. I never saw a more pugnacious assembly: a look sufficed for a quarrel. Once a Wahhabi stood in front of us, and by pointing with his finger and other insulting gestures, showed his hatred to the chibuk,[3] in which I was peaceably indulging. It was impossible to refrain from chastising his insolence by a polite and smiling offer of the offending pipe.

[†] When Indians would say "he was killed upon the spot," they use the picturesque phrase, "he asked not for water."

---

[2] A type of rock, often purple or dark red and embedded with crystals.

[3] A long-stemmed Turkish tobacco pipe.

This made him draw his dagger without a thought; but it was sheathed again, for we all cocked our pistols, and these gentry prefer steel to lead. We had travelled about seventeen miles, and the direction of Al-Sufayna from our last halting place was South-East five degrees. Though it was night when we encamped, Shaykh Mas'ud set out to water his moaning camels: they had not quenched their thirst for three days. He returned in a depressed state, having been bled by the soldiery at the well to the extent of forty piastres, or about eight shillings.

After supper we spread our rugs and prepared to rest. And here I first remarked the coolness of the nights, proving, at this season of the year, a considerable altitude above the sea. As a general rule the atmosphere stagnated between sunrise and ten A.M., when a light wind rose. During the forenoon the breeze strengthened, and it gradually diminished through the afternoon. Often about sunset there was a gale accompanied by dry storms of dust. At Al-Sufayna, though there was no night-breeze and little dew, a blanket was necessary, and the hours of darkness were invigorating enough to mitigate the effect of the sand and Samum-ridden day. Before sleeping I was introduced to a namesake, one Shaykh Abdullah, of Meccah. Having committed his Shugduf[4] to his son, a lad of fourteen, he had ridden forward on a dromedary, and had suddenly fallen ill. His objects in meeting me were to ask for some medicine, and for a temporary seat in my Shugduf, the latter I offered with pleasure, as the boy Mohammed was longing to mount a camel. The Shaykh's illness was nothing but weakness brought on by the hardships of the journey: he attributed it to the hot wind, and to the weight of a bag of dollars which he had attached to his waist-belt. He was a man about forty, long, thin, pale, and of a purely nervous temperament; and a few questions elicited the fact that he had lately and suddenly given up his daily opium pill. I prepared one for him, placed him in my litter, and persuaded him to stow

---

[4] Those who were better off did not ride directly on the camel's back but in a shug-duf, a miniature tent mounted on the camel's panniers in which there were usually two seats.

away his burden in some place where it would be less troublesome. He was my companion for two marches, at the end of which he found his own Shugduf. I never met amongst the Arab citizens a better bred or a better informed man. At Constantinople he had learned a little French, Italian, and Greek; and from the properties of a shrub to the varieties of honey,† he was full of "useful knowledge," and openable as a dictionary. We parted near Meccah, where I met him only once, and then accidentally, in the Valley of Muna.

At half-past five A.M. on Tuesday, the 6th of September, we arose refreshed by the cool, comfortable night, and loaded the camels. I had an opportunity of inspecting Al-Sufayna. It is a village of fifty or sixty mud-walled, flat-roofed houses, defended by the usual rampart. Around it lie ample date-grounds, and fields of wheat, barley, and maize. Its bazar at this season of the year is well supplied: even fowls can be procured.

We travelled towards the South-East, and entered a country destitute of the low ranges of hill, which from Al-Madinah southwards had bounded the horizon. After a two miles' march our camels climbed up a precipitous ridge, and then descended into a broad gravel plain. From ten to eleven A.M. our course lay southerly over a high table-land, and we afterwards traversed, for five hours and a half, a plain which bore signs of standing water. This day's march was peculiarly Arabia It was a desert peopled only with echoes,—a place of death for what little there is to die in it,—a wilderness where, to use my companion's phrase, there is nothing but He.†† Nature scalped, flayed, discovered all her skeleton to the gazer's eye. The horizon was a sea of mirage; gigantic sand-columns whirled over the plain; and on both sides of our road were huge piles of

---

† The Arabs are curious in and fond of honey: Meccah alone affords eight or nine different varieties. The best, and in Arab parlance the "coldest," is the green kind, produced by bees that feed upon a thorny plant called "sihhah." The white and red honeys rank next. The worst is the Asal Asmar (brown honey), which sells for something under a piastre per pound. The Abyssinian mead is unknown in Al-Hijaz, but honey enters into a variety of dishes.

†† "La Siwa Hu," *i.e.*, where there is none but Allah.

bare rock, standing detached upon the surface of sand and clay. Here they appeared in oval lumps, heaped up with a semblance of symmetry; there a single boulder stood, with its narrow foundation based upon a pedestal of low, dome-shapen rock. All were of a pink coarse-grained granite, which flakes off in large crusts under the influence of the atmosphere. I remarked one block which could not measure fewer than thirty feet in height. Through these scenes we travelled till about half-past four P.M., when the guns suddenly roared a halt. There was not a trace of human habitation around us: a few parched shrubs and the granite heaps were the only objects diversifying the hard clayey plain. Shaykh Mas'ud correctly guessed the cause of our detention at the inhospitable "halting-place of the Mutayr" (Badawin). "Cook your bread and boil your coffee," said the old man; "the camels will rest for awhile, and the gun will sound at nightfall."

We had passed over about eighteen miles of ground; and our present direction was South-west twenty degrees of Al-Sufayna.

At half-past ten that evening we heard the signal for departure, and, as the moon was still young, we prepared for a hard night's work. We took a south-westerly course through what is called a Wa'ar—rough ground covered with thicket. Darkness fell upon us like a pall. The camels tripped and stumbled, tossing their litters like cockboats in a short sea; at times the Shugdufs were well nigh torn off their backs. When we came to a ridge worse than usual, old Mas'ud would seize my camel's halter, and, accompanied by his son and nephew bearing lights, encourage the animals with gesture and voice. It was a strange, wild scene. The black basaltic field was dotted with the huge and doubtful forms of spongy-footed camels with silent tread, looming like phantoms in the midnight air; the hot wind moaned, and whirled from the torches flakes and sheets of flame and fiery smoke, whilst ever and anon a swift-travelling Takht-rawan,[5] drawn by mules, and surrounded by runners bearing gigantic

[5] Also translated as "takhtrawn," this is a brightly painted litter carried by mules or horses. These were used only by the very wealthy.

mashals or cressets,[†] threw a passing glow of red light upon the dark road and the dusky multitude. On this occasion the rule was "every man for himself." Each pressed forward into the best path, thinking only of preceding his neighbour. The Syrians, amongst whom our little party had become entangled, proved most unpleasant companions: they often stopped the way, insisting upon their right to precedence. On one occasion a horseman had the audacity to untie the halter of my dromedary, and thus to cast us adrift, as it were, in order to make room for some excluded friend. I seized my sword; but Shaykh Abdullah stayed my hand, and addressed the intruder in terms sufficiently violent to make him slink away. Nor was this the only occasion on which my companion was successful with the Syrians. He would begin with a mild "Move a little, O my father!" followed, if fruitless, by "Out of the way, O Father of Syria[††]!" and if still ineffectual, advancing to a "Begone, O he!" This ranged between civility and sternness. If without effect, it was supported by revilings to the "Abusers of the Salt," the "Yazid," the "Offspring of Shimr." Another remark which I made about my companion's conduct

---

[†] This article, an iron cylinder with bands, mounted on a long pole, corresponds with the European cresset of the fifteenth century. The Pasha's cressets are known by their smell, a little incense being mingled with the wood. By this means the Badawin discover the dignitary's place.

[††] "Abu Sham," a familiar address in Al-Hijaz to Syrians. They are called "abusers of the salt," from their treachery, and "offspring of Shimr" (the execrated murderer of the Imam Hosayn), because he was a native of that country. Such is the detestation in which the Shi'ah sect, especially the Persians, hold Syria and the Syrians, that I hardly ever met with a truly religious man who did not desire a general massacre of the polluted race. And history informs us that the plains of Syria have repeatedly been drenched with innocent blood shed by sectarian animosity. Yet Jalal al-Din (History of Jerusalem) says, "As to Damascus, all learned men fully agree that it is the most eminent of cities after Meccah and Al-Madinah." Hence its many titles, "the Smile of the Prophet," the "Great Gate of Pilgrimage," "Sham Sharif," the "Right Hand of the Cities of Syria," &c., &c. And many sayings of Mohammed in honour of Syria are recorded. He was fond of using such Syriac words as "Bakh[un]! Bakh[un]!" to Ali, and "Kakh[un]! Kakh[un]!" to Hosayn. I will not enter into the curious history of the latter word, which spread to Egypt, and, slightly altered, passed through Latin mythology into French, English, German, Italian, and other modern European tongues.

well illustrates the difference between the Eastern and the Western man. When traversing a dangerous place, Shaykh Abdullah the European attended to his camel with loud cries of "Hai! Hai†!" and an occasional switching. Shaykh Abdullah the Asiatic commended himself to Allah by repeated ejaculations of *Yá Sátir! Yá! Sattár*††

The morning of Wednesday (September 7th) broke as we entered a wide plain. In many places were signs of water: lines of basalt here and there seamed the surface, and wide sheets of the tufaceous gypsum called by the Arabs *Sabkhah* shone like mirrors set in the russet frame-work of the flat. This substance is found in cakes, often a foot long by an inch in depth, curled by the sun's rays and overlying clay into which water had sunk. After our harassing night, day came on with a sad feeling of oppression, greatly increased by the unnatural glare:—

> "In vain the sight, dejected to the ground,
> Stoop'd for relief: thence hot ascending streams
> And keen reflection pain'd."

We were disappointed in our expectations of water, which usually abounds near this station, as its name, *Al-Ghadir*, denotes. At ten A.M. we pitched the tent in the first convenient spot, and we lost no time in stretching our cramped limbs upon the bosom of mother Earth. From the halting-place of the Mutayr to Al-Ghadir is a march of about twenty miles, and the direction south-west twenty-one degrees. Al-Ghadir is an extensive plain, which probably presents the appearance of a lake after heavy rains. It is overgrown in parts with Desert vegetation, and requires nothing but a regular supply of water to make it useful to man. On the East it is bounded by a wall of rock, at whose base are three wells, said to

---

† There is a regular language to camels. "Ikh! ikh!" makes them kneel; "Yáhh! Yáhh!" urges them on; "Hai! Hai!" induces caution, and so on.

†† Both these names of the Almighty are of kindred origin. The former is generally used when a woman is in danger of exposing her face by accident, or an animal of falling.

have been dug by the Caliph Harun. They are guarded by a Burj, or tower, which betrays symptoms of decay.

In our anxiety to rest we had strayed from the Damascus Caravan amongst the mountaineers of Shammar. Our Shaykh Mas'ud manifestly did not like the company; for shortly after three P.M. he insisted upon our striking the tent and rejoining the Hajj, which lay encamped about two miles distant in the western part of the basin. We loaded, therefore, and half an hour before sunset found ourselves in more congenial society. To my great disappointment, a stir was observable in the Caravan. I at once understood that another night-march was in store for us.

At six P.M. we again mounted, and turned towards the Eastern plain. A heavy shower was falling upon the Western hills, whence came damp and dangerous blasts. Between nine P.M. and the dawn of the next day we had a repetition of the last night's scenes, over a road so rugged and dangerous, that I wondered how men could prefer to travel in the darkness. But the camels of Damascus were now worn out with fatigue; they could not endure the sun, and our time was too precious for a halt. My night was spent perched upon the front bar of my Shugduf, encouraging the dromedary; and that we had not one fall excited my extreme astonishment. At five A.M. (Thursday, 8th September) we entered a wide plain thickly clothed with the usual thorny trees, in whose strong grasp many a Shugduf lost its covering, and not a few were dragged with their screaming inmates to the ground. About five hours afterwards we crossed a high ridge, and saw below us the camp of the Caravan, not more than two miles distant. As we approached it, a figure came running out to meet us. It was the boy Mohammed, who, heartily tired of riding a dromedary with his friend, and possibly hungry, hastened to inform my companion Abdullah that he would lead him to his Shugduf and to his son. The Shaykh, a little offended by the fact that for two days not a friend nor an acquaintance had taken the trouble to see or to inquire about him, received Mohammed roughly; but the youth, guessing the grievance, explained it away by swearing that he and all the party had tried in vain to find us. This wore the semblance of truth: it is almost impossible to come upon any one who strays from his place in so large and motley a body.

At eleven A.M. we had reached our station. It is about twenty-four miles from Al-Ghadir, and its direction is South-east ten degrees. It is called Al-Birkat (the Tank), from a large and now ruinous cistern built of hewn stone by the Caliph Harun.[†] The land belongs to the Utaybah Badawin, the bravest and most ferocious tribe in Al-Hijaz; and the citizens denote their dread of these banditti by asserting that to increase their courage they drink their enemy's blood.[††] My companions shook their heads when questioned upon the subject, and prayed that we might not become too well acquainted with them—an ill-omened speech!

The Pasha allowed us a rest of five hours at Al-Birkat: we spent them in my tent, which was crowded with Shaykh Abdullah's friends. To requite me for this inconvenience, he prepared for me an excellent water-pipe, a cup of coffee, which, untainted by cloves and by cinnamon, would have been delicious, and a dish of dry fruits. As we were now near the Holy City, all the Meccans were busy canvassing for lodgers and offering their services to pilgrims. Quarrels, too, were of hourly occurrence. In our party was an Arnaut, a white-bearded old man, so decrepit that he could scarcely stand, and yet so violent that no one could manage

[†] A "birkat" in this part of Arabia may be an artificial cistern or a natural basin; in the latter case it is smaller than a "ghadir." This road was a favourite with Harun al-Rashid, the pious tyrant who boasted that every year he performed either a pilgrimage or a crusade. The reader will find in d'Herbelot an account of the celebrated visit of Harun to the Holy Cities. Nor less known in Oriental history is the pilgrimage of Zubaydah Khatun (wife of Harun and mother of Amin) by this route.

[††] Some believe this literally, others consider it a phrase expressive of blood-thirstiness. It is the only suspicion of cannibalism, if I may use the word, now attaching to Al-Hijaz. Possibly the disgusting act may occasionally have taken place after a stern fight of more than usual rancour. Who does not remember the account of the Turkish officer licking his blood after having sabred the corpse of a Russian spy? It is said that the Mutayr and the Utaybah are not allowed to enter Meccah, even during the pilgrimage season.

him but his African slave, a brazen-faced little wretch about fourteen years of age. Words were bandied between this angry senior and Shaykh Mas'ud, when the latter insinuated sarcastically, that if the former had teeth he would be more intelligible. The Arnaut in his rage seized a pole, raised it, and delivered a blow which missed the camel-man, but, which brought the striker headlong to the ground. Mas'ud exclaimed, with shrieks of rage, "Have we come to this, that every old-woman Turk smites us?" Our party had the greatest trouble to quiet the quarrelers. The Arab listened to us when we threatened him with the Pasha. But the Arnaut, whose rage was "like red-hot steel," would hear nothing but our repeated declarations, that unless he behaved more like a pilgrim, we should be compelled to leave him and his slave behind.

At four P.M. we left Al-Birkat, and travelled Eastwards over rolling ground thickly wooded. There was a network of footpaths through the thickets, and clouds obscured the moon; the consequence was inevitable loss of way. About 2 A.M. we began ascending hills in a south-westerly direction, and presently we fell into the bed of a large rock-girt Fiumara, which runs from east to west. The sands were overgrown with saline and salsolaceous plants; the Coloquintida, which, having no support, spreads along the ground;† the Senna, with its small green leaf; the Rhazya stricta;†† and a large luxuriant variety of the Asclepias gigantea,††† cottoned over with mist and dew. At 6 A.M. (Sept. 9th) we left the Fiumara,

---

† Coloquintida is here used, as in most parts of the East, medicinally. The pulp and the seeds of the ripe fruit are scooped out, and the rind is filled with milk, which is exposed to the night air, and drunk in the morning.

†† Used in Arabian medicine as a refrigerant and tonic. It abounds in Sind and Afghanistan, where, according to that most practical of botanists, the lamented Dr. Stocks, it is called "ishwarg."

††† Here called Ashr. According to it Seetzen bears the long-sought apple of Sodom. Yet, if truth be told, the soft green bag is as unlike an apple as can be imagined; nor is the hard and brittle yellow rind of the ripe fruit a whit more resembling. The Arabs use the thick and acrid milk of the green bag with steel filings as a tonic, and speak highly of its effects; they employ it also to intoxicate or narcotise monkeys

and, turning to the West, we arrived about an hour afterwards at the station. Al-Zaribah, "the valley," is an undulating plain amongst high granite hills. In many parts it was faintly green; water was close to the surface, and rain stood upon the ground. During the night we had travelled about twenty-three miles, and our present station was south-east 56° from our last.

Having pitched the tent and eaten and slept, we prepared to perform the ceremony of *Al-Ihram* (assuming the pilgrim-garb), as Al-Zaribah is the Mikat, or the appointed place.† Between the noonday and the afternoon prayers a barber attended to shave our heads, cut our nails, and trim our mustachios. Then, having bathed and perfumed ourselves,—the latter is a questionable point,—we donned the attire, which is nothing but two new cotton cloths, each six feet long by three and a half broad, white, with narrow red stripes and fringes: in fact, the costume called *Al-Eddeh,* in the baths at Cairo.†† One of these sheets, technically termed the *Rida,* is thrown over the back, and, exposing the arm and shoulder, is

---

and other animals which they wish to catch. It is esteemed in Hindu medicine. The Nubians and Indians use the filaments of the fruit as tinder; they become white and shining as floss-silk. The Badawin also have applied it to a similar purpose. Our Egyptian travellers call it the "Silk-tree"; and in Northern Africa, where it abounds, Europeans make of it stuffing for the mattresses, which are expensive, and highly esteemed for their coolness and cleanliness. In Bengal a kind of gutta percha is made by boiling the juice. This weed, so common in the East, may one day become in the West an important article of commerce.

† "Al-Ihram" literally meaning "prohibition" or "making unlawful," equivalent to our "mortification," is applied to the ceremony of the toilette, and also to the dress itself. The vulgar pronounce the word "heram," or "l'ehram." It is opposed to "ih!al," "making lawful" or "returning to laical life." The further from Meccah it is assumed, provided that it be during the three months of Hajj, the greater is the religious merit of the pilgrim; consequently some come from India and Egypt in the dangerous attire. Those coming from the North assume the pilgrim-garb at or off the village of Rabigh.

†† These sheets are not positively necessary; any clean cotton cloth not sewn in any part will serve equally well. Servants and attendants expect the master to present them with an "ihram."

knotted at the right side in the style *Wishah.* The *Izar* is wrapped round the loins from waist to knee, and, knotted or tucked in at the middle, supports itself. Our heads were bare, and nothing was allowed upon the instep.† It is said that some clans of Arabs still preserve this religious but most uncomfortable costume; it is doubtless of ancient date, and to this day, in the regions lying west of the Red Sea, it continues to be the common dress of the people.

After the toilette, we were placed with our faces in the direction of Meccah, and ordered to say aloud,†† "I vow this Ihram of Hajj (the pilgrimage) and the Umrah (the Little pilgrimage) to Allah Almighty!" Having thus performed a two-bow prayer, we repeated, without rising from the sitting position, these words, "O Allah! verily I purpose the Hajj and the Umrah, then enable me to accomplish the two, and accept them both of me, and make both blessed to me!" Followed the *Talbiyat,* or exclaiming—

> "Here I am! O Allah! here am I—
> No partner hast Thou, here am I;
> Verily the praise and the grace are Thine, and the empire—
> No partner hast Thou, here am I†††!"

---

† Sandals are made at Meccah expressly for the pilgrimage: the poorer classes cut off the upper leathers of an old pair of shoes.

†† This Niyat, as it is technically called, is preferably performed aloud. Some authorities, however, direct it to be meditated *sotto-voce.*

††† "Talbiyat" is from form the word Labbayka ("here I am") in the cry—!"
	"Labbayk' Allahumma, Labbayk'!
(Labbayka)	Lá Sharika laka, Labbayk'!
	Inna 'l-hamda wa 'l ni'amata laka wa 'l mulk!
	La Sharika laka, Labbayk'!"

Some add, "Here I am, and I honour thee, I the son of thy two slaves: beneficence and good are all between thy hands." A single Talbiyah is a "Shart" or positive condition, and its repetition is a Sunnat or Custom of the Prophet. The "Talbiyat" is allowed in any language, but is preferred in Arabic. It has a few varieties; the form above given is the most common.

And we were warned to repeat these words as often as possible, until the conclusion of the ceremonies. Then Shaykh Abdullah, who acted as director of our consciences, bade us be good pilgrims, avoiding quarrels, immorality, bad language, and light conversation. We must so reverence life that we should avoid killing game, causing an animal to fly, and even pointing it out for destruction;† nor should we scratch ourselves, save with the open palm, lest vermin be destroyed, or a hair uprooted by the nail. We were to respect the sanctuary by sparing the trees, and not to pluck a single blade of grass. As regards personal considerations, we were to abstain from all oils, perfumes, and unguents; from washing the head with mallow or with lote leaves; from dyeing, shaving, cutting, or vellicating a single pile or hair; and though we might take advantage of shade, and even form it with upraised hands, we must by no means cover our sconces. For each infraction of these ordinances we must sacrifice a sheep;†† and it is commonly said by Moslems that none but the Prophet could be perfect in the intricacies of pilgrimage. Old Ali began with an irregularity: he declared that age prevented his assuming the garb, but that, arrived at Meccah, he would clear himself by an offering.

The wife and daughters of a Turkish pilgrim of our party assumed the Ihram at the same time as ourselves. They appeared dressed in white garments; and they had exchanged the Lisam, that coquettish fold of muslin which veils without concealing the lower part of the face, for a hideous mask, made of split, dried, and plaited palm-leaves, with two "bulls'-eyes" for light.††† I could not help laughing when these strange figures met my

---

† The object of these ordinances is clearly to inculcate the strictest observance of the "truce of God." Pilgrims, however, are allowed to slay, if necessary, "the five noxious," viz., a crow, a kite, a scorpion, a rat, and a biting dog.

†† The victim is sacrificed as a confession that the offender deems himself worthy of death: the offerer is not allowed to taste any portion of his offering.

††† The reason why this "ugly" must be worn, is, that a woman's veil during the pilgrimage ceremonies is not allowed to touch her face.

sight; and, to judge from the shaking of their shoulders, they were not less susceptible to the merriment which they had caused.

At three P.M. we left Al-Zaribah, travelling towards the South-West, and a wondrously picturesque scene met the eye. Crowds hurried along, habited in the pilgrim-garb, whose whiteness contrasted strangely with their black skins; their newly shaven heads glistening in the sun, and their long black hair streaming in the wind. The rocks rang with shouts of *Labbayk! Labbayk!* At a pass we fell in with the Wahhabis, accompanying the Baghdad Caravan, screaming "Here am I"; and, guided by a large loud kettle-drum, they followed in double file the camel of a standard-bearer, whose green flag bore in huge white letters the formula of the Moslem creed. They were wild-looking mountaineers, dark and fierce, with hair twisted into thin Dalik or plaits: each was armed with a long spear, a matchlock, or a dagger. They were seated upon coarse wooden saddles, without cushions or stirrups, a fine saddle-cloth alone denoting a chief. The women emulated the men; they either guided their own dromedaries, or, sitting in pillion, they clung to their husbands; veils they disdained, and their countenances certainly belonged not to a "soft sex." These Wahhabis were by no means pleasant companions. Most of them were followed by spare dromedaries, either unladen or carrying water-skins, fodder, fuel, and other necessaries for the march. The beasts delighted in dashing furiously through our file, which being lashed together, head and tail, was thrown each time into the greatest confusion. And whenever we were observed smoking, we were cursed aloud for Infidels and Idolaters.

Looking back at Al-Zaribah, soon after our departure, I saw a heavy nimbus settle upon the hill-tops, a sheet of rain being stretched between it and the plain. The low grumbling of thunder sounded joyfully in our ears. We hoped for a shower, but were disappointed by a dust-storm, which ended with a few heavy drops. There arose a report that the Badawin had attacked a party of Meccans with stones, and the news caused men to look exceeding grave.

At five P.M. we entered the wide bed of the Fiumara, down which we were to travel all night. Here the country falls rapidly towards the sea, as the increasing heat of the air, the direction of the watercourses, and signs of violence in the torrent-bed show. The Fiumara varies in breadth from a hundred and fifty feet to three-quarters of a mile: its course, I was told, is towards the South-West, and it enters the sea near Jeddah. The channel is a coarse sand, with here and there masses of sheet rock and patches of thin vegetation.

At about half-past five P.M. we entered a suspicious-looking place. On the right was a stony buttress, along whose base the stream, when there is one, swings; and to this depression was our road limited by the rocks and thorn trees which filled the other half of the channel. The left side was a precipice, grim and barren, but not so abrupt as its brother. Opposite us the way seemed barred by piles of hills, crest rising above crest into the far blue distance. Day still smiled upon the upper peaks, but the lower slopes and the Fiumara bed were already curtained with grey sombre shade.

A damp seemed to fall upon our spirits as we approached this Valley Perilous. I remarked that the voices of the women and children sank into silence, and the loud Labbayk of the pilgrims were gradually stilled. Whilst still speculating upon the cause of this phenomenon, it became apparent. A small curl of the smoke, like a lady's ringlet, on the summit of the right-hand precipice, caught my eye; and simultaneous with the echoing crack of the matchlock, a high-trotting dromedary in front of me rolled over upon the sands,—a bullet had split its heart,—throwing the rider a goodly somersault of five or six yards.

Ensued terrible confusion; women screamed, children cried, and men vociferated, each one striving with might and main to urge his animal out of the place of death. But the road being narrow, they only managed to jam the vehicles in a solid immovable mass. At every matchlock shot, a shudder ran through the huge body, as when the surgeon's scalpel touches some more sensitive nerve. The Irregular horsemen, perfectly useless, galloped up and down over the stones, shouting to and ordering one another. The Pasha of the army had his carpet spread at the foot of the left-hand precipice, and debated over his pipe with the officers what ought to be done. No good genius whispered "Crown the heights."

Then it was that the conduct of the Wahhabis found favour in my eyes. They came up, galloping their camels,—

"Torrents less rapid, and less rash,—"

with their elf-locks tossing in the wind, and their flaring matches casting a strange lurid light over their features. Taking up a position, one body began to fire upon the Utaybah robbers, whilst two or three hundred, dismounting, swarmed up the hill under the guidance of the Sharif Zayd. I had remarked this nobleman at Al-Madinah as a model specimen of the pure Arab. Like all Sharifs, he is celebrated for bravery, and has killed many with his own hand.† When urged at Al-Zaribah to ride into Meccah, he swore that he would not leave the Caravan till in sight of the walls; and, fortunately for the pilgrims, he kept his word. Presently the firing was heard far in our rear, the robbers having fled. The head of the column advanced, and the dense body of pilgrims opened out. Our forced halt was now exchanged for a flight. It required much management to steer our Desert-craft clear of danger; but Shaykh Mas'ud was equal to the occasion. That many were not, was evident by the boxes and baggage that strewed the shingles. I had no means of ascertaining the number of men killed and wounded: reports were contradictory, and exaggeration unanimous. The robbers were said to be a hundred and fifty in number; their object was plunder, and they would eat the shot camels. But their princi-

---

† The Sharifs are born and bred to fighting: the peculiar privileges of their caste favour their development of pugnacity. Thus, the modern diyah, or price of blood, being 800 dollars for a common Moslem, the chiefs demand for one of their number double that sum, with a sword, a camel, a female slave, and other items; and, if one of their slaves or servants be slain, a fourfold price. The rigorous way in which this custom is carried out gives the Sharif and his retainer great power among the Arabs. As a general rule, they are at the bottom of all mischief. It was a Sharif (Hosayn bin Ali) who tore down and trampled upon the British flag at Mocha; a Sharif (Abd al-Rahman of Waht) who murdered Captain Mylne near Lahedge. A page might be filled with the names of the distinguished ruffians

pal ambition was the boast, "We, the Utaybah, on such and such a night, stopped the Sultan's Mahmil one whole hour in the Pass"

At the beginning of the skirmish I had primed my pistols, and sat with them ready for use. But soon seeing that there was nothing to be done, and wishing to make an impression,—nowhere does Bobadil now "go down" so well as in the East,—I called aloud for my supper. Shaykh Nur, exanimate with fear, could not move. The boy Mohammed ejaculated only an "Oh, sir!" and the people around exclaimed in disgust, "By Allah, he eats!". Shaykh Abdullah, the Meccan, being a man of spirit, was amused by the spectacle. "Are these Afghan manners, Effendim?" he enquired from the Shugduf behind me. "Yes," I replied aloud, "in my country we always dine before an attack of robbers, because that gentry is in the habit of sending men to bed supperless." The Shaykh laughed aloud, but those around him looked offended. I thought the bravado this time *mal placé* but a little event which took place on my way to Jeddah proved that it was not quite a failure.

As we advanced, our escort took care to fire every large dry Asclepias, to disperse the shades which buried us. Again the scene became wondrous wild:—

> "Full many a waste I've wander'd o'er,
> Clomb many a crag, cross'd many a shore,
>   But, by my halidome,
> A scene so rude, so wild as this,
> Yet so sublime in barrenness,
> Ne'er did my wandering footsteps press,
>   Where'er I chanced to roam."

On either side were ribbed precipices, dark, angry, and towering above, till their summits mingled with the glooms of night; and between them formidable looked the chasm, down which our host hurried with shouts and discharges of matchlocks. The torch-smoke and the night-fires of flaming Asclepias formed a canopy, sable above and livid red below; it hung over our heads like a sheet, and divided the cliffs into two equal parts. Here the fire flashed fiercely from a tall thorn, that crackled and shot up showers of sparks into the air; there it died away in lurid gleams, which lit up a truly Stygian scene. As usual, however, the picturesque had its inconveniences. There was no path. Rocks, stone-banks, and trees obstructed our passage. The camels, now blind in darkness, then dazzled by a flood of light, stumbled frequently; in some places slipping down a steep descent, in others sliding over a sheet of mud. There were furious quarrels and fierce language between camel-men and their hirers, and threats to fellow-travellers; in fact, we were united in discord. I passed that night crying, "Hail! Hail!" switching the camel, and fruitlessly endeavouring to fustigate Mas'ud's nephew, who resolutely slept upon the water-bags. During the hours of darkness we made four or five halts, when we boiled coffee and smoked pipes; but man and beasts were beginning to suffer from a deadly fatigue.

Dawn (Saturday, Sept. 10th) found us still travelling down the Fiumara, which here is about a hundred yards broad. The granite hills on both sides were less precipitous; and the borders of the torrent-bed became natural quays of stiff clay, which showed a water-mark of from twelve to fifteen feet in height. In many parts the bed was muddy; and the moist places, as usual, caused accidents. I happened to be looking back at Shaykh Abdullah, who was then riding in old Ali bin Ya Sin's fine Shugduf; suddenly the camel's four legs disappeared from under him, his right side flattening the ground, and the two riders were pitched severally out of the smashed vehicle. Abdullah started up furious, and with great zest abused the Badawin, who were absent. "Feed these Arabs," he exclaimed, quoting a Turkish proverb, "and they will fire at Heaven!" But I observed that, when Shaykh Mas'ud came up, the citizen was only gruff.

We then turned Northward, and sighted Al-Mazik, more generally known as Wady Laymun, the Valley of Limes. On the right bank of the Fiumara stood the Meccan Sharif's state pavilion, green and gold: it was surrounded by his attendants, and he had prepared to receive the Pasha of the Caravan. We advanced half a mile, and encamped temporarily in a hill-girt bulge of the Fiumara bed. At eight A.M. we had travelled about twenty-four miles from Al-Zaribah, and the direction of our present station was South-west 50°.

Shaykh Mas'ud allowed us only four hours' halt; he wished to precede the main body. After breaking our fast joyously upon limes, pomegranates, and fresh dates, we sallied forth to admire the beauties of the place.

· · ·

We again mounted, and night completed our disappointment. About one A.M. I was aroused by general excitement. "Meccah! Meccah!" cried some voices; "The Sanctuary! O the Sanctuary!" exclaimed others; and all burst into loud "Labbayk," not unfrequently broken by sobs. I looked out from my litter, and saw by the light of the Southern stars the dim outlines of a large city, a shade darker than the surrounding plain.

JOHN L. STEPHENS

(1805–1852)

From *Incidents of Travel in Central America, Chiapas, and Yucatan*

It is a curious fact that some of the strongest travel writing of the nine-teenth century came from those with the weakest constitutions, as if those who survived a tenuous childhood could throw themselves into the unknown with ever greater abandon, clear-eyed curiosity, and dis-arming optimism. John Stephens possessed all these qualities in droves.

Stephens began to roam the globe in search of better health in 1834, going first to Europe, Egypt, Syria, and Russia. That first journey spawned two books, Incidents of Travel in Egypt, Arabia, Patraea, and the Holy Land, *followed by* Incidents of Travel in Greece, Turkey, Russia, and Poland. *Both were instant bestsellers in his native America and abroad. In 1839, Stephens set out on what was to be the most important and thrilling adventure of his life, a hunt for the ruins of the Mayan civilization in the jungles of Central America. He went with his friend Frederick Catherwood, whose magnificent and detailed drawings of the temples and artifacts of the Mayan world became the first visual renditions of many of these ancient cities. He and Cather-wood returned to the region several times, and Stephens's two volumes*

about his travels were again wildly popular. Stephens died some years
later in Panama, where he was overseeing the construction of a rail
line to span the isthmus.

In the following passage, Catherwood and Stephens go by mule to
Copan and are amazed by what they find when they begin to hack
away at the lush tropical forest growing over the mounds of the temple.

With an interest perhaps stronger than we had ever felt in wandering among the ruins of Egypt, we followed our guide, who, sometimes missing his way, with a constant and vigorous use of his machete, conducted us through the thick forest, among half-buried fragments, to fourteen monuments of the same character and appearance, some with more elegant designs, and some in workmanship equal to the finest monuments of the Egyptians; one displaced from its pedestal by enormous roots; another locked in the close embrace of branches of trees, and almost lifted out of the earth; another hurled to the ground, and bound down by huge vines and creepers; and one standing, with its altar before it, in a grove of trees which grew around it, seemingly to shade and shroud it as a sacred thing; in the solemn stillness of the woods, it seemed a divinity mourning over a fallen people. The only sounds that disturbed the quiet of this buried city were the noise of monkeys moving among the tops of the trees, and the cracking of dry branches broken by their weight. They moved over our heads in long and swift processions, forty or fifty at a time, some with little ones wound in their long arms, walking out to the end of boughs, and holding on with their hind feet or a curl of the tail, sprang to a branch of the next tree, and, with a noise like a current of wind, passed on into the depths of the forest. It was the first time we had seen these mockeries of humanity, and, with the strange monuments around us, they seemed like wandering spirits of the departed race guarding the ruins of their former habitations.

We returned to the base of the pyramidal structure, and ascended by regular stone steps, in some places forced apart by bushes and saplings, and in others thrown down by the growth of large trees, while some remained entire. In parts they were ornamented with sculptured figures and rows of death's heads. Climbing over the ruined top, we reached a terrace overgrown with trees, and, crossing it, descended by stone steps into an area so covered with trees that at first we could not make out its form, but which, on clearing the way with the machete, we ascertained to be a square, and with steps on all the sides almost as perfect as those of the Roman amphitheatre. The steps were ornamented with sculpture, and on the south side, about half way up, forced out of its place by roots, was a colossal head, evidently a portrait. We ascended these steps, and reached a broad terrace a hundred feet high, overlooking the river, and supported by the wall which we had seen from the opposite bank. The whole terrace was covered with trees, and even at this height from the ground were two gigantic Ceibas, or wild cotton-trees of India, above twenty feet in circumference, extending their half-naked roots fifty or a hundred feet around, binding down the ruins, and shading them with their wide-spreading branches. We sat down on the very edge of the wall, and strove in vain to penetrate the mystery by which we were surrounded. Who were the people that built this city? In the ruined cities of Egypt, even in the long-lost Petra, the stranger knows the story of the people whose vestiges are around him. America, say historians, was peopled by savages; but savages never reared these structures, savages never carved these stones. We asked the Indians who made them, and their dull answer was "Quien sabe?" "who knows?"

There were no associations connected with the place; none of those stirring recollections which hallow Rome, Athens, and

"The world's great mistress on the Egyptian plain,"

but architecture, sculpture, and painting, all the arts which embellish life, had flourished in this overgrown forest; orators, warriors, and statesmen, beauty, ambition, and glory, had lived and passed away, and none knew that such things had been, or could tell of their past existence. Books, the records of knowledge, are silent on this theme. The city was desolate. No remnant of this race hangs round the ruins, with traditions handed down from father to son, and from generation to generation. It lay before us like a shattered bark in the midst of the ocean, her masts gone, her name effaced, her crew perished, and none to tell whence she came, to whom she belonged, how long on her voyage, or what caused her destruction; her lost people to be traced only by some fancied resemblance in the construction of the vessel, and, perhaps, never to be known at all. The place where we sat, was it a citadel from which an unknown people had sounded the trumpet of war? or a temple for the worship of the God of peace? or did the inhabitants worship the idols made with their own hands, and offer sacrifices on the stones before them? All was mystery, dark, impenetrable mystery, and every circumstance increased it. In Egypt the colossal skeletons of gigantic temples stand in the unwatered sands in all the nakedness of desolation; here an immense forest shrouded the ruins, hiding them from sight, heightening the impression and moral effect, and giving an intensity and almost wildness to the interest.

Late in the afternoon we worked our way back to the mules, bathed in the clear river at the foot of the wall, and returned to the hacienda. Our grateful muleteer-boy had told of his dreadful illness, and the extraordinary cure effected by Mr. Catherwood;[1] and we found at the hacienda a ghastly-looking man, worn down by fever and ague, who begged us for "remedios." An old lady on a visit to the family, who had intended to go home that day, was waiting to be cured of a malady from which she had suffered twenty years. Our medicine-chest was brought out, and this converted the wife of the don into a patient also. Mr. C.'s reputation rose with the medicines he distributed; and in the course of the evening he had under his hands four or five women and as many men. We wanted very much to practice on the don, but he was cautious. The percussion caps of our pistols attracted the attention of the men; and we showed them the compass and other things, which made our friend at San Anto-

[1] He had a fever, for which Catherwood gave him a dose of "medicine."

nio suppose we were "very rich," and "had many ideas." By degrees we became on social terms with all the house except the master,[2] who found a congenial spirit in the muleteer. He had taken his ground, and was too dignified and obstinate to unbend. Our new friends made more room for our hammocks, and we had a better swing for the night.

In the morning we continued to astonish the people by our strange ways, particularly by brushing our teeth, an operation which, probably, they saw then for the first time. While engaged in this, the door of the house opened, and Don Gregorio appeared, turning his head away to avoid giving us a buenos dios. We resolved not to sleep another night under his shed, but to take our hammocks to the ruins, and, if there was no building to shelter us, to hang them up under a tree. My contract with the muleteer was to stop three days at Copan; but there was no bargain for the use of the mules during that time, and he hoped that the vexations we met with would make us go on immediately. When he found us bent on remaining, he swore he would not carry the hammocks, and would not remain one day over, but at length consented to hire the mules for that day.

Before we started a new party, who had been conversing some time with Don Gregorio, stepped forward, and said that he was the owner of "the idols"; that no one could go on the land without his permission; and handed me his title papers. This was a new difficulty. I was not disposed to dispute his title, but read his papers as attentively as if I meditated an action in ejectment; and he seemed relieved when I told him his title was good, and that, if not disturbed, I would make him a compliment at parting. Fortunately, he had a favour to ask. Our fame as physicians had reached the village, and he wished remedios for a sick wife. It was important to make him our friend; and, after some conversation, it was arranged that Mr. C., with several workmen whom we had hired, should go on to the ruins, as we intended, to make a lodgment there, while I would go to the village and visit his wife.

[2] Don Gregorio, a churlish host.

Our new acquaintance, Don Jose Maria Asebedo, was about fifty, tall, and well dressed; that is, his cotton shirt and pantaloons were clean; inoffensive, though ignorant; and one of the most respectable inhabitants of Copan. He lived in one of the best huts of the village, made of poles thatched with corn-leaves, with a wooden frame on one side for a bed, and furnished with a few pieces of pottery for cooking. A heavy rain had fallen during the night, and the ground inside the hut was wet. His wife seemed as old as he, and, fortunately, was suffering from a rheumatism of several years' standing. I say fortunately, but I speak only in reference to ourselves as medical men, and the honour of the profession accidentally confided to our hands. I told her that if it had been a recent affection, it would be more within the reach of art; but, as it was a case of old standing, it required time, skill, watching of symptoms, and the effect of medicine from day to day; and, for the present, I advised her to take her feet out of a puddle of water in which she was standing, and promised to consult Mr. Catherwood, who was even a better medico than I, and to send her a liniment with which to bathe her neck.

This over, Don Jose Maria accompanied me to the ruins, where I found Mr. Catherwood with the Indian workmen. Again we wandered over the whole ground in search of some ruined building in which we could take up our abode, but there was none. To hang up our hammocks under the trees was madness; the branches were still wet, the ground muddy, and again there was a prospect of early rain; but we were determined not to go back to Don Gregorio's. Don Mariano said that there was a hut near by, and conducted me to it. As we approached, we heard the screams of a woman inside, and, entering, saw her rolling and tossing on a bull's-hide bed, wild with fever and pain; and, starting to her knees at the sight of me, with her hands pressed against her temples, and tears bursting from her eyes, she begged me, for the love of God, to give her some remedios. Her skin was hot, her pulse very high; she had a violent intermitting fever. While inquiring into her symptoms, her husband entered the hut, a white man, about forty, dressed in a pair of dirty cotton drawers, with a nether garment hanging outside, a handkerchief tied around his head, and barefooted; and his name was *Don* Miguel. I told him that we wished to pass a few days among the ruins, and asked permission to stop at this hut. The woman, most happy at having a skilful physician near her, answered for him, and I returned to relieve Mr. Catherwood, and add another to his list of patients. The whole party escorted us to the hut, bringing along only the mule that carried the hammocks; and by the addition of Mr. C. to the medical corps, and a mysterious display of drawing materials and measuring rods, the poor woman's fever seemed frightened away.

The hut stood on the edge of a clearing, on the ground once covered by the city, with a stone fragment, hollowed out and used as a drinking-vessel for cattle, almost at the very door. The clearing was planted with corn and tobacco, and bounded on each side by the forest. The hut was about sixteen feet square, with a peaked roof, thatched with husks of Indian corn, made by setting in the ground two upright poles with crotches, in which another pole was laid to support the peak of the roof, and similar supports on each side, but only about four feet high. The gable end was the front, and one half of it was thatched with corn-leaves, while the other remained open. The back part was thatched, and piled up against it was Indian corn three ears deep. On one side the pile was unbroken, but on the other it was used down to within three or four feet of the ground. In the corner in front was the bed of Don Miguel and his wife, protected by a bull's hide fastened at the head and side. The furniture consisted of a stone roller for mashing corn, and a comal or earthen griddle for baking tortillas; and on a rude shelf over the bed were two boxes, which contained the wardrobe and all the property of Don Miguel and his wife, except Bartalo, their son and heir an overgrown lad of twenty, whose naked body seemed to have burst up out of a pair of boy's trousers, disdaining a shirt, his stomach swollen by a distressing liver complaint, and that and his livid face clouded with dirt. There was only room enough for one hammock, and, in fact, the cross-sticks were not strong enough to support two men. The pile of corn which had been used down was just high and broad enough for a bed; by consent, I took this for my sleeping-place, and Mr. Catherwood hung up his hammock; we

were so glad at being relieved from the churlish hospitality of Don Gregorio, and so near the ruins, that all seemed snug and comfortable.

After a noonday meal I mounted the luggage-mule, with only a halter
to hold her, and, accompanied by Augustin[3] on foot, set out for Don Gregorio's, for the purpose of bringing over the luggage. The heavy rains had
swollen the river, and Augustin was obliged to strip himself in order to
ford it. Don Gregorio was not at home; and the muleteer, as usual, glad
of a difficulty, said that it was impossible to cross the river with a cargo
that day. Regularly, instead of helping us in our little difficulties, he did
all that he could to increase them. He knew that, if we discharged him,
we could get no mules in Copan except by sending off two days' journey;
that we had no one on whom we could rely to send; and that the delay
would be at least a week. Uncertain at what moment it might be advisable to leave, and not wishing to be left destitute, I was compelled to hire
him to remain, at a price which was considered so exorbitant that it gave
me a reputation for having "mucha plata," which, though it might be useful at home, I did not covet at Copan; and, afraid to trust me, the rascal
stipulated for daily payments. At that time I was not acquainted with the
cash system of business prevailing in the country. The barbarians are not
satisfied with your custom unless you pay them besides; and the whole,
or a large portion, must be in advance. I was accidentally in arrears to the
muleteer; and, while I was congratulating myself on this only security for
his good behaviour, he was torturing himself with the apprehension that I
did not mean to pay at all.

In the mean time it began to rain; and, settling my accounts with the
señora, thanking her for her kindness, leaving an order to have some
bread baked for the next day, and taking with me an umbrella and a blue
bag, contents unknown, belonging to Mr. Catherwood, which he had
particularly requested me to bring, I set out on my return. Augustin followed with a tin teapot, and some other articles for immediate use.
Entering the woods, the umbrella struck against the branches of the
trees, and frightened the mule; and, while I was endeavouring to close it,

[3] Their servant; a French "Spainard."

she fairly ran away with me. Having only a halter, I could not hold her; and, knocking me against the branches, she ran through the woods, splashed into the river, missing the fording-place, and never stopped till she was breast-deep. The river was swollen and angry, and the rain pouring down. Rapids were foaming a short distance below. In the effort to restrain her, I lost Mr. Catherwood's blue bag, caught at it with the handle of the umbrella, and would have saved it if the beast had stood still; but as it floated under her nose she snorted and started back. I broke the umbrella in driving her across; and, just as I touched the shore, saw the bag floating toward the rapids, and Augustin, with his clothes in one hand and the teapot in the other, both above his head, steering down the river after it. Supposing it to contain some indispensable drawing materials, I dashed among the thickets on the bank in the hope of intercepting it, but became entangled among branches and vines. I dismounted and tied my mule, and was two or three minutes working my way to the river, where I saw Augustin's clothes and the teapot, but nothing of him, and, with the rapids roaring below, had horrible apprehensions. It was impossible to continue along the bank; so, with a violent effort, I jumped across a rapid channel to a ragged island of sand covered with scrub bushes, and, running down to the end of it, saw the whole face of the river and the rapids, but nothing of Augustin. I shouted with all my strength, and, to my inexpressible relief, heard an answer, but, in the noise of the rapids, very faint; presently he appeared in the water, working himself around a point, and hauling upon the bushes. Relieved about him, I now found myself in a quandary. The jump back was to higher ground, the stream a torrent, and, the excitement over, I was afraid to attempt it. It would have been exceedingly inconvenient for me if Augustin had been drowned. Making his way through the bushes and down to the bank opposite with his dripping body, he stretched a pole across the stream, by springing upon which I touched the edge of the bank, slipped, but hauled myself up by the bushes with the aid of a lift from Augustin. All this time it was raining very hard; and now I had forgotten where I tied my mule. We were several minutes looking for her; and wishing everything but good luck to the old bag, I mounted. Augustin, principally because he could carry them more conveniently on his back, put on his clothes.

Reaching the village, I took shelter in the hut of Don Jose Maria, while Augustin, being in that happy state that cannot be made worse, continued through the rain. There was no one in the hut but a little girl, and the moment the rain abated I followed. I had another stream to cross, which was also much swollen, and the road was flooded. The road lay through a thick forest; very soon the clouds became blacker than ever; on the left was a range of naked mountains, the old stone quarries of Copan, along which the thunder rolled fearfully, and the lightning wrote angry inscriptions on its sides. An English tourist in the United States admits the superiority of our thunder and lightning. I am pertinacious on all points of national honour, but concede this in favour of the tropics. The rain fell as if floodgates were opened from above; and while my mule was slipping and sliding through the mud I lost my road. I returned some distance, and was again retracing my steps, when I met a woman, barefooted, and holding her dress above her knees, who proved to be my rheumatic patient, the wife of Don Jose Maria. While inquiring the road, I told her that she was setting at naught the skill of the physician, and added, what I believed to be very true, that she need not expect to get well under our treatment. I rode on some distance, and again lost my way. It was necessary to enter the woods on the right. I had come out by a footpath which I had not noticed particularly. There were cattle-paths in every direction, and within the line of a mile I kept going in and out, without hitting the right one. Several times I saw the print of Augustin's feet, but soon lost them in puddles of water, and they only confused me more; at length I came to a complete stand-still. It was nearly dark; I did not know which way to turn; and as Mr. Henry Pelham did when in danger of drowning in one of the gutters of Paris, I stood still and hallooed. To my great joy, I was answered by a roar from Augustin, who had been lost longer than I, and was in even greater tribulation. He had the teapot in his hand, the stump of an unlighted cigar in his mouth, was plastered with mud from his head to his heels, and altogether a most distressful object. We compared notes, and, selecting a path, shouting as we went, our united voices were answered by barking dogs and Mr. Catherwood, who, alarmed at our absence, and apprehending what had happened, was coming out with Don Miguel to look for us. I had no change of clothes, and therefore stripped and rolled myself up in a blanket in the style of a North American Indian. All the evening peals of thunder crashed over our heads, lightning illuminated the dark forest and flashed through the open hut, the rain fell in torrents, and Don Miguel said that there was a prospect of being cut off for several days from all communication with the opposite side of the river and from our luggage. Nevertheless, we passed the evening with great satisfaction, smoking cigars of Copan tobacco, the most famed in Central America, of Don Miguel's own growing and his wife's own making.

. . .

At daylight the clouds still hung over the forest; as the sun rose they cleared away; our workmen made their appearance, and at nine o'clock we left the hut. The branches of the trees were dripping wet, and the ground very muddy. Trudging once more over the district which contained the principal monuments, we were startled by the immensity of the work before us, and very soon we concluded that to explore the whole extent would be impossible. Our guides knew only of this district; but having seen columns beyond the village, a league distant, we had reason to believe that others were strewed in different directions, completely buried in the woods, and entirely unknown. The woods were so dense that it was almost hopeless to think of penetrating them. The only way to make a thorough exploration would be to cut down the whole forest and burn the trees. This was incompatible with our immediate purposes, might be considered taking liberties, and could only be done in the dry season. After deliberation, we resolved first to obtain drawings of the sculptured columns. Even in this there was great difficulty. The designs were very complicated, and so different from anything Mr. Catherwood had ever seen before as to be perfectly unintelligible. The cutting was in very high relief, and required a strong body of light to bring up the figures; and the foliage was so thick, and the shade so deep, that drawing was impossible.

After much consultation, we selected one of the "idols," and determined to cut down the trees around it, and thus lay it open to the rays of the sun. Here again was difficulty. There was no axe; and the only instrument which the Indians possessed was the machete, or chopping-knife, which varies in form in different sections of the country; wielded with one hand, it was useful in clearing away shrubs and branches, but almost harmless upon large trees; and the Indians, as in the days when the Spaniards discovered them, applied to work without ardour, carried it on with little activity, and, like children, were easily diverted from it. One hacked into a tree, and, when tired, which happened very soon, sat down to rest, and another relieved him. While one worked there were always several looking on. I remembered the ring of the woodman's axe in the forests at home, and wished for a few long-sided Green Mountain boys. But we had been buffeted into patience, and watched the Indians while they hacked with their machetes, and even wondered that they succeeded so well. At length the trees were felled and dragged aside, a space cleared around the base, Mr. C.'s frame set up, and he set to work. I took two Mestitzoes, Bruno and Francisco, and, offering them a reward for every new discovery, with a compass in my hand set out on a tour of exploration. Neither had seen "the idols" until the morning of our first visit, when they followed in our train to laugh at los Ingleses; but very soon they exhibited such an interest that I hired them. Bruno attracted my attention by his admiration, as I supposed, of my person; but I found it was of my coat, which was a long shooting-frock, with many pockets; and he said that he could make one just like it except the skirts. He was a tailor by profession, and in the intervals of a great job upon a roundabout jacket, worked with his machete. But he had an inborn taste for the arts. As we passed through the woods, nothing escaped his eye, and he was professionally curious touching the costumes of the sculptured figures. I was struck with the first development of their antiquarian taste. Fran-

cisco found the feet and legs of a statue, and Bruno a part of the body to
match, and the effect was electric upon both. They searched and raked
up the ground with their machetes till they found the shoulders, and set
it up entire except the head; and they were both eager for the possession
of instruments with which to dig and find this remaining fragment.

It is impossible to describe the interest with which I explored these
ruins. The ground was entirely new; there were no guide-books or guides;
the whole was a virgin soil. We could not see ten yards before us, and
never knew what we should stumble upon next. At one time we stopped-
to cut away branches and vines which concealed the face of a monument, and then to dig around and bring to light a fragment, a sculptured
corner of which protruded from the earth. I leaned over with breathless
anxiety while the Indians worked, and an eye, an ear, a foot, or a hand
was disentombed; and when the machete rang against the chiselled
stone, I pushed the Indians away, and cleared out the loose earth with
my hands. The beauty of the sculpture, the solemn stillness of the
woods, disturbed only by the scrambling of monkeys and the chattering
of parrots, the desolation of the city, and the mystery that hung over it, all
created an interest higher, if possible, than I had ever felt among the
ruins of the Old World. After several hours' absence I returned to Mr.
Catherwood, and reported upward of fifty objects to be copied.

I found him not so well pleased as I expected with my report. He was
standing with his feet in the mud, and was drawing with his gloves on, to
protect his hands from the moschetoes. As we feared, the designs were
so intricate and complicated, the subjects so entirely new and unintelligible, that he had great difficulty in drawing. He had made several
attempts, both with the camera lucida[4] and without, but failed to satisfy
himself or even me, who was less severe in criticism. The "idol" seemed
to defy his art; two monkeys on a tree on one side appeared to be laughing at him, and I felt discouraged and despondent. In fact, I made up my

[4] A camera lucida, through the use of a mirror or prism, reflected an image onto a
flat surface so that it could be traced.

mind, with a pang of regret, that we must abandon the idea of carrying away any materials for antiquarian speculation, and must be content with having seen them ourselves. Of that satisfaction nothing could deprive us. We returned to the hut with our interest undiminished, but sadly out of heart as to the result of our labours.

SVEN HEDIN

(1865–1952)

From *My Life as an Explorer*

Perhaps more than anyone else in the last decade of the nineteenth century, Swedish geographer, explorer, and scholar Sven Hedin embodied the spirit of adventure. The more mysterious, dangerous, or seemingly impossible the journey, the more it thrilled him. These words, written as he prepared a 1897 journey across "the murderous labyrinth" of the Lop-nor desert in central Asia, say a great deal about his indomitable and exuberant personality: "Not wishing to return to Khotan, my headquarters, along roads that I knew already, I decided to take the long, roundabout route, across the Lop-nor, in the east, and then ride back to Khotan along the southern road, once traversed by Marco Polo. It was a route of some twelve hundred miles. Our provisions were used up; but we could live on the same food as the natives. I had not brought any maps of the eastern regions; but I was prepared to make new ones myself. I had left my Chinese passport in Khotan, but we might possibly manage without it. . . . [Then] Temir Bek, the chieftain of Shah-yar, asked to see my Chinese passport. As it was impossible for me to show it, he declared that the road to the east was closed to us. But we outwitted him, and escaped surreptitiously into the thickets of the Tarim, leaving no trace."

After five long expeditions crisscrossing Asia and the Middle East, Hedin had single-handedly surveyed many of Asia's "blank spaces" on the map of the world. In 1897 the Royal Geographic Society awarded Hedin a Founder's Medal, their highest honor.

In 1899, in the tradition of many Western adventure-seekers before and after, Hedin tried to slip into Tibet and all the way to Lhasa disguised as a pilgrim. It was a wild and stormy journey. He didn't pull it off, but part of the charm of this excerpt is his obvious delight in the intrigue and high drama of his situation.

Our new headquarters, 16,800 feet high, was designated Number 44. From there we were to start our wild ride toward Lhasa. I had intended to rest a week, for the sake of the animals, but Sirkin having noticed, near by, fresh footprints of a man leading a horse, I decided to break camp immediately.[1] Were we already being watched? I also decided that only Shereb Lama and Shagdur should accompany me. This was hard on Cherdon, who, too, was of the Lamaist faith; but our headquarters needed every possible defense in case the Tibetans should use armed force against us.

We were three Buriat[2] pilgrims, bound for Lhasa. Our caravan was to be as light and mobile as possible, only five mules and four horses, all newly shod for the trip. Rice, flour, toasted flour, dried meat, and Chinese brick tea constituted our provisions. My Mongolian cloak, ox-blood red, had secret pockets for my aneroid, compass, watch, note-book, and a book in which I sketched a map of the route. In my left boot was a pocket for the thermometer. I also took shaving-utensils, a lantern, some

[1] Hedin and his Mongolian friends were already in Tibet at this point, and are in constant fear of being attacked by horse thieves or turned back by Tibetan guards.

[2] The men with Hedin came from Buriat, a province of Russia adjacent to Mongolia.

candles, matches, an axe, Mongolian pots and pans, and ten silver *yam-bas*. Two Mongolian leather cases held most of these things. I wore a Chinese skull-cap, with ear-laps, and round my neck a rosary, with one hundred and eight beads, and a copper case containing an image of Buddha. A dagger, chop-sticks, a fire-steel, etc., hung in my girdle. We also had furs and blankets of Mongolian make, but no beds. The smallest of our tents was to shelter us.

On the last evening I addressed the men. Sirkin was appointed commander of headquarters, and received the keys to the boxes of silver. If we were not back within two and a half months, he was to return to Charkhlik and Kashgar[3] with the whole caravan. Twenty ravens circled round our tents. Night came and we went to bed.

At sunrise, on July 27, Shagdur roused me. I shall never forget that day. Off for Lhasa! Whether we succeeded or not, the experience would be something extraordinary. If successful, we would see the Holy City, unvisited by Europeans since Huc and Gabet, two French abbés, had spent two months there, in 1847, or fifty-four years before. And if we failed, we would be entirely at the mercy of the Tibetans, becoming their prisoners, with no inkling of how that captivity might end. However, when Shagdur woke me, I rose eagerly to the great adventure; and in less than a quarter of an hour, I was a thorough Mongol, from head to foot.

At the last moment, it was decided that Ordek should accompany us for a day or two, in order to guard our animals at the camp, and thus allow us a good sleep before our night-vigils began. I rode my white horse, Shagdur his yellow one, Shereb Lama the smallest mule, and Ordek one of the other horses. Malenki and Yolbars were to go along. Yolbars had once been lacerated by a boar; he was the largest and the wildest of our dogs.

When everything was ready, and we were already in the saddle, I asked Shereb Lama if he preferred to stay at headquarters.

"No, never!" was his answer.

---

[3] Cities in western China.

We said our farewells. Those we left behind thought that they would never see us again. Sirkin turned away and wept. It was a solemn moment; but, secure in the protection of the Eternal, my calm was unshaken.

We went down the valley at great speed. Hunters had recently been camping on the shore of its stream. The skeleton of a yak lay there. A bear had been foraging about. We rode southeastwards. At an open spring we made our camp. The animals were released to graze, and Ordek tended them. We gave our blessing to the moon that illuminated the silent wilderness, but went early to sleep in the narrow tent.

On the second day, we rode twenty-four miles across fairly level ground, as far as two small lakes, one of them salt, the other of fresh water. Tent was pitched on the narrow strip of land between the lakes. It was a lovely evening. Seated outdoors before the fire, I underwent treatment by Shagdur and Shereb Lama. The former shaved my head, and even my moustache, till I was as smooth as a billiard-ball; the latter rubbed a mixture of fat, soot, and brown pigment into me. I became almost frightened at the sight of myself in my polished watchcase, my only mirror. We were in high spirits, laughing and chatting like schoolboys.

We ate and had tea by the fire, and went to rest early. The animals were grazing on the shore, two hundred paces away. Ordek watched over them. In the evening a storm blew up. At midnight Ordek put his head inside the tent, and said: "There is a man."

We rushed out with the two rifles and revolver that constituted our arsenal. The tempest howled. The moon spread a pale light amid dark, flying clouds. On a small hill to the southwest, we perceived two galloping horsemen, urging two free horses before them. Shagdur directed a few shots at them, but they disappeared in the dark.

What was to be done? First we counted our animals. There were seven of them. My white horse and Shagdur's yellow one were missing. It was evident from the footprints that one of the thieves had stolen upon the outermost horses and frightened them down to the shore, where two mounted Tibetans had taken them in charge. They had been lying in wait for us like wolves, and were assisted by the storm. I was furious at this skulking attack, and my first impulse was to pursue them night and day. But could we leave our camp and the rest of the animals? Perhaps we were surrounded by a whole band of robbers. We lit the fire, and our pipes, and sat in conversation until dawn. Peace was gone. Our hands were on our daggers. Sunrise found Ordek weeping. He was to go back to headquarters alone. On a leaf torn from my note-book, I wrote Sirkin to strengthen the guard.

Afterwards we learned that Ordek had arrived half dead at headquarters. He had sneaked like a cat in hollows and river-beds, taking every shadow for a robber, and two docile wild asses for hostile horsemen. And when at last he reached the camp, he came near being shot by the guard. When the others heard that we had been attacked by robbers, after only two days' journey, their fears grew, and they were convinced we would never come back alive.

We continued southeast; and the lone Ordek, after helping us load the beasts, disappeared. We came upon a huge herd of yaks on a plain. Were they tame? No; they fled. We pitched our tent in open terrain, and I gathered yak-droppings for the fire. From this moment on, not a word of Russian was to be spoken, only Mongolian. Shagdur was ordered to act the part of our leader. I was his servant, and he was to treat me as a servant in the presence of Tibetans.

I slept till eight o'clock in the evening. Then Shagdur and Shereb Lama came driving our seven animals up to the tent. They were in a serious mood; for they had seen three Tibetan horsemen, who were on the lookout. The animals were immediately tethered in the lee of the tent, the entrance of which was open. Yolbars was tied beyond the animals, and Malenki to windward of the tent. The night was divided into three watches. Mine was the first, from nine o'clock to twelve; Shagdur's the second, from twelve to three; and Shereb Lama's the last, to six o'clock.

Thus my two comrades went to sleep while I stood watch. I walked from Yolbars to Malenki, and back, and alternated between playing with them and stroking the exhausted horses and mules. At nine-thirty an infernal storm broke—coal-black clouds, lightning and thunder, and a rattling, pouring rain. I took refuge in the entrance to the tent. The rain battered the canvas, and a fine drizzle sifted through. I lit my pipe and the candle in the lantern, and took out my note-book. But every ten minutes I patrolled the space between the dogs. The rain splashed dully and monotonously. It ran in jets from the animals' manes and tails, and from the pack-saddles. It ran from my skin-coat. The Chinese cap stuck to my bald head like glue.

I heard a plaintive sound in the distance, and hurried out. "Oh," thought I, "that is only Yolbars, expressing anger at the rain." My eyelids grew heavy. A thunderbolt roused me. The dogs growled, and I went out again. There was a clacking and swishing, as I trod in the mud. The hours seemed endless. Would my spell never come to an end? But at last the midnight-hour struck. I was just about to wake Shagdur, when the two dogs began to bark furiously. Shereb Lama woke up and rushed out. We took our arms, and all three of us stole away to leeward. The tramping of horses was audible. There were horsemen near by, and we hurried in their direction. But then they disappeared, and again all was quiet. The rain beat the ground. I lay down in my wet clothes. For a while, I heard the splashing steps of Shagdur in the wet; but then I fell sound asleep.

We broke camp at daybreak, crossed a ridge of the pass, entered a beaten path, saw many old camping-places, but no people, and halted again on a strip of land between two small lakes. As soon as camp was made, two of us lay down to sleep. We tethered the animals as on the night before, and I began my watch. Merciless rain fell all night long. One mule tore herself loose, and trotted off to the pasturage. I followed. At least she kept me awake. After many vain attempts, I managed to seize her halter, and tied her up.

On July 31, we set out in a pouring rain. It made us and our animals glisten. It dripped and spouted in streams. The road became wider. No doubt it led to Lhasa. We followed the trail of a large yak-caravan across five small passes. The yak-caravan was encamped on the roadside. Shereb Lama went up to them. The travellers were Tanguts from Kumbum on their way to Lhasa. They questioned Shereb Lama about us and our errand. Meanwhile, our dogs and theirs began to fight. I felt sorry for the dogs that got into a scuffle with Yolbars.

A little further on, we encamped in a glen, quite close to a Tibetan tent, where a young man and two women were living. The owner came home soon. We invited him to our tent, and he gave us an armful of yak-droppings and a wooden vessel, with milk. His name was Sampo Singi, and the place was Gom-jima. Sampo Singi was black with dirt, bare-headed, had long hair, no trousers, yet sat down, right in the wet, outside the tent. He took snuff offered by Shereb Lama, and after sneezing about a hundred times asked whether there used to be pepper in our snuff. He thought it was nice of us, who lived so far away, to make a pilgrimage to Lhasa. We were still eight days distant from there.

All of a sudden Shagdur roared at me to drive our animals in, and I obeyed straightway. The sun went down and the moon peeped out. But during the night it poured again. I felt secure in the vicinity of the nomads.

The next morning, Sampo Singi and one of the women brought us sheep-fat, sour and sweet milk, cheese-powder and cream, and a sheep. He would not accept money; but we had a piece of blue Chinese silk, over which the woman nearly went crazy. The man killed the sheep by choking it; he wound a strap around its nose, and thrust his thumb and index-finger in its nostrils. Then he slaughtered it. We allowed him to retain the skin. Thereupon we took leave of the kind nomads, threw ourselves into our saddles, and rode on.

At the same moment the rain began again. It poured from the sky in jets, and it was like riding through dense clusters of glass. A big body of water was dimly seen through the mist. At first we believed it to be a lake; but upon reaching the shore, we found a gigantic river, the yellow-grey, thick, muddy water-masses of which rolled south-west with a hollow and sinister roar. I knew at once that it was the Sachu-tsangpo, which Bonvalet and Rockhill[4] had once crossed. The opposite (left) bank was not visible at all. The road to Lhasa had taken us down to the right bank. But where was the ford? Before one could say Jack Robinson, Shereb Lama led the way into the river, leading the pack-mules. Shagdur and I followed.

In the middle of the river we halted for a minute on a sand-bank, in water about a foot deep. From there, neither the right nor the left bank could be seen. The water rolled by in great volume, seething and rumbling. Owing to the constant rain, the river was rising rapidly. If we stayed too long, we risked being cut off in both directions. Shereb Lama went on. It began to look bad when the water rose above the root of his little mule's tail. And now one of the pack-mules slipped. The two Mongol boxes tied to her back acted as cork-cushions and kept her afloat. The swift current swept her along at breakneck speed. I thought she was lost. Only her head and the edges of the boxes were visible above the water. She swam, however, and after a while touched ground again. Far away she righted herself and scrambled up on the left bank.

Lama rode on alone. The water got deeper and deeper. We called out to him at the top of our lungs; but he continued, bold and fearless. The rain beat the river; all was water. I rode last, and my horse fell behind. I saw the other two, and the pack-animals, rising above the surface of the water. I had a glimpse of the left shore. They managed to make it safely. I dug my heels into my horse. But we happened to strike a little below the ford, and sank deeper and deeper. I felt dizzy, as the water filled my boots. Presently it rose above my knees and the saddle. I loosened my girdle and pulled off my skin coat. Lama and Shagdur shouted and pointed; but in the roar of the water I did not hear them. Now it reached my waist. Now I saw no more of my horse than his head and neck. I prepared to throw myself from the saddle and let go of the horse. But at that very moment he began to swim. Involuntarily I grasped his mane. He was

---

[4] Almost certainly the French geographer Gabriel Benvalot and the English explorer William Woodville Rockhill, both of whom ventured into Tibet.

carried along by the current, and almost choked. But the next moment he touched bottom, got his footing, and heaved himself onto the shore. I never experienced a worse river-crossing in Asia. It was nothing less than a miracle that no one was drowned. Neither Shagdur nor Shereb Lama could swim.

Our little caravan looked tragi-comic in the teeming rain. Lama, who always led the way, continued as though the river had not existed. I pulled off my boots, poured the water out, and hung them behind my saddle. It rained heavily, and everything was soaking-wet. The water streamed out of the two boxes.

At last our honourable monk stopped in a field, where there were yak-droppings. By scraping away the wettest layer, we managed after much trouble to ignite the cakes. And when the fire was burning properly, in spite of the rain sizzling in the flames, I undressed, bit by bit, and wrung the water out of my Mongolian clothes. Had any Tibetans happened by, they would have been dumbfounded at the sight of my white body.

Night came, with its cloak of darkness, its rattling rain, and its mysterious sounds. I heard steps, the tramp of horses, human voices, shouts, and rifle-shots. I waked Shagdur at twelve o'clock sharp, slipped into the tent, and lay down in my still-wet clothes. I was so tired that I almost longed to be captured and get a thorough rest.

On August 2, it did not rain. We entered populated regions. We rode past two nomad-tents, where there were sheep and yaks, and passed a caravan of three hundred yaks, laden with brick tea for the famous Tashi-lunpo monastery. The drivers built their fires close to the roadside; and as we rode past, the men approached us, asking many questions. One old man pointed at me and said, "peling" (European). The region was called Amdo-mochu.

We proceeded to a spring and a field, and spread our clothes out on the ground in the evening sun. But then came a hail-storm and a downpour, and we stowed everything in the tent. The thunder pealed with a ringing sound, strangely reminiscent of church-bells.

The next morning I enjoyed a complete rest. I was waked at nine

o'clock by the other two, who advised me to take a look at the tea-cara-
van. It was really amusing. The men were all afoot, their rifles on their
shoulders. They looked like robbers, every one of them black, men as
well as yaks. They whistled, shouted, and sang.

We stayed there all day to get dry. I filled my boots with warm, dry
sand, to get the moisture out of them. While the animals grazed, we took
turns in sleeping. The night was clear, the moon was up, and the stars
twinkled.

The fourth of August saw us on the main road to Lhasa. We were constantly passing nomads' tents and herds, meeting large caravans, and riding past others. And now we also passed cairns of holy *mani* stones. We
stopped for the night, and a young Tibetan dropped in to see us.

On the fifth, we rode twenty and a half miles, brushing past the Tso-
nek (the Black Lake), where tents and herds were numerous, till at last
we reached a plain, on which there were twelve tents. There we established our Camp No. 53, having covered one hundred and sixty-two
miles since leaving headquarters.

AT DUSK, THREE Tibetans came walking toward our tent, and Shereb
Lama and Shagdur went out to meet them. They conversed for a long
time, and it was dark in every sense when my two comrades returned.
One of the Tibetans had told them, in a magisterial tone, that three days
before a messenger had come from a yak-hunter in the north, who
reported having seen an enormous caravan proceeding toward Lhasa.

"Are you associated with them?" he asked. "Tell the truth. Remember
that you are a lama."

Shereb Lama's knees trembled, and he stated the facts, without mentioning my presence. But Shagdur assured me that the magisterial
Tibetan had several times used the expression "shved peling," or
"Swedish European." The pilgrims from Temirlik or Charkhlik had probably ascertained my nationality through their questioning, though none of
them had the slightest knowledge of Sweden. They had only very hazy

ideas about China, British India, and Russia. Shagdur thought that Shereb Lama had betrayed us, but I could not share his suspicions. And even if it were true, all is now forgotten and forgiven. The Tibetan had finally said: "You will stay here to-morrow."

We sat up long, pondering over our prospects. All through the night, watch-fires surrounded our tents at a little distance.

Shortly after daybreak, three other Tibetans came to our tent. I always wore blue Mongolian eye-glasses. The newcomers asked to see my eyes, and were much surprised to find them as dark as their own. Their wish to see our weapons was granted with pleasure. After that lesson they backed towards their horses.

A while later, an old white-haired lama and three other men visited us. The former asked a number of questions about our headquarters, and informed us that couriers had been sent to Kamba Bombo, the Governor of Nakchu. We were prisoners until his instructions came.

The next number on the day's program was not reassuring. Fifty-three horsemen, in red, black, or grey cloaks, wearing high white hats or red bandannas around their heads, and armed with spears, lances, swords, and muskets, decorated with streamers, gathered at a tent-settlement a few hundred yards away. They dismounted, held a consultation by a fire, right in the rain, and then sprang into their saddles. Seven of them rode east on the road to Nakchu, two went south along the main road to Lhasa. The rest galloped off, making straight for our tent, emitting wild war-cries, and swinging their swords or muskets above their heads. Shereb Lama believed that our hours were numbered. We took our stand in front of the tent, with finger on trigger. Like an avalanche the Tibetans rushed forward. The hoofs of the horses smacked in the wet. When so close that the nearest horses splashed us, they divided into two squads, and swung back in two wide curves to their starting-point.

Having repeated this warlike manœuvre twice, they dismounted and shot at a target. They evidently intended to inspire us with awe. Finally they rode toward the northwest, and I wondered if they would dare to attack our headquarters.

All day long new visitors came. They brought us little gifts of fat, milk, or sour milk, and none of them would accept payment. During a shower we had four fellows in our tent, where we sat packed like sardines. But when a small stream of rain-water found its way into our shelter, I sent them out to dig a ditch around the tent. In the evening we counted thirty-seven watch-fires around us, faintly gleaming through the rain.

The next day new spies arrived. One of them presented us with an armful of yak-droppings and a bellows, and told us that Lhasa was five days off, but that the mounted postman made the journey in a day. The district where we were was named Yallok. Our seven pack-animals had been led away, probably to prevent our flight. We saw horsemen in every direction, riding singly or in squads. At times the place swarmed with mounted, armed men. It looked like a mobilization. We were but three against this superior force. We were prisoners and in the midst of a great adventure.

On the morning of August 8, five men came up and presented us with a sheep. A message had arrived that Kamba Bombo, the All-Highest, was himself on his way to see us. Shereb Lama was afraid that the Governor would recognize him. By way of punishment for a dereliction, a lama had once been sentenced to travel the entire distance from Urga to Lhasa in a prostrate position, i. e., he had to measure the road with the length of his body. It had taken him six years. Shereb Lama believed that he would suffer a like penalty.

We could not take fifty steps from the tent without spies coming forth to watch us. Ben Nursu seemed to be a sort of chief spy. His tent was close to ours. He sat with us for hours, and ate his meals with us.

In the afternoon we were seated with seven Tibetans around our fire in the open, when a troop of horsemen came galloping straight up to us from the east. It was Kamba Bombo's interpreter, who spoke a poorer Mongolian than I, but was otherwise a decent fellow. He questioned us thoroughly, and was most interested in our headquarters. Apparently they had illusions of a Russian invasion, with thousands of Cossacks. The interpreter told us that the Dalai Lama received daily reports about us. I asked him harshly how they dared to detain peaceful pilgrims from the Buriat provinces of the Russian Czar. "Your subjects steal our horses at night; but you treat us, who do you no harm, like robbers." The interpreter looked pensive, but answered that the road to Lhasa was closed to everyone who had no proper passport.

On the ninth, in the morning, the scene became animated. The whole plain swarmed with horsemen and pack-animals, and a new tent-village was growing up not far away. So much ado because of us, three poor pilgrims! One large tent was white, with blue ribbons. None but a chief could lodge thus.

Accompanied by a squad of horsemen, the interpreter came to our tent, and announced that Kamba Bombo had arrived, and was expecting me to a feast. Everything was prepared. Each of us was to receive a *haddik,* a long piece of thin white gauze cloth, symbolizing welcome. There were viands, including an entire sheep.

I answered stiffly: "People of good manners first pay a visit before inviting guests to a party. If Kamba Bombo wants anything of us, let him come here. We have nothing to withhold from him. All that we wish to know is whether the road to Lhasa is open to us or not. If not, Kamba Bombo will have to take the consequences on himself."

The interpreter was in despair. For two hours he sat begging and imploring us to come to the feast.

"I shall be dismissed if you do not come," he pleaded.

Even when he was in his saddle, he continued his persuasion. Finally he rode off.

Another two hours passed, when a troop of sixty-seven horsemen came dashing up from the new tent-village. They presented a splendid picture in their deep-blue and dark-red attire, their swords in scabbards ornamented with silver, coral, and torquoises, their cases holding an image of Buddha, their rosaries, and the rattling silver accoutrement at their sides. Kamba Bombo rode in the centre on a milk-white she-mule. He was a small, pale man, perhaps forty years old, with eyes that blinked roguishly; and he wore a red cloak and red *bashlik* over a yellow silk robe, with skunk sleeves, green velvet boots, and a blue Chinese cap.

He dismounted in front of my tent. His servant spread a rug on the ground and placed cushions on it. Here he and another high official, Nanso Lama, a monk, settled down.

I invited the two gentlemen into my tent, where each found a seat on a bag of flour.

Kamba Bombo was polite and kind, notwithstanding that we had tried to deceive him, had responded uncivilly to his invitation to a party, and were in his power. The interrogations were renewed, the Governor's secretary recording all my answers. To my request for permission to continue, see the Holy City, and then return to headquarters, Kamba Bombo answered with a significant gesture of his hand toward his neck.

"No; not one step further toward Lhasa. That would cost your heads— and mine, too. I do my duty. I get orders from the Dalai Lama every day."

He was immovable, inexorable. He did not lose control of himself for one moment. He was at once dignified and jovial. When we spoke of the two horses that had been stolen, he laughed and said: "You shall get two others from me. When you return to your headquarters, you shall be escorted to the border of my province, you shall have provisions, sheep, and everything you need. You have but to give your orders. But not *one* step farther toward the south."

In those days it was impossible for a European to travel to Lhasa. Przhevalsky, Bonvalot, De Rhins, Rockhill, Littledale, all had met with the same insurmountable resistance. Two years later, Lord Curzon sent his Anglo-Indian army to Lhasa. It opened the southern road to the Holy City by force, and four thousand Tibetans were killed. That was called war. But the Tibetans had asked nothing but to be left in peace. When the Tibetans under Kamba Bombo outwitted me, they too used peremptory means, but no violence, and they made their will effective without staining their hands with blood. On the contrary, they treated me with the utmost consideration. As for myself, I had the satisfaction of going to the limit of the adventure without capitulating until the opposition proved absolutely unconquerable. In the end, Kamba Bombo rode back to his tent. I told him it was my purpose to start off for headquarters already on the following day.

Early in the morning, I mounted my horse, and rode—much to the dismay of Shagdur and Shereb Lama—quite alone to Kamba Bombo's tent. But I had not gone half-way, when twenty horsemen surrounded me and asked me to dismount. After some waiting, Kamba Bombo appeared with his escort. Rugs and cushions were spread out, and we settled down to converse on neutral ground. I asked him jokingly how it would be if he and I should ride to Lhasa, only we two together? He laughed, shook his head, and said that it would be a pleasure to him to travel in my company, provided the Dalai Lama gave his permission.

"Well, let us send a courier to the Dalai Lama. I am willing to wait a couple of days."

"No," he answered determinedly. "I should be dismissed immediately after such a question."

Kamba Bombo screwed up his eyes, and pointing at me, said: "Sahib!"

I asked him how he could think that an Englishman from India could come from the north with Russian and Buriat Cossacks in his service, and I tried to explain to him where Sweden was.

Presently two horses were brought forth as compensation for the stolen ones. They were poor stock, and I said that I did not want them. Thereupon two perfect animals were produced, and I declared myself satisfied.

Finally I asked Kamba Bombo why he came with sixty-seven men, when we were only three, nay, I was quite alone now. Was he afraid of me?

"No, not at all, but I have orders from Lhasa to treat you as we treat the highest dignitaries in our own country."

We mounted again, and Kamba Bombo and his gentlemen accompanied me to my tent. There our weapons were examined and the escort was introduced to us. It consisted of two officers—Solang Undy and Ana Tsering—a non-commissioned officer, fourteen men, and six men for the Tibetans' belongings. They brought ten sheep for themselves. Kamba Bombo gave us six besides; also fat, flour, and milk. Thereupon I said farewell, and we parted, the very best of friends.†

Our procession looked like the transfer of prisoners. We were flanked by Tibetans, and they rode before us and behind us. When we encamped, they pitched two of their tents immediately next to ours, and kept watch during the night. We slept the whole night, and gave no thought to our pack-animals. Yolbars inspired them with the greatest awe, and had con-

---

† Edmund Candler, Reuter's correspondent in the British-Indian military expedition against Lhasa, relates in his book, "The Unveiling of Lhasa," that a small British force was attacked unexpectedly in the beginning of May, 1904, by one thousand Tibetans under the command of that same Kamba Bombo who, three years earlier, had checked my advance near Nakchu. After ten minutes' violent shooting, the Tibetans retired, leaving behind one hundred and forty dead. The British lost five. It is probable that my friend Kamba Bombo was among those killed. On that occasion as when we met him, he did only his duty to his country. I was not angry with him in 1901. After what happened in 1904, I admire him and honour his memory.

stantly to be held in leash. The escort included two lamas, who constantly swung their prayer-wheels, mumbling "om mani padme hum."

The day's journey was divided into two stages, with an interval for tea. Then the Tibetans cut three chunks of earth out of the ground, with their swords, and made a triangular support for the saucepan over a fire. Their lunch consisted of boiled mutton, *tsamba,* and tea. Their horsemen looked handsome, with queues rolled round their heads, and red turban-like sashes. Their right arms and shoulders were bare, the skin coat being allowed to slip half-way down their backs. All the horses wore bell-collars, and they made the valleys gay with their tinkling.

After we had ridden across the Sachutsangpo, which had fallen considerably, the escort bade us farewell, and we were once more left to ourselves. It seemed lonely and desolate after they abandoned us, and our night-watches began again. Once Malenki stood barking on a small hillock by the roadside. I rode thither and saw a bear digging up a marmot-hole. He was so absorbed in his work that he did not notice me until I was quite close upon him. Then he left the hole and slunk away. The dogs chased him, he turned round and held his ground, and there was a gay dance before both sides tired.

On August 20, only a few miles remained to be covered. We heard rifle-shots in a glen, and beheld two horsemen—Sirkin and Turdu Baï—who were out getting meat for the caravan. They wept with joy on seeing us.

And then we rode up to the camp, where everything was quiet. Chernoff had arrived with the rear-guard, having lost only two camels and two horses. To me it was like coming back to civilization. Using the caravan-buckets, I took a hot bath. I had not washed in twenty-five days, and the water had to be changed several times. Afterwards it was pleasant to lie undressed in one's clean, dry bed, while some of the men gave a concert with a *balalaika,* a flute, a temple-bell, my music-box, and two improvised drums. We had not reached Lhasa, but we had tasted the enchantment of the great adventure as never before.

Bibliography

Allen, Thomas Gaskell, Jr., and William Lewis Sachtleben. *Across Asia on a Bicycle*. New York: The Century Co., 1894.

Bird, Isabella. *A Lady's Life in the Rocky Mountains*. London: John Murray, 1879.

Bullen, Frank T. *The Cruise of the Cachalot: Round the World After Sperm Whales*. London: Smith, Elder & Co., 1898.

Burton, Richard Francis, Sir. *Personal Narrative of a Pilgrimage to Al-Madinah and Meccah*. London: G. Bell & Sons, 1913.

Dana, Richard Henry, Jr. *Two Years Before the Mast*. Boston: Houghton Mifflin Company, 1895.

Darwin, Charles. *Voyage of the* Beagle. Edited by Janet Browne and Michael Neve. London: Penguin Books Ltd, 1989. First published by Henry Colburn, London, 1839.

De Filippi, Filippo. *The Ascent of Mount St. Elias*. Westminster: Archibald Constable, 1900.

Hedin, Sven. *My Life as an Explorer*. Translated by Alfhild Huebsch. New York: Boni & Liveright, 1925.

Kennan, George. *Tent Life in Siberia*. New York: G. P. Putnum's Sons, 1910.

King, Clarence. *Mountaineering in the Sierra Nevada*. Boston: James R. Osgood and Company, 1872.

Kingsley, Mary. *Travels in West Africa*. London: Macmillian and Company, 1897.

Landor, A. Henry Savage. *In the Forbidden Land*. London: William Heinemann, 1898.

Le Blond, Elizabeth Alice Frances Hawkins-Whitshed. *Adventures on the Roof of the World.* London: T. Fisher Unwin, 1904.

Lewis, Meriwether, and William Clark. *Original Journals of the Lewis and Clark Expedition, 1804–1806.* Edited by Gary E. Moulton. Lincoln, Nebr.: University of Nebraska, 1987.

Melville, George Wallace. *In the Lena Delta.* Boston: Houghton, Mifflin, 1885.

Muir, John. *Travels in Alaska.* Boston: Houghton-Mifflin, 1915.

Mummery, Alfred F. *My Climbs in the Alps and Caucasus.* London: T. Fisher Unwin, 1895.

Nansen, Fridtjof. *Farthest North.* Westminster, England: Archibald Constable and Company, 1897.

Parkman, Francis. *The Oregon Trail.* Boston: Little, Brown and Company, 1872.

Powell, John Wesley. *The Exploration of the Colorado River and Its Canyons.* New York: Penguin Books, 1987. First published by the Government Printing Office, 1875.

Slocum, Captain Joshua. *Voyage of the* Liberdade. London: Rupert Hart-Davis, 1948.

Stanley, Henry M. *Through the Dark Continent.* New York: Harper and Brothers, 1878.

Stephens, John L. *Incidents of Travel in Central America, Chiapas, and Yucatan.* New York: Harper & Brothers, 1841.

Stevenson, Robert Louis. *Travels with a Donkey in the Cevénnes.* Boston: Roberts Brothers, 1879.

Thoreau, Henry David. *The Maine Woods.* Boston: Ticknor and Fields, 1864.

Twain, Mark (Samuel L. Clemens). *Roughing It.* Hartford, Conn.: American Publishing Company, 1872.

Voss, Captain John Claus. *The Venturesome Voyages of Captain Voss.* London, 1926. Reprint, Sidney, Canada: Grays Publishing Ltd., 1976.

Wallace, Alfred Russel. *The Malay Archipelago.* London: Ward, Lock, 1890.

Wallace, Dillon. *The Lure of the Labrador Wild.* New York: Fleming H. Revell Company, 1905.

Whymper, Edward. *The Ascent of the Matterhorn.* London: John Murray, 1880.

Wills, William John. *An Account of the Crossing of the Continent of Australia.* London: Wilson & MacKinnon, 1861.

Younghusband, Captain Francis. *Among the Celestials.* London: John Murray, 1898.